Contents

APPENDICES

Law Society guidance

Statutory legislation

Software suppliers

Preface

This is the fifth edition of the Handbook. I hope that it will be as useful to the profession as the previous ones. Practice in general is changing with frightening speed and probate practice particularly so. The changes to the IHT treatment of trusts introduced by the Finance Act 2006 represented a seismic shift.

Practitioners need to be aware of recent developments in law, tax, practice and client care. At the same time they have to be able to market themselves and their firms effectively. It is a daunting task, and I hope that this Handbook will assist by gathering together the different areas into one book.

This edition contains more information than previous ones on obligations in relation to money laundering and proceeds of crime. It has been updated to deal with the impact of the Civil Partnership Act 2004, Gender Recognition Act 2004 and Mental Capacity Act 2005, and current thinking on the effect of Charities Act 1993, s.33 on personal representatives dealing with 'charity land'.

I am very grateful for all the help I have received from the Law Society, and from the contributors who have been so generous with their time.

Professor Lesley King
October 2006

Abbreviations

1994 Order	Solicitors' (Non-Contentious Business) Remuneration Order 1994, SI 1994/2616
ACTAPS	Association of Contentious Trusts and Probate Specialists
AEA 1925	Administration of Estates Act 1925
AIDA rule	Attention, Interest, Desire and Action
AIEDPO 1986	Administration of Insolvent Estates of Deceased Persons Order 1986, SI 1986/1999
BMA	British Medical Association
CA 1989	Children Act 1989
CCS	Consumer Complaints Service
CGT	capital gains tax
COB Rules	Solicitors' Financial Services (Conduct of Business) Rules 2001
Code	Solicitors' Costs Information and Client Care Code 1999
CPR	Civil Procedure Rules 1998, SI 1998/3132
CRM	customer relationship management
DPA 1998	Data Protection Act 1998
DPB	designated professional body
ECA 2000	Electronic Communication Act 2000
E-Commerce Directive	Electronic Commerce Directive 2001/31/EC
FSA	Financial Services Authority
FSMA 2000	Financial Services and Markets Act 2000
Guidance	Law Society's Money Laundering Guidance – Pilot 2004
Guide	*The Guide to the Professional Conduct of Solicitors 1999*
HMRC	HM Revenue and Customs
ICO	Information Commissioner's Office
IFA	independent financial adviser
IHT	inheritance tax
IHTA 1984	Inheritance Tax Act 1984

IIP	Investors in People
ILM	Institute of Legacy Management
IPFDA 1975	Inheritance (Provision for Family and Dependants) Act 1975
IPS	inadequate professional services
IT	information technology
LLP	limited liability partnership
LSC	Legal Services Commission
NCIS	National Criminal Intelligence Service
NCPR 1987	Non-Contentious Probate Rules 1987, SI 1987/2024
PI insurance	professional indemnity insurance
PMS	Practice Management Standards
POCA 2002	Proceeds of Crime Act 2002
PR	personal representative
RAO 2001	Financial Services and Markets Act 2000 (Regulated Activities) Order 2001, SI 2001/544
ROI	return on investment
Rules	Solicitors' Accounts Rules 1998
SAS	Solicitors Assistance Scheme
Scope Rules	Solicitors' Financial Services (Scope) Rules 2001
SIF	Solicitors' Indemnity Fund
SOCA	Serious and Organised Crime Agency
STEP	Society of Trust and Estate Practitioners
TCGA 1992	Taxation of Chargeable Gains Act 1992
TLATA 1996	Trusts of Land and Appointment of Trustees Act 1996
TMA 1970	Taxes Management Act 1970

Notes on contributors

Meg Andrews is a partner at Hartley & Worstenholme Solicitors, West Yorkshire and chair of the Law Society's Wills and Equity Committee.

Peter Camp runs his own training consultancy, Educational and Professional Services and is a visiting Professor of Ethics at the College of Law.

Charles Christian is an ex-barrister who has been writing about IT for 30 years. He is the editor of the *Legal Technology Insider* newsletter and The Orange Rag.com blog.

Helen Clarke is a solicitor, Law Society council member and member of both the Probate Section and the Wills and Equity Committee.

Gillian E. Cockburn runs her own practice, Cockburns, Guildford.

Henry Frydenson is a consultant at Baker & Mackenzie LLP, London.

Dawn Goodman is a principal at Withers LLP, London.

David Hodson is a family law solicitor and mediator with Panorama Legal Services, Guildford, and a Deputy District Judge at the Principal Registry of the Family Division, London.

Professor Lesley King is a solicitor and principal lecturer at the College of Law, and a member of the Law Society's Wills and Equity Committee.

Alexander Learmonth is a barrister at Hogarth Chambers, where he practises in chancery and intellectual property law.

Sue Medder is a solicitor at Withers LLP, London.

Adrian O'Loughlin is a partner at TWM Solicitors LLP, Guildford, and chair of the Law Society's Probate Section.

Gill Steel is a solicitor and director of LawSkills Ltd, consultants and trainers, and a member of the Law Society's Wills and Equity Committee.

Heather Stewart worked as a solicitor in private practice before completing a doctorate on research into client evaluation of legal services and is currently a management consultant with Otterburn Legal Consulting.

Kim Tasso is a marketing consultant and freelance journalist specialising in marketing the professions.

Table of cases

xix

Table of statutes

Table of statutory instruments

EUROPEAN LEGISLATION

LAW SOCIETY RULES AND CODES

PART I

Probate and the Professional Rules

This Part covers the interaction of the professional rules with probate and estate administration work and deals particularly with some of the aspects of those rules which have caused difficulty to practitioners in the past.

The Professional Ethics Division of the Law Society (see **Useful addresses**) may be able to help you with difficult matters. Professional Ethics can be contacted in writing or by telephone, and help is confidential.

Please note that in this Handbook references are made to *The Guide to the Professional Conduct of Solicitors 1999*. Updates to the Guide are available on the Law Society website (see **www.guide-on-line.lawsociety.org.uk**).

The Law Society's draft Code of Conduct [2004] is expected to come into force in 2007 and will replace the Guide.

CHAPTER 1

Solicitors and instructions

Adrian O'Loughlin

1.1 WHO IS THE CLIENT?

1.1.1 Personal representatives

In probate and estate administration, the solicitor's clients are the personal representatives (PRs) and not the beneficiaries or friends and family of the PR. Problems can arise if a PR is elderly and a son or daughter offers to help him or her, because here as in other legal work, a solicitor's instructions should come directly from the client. Otherwise, the PR should consider renunciation, allowing those next entitled to apply for the grant, or the appointment of an attorney (the relative or perhaps you as solicitor to act on their behalf). There are circumstances in which it may well be preferable for an executor to renounce. In a useful article in [1995] *Solicitors Journal*, 13 January, Philip Rossdale identified five situations in which an executor or executrix should consider renouncing.

1. Where there is a danger that the executor or executrix would infringe the rule against self-dealing, typically where the named executor or executrix was the deceased's business partner or a trustee of a trust under which the deceased was a beneficiary.
2. Where the executor or executrix is a debtor of the deceased whose debt is statute barred.
3. Where the deceased was an executor or executrix (because of the possibility of the chain of representation applying).
4. Where the deceased was a sole trader.
5. Where there are substantial overseas assets and modest UK ones (because the executor or executrix may find himself or herself facing a UK tax liability with insufficient UK assets to discharge it).

A PR may be replaced under Administration of Justice Act 1985, s.50 or passed over under Supreme Court Act 1981, s.116.

As an alternative to renunciation, one of two or more executors may choose to have power reserved to him or her which gives that person the option to get involved later (the power reserved process is simpler than that

3

for renunciation). Renunciation or the reservation of power might also be considered by prospective PRs who plan to be away for long periods of time, or who clearly do not wish to be involved in the administration. If this is suggested, the pros and cons should be clearly pointed out to those concerned.

Problems can arise where the two PRs cannot agree on a solicitor to represent them. If it is not practicable for the solicitors to represent both PRs it makes no sense for both solicitors to fully replicate the work required to obtain a grant and administer the estate. Instead, the solicitors acting should seek to come to some kind of agreement which will allow one solicitor to deal with the administration of the estate, while the other will review what has been done on behalf of his or her client.

1.1.2 Beneficiaries

Some recent cases may point the way to an extension of the liability of professionals to third parties. (Aspects of liability are considered in **Chapter 6**.) However, in general, beneficiaries' rights in estate administration are limited. They have the right to have the estate properly administered, but are not entitled, unless they are also PRs, to make decisions about the conduct of the administration, nor to be involved in the day-to-day business of administering the estate. (Residuary beneficiaries have the right to obtain remuneration certificates in certain cases, see **Chapter 2**.)

Beneficiaries who are not PRs are not clients of the solicitor acting for the PRs, so it is not up to them to instruct those solicitors. It is for the PRs. Where appropriate, of course, beneficiaries' wishes, and particularly those of residuary beneficiaries, can be taken into account. This may be of particular relevance if the beneficiary is a charity and can, for example, reclaim income tax paid or avoid capital gains tax where assets are appropriated to the charity prior to sale so that they may then be sold on behalf of the charity as bare trustee. (Charitable beneficiaries are considered further at **16.8** below.)

Bear in mind that most beneficiaries will have no idea of what needs to be done to complete the winding up of an estate and how long it can take to do it. They may expect payment of their legacies or to be able to take possession of their gifts within an unrealistically short time frame. This, together with their lack of involvement in the administration, can mean worry and uncertainty for them and may possibly result in expression of unjustified dissatisfaction with the firm involved. Accordingly, obtaining the PRs' consent to informing the beneficiaries briefly of the expected timescale for completing the administration, or how long an unexpected hold-up may take to resolve, is likely to be beneficial to all concerned. It is a good idea, when establishing the terms of the retainer with the PRs, for solicitors to agree the extent of any communication with beneficiaries and the specific information which may be divulged.

4

It is the usual practice of many firms to notify all beneficiaries of their entitlements or legacies at an early stage. Legatees may simply be informed or sent a copy of the relevant part of the will, and residuary beneficiaries may be sent a copy of the whole will. Taking this action, and including an indication of the realistic likely date of payment, may put the beneficiaries' minds at rest and avoid unrealistic expectations, as well as saving time and costs in unnecessary correspondence. However if the anticipated timetable changes, those people who are still working to the original dates will need to be updated.

Solicitors approached for information by beneficiaries during the administration may wish to agree with the PRs as to the information to be given, and to advise the PRs on what would be appropriate. This will depend on factors such as the beneficiaries' status and relationship to the PRs (and the deceased), the nature of the questions, and the costs which would be involved in dealing with them. Although beneficiaries are not clients, the Consumer Complaints Service (CCS) would expect replies to letters of enquiry to be courteous and as informative as they can be in the circumstances, and for these to be sent reasonably promptly.

More information about trustees and beneficiaries, and the information which beneficiaries are entitled to have, is available in works such as Hayton, *Underhill and Hayton: Law Relating to Trustees*, 16th edn (2002, LexisNexis).

What is most important in any administration is to establish good communication with the executors and residuary beneficiaries. The vast majority of complaints against solicitors arise out of inadequate communication. It makes sense, therefore, for solicitors to try and agree with the executors and any residuary beneficiaries how often the solicitor will communicate with them so that their expectations can be met.

Solicitors should be aware of the dangers of committing a money laundering offence when administering an estate. See the Law Society's Anti-Money Laundering Guidance for Solicitors Conducting Private Client Work (see **Appendix A1**) and the discussion in **Chapter 6**.

See the remainder of this chapter and also **Chapter 2**, and Mike Frith's article 'Who is the probate client?' [2000] *Gazette,* 10 February, 38, reproduced in **Appendix A3**.

1.2   INSTRUCTIONS

1.2.1   General reminders

Generally, see the Law Society's *The Guide to the Professional Conduct of Solicitors 1999* (the Guide), ch.13 on client care.

Solicitors need to be as sure as they can be that the person purporting to instruct them has authority to do so. Remember that if the next of kin are to be administrators under an intestacy, there might be an as yet untraced will appointing others as executors. Next, the solicitor needs to establish exactly what the client wants him or her to do, and it is important to agree with the client precisely what is possible and what the firm can do. Making a summary of the client's instructions for the front of the file can be a useful reminder of the extent of the original retainer, particularly if more than one person is likely to be working on the file or if there are unusual instructions which might get buried in a thick file. Extensions or alterations to the retainer can be dealt with in the same way, together with the date. As a matter of routine, instructions and alterations should, of course, be confirmed in writing as soon as possible.

The case of *Cancer Research Campaign* v. *Ernest Brown & Co* [1997] STC 1425 illustrates the importance of identifying the scope of the retainer.

At this stage, it is also appropriate for solicitors to consider what information the client needs from them. This Handbook contains some specimen materials which solicitors in private practice may adapt or adopt. They are intended to cover certain basic points relating to succession and estate administration work.

Other materials for clients can be obtained from the Law Society (see **Useful addresses**), and details of relevant leaflets can be found under **Further reading**.

1.2.2   Difficulty with instructions

If difficulty is experienced, it may be possible to shed some light by going back to the beginning and finding exact answers to the following questions:

* Who is my client? (usually, but not always, this will be the same as the answer to the question 'Who will pay my bill?')
* What have I been instructed to do?
* What is my role – professional, legal, practical?

The answer to the first question will help disentangle conflicts in areas where these might arise; contradictory or unacceptable instructions can be revealed by the answer to question two; and the answer to the third question can often pinpoint where the difficulty lies.

Some of the problems which can arise in the course of estate administration are dealt with in **Chapter 15**.

1.3   CONFLICTS AND DISPUTES

Clients sometimes find that conflicts arise between their roles as beneficiary and PR. It may be preferable for a PR to renounce before taking the grant if there are reasons to suspect that a conflict is likely to arise which cannot be addressed in any other way. A renunciation can only take place before the executor or executrix has acted in the administration. If the conflict arises at a later stage an alternative way to address the conflict will need to be found. Another problem, particularly where an intestacy or a step-relationship is involved, is that one PR may feel left out or that the other is being favoured, especially if the firm acting is the other PR's usual solicitor. Both PRs should be involved in the decision taking and it may be helpful, in these sensitive situations, to ensure that the content of conversations and correspondence with one PR is fully and promptly reported to the other.

Disputes can, of course, arise on any number of grounds, for example because a will is challenged, through disappointment on the part of the family about the disposition of the estate, or regarding the identity of the PRs. It may be appropriate to advise the client what steps the other side may take, whether seeking an opinion from counsel or a specialist solicitor or even commencing litigation, and about the costs and time implications. Clear preliminary instructions need to be obtained and confirmed in writing. Family companies, in particular, can be a fertile source of difficulty. Firms who have acted for the founder and members of his or her family personally and on behalf of the business may find that the various parties are at loggerheads after the death. This may result in the firm having to cease to act for some or all of those involved.

There is a new practice rule on conflicts of interest, Rule 16D and there is also for the first time a rule on confidentiality, Rule 16E. Solicitors must not put their duty of confidentiality to a client or former client at risk by accepting instructions to act for another client with an adverse interest.

Problems of conflict and confidentiality may arise where a solicitor has drafted wills for a husband and wife, and one party later asks for a new will to be drafted without disclosing this fact to the other. See Duncan Bailey, 'Serving two masters' [2006] *Trusts and Estates Law and Tax Journal*, January/February.

1.3.1 Independent advice

From time to time, beneficiaries or PRs may seek independent advice about their position, perhaps because they think a lay or co-PR is mishandling an administration, or because they consider a solicitors' firm is working too slowly. Such a move creates some practical difficulties, the main issue usually relating to costs. The opinion set out at **15.10** below, although it relates to PRs seeking independent advice only, may be of interest in this connection. In any event, solicitors may wish to discuss the costs issue with those involved early on. It may also be appropriate to discuss the implications for the administration of what has happened.

Another difficulty may relate to access to papers, particularly if the disagreement centres on dissatisfaction with the firm of solicitors handling the administration. The solution to these problems is difficult, but dealing with the following questions may shed some light on the matter:

- Who is the original client of the firm?
- Has the retainer been terminated? By whom?
- To whom will duties, such as the duty of confidentiality, be owed?
- To whom should reports be made?
- If a conflict appears to have arisen, is there a conflict for the firm, or is it in fact a conflict for the PR?

The Guide deals with termination of retainers in ch.12.

A solicitor may have to advise a client to seek independent advice if he or she has made a mistake or there is concern that a mistake may have been made by the solicitor: see **15.18** below. Solicitors should remember that they must comply with the terms of their insurance contract in informing insurers of possible claims against them.

1.3.2 Solicitors giving evidence as to circumstances in which will was made

Solicitors may be drawn into disputes about a will after a death, for example if it is questioned whether the testator or testatrix had capacity.

Some years ago the Council of the Law Society obtained the opinion of leading counsel as a result of *Larke* v. *Nugus* on the duty of a solicitor who had acted for a testator in drawing up his will which, after the death, had been the subject of a dispute.

It was decided that a solicitor should make available a statement of his or her evidence regarding the execution of the will and circumstances surrounding it, to a person who is either a party to probate proceedings or whom the solicitor believes to have a reasonable claim under the will but who is not yet a party to any proceedings, whether or not the solicitor acted for those propounding the will. Further guidance on the position of a solicitor who may be a material witness can be found in the Guide, Principle 21.12. (Also see **Chapter 11** on contentious probate.) While the facts of each matter will differ, the principle that the available information should be made accessible impartially to both sides is likely to be of value.

The advice of Professional Ethics (see **Useful addresses**) on all such points may be sought.

1.4 EXECUTORS IN THE OFFICE

1.4.1 Retired and non-practising solicitors

Many solicitors take up executorships during retirement or during a period in which they are consultants to their previous firms. As far as charging clauses are concerned, these will need to be interpreted to see whether they are wide enough to cover charging by a person not involved in any business. A person may not act as a solicitor, of course, unless he or she holds a current practising certificate. Solicitors merely on the Roll, i.e. non-practising and retired solicitors not holding practising certificates, may not describe themselves as solicitors or act as such, by, for example, making an application for the grant of representation as a solicitor. See the decision in *Glenister* vs. *Moody* [2005] WTLR 1205 for a discussion of when an accountant who was winding down his practice could be said to have retired.

1.4.2 Fee earners about to retire or move firms

When a fee earner leaves the firm, it may be necessary to resolve the question of his or her appointment as executor or executrix. What is to happen? Was the appointment of the individual personally (so that the testator or testatrix will probably wish the fee earner to continue to act after going to the new firm) or was it, in effect, appointment of the firm (so that someone else in the original firm should now be appointed)? Ideally the client's instructions should be obtained. Making contact in this way can also usefully remind the client that other aspects of the will may need review and revision. From a marketing point of view, it might be useful to include an invitation to make an appointment for this; and why not send a copy of the firm's brochure too? (For more on marketing, see **Chapter 20**.)

1.4.3 Supervision of employee personal representatives

The following (updated) guidance was first issued in 1991 by the Property and Commercial Services and the Standards and Guidance Committees of the Council of the Law Society:

> **Solicitor's clerk appointed executor of a client's will: duty of supervision**
>
> The Solicitors Complaints Bureau [as it then was] has recently had to deal with a case involving the misappropriation of trust funds by an unqualified employee of a solicitor who drafted a will for a client and was appointed under that will as sole executor. The clerk in that case administered the estate through the firm by which he was employed but the monies were held outside the firm. The Standards and Guidance Committee, in conjunction with the Property and Commercial Services Committee and the Wills and Equity Committee wish to remind solicitors of their obligation to supervise both their admitted and unadmitted staff. Principle 3.01 of

the Guide states, 'A solicitor is responsible for exercising proper supervision over both admitted and unadmitted staff' and at 3.13 'As a matter of conduct a partner is prima facie responsible for the acts or omissions of the firm and this extends to the acts or omissions of staff'. In particular a solicitor should take special care when exercising these functions in circumstances where a clerk is an executor or executrix whether alone or with a lay person and is administering the estate through the firm, but the money involved is being paid into an account which is outside the Accounts Rules.

Firms may wish to consider whether it would be appropriate to prohibit unqualified staff from being appointed executor or executrix for clients of the firm by inserting appropriate clauses into the contracts of employment of those staff. However, the solicitor's duty to act in the best interest of the client may mean that such a blanket prohibition would be inappropriate, for example where the client was a close friend or relative of the member of staff. Therefore consideration should be given to clauses restricting unqualified staff from being named as executor or executrix unless prior approval of a partner is obtained. Any such restrictions must not prejudice the interest of the firm's client. The contract could also provide that where an unqualified member of staff becomes executor or executrix on the death of a client, all estate monies should be paid into the firm's client account. In practice, a client who is not a close friend or relative of a staff member is unlikely to be prejudiced by such a restriction.

Similar points should be borne in mind where an unqualified member of staff is asked to be appointed attorney or enduring attorney for a client. It is better for a solicitor to be appointed, even if the day-to-day work is delegated to the member of staff.

It is worth noting that the Solicitors' Accounts Rules 1998 impose some record-keeping requirements where money is held outside a firm's client bank account (e.g. where a client's own bank account is operated). See **Chapter 5** for a fuller discussion.

10

CHAPTER 2

Costs and charging

Adrian O'Loughlin

2.1 SOURCES OF INFORMATION

The following sources of information are available:

- Solicitors' Practice Rule 15 (Costs information and client care);
- Solicitors' Costs Information and Client Care Code 1999;
- Solicitors' (Non-Contentious Business) Remuneration Order 1994;
- Non-Contentious Costs (Law Society Practice Advice Service, 2005).

See also **Chapter 3** on client care.

2.2 COSTS AND THE CLIENT

The Law Society wants openness about costs. The final charge for the administration of an estate may be difficult to predict at the outset, but most clients will not understand the reasons why, and are likely to interpret vagueness and uncertainty about costs as a signal that the costs will be enormous, or that the firm is not being frank. Either way, it is in the firm's interests (as well as in accordance with the obligations imposed by the Law Society) to give clients the facts as far as is possible. If an indication of the cost for the whole administration cannot be given, the solicitor can tell the client why, as well as what work will have to be done before the total costs can be estimated and how much it will cost the client to reach that point. If nothing else, clients can be told the hourly charging rate of the person handling their work, and given an idea of the number of hours involved, plus details of any known disbursements or a range within which their costs are likely to fall.

Such evidence as is available indicates that most clients feel they get good value from solicitors. Do not shrink from discussing fees and do include everything the client is likely to have to pay for, including disbursements. Plain speaking about costs is in everyone's interests. (See **2.7** below and also **Chapter 3**.)

Solicitors should always remember Practice Rule 1 when it comes to billing, and they should never put their own interests before those of the client. This is particularly important in a contentious probate when a client is proposing to spend a lot of money on legal work when there may be very little at stake.

2.3 CHARGING FOR WILLS

Although this Handbook is primarily about estate administration, will drafting is, of course, closely related. A number of general points about wills are included in **Chapter 12**. As with estate administration, there is a need to be open with clients and potential clients about the cost involved. However, it is often feasible to quote a definite fee for drafting a will.

Some firms offer will preparation at a price similar to the unregulated will-selling services; making this known may encourage clients to consult solicitors, but if this is the case, it is important that solicitors do not compromise the quality of their advice. If your firm's charges are higher, be open about the cost and explain why the service offered is good value. What solicitors have, which is of great value to most clients, is the ability to advise in the broader area of what happens when someone dies and also any tax issues, and it may be helpful to explain to a potential client all the reasons why seeing a solicitor is worth the extra amount. Where the solicitor has a Legal Help contract with the Legal Services Commission, some clients can still get help with will drafting under the Legal Help scheme (see **12.1.7**).

2.4 SOLICITORS' (NON-CONTENTIOUS BUSINESS) REMUNERATION ORDER 1994

Note: Paragraphs 2.4–2.6 are based on an article which originally appeared in [1994] *Gazette*, 28 September, 31.

The main text of the Solicitors' (Non-Contentious Business) Remuneration Order 1994 (the 1994 Order) is set out in **Appendix B4** and an article-by-article commentary follows below. A specimen of the information that you must give to entitled persons is provided at **2.6**.

2.5 LAW SOCIETY'S COMMENTARY ON THE 1994 ORDER

2.5.1 Article 1: citation, commencement and revocation

The Order came into force on 1 November 1994 and applies only to matters for which bills are delivered on or after 1 November 1994.

2.5.2 Article 2: interpretation

Although it is not stated, the Interpretation Act 1978 applies in the 1994 Order where art.2 is silent. 'Client', 'paid disbursements', 'recognised body', 'remuneration certificate', 'solicitor' and 'the Council' are defined. 'Costs' is defined as the amount charged exclusive of VAT and disbursements. 'Residuary beneficiary' is defined as including a person entitled to all or part of the residue of an intestate estate.

'Entitled third party' is defined as a residuary beneficiary who is entitled to ask the solicitor to obtain a remuneration certificate. The definition has the following effect:

- A residuary beneficiary of an estate where there is at least one lay executor or executrix is not an entitled third party.
- A residuary beneficiary of an estate in which all the PRs are solicitors would be able to ask the solicitor billing the estate to obtain a remuneration certificate, even if the bill is from another solicitor (not a PR) instructed by the PRs to do the work.
- A residuary beneficiary who will become entitled only upon the happening of some event (for example a person entitled subject to a life interest, or a minor entitled only on majority) is not an entitled third party.

'Entitled person' is defined as a person entitled to a remuneration certificate – a client or an entitled third party.

2.5.3 Article 3: matters taken into account 'in particular'

Note the importance of an entitled person's express or implied approval, or a testator's or testatrix's express approval, of the amount of the costs or any particular work giving rise to the costs. If, for example, the file shows compliance with the written professional standards, recorded discussions with the client authorising unusual work, or an express provision in a will or in a document referred to in a will, this could operate in a solicitor's favour in assessing the reasonableness of the costs.

2.5.4 Article 4: right to certification

Note the £50,000 limit.

2.5.5 Article 5: disciplinary and other measures

Note the reference to the general disciplinary powers of the Law Society.

2.5.6 Article 6: obligation to give information before suing on a bill

Note the information required to be given. (See the specimen 'Notice of Rights' at **2.6** below.)

2.5.7 Article 7: obligation to give information when costs have been taken by deduction

Note there is no *automatic* obligation in deduction cases to send out the information which a solicitor must send to a client before suing on an unpaid bill. There is an obligation, where costs have been taken by deduction from money held by the solicitor on behalf of a client or on behalf of an estate, and an entitled person (client or residuary beneficiary) raises written objections to the amount of the costs within three months, that information must be given 'immediately' to the person raising the objections.

The normal time which must be allowed for the entitled person to raise objections is three months. The solicitor may, however, stipulate a shorter time when sending the bill or notification of costs. The shorter time must not be less than one month.

2.5.8 Article 8: information to be given to the entitled person

If required to do so under arts.6 or 7 the solicitor must inform the entitled person:

- of the right to ask for a remuneration certificate;
- that the entitled person must ask for a remuneration certificate within one month of receipt of the information about their rights, or within one month of receipt of the bill or notification of the costs if later;
- that the client may apply to the Society for a waiver of the requirement to pay half the amount of the bill, VAT and paid disbursements, when requesting a remuneration certificate, if exceptional circumstances apply (the solicitor can, of course, waive the advance payment, and this may reduce delay in obtaining the certificate and eventual payment of costs);
- of the entitled person's rights in connection with taxation of the bill; and
- of the solicitor's right to charge interest on the outstanding bill.

2.5.9 Article 9: loss by client of the right to a remuneration certificate

Note the situations in which a client loses this right and, in particular:

- where there is a non-contentious business agreement; and

- where the client has not paid half the costs in advance of the application as required by art.11, and has not obtained or applied in writing for a waiver.

2.5.10 Article 10: loss by entitled third party of the right to a remuneration certificate

The provisions of this article are, with the appropriate modifications, the same as those applying in respect of clients, except that there is no mention of the bill being delivered and paid, or of the requirement that half the costs be paid, as costs will have been taken by deduction from the estate. There is no mention of a non-contentious business agreement; normally there could be no such agreement as a person cannot enter into a contract with himself or herself.

2.5.11 Article 11: requirement to pay a sum towards the costs

As a prerequisite to obtaining a remuneration certificate, a client who has not already done so must pay half the costs and all the VAT and paid disbursements before the solicitor is obliged to apply for a remuneration certificate. The requirement may be waived by the solicitor or by the Law Society on application by the client if the solicitor has refused to do so, providing exceptional circumstances exist to justify waiving the requirement. The Law Society will have regard to the fact that a remuneration certificate rarely reduces the solicitor's costs by more than half, so normally a client will in the end pay at least half of the costs.

2.5.12 Article 12: miscellaneous

This article sets out various provisions which are not easy to classify. Note in particular that:

- if the application for a certificate has been made the client can pay the bill without invalidating the application;
- if the solicitor and client agree in writing, the client will not lose his or her right to a remuneration certificate by paying the bill or by asking 'out of time' for the solicitor to obtain a remuneration certificate;
- the solicitor has the right to take security for the payment of costs.

2.5.13 Article 13: refunds of money due to an entitled person, and interest on refund monies

This article specifies the implied duty to refund any overpayment arising from a remuneration certificate being issued for a smaller sum than that shown on the certificate, where costs have already been paid in full. The solicitor must make the refund immediately unless he or she 'appeals' the certificate by applying for taxation of the bill within one month of receiving the certificate.

It also flags up the possibility that the refund may carry interest under the Solicitors' Accounts Rules or under trust law, since the money to be refunded will have been held by the solicitor for a period 'on behalf of' the client or the estate.

2.5.14 Article 14: interest payable on unpaid costs

Since in estate cases money will have been taken by deduction these provisions only apply in respect of clients who have not paid the whole of the bill. A solicitor who has given a client the information required before suing on the bill may charge interest at the judgment debt rate on the unpaid amount from one month after delivery of the bill. Note in particular:

- the solicitor and client may agree that interest will run from before or after the date of delivery of the bill, or that interest will be charged at a higher or lower rate than the judgment debt rate (interest runs from one month after the date of delivery of the bill unless the solicitor and client agree otherwise);
- if the solicitor delays in applying for a remuneration certificate interest may not be charged for the period between one month after the client's request and the date on which the solicitor makes the application to the Law Society;
- interest is chargeable on the amount certified unless either the application is withdrawn or there is a taxation of the bill; in which case it is chargeable on the full amount in the bill or the taxed amount respectively.

2.5.15 Article 15: applications

This article requires the solicitor to supply the file and any other information or documentation required for the purpose of providing a remuneration certificate.

2.6 SPECIMEN 'NOTICE OF RIGHTS'

This specimen information for entitled persons is not part of the Order and any form of words which complies with the requirements of the Order may be used.

Remuneration certificates

(1)   If you are not satisfied with the amount of our fee you have the right to ask us to obtain a remuneration certificate from the Law Society.

(2)   The certificate will either say that our fee is fair and reasonable, or it will substitute a lower fee.

(3)   If you wish us to obtain a certificate you must ask us to do so *within a month* of receiving this notice.

(4)   We may charge interest on unpaid bills and we will do so at [the rate payable on judgment debts, from one month after delivery of our bill].

(5)   (a)   If you ask us to obtain a remuneration certificate, then, unless we already hold the money to cover these, you must first pay:

- half our fee shown in the bill;
- all the VAT shown in the bill;
- all the expenses we have incurred shown in the bill – sometimes called 'paid disbursements'.

(b)   However, you may ask the Law Society [see **Useful addresses** for contact details] to waive this requirement so that you do not have to pay anything for the time being. You would have to show that exceptional circumstances apply in your case.

(6)   Your rights are set out more fully in the Solicitors' (Non-Contentious Business) Remuneration Order 1994.

Assessment of costs

You may be entitled to have our charges reviewed by the court. (This is called 'assessment of costs'.) The procedure is different from the remuneration certificate procedure and it is set out in Solicitors Act 1974, ss.70, 71 and 72. Where appropriate it refers to the new Practice Rule 15.

2.7   RELEVANT FACTORS WHEN GIVING COST INFORMATION FOR NON-CONTENTIOUS WORK

2.7.1   Introduction

This section draws together and updates the existing guidance available to the profession about giving costs information to clients, particularly with regard to estimates, quotations, or other costs indications.

2.7.2   Solicitors' Costs Information and Client Care Code 1999

The Solicitors' Costs Information and Client Care Code 1999 (the Code) is designed to ensure that clients know the name and status of the person(s) responsible for both the day-to-day conduct and overall supervision of their matters. This is an ongoing requirement that lasts throughout

17

the retainer. It also requires that clients are at all relevant times given appropriate information as to the issues raised and progress of those matters.

Firms are required to maintain their own procedures for dealing with complaints about the service received and in practical terms, such complaints usually manifest themselves at the time of billing. The Code requires that, in addition to the requirement to inform the client of the name of the person handling the case and to operate a complaints handling procedure, solicitors will also be required to give 'appropriate' information as to the costs of any matter (both professional fees and disbursements). What is 'appropriate' is explained in the Code.

2.7.3 Lexcel

The Practice Management Standards under Lexcel were last revised in 2004. The standards encourage compliance with the Code (see **www.lexcel. lawsociety.org.uk**).

2.7.4 Client care letter

The best way of ensuring compliance with Rule 15 and the Code is to send the client, as soon as possible after instructions are taken, a comprehensive client care or terms of business letter.

The Law Society has designed a series of sample letters to assist with compliance with the new Code. There is no reason why practitioners should not devise their own letter to suit the particular needs or circumstances of the client. From the Committee's standpoint, the existence of such a letter is *prima facie* evidence of compliance with the Code.

2.7.5 Agreements under Solicitors Act 1974, s.57 (as amended)

Solicitors who enter into a written agreement signed by the client concerning their costs or remuneration (including hourly rates) will find that these can only be challenged through the courts as they are outside the scope of the remuneration certifying procedure. However, to qualify as such an agreement, the terms must be precise and unambiguous (*Chamberlain* v. *Boodle & King* [1982] 3 All ER 188).

Depending on the wording used, solicitors may find that if the client signs and returns a client care or terms of business letter of the type referred to above, then a s.57 agreement may have been entered into.

If a solicitor is involved in a costs dispute, care should be taken by the solicitor to make sure there is no s.57 agreement in existence. If there is, then the solicitor may be inviting further difficulties with the client by telling them about remedies which are not, in fact, available.

2.7.6   Non-Contentious Costs Guidance 2005

The following is an extract from Non-Contentious Costs (Law Society Practice Advice, 2005). Text within square brackets has been inserted by the Editor of this book.

CHARGING IN PROBATE AND IN THE ADMINISTRATION OF ESTATES

Fair and reasonable

[It may be appropriate to include a value element in the method of charging.] In all cases the overall consideration must be that the charges are fair and reasonable, having regard to all the circumstances of the matter. The figures below should not be regarded as scale charges in any way and must always be exercised with discretion. In *Jemma Trust* v. *Liptrott* [2003] EWCA Civ 1476 . . . the Court of Appeal held that a value charge can either be made in addition to an hourly rate, or it can be included in the hourly rate, but the value element must not be reflected in both charges. The comments of the court are reproduced in Appendix 5 [of the *Non-Contentious Costs* Guidance] but it is recommended that practitioners read the Jemma Trust judgment in its entirety. [The Court of Appeal recommended that the charging regime be agreed with the residuary beneficiaries as well as the executors.]

Where appropriate, charges may consist of two elements:

(a)   Hourly Rate

This should be an inclusive figure incorporating the fee earner's expense rate and any appropriate care and conduct uplift.

(b)   Value Element

Account may be taken of the value of the assets in the estate. In calculating the value element of the charge, the following approach may be helpful:

Consider the value nature and number of assets

It is usual to divide the estate (i.e. total value of the assets left after death) into two parts:

(i)   The deceased's residence
       The value of the deceased's home, or as much of it as he or she owned, if it was shared with another person. For example, where the property is jointly owned, the value is reduced by half.
(ii)   Value of rest of the estate

Apply an appropriate percentage

An appropriate percentage should be considered in the light of the circumstances of the case but the following may be helpful.

Solicitor not acting as an executor

Value of gross estate less residence	1 %
Value of residence	0.5%

[The guidance provides worked examples of calculating a value element in the following situations:

- Solicitor not acting as an executor;
- Solicitor acting as an executor, either solely or with another person;
- Solicitor not acting as an executor but for a corporate executor;
- Solicitor acting as a joint executor with a corporate executor.]

High value estates

When dealing with high value estates, consideration should be given to reducing the value element percentage charged in order to ensure that the overall level of charge is fair and reasonable. For general guidance on this point, see the case of *Jemma Trust* v. *Liptrott* [2003] EWCA Civ 1476 . . .

While accepting in the *Jemma Trust* case that a value element charge was allowable in principle, the Court of Appeal held that there should be a regressive charging regime in respect of high value non-contentious cases, suggesting that the appropriate bands for bills rendered for work done in 2003 would be:

Value	Solicitor-executor	Solicitor not executor
Up to £1 million	1.5%	1.0%
£1 million – £4 million	0.5%	0.33%
£4 million – £8 million	0.1666%	0.1111%
£8 million – £12 million	0.0833%	0.0555%
Over £12 million	0.0416%	0.0275%

Individual practitioners must exercise their own professional judgment as to whether or not to apply the value element when charging for the administration of an estate. In the *Jemma* case, clarity of billing was encouraged and if time plus value is charged, the value element must be identified separately on the face of the bill.

2.7.7 Estimates, quotations or other indications of cost

The word 'indication' is used where appropriate to include quotations and estimates. It is advisable that indications are given by an authorised responsible member of a firm and that a standard procedure for giving indications is adopted within the firm. All such indications should be readily visible on the file.

All indications should be confirmed in writing to the client. The final amount payable should not vary substantially from the relevant indication unless the client was informed in writing at the time that there was a change of circumstances.

A solicitor may wish to give a qualified indication, for example by stating that it may be reviewed if the matter develops in an unforeseen manner or turns out to be more complex or difficult than originally envisaged. However, even if such complications arise, the original indication will still be binding on the solicitor unless the solicitor informs the client immediately and in writing of the change in circumstances. The solicitor should point out that the original indication no longer stands and/or the client's instructions to proceed should be sought.

In cases where the solicitor's fee is to be paid by a third party, it may be that the indication has only been given to the third party and not to the client. In such cases (depending on the overall circumstances) the same principles as set out above in relation to solicitor and own client indications will generally apply.

2.7.8   Consumer Protection Act 1987, Part III

Practitioners are reminded that indications could fall within Consumer Protection Act 1987, s.20. Section 20 sets out the circumstances in which a misleading indication could give rise to a criminal offence.

2.7.9   Solicitors' (Non-Contentious Business) Remuneration Order 1994

Article 3 states that a solicitor's remuneration in non-contentious business 'shall be such sum as may be fair and reasonable having regard to all the circumstances of the case'.

The normal practice of the Appeals and Adjudication Committee would be to regard any indication of the likely cost of the matter as a material consideration to be taken into account in the giving of a certificate if it appears that the indication was given as an incentive to the client to give instructions to that solicitor, or that the client relied on the indication.

The Committee will therefore normally hold an indication (whether oral or written) to be binding upon the solicitor giving it. Similarly, it is the policy of the Committee to view a material breach of Rule 15 and the Solicitors' Costs Information and Client Care Code 1999 as a circumstance to be taken into account in assessing a fair and reasonable fee under the above Order.

Where there is a dispute as to whether an oral indication has been given, the Committee will try to ascertain from the available documentation and circumstances whether the claim that an oral indication was given can be justified.

2.7.10   Consumer Complaints Service

A material breach of Rule 15 and the Code could lead to a finding (by the Committee) that the solicitor has provided inadequate professional services (IPS). Similarly, the exceeding of costs without appropriate notice or warning could, depending on the particular circumstances of the case, result in the fee being reduced to the indication figure if the matter is subject to an IPS investigation.

It therefore follows that the principles applied to remuneration certificates apply equally to IPS investigations in the context of costs indications.

Complaints primarily concerning a breach of professional conduct are dealt with by the Compliance Directorate of the Law Society.

2.7.11   Change of circumstance

A solicitor is required to notify the client immediately, and in writing, if a change of circumstances has occurred so that the original qualified indication no longer applies. It is appreciated that some special circumstances, e.g. a contract race, may make it impractical for the solicitor to revise the indication in the way contemplated by the statement.

Solicitors should take extra care in these circumstances to ensure that the client does not rely on the indication if it has become misleading.

2.7.12   Split transactions

Where a transaction has a number of parts (e.g. the purchase of a property, the creation or discharge of a mortgage or the registration of title) the indication, unless it states otherwise, will be deemed to include all of these matters. The view that an indication only covers the basic transaction and that a charge can be raised in addition for ancillary matters such as registration of title is not acceptable and this may well be (depending on the circumstances) a misleading indication.

2.7.13   Petty disbursements

The practice of adding petty disbursements such as postage, telephone calls and faxes to the final bill is generally unacceptable. Petty disbursements are considered to be part of the overheads of the firm. They are expenses of the firm and should be included in the calculation of the fee even if there is an indication that petty disbursements will not normally be allowed, unless there is a specific agreement to the contrary.

Where a transaction is likely to involve substantial telephone work, faxing or photocopying, it should be made clear to the client if such items are to be charged in addition to any indication of costs.

2.7.14   Abortive matters

In general, where an indication has been given for a completed transaction and it does not proceed to completion, the charge for the abortive work should be made on a *pro rata* basis. In the context of conveyancing, an indication given for a sale will normally be held to include all abortive sales unless the solicitor has revised the indication at the appropriate time.

In a purchase transaction, it is in both the solicitor's and the client's interests that the extent of the indication is revised in writing as soon as abortive matters make it clear that the original indication is no longer appropriate.

In all abortive matter cases, the Appeals and Adjudication Committee will look closely at the available evidence and decide the scope of the indication.

See **15.9** in connection with estates which turn out to be insolvent.

2.7.15   Approximations

Where an indication is expressed in forms such as 'about £500', or 'approximately £500', it would normally be expected that the final fee charged would be within 10 per cent of the indicated figure. Any fee outside that tolerance may (depending on the circumstances) be viewed as a substantial variation resulting in the original approximation restricting the solicitor's fee.

2.7.16   Time limits

When confirming an indication, it is advisable to make clear the time period within which the indication will remain valid. Failure to do so may well (depending on the circumstances of the case) result in solicitors being held to what they consider to be an out-of-date figure, particularly where it is clear that the client still viewed the indication as an incentive to instruct the solicitor and relied upon it.

CHAPTER 3

Client care

Heather Stewart

3.1   INTRODUCTION

Legal practices are the same as any other business – you have services that you wish to sell in order to make the desired level of return on your investment. In the case of a probate department, these services will include wills, trusts, tax planning and estate administration. Clients will only buy these services and the department will only make that return if its products are what clients want and they consider the price charged to be fair. Expectations of, and attitudes towards, legal services have changed significantly in the last 25 years. Many legal services are now regarded as commodities by clients, which impacts on the price sensitivity of the service. The marketplace has hardened and solicitors have had to accept that adversity and intense competition are here to stay and managing them is not a one-off but a continuous process.

Solicitors already operate in mature markets for most of their services – there are numerous other legal practices offering the same technical skills. Successful firms have differentiated themselves on their service package, the way in which they deliver advice, and on their culture, in order to attract and retain clients who feel comfortable dealing with like-minded people. But, by and large, solicitors have been aware of their competition and the parameters within which they have had to operate.

Now, post Clementi (*Review of the Regulatory Framework for Legal Services in England and Wales – Final Report by Sir David Clementi*, December 2004) and the Government White Paper *The Future of Legal Services: Putting the Consumer First*, the potential marketplace has broadened significantly. Section 55 of Courts and Legal Services Act 1990 was implemented in Autumn 2004, which meant that bodies could apply to become 'approved' for the purposes of applying for grants of representation, further indicating the Government's intention to open up the provision of legal services, and probate services in particular.

It is no longer a question of whether external suppliers will enter the market, but rather *when* they will do so. Some potential entrants may not have experience of delivering legal services but are exceptionally good at understanding their markets and customers. Will solicitors be able to compete? Although some legal firms have excellent senior management, the external competition is likely to have superior management skills throughout their organisation. Even if they do not compete directly against you, the impact of those skills will gradually be felt across all firms. They will have a more commercial approach and deeper pockets, and the way in which services are provided may be quite different from what we have seen in the past. Clients will see how the new suppliers deliver their services and their expectations of all legal firms are likely to rise even further.

To compete, firms are going to have to become more agile, be in tune with continuous change, and be proactive about change. Being receptive to change, constantly ensuring that the service provided actually meets clients' needs, continuously considering how profitability can be maintained or enhanced while meeting those needs, being willing to adopt new ways of working, working in teams, being innovative – these will become absolutely essential.

3.2 CULTURE AND LEADERSHIP

The critical difference between successful and less successful firms irrespective of size is often culture, the intangible issue that affects the behaviour of every person within a firm because it is 'the way we do things round here'. Culture is something that a firm 'is' rather than 'has', but it does not just happen. Although partly derived from a firm's history, culture is in fact managed on a daily basis by the attitudes, behaviours and leadership demonstrated by a firm's partners, the organisational structures and processes by which it is managed and success measured, and the decisions taken in running the firm. Culture provides the guidelines for the behaviour of everyone in the firm, for their attitudes towards work and the way in which it is undertaken, for relationships within the firm and with clients. Firms that have a distinctive culture have a real advantage because this is what differentiates them from other firms. Aspects of service that create confidence and value for clients relate back to a firm's ethos and the way its people consistently treat clients and build relationships with them. Solicitors might profess to care for their clients but, unless their attitude and behaviour actually backs that up, they will fail as far as their clients are concerned.

Good, well-respected team leadership from all partners, the implementation of relevant procedures backed up by training, appropriate supervision and performance review and (as what gets measured gets managed) appropriate changes in targets, are the ways forward to achieve buy-in to a culture in which clients are put first. It is then up to every fee earner to understand the expectations of individual clients and either to deliver a service that meets these expectations or to manage the expectations appropriately. Probate departments have traditionally been staffed with a range of fee earners, many of whom are experienced and therefore may not be supervised to any great extent. In some instances this can lead to fee earners carrying far too heavy a workload to be able to handle files effectively and efficiently, which may lead to poor client service, complaints and potential negligence claims.

Quality accreditation schemes such as Lexcel can act as a catalyst for a change of behaviour, in addition to promoting better management of the firm and greater effectiveness in the way in which work is handled.

3.3 PROFESSIONAL CONDUCT

Practitioners must accept that the Law Society regulations in respect of client care exist to assist with meeting a client's needs from a legal service. They should not be regarded as yet another hurdle, but instead should be embraced and followed to help ensure satisfied clients.

3.3.1 Rule 15 and the Solicitors' Costs Information and Client Care Code 1999

The professional standards in respect of client care are currently embodied in Practice Rule 15 (Costs information and client care) and the Solicitors' Costs Information and Client Care Code 1999 (see **Appendix A4**).

3.3.2 Draft Code of Conduct

The proposed Law Society Code of Conduct is anticipated to come into effect in 2007.

3.4 UNDERSTANDING YOUR CLIENTS' PERSPECTIVE

For some clients, either making a will or dealing with a relative's estate may be their first contact with a lawyer, while other clients may be sophisticated users of legal services. However, for all clients, the matters that a solicitor will be dealing with on their behalf are likely to be of immense personal importance to them. Clients are members of a consumerist society and they will anticipate a certain level of service. They want to feel confident they are receiving the best advice and that your charges are fair and reasonable. Unfortunately they cannot assess either of those issues beforehand and so may approach a solicitor's service with a feeling of uncertainty. Their lack of knowledge manifests itself in a need for information, particularly in a long-running probate matter. Unfamiliarity with what could or should happen, or the time that each stage should take, often makes clients feel that things are out of their control. Nor can they anticipate the likely level of costs, which increases their feeling of vulnerability. They may also find it hard to under-stand the concept of a 'value' element in addition to what they may consider to be a high hourly rate.

Clients cannot judge the accuracy of the advice given and therefore will focus on what they understand: how it is delivered. Complaints rarely arise from poor advice. Each interaction between firm and client is a chance to get the service right, or to get it wrong; there will not be another opportu-nity. Client expectations may be quite unrealistic but unless solicitors explain what they can and cannot do for them, the likely timescale involved in each stage of the matter, and give an explanation of the cost estimate, the clients will continue to hold these unrealistic expectations, and will probably become dissatisfied. Managing a matter should be a two-way process: solic-itors need their clients' instructions, and, although solicitors have the profes-sional knowledge and skill, they have to manage the relationship to their clients' satisfaction. Both service levels and costs information need careful management throughout.

3.5 SERVICE LEVELS AND CLIENT EXPECTATIONS

Several aspects of service delivery are key in building a client's confidence and giving a sense of involvement. Communication does not only involve giving advice, and clients often complain that lawyers are poor listeners and assume that they know what the client wants. It is essential to listen to clients in order to understand, or to help them to formulate, their wishes and to ensure that you understand their concerns. Whenever talking about a complicated issue, solicitors should feed back to their client what the client has said and the implications of the proposed course of action, to allow the client to consider whether that is really what they intend. Summarise discussions periodically to ensure that both sides fully understand each other and always write to confirm instructions where there may be any cause for doubt. Bear in mind that a client's emotional or distressed state after a bereavement may affect the ability to absorb information.

Clients will rarely be familiar with the technical language often used in wills and trusts or the intricacies of an inheritance tax calculation. It is essen-tial that the terms are explained to all clients in clear and simple language. Wherever possible, straightforward language should be used in documents, as clients will want to be able to understand them when they revisit them in several years' time. If the provisions are complicated, provide a separate written note giving an explanation in simple terms together with the reason for their inclusion.

Solicitors cannot assume that a client is aware that they are working on their file; clients need to receive information about progress in a timely way. Nor can a client assess the extent of the work that the solicitor may have to undertake. Solicitors should agree when and how they will communicate at the outset and be proactive with information. Case planning at each stage of a matter in which the solicitor identifies with the client the steps involved and agrees how issues are to be dealt with serves to give the client a sense of involvement and an awareness of progress. Whether information should be given to beneficiaries is discussed later in this chapter, but providing information at least on timescales is likely to promote better understanding on their part and give them a better impression of the firm.

Clients need to feel able to contact their solicitors easily. Whilst they understand solicitors may not be available on demand, they expect either their call to be returned on the same day or to receive a holding call. Voice mail is not necessarily the answer, as far too many voice mail messages go unreturned. Departments need to set standards for a prompt response to calls and letters and e-mails, and to enforce these standards.

All clients need to feel supported and valued as clients and here it is the small things that can have the greatest impact. Always bear in mind the emotional state of the client. Greeting clients in reception for instance, helps them to feel at ease and therefore more able to discuss any issues.

In summary, solicitors should do the following:

- Listen to the client; ensure that all relevant information is obtained to enable draft documentation to be prepared which gives effect to the client's wishes.
- Communicate with the client clearly, simply and in a timely way.
- Agree when and how the client will be updated with progress.
- Give an indication of timescales for each stage of the matter.
- Be proactive in explaining any delay.
- Return phone calls, voice mails and e-mails promptly.
- Always keep the client informed of the process and involved in the decision making of the matter.
- Ensure that the client feels that he or she can easily contact either the solicitor or a member of his or her team.
- Follow the client's instructions and deliver the service when and how agreed.
- Keep promises and be reliable and efficient, including in relation to billing.
- Reassure clients on the safety of their documents.
- Treat clients with respect and show genuine interest in them and their concerns.
- Demonstrate the effort put in on the client's behalf.

On a practical note, solicitors should:

- Establish the client's objectives at the outset and at significant stages in a long-running matter. Case planning with the client is a discipline and an opportunity to ensure that this is addressed.

- Where appropriate, consider whether the likely outcome justifies the expense or risk involved.
- Identify any special client needs and discuss and manage the client's expectations.
- Agree with the client how frequently they will be in touch and the most convenient method to do so.
- Outline the likely steps to be involved in the matter overall and explain the immediate stage in detail.
- Explain the responsibilities of the solicitor and those of the client in the next stage of the matter.
- Discuss the likely timescales involved. For example, agree a timescale with the client for drafting, engrossing and executing a will. Operate a reminder system and ensure the will is executed, or the file is closed and the client notified.
- Explain when a client can expect a distribution of assets, if appropriate.
- Use diary systems and file review systems to maintain regular contact with clients.
- Do not delay in acting on instructions, for example the sale of assets, as their value may go down.
- Ensure beneficiaries are correctly identified and that correspondence is sent to the correct address.
- Write to confirm as soon as a matter is completed.
- Bill promptly, while a client still remembers the value of their efforts. (See Principle 14.07 in *The Guide to Professional Conduct of Solicitors 1999*.)
- Account promptly for all client-related funds held (together with interest if appropriate).
- Hand over all papers and property to which the client is entitled (subject to any lien for unpaid bills).
- Handle all post-completion matters speedily.
- Ask clients whether the matter has been completed to their satisfaction and whether the service provided might have been improved in any way.
- Maintain an accurate record of all wills kept. If records are computerised, ensure regular back up, including off site.
- If a will is released, obtain a receipt and ensure that the recipient and his or her address is noted on the register.
- If the original will is sent to the client, make a file note and ensure that a completed copy is retained.
- Ensure that clients are aware where their papers are located, particularly if the firm moves office, merges or changes name.

Effective teams need good leadership. If standards for service are discussed and agreed by members of a team, they are more likely to be complied with than if merely imposed. The following pointers will assist in ensuring a consistent service within a department:

- Agree standards for delegation of work within a team and adhere to them.
- Maintain both written and computerised files and systems in a common format.
- Use key date central diary systems.
- Set up and use regular bring-forward and reporting systems.
- Have a departmental protocol by which all letters/e-mails are answered within a set time.
- Always use attendance notes, whether written or online.
- Engender a culture of discussing files and any difficulties encountered with either clients or the work itself, and make time to do it.
- Undertake file reviews for all fee earners and appropriate supervision for non-partners.

3.6   COSTS INFORMATION

Some practitioners remain reluctant to talk about money with clients; they fail to recognise that clients are often anxious about costs and need that information. Probate clients may be extremely distressed and it may be difficult to discuss costs at an initial meeting, but it should not be avoided. It may not be possible to give an estimate of the likely overall cost or of the timescale involved in a complicated matter until what is involved has been fully investigated, but an estimate can be given for the first investigatory stage and the client informed that you will be in a better position to discuss costs fully after that.

Practitioners will meet clients' needs on costs if they comply with the Solicitors' Costs Information and Client Care Code 1999 (the Code), which is reproduced in **Appendix A4**. Being willing to discuss costs and billing, providing 'the best possible information' on an agreed and regular basis, and undertaking cost/benefit analyses are of enormous benefit to clients. Corporate executors may insist on total transparency and for matters to be billed strictly in accordance with their agreement with the firm. That is what all clients would like, but few receive.

The Law Society's Practice Advice Service has published Non-Contentious Costs (May 2005), extracts from which are reproduced in **Chapter 2**. Both the Practice Advice and Professional Ethics departments at the Law Society provide helplines which are staffed by knowledgeable and helpful solicitors (see **Useful addresses**). The Lexcel accreditation standard embodies the Code and provides a framework for the consistent delivery of excellent service to clients. Client care guidance published by the Law Society in May 2006 entitled Your Clients – Your Business can be downloaded from its website (**www.lawsociety.co.uk**) and provides a checklist of the Code in an easy-to-read format (although the Code itself should always be referred to when considering whether you have complied with its provisions). Extracts from this guidance are reproduced below.

3.7   WHO IS THE CLIENT?

Identifying the client may be problematic when handling an estate, particularly as a solicitor-executor. What relationship should the solicitor have with the beneficiaries? How much information should be given in respect of costs or the conduct of the matter in general? See **Chapters 1** and **2** and Mike Frith's article 'Who is the probate client?' [2000] *Gazette*, 10 February, 38, reproduced in **Appendix A3**.

In *Jemma Trust* v. *Liptrott* [2003] EWCA Civ 1476, the Court of Appeal stated that it would be best practice to agree the charging regime in advance not only with the executors but also, where appropriate, with any residuary beneficiary who is an entitled third party under the Solicitors' (Non-Contentious Business) Remuneration Order 1994. The clear message was the need for transparency between solicitor, executor and residuary beneficiary.

However, in the case of *Barrett* v. *Father Benjamin Rutt-Field* (SCCO, 29 January 2004), Costs Judge Rogers ruled that the sole beneficiary had the status neither of a client nor of an entitled person and was thus unable to challenge the costs of the administration. Father Ben and the deceased's solicitor were appointed executors of the estate and, although the solicitors had supplied a costs information letter to both Father Ben and the beneficiary, Mrs Barrett, they supplied copies of interim bills and revised estimates to him but not to her. The solicitors were criticised for not doing so and Costs Judge Rogers referred to the message for transparency from the *Jemma* case.

Compare the guidance of the proposed Rule 2 in the draft Law Society Code of Conduct [2004]:

> Where you are, in effect, your firm's client – for example, as an executor administering a deceased's estate or a trustee of a trust – you should consider what information, if any, should be given to interested parties. There is no requirement, for example, that beneficiaries under a will or trust should be treated as though they were clients. It may, however, be good practice to provide some information – for example about the type of work to be carried out and approximate time scales.

3.8   CLIENT CARE LETTERS/TERMS AND CONDITIONS

The Law Society has recently published guidance on client care letters and terms and conditions of business: Your Clients – Your Business (Law Society, 2006). Section 2 of the guidance states:

Since the client care rule came into force, solicitors have adopted a number of different approaches and styles in their client care letters. Some solicitors put their terms and conditions in their client care letter. The result is a letter that may extend to several pages. Other solicitors create a relatively brief letter and append a separate terms and conditions document that will run to several pages. In regulatory terms, neither approach is wrong. It is for the individual solicitor to decide what best suits them and their client.

However, as we seem to be moving to the position where more terms and conditions may be appropriate because of the complexity of practice, we believe that more solicitors will proceed on the basis of a separate terms and conditions document. The guidance is, therefore, based on that premise, although clearly solicitors who do not favour that approach can simply import the required terms and conditions into their letters.

We have tried to provide a comprehensive list of general terms and conditions to be considered. Not all of them may apply to each practice. Solicitors are encouraged to be selective in deciding which ones to include in their terms and conditions. Also, consider whether the capability of the client means that they will understand the terms and conditions, and if not try to express them in such a way that they are made clear to the client. Consideration should also be given to whether additional terms and conditions are appropriate given the nature of the work being dealt with.

Paragraph 2.3 in Your Clients – Your Business advises on costs:

How you address costs information will vary depending on the matter and how costs are being funded. However, our suggested approach is for the costs information which appears in your client care letter to be tailored to the circumstances of that particular client. It may be appropriate to include in your general terms and conditions document other standard information about costs.

The guidance also suggests that a good client care letter should do the following:

1. Clearly identify the client.
2. State what the solicitor is instructed to do (and what is not included in the retainer if appropriate) and, if possible, give timescales.
3. Give an overall estimate of costs, broken down between fees, VAT and disbursements. Make it clear how the costs have been calculated and refer the client to any additional information on costs in the terms and conditions document, if there are any.
4. Give the name and status of the person who will be dealing with the matter in the firm and the name of the principal responsible for its overall supervision.
5. Give the name and status of the person whom the client should approach if there is a problem.

Some solicitors ask the client to sign, date and return either the client care letter or their terms and conditions document. This is not a regulatory requirement, but could assist solicitors if they are subsequently faced with a client denying he or she has received this information.

In general, clients seem willing to sign and return a copy of such a letter because they are familiar with commercial organisations' terms and conditions in this format.

3.9 CLIENT CARE CHECKLIST

Your Clients – Your Business provides a client care checklist, reproduced below.

2.1 Client care

– Identify who will conduct the matter.
– Give the person's status.
– Name the partner with overall supervisory responsibility for the work (unless the fee earner is a partner).
– Name a person the client should contact in the event of a problem.

2.2 The matter

– Give a clear explanation of the issues and the extent of your retainer. Make it clear if you will not be advising on a particular issue.
– Give an explanation of the likely timescale.
– Confirm the instructions received and advice given (including key dates, where appropriate).
– Outline the next steps to be taken by the firm and the client, as appropriate.

2.3 Costs

How you address costs information will vary depending on the matter and how costs are being funded. However, our suggested approach is for the costs information which appears in your client care letter to be tailored to the circumstances of that particular client. It may be appropriate to include in your general terms and conditions document other standard information about costs.

2.4 General costs information

– Give the best information possible about the likely overall costs, broken down between fees, VAT and disbursements.
– Explain the time likely to be spent, if time is a factor in calculating the fees.
– The best information possible can include:
  – agreeing a fixed-fee; or
  – giving a realistic estimate; or
  – giving a forecast within a possible range of costs; or
  – explaining why it is not possible to give the above; and instead give the best possible information about the costs of the next stage of the matter.
– Explain the client's ability to set upper limits on fees to a privately paying client.
– Make clear at the outset if it is an estimate or a quotation and ensure that the client understands the difference.

- Explain how fees are calculated (for example, by giving hourly rates) – this is unnecessary where the fees are fixed or clear.
- State if charging rates may be increased.
- State how the firm will charge if the matter is not completed.
- Outline what reasonably foreseeable payments the client may have to make (to any party) and when.
- Agree times or stages in the transaction when the client will be updated in relation to costs information (including not only costs incurred, but also addressing when a costs estimate or agreed upper limit may be exceeded) and any changed circumstances affecting the client's potential liability for costs, risk or cost-benefit position. Costs information should be updated at least every six months, or sooner, if it appears that a costs estimate or agreed upper limit may or will be exceeded.
- Explain the firm's billing arrangements.
- Explore the availability of alternative funding arrangements, even if the firm does not take on work on that basis.
- Advise the client of the cost-benefit risk analysis of pursuing their matter.
- Disclose any relevant arrangement with a third party such as a funder, fee-sharer, or introducer that may affect the client or the solicitor's conduct of the matter – including the amount of any referral fee where appropriate.
- Advise the client if money is needed on account.

2.5 ...

2.6 A privately paying client in a contentious matter (and potentially contentious matter)

Explain to the client their potential liability for their own costs and for those of any other party, including:

- The fact that the client will be responsible for paying the firm's bill in full regardless of any order for costs made against an opponent.
- Potential liability for opponent's costs as well as own costs, if the case is lost.
- The risk of an opponent not being ordered or able to pay costs.
- The implications of an opponent being legally aided.
- The possible cost implications of the client rejecting Alternative Dispute Resolution (ADR).
- The costs and risk of enforcing judgments.
- The costs implications if the client withdraws, or rejects a reasonable offer of settlement.

2.7 Liability for third party costs in non-contentious matters

The solicitor should explain to the client any liability they may have for the payment of third party costs, for example, landlords' fees.

3.10 RULE 2.02 DRAFT CODE OF CONDUCT

Rule 2.02 of the draft Code of Conduct is more specific than the Solicitors' Costs Information and Client Care Code 1999:

(1) You must:

    (a) identify clearly the client's objectives in relation to the work done for the client;

    (b) give the client a clear explanation of the issues involved and the options available to the client;

    (c) agree with the client the next steps to be taken; and

    (d) keep the client informed of progress, unless otherwise agreed.

(2) You must, both at the outset and, as necessary, during the course of the matter:

    (a) agree an appropriate level of service;

    (b) explain your responsibilities;

    (c) explain the client's responsibilities;

    (d) ensure that the client is given, in writing, the name and status of the person dealing with the matter and the name of the person responsible for its overall supervision; and

    (e) explain any constraints or conditions resulting from your relationship with a third party (eg a funder, fee sharer, introducer) which affect the steps that you can take on the client's behalf.

Although the information under this rule does not have to be in writing, it is recommended that there is a written record.

3.11 ADDITIONAL ISSUES RELATING TO COSTS

1. The ruling in *Pilbrow* v. *Pearless de Rougement* [1999] 3 All ER 355 means that firms should give the status of the fee earner dealing with the matter immediately on receipt of instructions. Be particularly clear about this status: for example do not describe a fee earner as a legal executive unless that person is a member of the Institute of Legal Executives.

2. All information given orally should be confirmed in writing to the client as soon as possible.

3. Do not anticipate that even the most experienced client will fully comprehend complicated funding issues. Costs information must not be 'inaccurate or misleading' and 'must be given clearly, in a way and at a level which is appropriate for the particular client'. Any terms should be explained in simple, non-legal jargon to all clients.

4. Merely setting out the hourly rate in your terms of business or retainer letter, even if supported by information leaflets, does not comply with the requirement to give your client 'the best information possible about the likely overall costs'. All possible options should be considered, discussed and then confirmed in a client care letter that accompanies your terms and conditions of business or retainer letter.

5. An indication of the probable timescale along with the number of hours the matter is likely to take must be given to the client.

6. Solicitors are expected to give the client the opportunity to set an upper limit on costs and are required to state whether any estimate or quote provision is intended to be fixed.
7. Solicitors must get back to their clients and revise their estimates and secure the client's acceptance to the new figure before it is exceeded. There have been a series of cases involving solicitor and client.

In *Wong* v. *Vizards (A Firm)* [1997] 2 Costs LR 46, the defendants were allowed a 15 per cent margin over the estimate as an acceptable margin of error. The claimant had sought a reliable estimate from his solicitors as to his potential costs exposure before deciding to take the matter to trial. He was not required to pay 'a far greater amount without further warning or a proper explanation of the difference'. Following *Wong*, in *Anthony* v. *Ellis and Fairburn (A Firm)* [2000] 2 Costs LR 277, the defendants were limited to the same 15 per cent margin over their estimate.

With reference to *Wong* v. *Vizards*, the court in *Slade* v. *Boyes Turner Solicitors* (unreported) SCCO, 17 October 2003 held that the payment by clients of interim bills is not treated as implication of acceptance of either an increase in hourly rates or an increased level of costs. It was held to be 'incorrect for the notification to be given after the work is done, or the bulk of the fees incurred'.

In the case of *Barrett* v. *Father Benjamin Rutt-Field* (SCCO, 29 January 2004), Costs Judge Rogers made it clear that the breach of the requirement to tell the client in advance if a final bill is going to exceed an estimate applies just as much in non-contentious as in contentious work.

3.12 IMPLICATIONS FOR MANAGING PROBATE DEPARTMENTS AND COSTS

The recent cases raise difficult issues and it is of even greater importance that probate departments are organised to ensure that:

- fee earners who discuss costs with clients fully understand the obligations under the Code and of current costs issues; and
- costs information is disseminated to all members of the department.

3.13 COMPLAINTS

Many practitioners perceive a complaint to be the same as a negligence claim, but few complaints arise from bad advice. In an analysis of the reasons for complaints made to the former Office for the Supervision of Solicitors in 2004, over 50 per cent of complaints included failure to keep clients informed or to reply to their queries for information. A further 37 per cent of complaints included delay and 29 per cent failure to follow instructions. According to the Client Care Guide to Keeping Clients (Law Society, 2004, superseded by Your Clients – Your Business) some 60 per cent of complaints reaching the Office for the Supervision of Solicitors also concerned costs, the majority being in respect of the poor handling of costs information, largely arising from poor communication in respect of both terminology and transparency.

Complaints are expensive, not only in terms of loss of fees, potential loss of reputation, and loss of future work but also because of the hassle and time that it takes to resolve them. However, if complaints are received, they should be seen from a positive stance and treated as contributing to the promotion of quality and continuous improvement. They provide valuable feedback on clients' perceptions of the firm's service and, if a complaint is handled well, may even result in increased client satisfaction and loyalty. In fact, it is far better that a client actually makes a complaint about perceived poor service because it presents an opportunity for redress. Many private clients do not have the courage to tell their lawyers of their dissatisfaction. Instead, they will tell their family, friends, colleagues, union representative or other referrer thereby doing untold damage to a firm's reputation and potentially resulting in the firm losing work.

To learn from complaints, consider how to collate and analyse the information they contain, whether within a department or centrally, and then review and use the information. What does it tell you? Dig deeper and find the underlying cause of the complaint. Are there any trends? What must be done to ensure that the complaint is not repeated? There may be a raft of reasons for a complaint arising: for example, too much work, poor supervision, poor delegation, lack of competence, or a breakdown of internal communication. When analysed, many problems are caused by indadequate management or lack of skills training, such as interviewing or listening skills, or the inadequate setting and enforcement of standards. No one is infallible, nor is any firm is immune from receiving complaints, irrespective of size.

It is far better to resolve a complaint in-house rather than to allow it to escalate and result in a complaint being made to the Consumer Complaints Service. The current professional standard for handling complaints is set out in Rule 15 and at para.7(b) of the Code. This states that every principal in private practice (or, in the case of a recognised body, the body itself) must:

(i) ensure that the client is told the name of the person in the firm to contact about any problem with the service provided;
(ii) have a written complaints procedure and ensure that complaints are handled in accordance with it;
(iii) ensure that the client is given a copy of the complaints procedure on request.

Material breaches of Rule 15 can amount to inadequate professional conduct and lead to findings in which all or part of the solicitor's costs are disallowed, or a direction for compensation of up to £15,000 to be paid to the client.

3.13.1 Draft Code of Conduct Rule 2.05

Complaints handling is set out in Rule 2.05 of the draft Code of Conduct. The draft rule is broadly similar to Practice Rule 15 but also covers the ongoing handling of complaints.

2.05 Complaints handling

(1) If you are a principal in a firm you must ensure:

    (a) that the firm has a written complaints procedure and that complaints are handled promptly, fairly and effectively in accordance with it;

    (b) that the client is told, in writing, at the outset:

        (i) that, in the event of a problem, the client is entitled to complain; and

        (ii) to whom the client should complain;

    (c) that the client is given a copy of the complaints procedure on request; and

    (d) that once a complaint has been made, that the person complaining is told in writing:

        (i) who the complaint will be handled, and

        (ii) within what time-scales they will be given an initial and/or substantive response.

(2) If you can demonstrate that it was inappropriate in the circumstances to meet some or all of these requirements, you will not breach of 2.05.

(3) You must not charge your client for the cost of investigating a complaint.

3.13.2 Complaints handling procedures

The content of each firm's complaints handling procedure is an internal matter, but the procedure must be in writing, clear and unambiguous. Merely informing the client about the persons with whom a client may take up any concern or complaint in the original Rule 15 letter does not constitute a written complaints procedure. The Law Society guidance, Handling Complaints Effectively (available from **www.lawsociety.org.uk**), gives examples of complaints handling procedures applicable to different sizes of firm. When defining a complaint, firms should ensure that their definition is not too wide to be unmanageable. The definition provided by Lexcel of 'any expression of client dissatisfaction which the fee earner is unable immediately to resolve' is realistic. Further assistance on the format of a central complaints record can be obtained from the Consumer Complaints Service.

Everyone in the firm should be aware of the obligation to ensure that clients know whom to contact if they have a problem, the information to give to the client if a complaint is made, and the importance of recording the stages of a complaint and its final outcome. Staff should be provided with regular training on the firm's system, and suitable training should be included as part of the firm's induction process.

3.13.3   Dealing with complaints

Most lawyers are articulate and have an assertive air of certainty when arguing a point which gives an impression of confidence and sometimes arrogance. However, this does not necessarily mean they are also thick skinned and able to take feedback easily. Many solicitors find it hard to acknowledge that they may be at fault and all too often they will become defensive when criticised, even constructively. They do not feel comfortable listening to feedback or reflecting upon it to see if it contains any element of truth. Instead, solicitors often adopt an aggressive stance in defence of their conduct, but this does nothing to assist client relations. A more constructive response is to be conciliatory. Few clients make complaints lightly and, even if you do not think a complaint is justified, you should at least acknowledge that the client is upset and apologise for this. The Law Society's Handling Complaints Effectively gives guidance on how to handle complaints and reminds solicitors:

Don't:
- Be aggressive or defensive, or suffer wounded pride.
- Reject the complaint immediately without a good reason.
- Forget clients are your livelihood and have needs and expectations you should care about.
- Give the impression that only you know all the answers.
- Be patronising.
- Be critical that your client expects money as a remedy. Clients are consumers and demand a direct approach.
- Let your client's complaint 'escape' from your office to ours.

CHAPTER 4

Estate administration and the Financial Services and Markets Act 2000: a review

Peter Camp

This review is intended to give a brief outline of the relevance of the Financial Services and Markets Act 2000 to wills and probate work and to raise the issues that should be considered. First, terminology and sources are covered; then where to find more information; finally, some of the basic points are outlined.

4.1 TERMINOLOGY AND SOURCES

The Financial Services and Markets Act 2000 (FSMA 2000) prohibits the undertaking of 'regulated activities' without authorisation. Since the Act came into force on 1 December 2001 the only regulating authority has been the Financial Services Authority (FSA). The Law Society is no longer able to regulate solicitors as a recognised professional body. However, exemptions and exclusions in the new legislation mean that few solicitors will need to be authorised by the FSA. It is, however, important for firms to identify the exact nature of the exemptions and exclusions. Undertaking regulated activities without authorisation and outside the statutory exemptions or exclusions is a criminal offence.

The main statutory exemption for professionals is contained in FSMA 2000, Part XX. Solicitors will be able to rely upon Part XX since the Law Society is a 'designated professional body' (DPB). However the Society has been required to issue rules regulating solicitors who use the Part XX exemption. The rules are the Solicitors' Financial Services (Scope) Rules 2001 (the Scope Rules) and the Solicitors' Financial Services (Conduct of Business) Rules 2001 (the COB Rules). Both sets of Rules have been amended in the light of the extension of financial services regulation to regulated mortgages and insurance work.

Solicitors conducting regulated activities (whether mainstream activities or exempt activities) must also comply with the Money Laundering Regulations 2003, SI 2003/3075, now contained in *The Guide to the Professional Conduct of Solicitors 1999* (the Guide) at Annex 3B. (For further details, see below, at **4.3.8**.)

4.2 MORE INFORMATION

Probate work is, generally speaking, the area where most solicitors come into contact with regulated activities, FSMA 2000, the Scope Rules and the COB Rules. It is, therefore, important that solicitors are aware of the compliance requirements and also the investment business opportunities involved. The publications listed at **4.3.8** would be useful if you wish to gain a wider knowledge of this area.

The Professional Ethics Division (see **Useful addresses**) offers confidential guidance on the Practice Rules, the Scope Rules and the COB Rules, including whether or not authorisation is required.

4.3 THE BASICS

What follows is, necessarily, a brief indication of the relevant aspects of this area. The guidance and rules will give more detailed information.

4.3.1 Do you need to be authorised?

Solicitors carrying out probate and trust work are likely to be potentially undertaking regulated activities. However the exclusions and exemptions contained in the legislation mean that most solicitors will not need to be authorised by the FSA.

4.3.2 What are 'investments' and what is a 'regulated activity'?

'Investments' are defined in the Financial Services and Markets Act 2000 (Regulated Activities) Order 2001, SI 2001/544 (RAO 2001) (as amended by the Financial Services and Markets Act 2000 (Regulated Activities) (Amendment) (No.1) Order 2003, SI 2003/1475 and the Financial Services and Markets Act 2000 (Regulated Activities) (Amendment) (No.2) Order 2003, SI 2003/1476). Examples include stocks and shares, unit trusts and life and other insurance policies. Further, regulated mortgage contracts will also be 'investments' for these purposes. (National Savings products are outside the scope of FSMA 2000.) The activities constituting 'regulated activities' are also defined in RAO 2001: examples include dealing and arranging deals in investments, giving investment advice and the discretionary management of investments. The activities of 'sending dematerialised instructions' and 'custody of investments' are also potentially regulated activities. 'Custody of investments' involves safeguarding *and* administering investments and this is likely to be relevant to firms conducting probate/trust work. Further guidance is available from the Professional Ethics Division.

4.3.3 What exclusions apply?

Under the terms of RAO 2001 there are exclusions for dealing and arranging deals where the activities are carried out using an authorised person, providing an authorised person has advised on that activity. However, of greater relevance to trust and probate practitioners are the exclusions contained in RAO 2001, art.66 which apply to arranging deals, discretionary management, investment advice, sending dematerialised instructions and custody of investments where the activity is being carried out by a trustee or PR. Note that these exclusions are not available where a firm is simply acting for outside trustees or PRs. However, where a member of the firm is a trustee or PR (whether alone, with another member of the firm or with an external trustee or PR) these exclusions are valuable. Practitioners must check carefully the conditions contained in art.66. Where they apply the firm will not be carrying on regulated activities and will be subject to no compliance requirements other than those applicable to solicitors generally. There is, however, a very important restriction on the use of the exclusions. The 'authorised person' exclusion and the 'trustee' exclusion do not, generally, apply where the investment is an insurance policy. Solicitors who advise on or make arrangements for a PR client to obtain, for example, a missing beneficiary insurance policy will not be able to benefit from any of these exclusions.

4.3.4 What exemptions apply?

As discussed in **4.3.3** above, whilst RAO 2001, art.66 is invaluable for those matters where a member of the firm is a trustee or PR, it will offer no assistance in those circumstances where the firm is simply acting for outside trustees or PRs or where an insurance policy is involved. Here, an alternative solution must be found to avoid the need for authorisation. Under Part XX of FSMA 2000 certain professionals can undertake 'exempt regulated activities' without the need for authorisation. The exempt regime is available where the member of the profession is regulated by a DPB, and the Law Society is such a body. Certain conditions must apply before regulated activities can be treated as exempt. These include the requirement that the activities must be incidental to the provision of other professional services, and that the activities are of a type not prohibited by the rules of the DPB. The Scope Rules of the Law Society contain a number of prohibitions. Most of these prohibitions will not be relevant to probate practitioners but one is worthy of note. The Scope Rules prohibit solicitors entering into a regulated mortgage contract (where credit is provided to an individual or trustees secured by a first legal charge over residential property) as lender unless it is done in the firm's capacity as a trustee or PR and the borrower is a beneficiary under the trust, will or intestacy.

Where the Part XX regime is relied upon, care must be taken to ensure that the specific prohibitions relating to 'packaged products', 'securities' and other 'relevant investments' are identified. In most cases these prohibitions apply to recommendations and arrangements to *buy* such investments. Investment activities undertaken by probate practitioners usually relate to the disposal of investments. However, trust practitioners may need to take care in relying upon the Part XX regime as a result of these Scope restrictions. Where policies other than life insurance policies are involved (e.g. advice on or arrangements made in respect of missing beneficiary policies) solicitors should be able to use the Part XX regime. However, any advice or arrangement relating to an insurance policy (life or general insurance) will amount to 'insurance mediation'. Where a firm undertakes insurance mediation, the Scope Rules require the firm to appoint a compliance officer and to ensure that the firm's name is registered in the FSA register.

4.3.5 The 'incidental' nature of probate

If a solicitor is involved only in winding up estates on behalf of outside PRs, then the investment business work is likely to be 'incidental' to the main activity, which is the administration. The effect of this is that the work will be capable of falling within Part XX of FSMA 2000 and the requirements for compliance relating to non-insurance products are very few: see below.

4.3.6 Compliance requirements

Where the statutory exclusions apply, as noted above, no special compliance requirements will apply. Where a solicitor relies upon the Part XX regime, the COB Rules will apply. These rules are designed to be simple and generally will not impose a major burden upon practitioners. However, it is necessary for probate practitioners who rely upon Part XX to familiarise themselves with the COB Rules. They cover obligations relating to status disclosure, record keeping, systems for safe custody and confirmation of execution only business. Where insurance mediation is undertaken, the status disclosure requirements include an obligation to provide the client with a statutory statement (see COB Rule 3) before undertaking any insurance mediation. Further, if the insurance mediation includes the recommendation of a policy to a client, the requirements of COB Rule 8A will apply. This rule requires firms to indicate whether or not a full market analysis of insurance products was undertaken before making any recommendation; ensuring that whether or not a full market analysis was undertaken, the recommendation was suitable to the client's demands and needs; and providing the client with a demands and needs statement.

43

4.3.7 Relevance of the Solicitors' Practice Rules

Solicitors who are involved in investment business activities (whether bene-fiting from a statutory exclusion or from the 'exempt' regime under Part XX of FSMA 2000) are bound by the Solicitors' Practice Rules 1990. As with any aspect of a solicitor's practice, the Solicitors' Practice Rules 1990 will apply, but of particular relevance to probate work and investment business services are Practice Rules 2, 3, 5, 10 and 12. (See the Guide, paras.27.19 onwards.)

4.3.8 Money laundering

Any compliance system should include appropriate anti-money laundering procedures. The Law Society has issued Anti-Money Laundering Guidance for Solicitors Conducting Private Client Work (February 2006) (see **Chapter 6** and **Appendix A1**). This confirms that solicitors could be at risk of money laundering where their work involves assisting with the management or distribution of assets. If the assets are (or include) 'criminal property' (defined as the benefit or representation of the benefit, from criminal conduct), the solicitor could be involved in one or more of the money laun-dering offences contained in Proceeds of Crime Act 2002 (POCA 2002), ss.327–329. Under these provisions it is an offence:

(a) to conceal, disguise, convert, transfer or remove from the UK the proceeds of criminal conduct (s.327);

(b) to be concerned in an arrangement which facilitates the acquisition, reten-tion, use or control of another person's proceeds of criminal conduct, where there is knowledge or suspicion that this is the case (s.328); or

(c) to acquire, use or possess the proceeds of criminal conduct (s.329).

Further, even if solicitors are not themselves involved in the management or distribution of assets, they may be subject to an obligation under POCA 2002, s.330 to report to the authorities, information which gives rise to knowledge or suspicion of money laundering where such knowledge or suspi-cion came into their possession as a result of business in the 'regulated sector'. The 'regulated sector' is defined as including 'regulated activities' under FSMA 2000 (i.e. where solicitors are relying upon the Part XX exclu-sion regime (see above)) and legal services which involve participation in a financial or real property transaction.

Probate practitioners are likely to be subject to the Money Laundering Regulations 2003, SI 2003/3075. These apply where the solicitor undertakes 'relevant business', which is defined in the same way as the 'regulated sector' (see above). Where the regulations apply, solicitors must establish procedures relating to:

(a) training;

(b) client identification;

(c)   record keeping; and

(d)   reporting procedures.

For further information, the following publications would be useful.

- P. Camp, *Solicitors and Money Laundering: A Compliance Handbook*, 2nd edn (Law Society, 2006).
- Money Laundering Guidance (January 2004) available from the Law Society website (**www.lawsociety.org.uk**) or from Professional Ethics as amended by Guidance on *Bowman* v. *Fels* [2005] EWCA 226 (September 2005).
- Financial Services and Solicitors (September 2004), an information pack available from the Law Society website or from Professional Ethics.

4.3.9   Solicitors' Accounts Rules 1998

Solicitors are also subject to the Solicitors' Accounts Rules 1998. Brief guidance on these can be found at **Chapter 5**.

4.3.10   Investment business opportunities

If a firm decides to offer investment services to its clients, either by seeking authorisation or by using an exclusion or exemption, then there are a number of investment business opportunities deriving from probate work. Examples include offering investment advice to beneficiaries and tax planning for beneficiaries.

CHAPTER 5

Solicitors' Accounts Rules 1998

Professional Ethics, Law Society

5.1 INTRODUCTION

The Solicitors' Accounts Rules 1998 (the Rules) were made by the Council of
the Law Society with the approval of the Master of the Rolls on 22 July 1998
and had to be implemented by 1 May 2000. They include explanatory notes
which form part of the Rules.

The Rules are published by the Law Society in the *Solicitors' Accounts
Manual*, 9th edn (Law Society, 2004) and the latest version of the Rules can
be downloaded from the Law Society's website (see **www.lawsociety.org.uk/
professional/conduct.law**; see also the Guide at **www.lawsociety.org.uk/
professional/conduct/guideonline.law**.).

From 17 March 2004, the following changes apply:

* note (ix) to Rule 15 has been updated to reflect the view of the Solicitors'
  Disciplinary Tribunal that the provision of banking facilities through a
  client account does not form part of a solicitor's practice;
* a new Rule 21(2), and new notes (vii)–(x), deal with regular payments
  from the Legal Services Commission under its civil and criminal
  contracting schemes (the new rule had to be implemented by 1 May 2005);
* an amended Rule 32(10), and new notes (xv)–(xvii), permit the retention
  of digital images of paid client account cheques in place of the original
  paper cheques (see also note (xiv) to Rule 32 as to the extent of the
  requirement to keep paid cheques).

5.2 AN OUTLINE OF THE RULES

5.2.1 Who is governed by the Rules?

The Rules apply to solicitors, registered European lawyers, registered foreign
lawyers and recognised bodies. They do not apply to solicitors who are
employed by, for example, a local authority or to a solicitor when carrying out
the function of a coroner or other judicial office or a sheriff or under-sheriff
(Rules 4 and 5).

All of the partners in a practice are required to ensure compliance with the Rules by fellow partners and everyone else in the practice, and to remedy breaches (Rules 6 and 7). (This duty extends to directors of recognised bodies which are companies, and to members of recognised bodies which are limited liability partnerships.) The case of *Weston* v. *The Law Society* (1998) *The Times*, 15 July is a reminder that solicitors are under a heavy obligation in securing compliance with the Rules. The Court of Appeal confirmed that it was appropriate to strike off a solicitor where no dishonesty was alleged but the partner in question was guilty of breaches through his partners' activities of which he was unaware. Lord Bingham referred to 'the duty of anyone holding anyone else's money to exercise a proper stewardship in relation to it'.

The Law Society's Guidelines (published as Appendix 3 to the Rules) state that compliance with the Rules is the equal responsibility of all partners. Responsibility for day-to-day supervision may be delegated to individual partner(s) but it is not acceptable to delegate total responsibility to a cashier or book-keeper.

Liquidators, trustees in bankruptcy, Court of Protection receivers and trustees of occupational pension schemes are subject to some of the record-keeping requirements of the Rules (Rule 9 and see **5.4** below). The reason for this extension of the Rules is to protect the vulnerable against defalcations and to protect the profession from claims on the Compensation Fund, but with a lighter regulatory touch because of the existence of other statutory regulatory frameworks.

Similarly, solicitors who operate joint accounts with clients, another solicitors' practice or another third party, or operate the accounts of clients, are subject to certain record-keeping requirements (Rules 10 and 11 and see **5.4** below).

The obligations on reporting accountants are set out in Part F of the Rules.

5.2.2 Classification of money (Rule 13)

All money held or received in the course of practice falls into one of the following categories.

Client money

Client money is money held or received for a client and all other money which is not controlled trust money or office money.

A 'client' is defined by Rule 2 as a person for whom the solicitor acts. However, client money includes money held as a bailee, agent, or donee of a power of attorney. It also extends to money held as stakeholder, liquidator, trustee in bankruptcy or Court of Protection receiver.

Client money also includes money received:

- for unpaid professional disbursements;
- for other unpaid disbursements where the solicitor has not incurred a liability to pay them (for example, stamp duty land tax, Land Registry registration fees, telegraphic transfer fees and court fees);
- on account of costs;
- as commission paid in respect of a client unless the solicitor is entitled to retain it (see Practice Rule 10).

Professional disbursements include the fees of counsel, other lawyers, and other professionals, agents or experts instructed by the solicitor – this will include interpreters, translators, process servers, surveyors and estate agents instructed by the solicitor. It does not include travel agents' charges.

Controlled trust money

Controlled trust money is money held or received for a 'controlled trust'. A controlled trust is one where the solicitor is the sole trustee or co-trustee only with one or more of his or her partners or employees. See Rule 2(2)(h) for controlled trusts and registered foreign lawyers, registered European lawyers and recognised bodies. Note that if the trust is not a controlled trust, for example because there is a 'lay' co-trustee, the money is client money.

Office money

Office money is money which belongs to the solicitor or practice. It includes:

- money held or received in connection with running the practice, for example PAYE or VAT on the firm's fees;
- interest on general client accounts;
- money received for profit costs where a bill or written notification of costs has been sent;
- money received to repay the solicitor for disbursements already paid;
- money received for disbursements which are unpaid but for which the solicitor has incurred a liability to pay (e.g. items settled by a credit account such as Land Registry search fees, taxi fares or courier charges); however, unpaid professional disbursements are expressly excluded and money received for them is client money (see above under 'Client money' for the definition of a professional disbursement);
- money received for an agreed fee (see Rule 19(5)); and
- money held in the client account but earmarked for costs and awaiting transfer (see Rule 19(3)).

5.3   USE OF CLIENT ACCOUNT

A solicitor who holds or receives client money and/or controlled trust money must keep one or more client accounts (see Rule 14(1)).

5.3.1   What is a client account? (Rule 14)

A client account is an account of the practice kept at a bank or building society in England and Wales. It must include the word 'client' in the title. There are two types of client account:

- a separate designated client account which is a deposit or share account for money relating to a single client, or a current, deposit or share account kept for a single controlled trust; or
- a general client account which is any other client account.

5.3.2   What money goes into the client bank account? (Rule 15)

Rule 15(1) states that all client money and controlled trust money must be paid without delay into a client account.

There are some exceptions, for example when a client instructs the solicitor not to pay in money (Rule 16(1)) or where a controlled trustee operating in accordance with his or her powers pays money into a non-client account or retains it as cash (Rule 18(c)).

Rule 15(2) states that no other money may be paid into the client account. Again there are exceptions so, for example, a solicitor can use his or her own money to open or maintain the client account and can advance money to the client where the solicitor is holding too little money for a client or controlled trust to fund a payment.

5.3.3   When can money come out of the client account?

This is governed by Rule 22. The situations in which solicitors can withdraw client money and controlled trust money include:

- making payments on behalf of the client or trust;
- paying disbursements on behalf of the client or trust;
- reimbursing themselves for money spent on behalf of the client or trust;
- transferring to another client account.

The money taken out of a general client account must not exceed the total held for that client or controlled trust in all the general client accounts.

There is one exception to this, which is where a solicitor holds money in a separate designated client account for a client or trust. A solicitor can withdraw from a general client account a sum in excess of the amount held there for the client or trust provided that a transfer is immediately made from the separate designated client account.

Note: A solicitor can withdraw money from the client account to meet the cost of disbursements that have already been paid from the office bank account without sending a bill. Solicitors can only withdraw money for their professional charges once they have sent the bill or other written notification of costs, or agreed a fee under Rule 19(5). Once the bill has been sent the money due for professional charges becomes office money and it must be transferred within 14 days. See **5.3.6** below.

5.3.4   Mixed receipts (Rule 20)

Where office money is received mixed with either client or controlled trust money, either the cheque must be split or the whole amount paid into the client account.

If it is all paid into the client account, all office money must be transferred out of the client account within 14 days. (But see also Rule 19 (at **5.3.5** below) in the case of costs payments.)

5.3.5   Special rules for dealing with money received for bills (or other notifications of costs) (Rules 19 and 21)

There are four possibilities:

1.   Identify the type of money received and deal with it appropriately:

      –   if the money is all office money, put it all in the office account;
      –   if the money is all client money, put it all in the client account;
      –   if the money is a mixture, deal with it under Rule 20 – either splitting it or paying it all into the client account and then transferring out the office element within 14 days of receipt.

2.   Where the money is all office money and/or client money in the form of unpaid professional disbursements for which the solicitor has incurred a liability to pay, in this one circumstance client money can be paid into the office bank account for a limited period (Rule 19(1)(b)). To fall within Rule 19(1)(b) the receipt must consist only of office money and client money for unpaid professional disbursements (see Rule 2(2)(s) for definition). The solicitor must have already incurred liability for the disbursement. If the disbursement is not paid by the end of the second working day following receipt, the client money must be transferred to the client bank account. The advantage of this option is that it simplifies dealing with receipts of costs, allowing more to be paid straight into the office bank account and resulting in fewer transfers between client and office bank accounts.

3. Irrespective of the type of money, pay it all into the client bank account and transfer out any office money within 14 days of receipt. This may be done where the person dealing with the money is uncertain as to its correct classification. This option allows the money to be banked promptly pending a decision as to how it should be treated. It is also a useful option where a client wishes to make direct payments into a bank account. The client can be given the number of the client bank account and all payments can be made into that account.

4. Follow Rule 21 in relation to payments from the Legal Services Commission (LSC):

    – a special dispensation for costs payments in relation to certificated work means that a payment for costs may be paid into the office bank account, even when mixed with client money for unpaid disbursements, provided the disbursements are paid or money representing them is transferred to the client bank account within 14 days of receipt (see Rule 21(1)(b) and note (iii) to Rule 21);

    – from 1 May 2005, Rule 21(2) replaced the Society's interim guidance on standard monthly payments from the LSC in respect of civil and criminal contracts. These regular payments are office money and must be paid into an office account at a bank or building society in England and Wales (Rule 21(2)(a)–(b) and note (vii) to Rule 21). Professional disbursements relating to a matter (see Rule 2(2)(s)) must be paid, or an amount for their settlement transferred to a client account, within 28 days of the solicitor reporting to the LSC on the completion of that matter (see Rule 21(2)(c) and notes (viii)–(ix) to Rule 21).

There is a special rule for payments from a third party (see Rule 21(3)). Where the LSC has already paid any costs to a solicitor (or has paid professional disbursements direct) and costs are subsequently settled by a third party, the entire third party payment must be paid into the client bank account.

Any balance belonging to the solicitor must be transferred to the office bank account within 14 days of the solicitor sending a report to the LSC containing details of the third party payment. The amount retained in the client bank account must be recorded as held for the LSC (either on the individual client's ledger account or on a separate ledger in the LSC's name).

It must be kept there until the LSC informs the solicitor that it has recouped an equivalent sum from subsequent legal aid payments due to the solicitor. The retained sum must be transferred to an office bank account within 14 days of notification of recoupment.

5.3.6 Time limit on transfers (Rules 19–21)

The Rules impose a standard 14-day time limit on all transfers needing to be made to or from the client bank account (apart from the two-day period for unpaid professional disbursements under Rule 19(1)(b), and the 28-day time limit for the payment of professional disbursements (or transfer to a client account of an equivalent sum) under Rule 21(2)(c)). The time limit on transfers is imposed in order to prevent unclaimed costs concealing a shortfall on the client account.

5.3.7 Transfers between clients (Rule 30(2))

Solicitors are required to obtain the written authority of both clients in the case of private loans between clients. This does not apply to loans made by an institutional lender.

5.3.8 Authority for withdrawals from client account (Rule 23)

A withdrawal of funds from client account may be made without the bank which actually makes the transfer having to hold a written authority, for example, it can be done by telephone. However, before the transfer is made there must be in existence a specific authority in respect of the particular withdrawal, signed by one of the persons specified in Rule 23(1). It is also of paramount importance that there are appropriate safeguards, such as passwords. Note that in the case of a withdrawal by cheque, the signature on the cheque is usually the specific authority. Signing a blank cheque is not a specific authority.

5.3.9 Who may authorise withdrawals from client account? (Rule 23)

Withdrawals from client account may be authorised by:

- a solicitor with a current practising certificate or a registered European lawyer;
- a three-year FILEX employed by a solicitor, registered European lawyer or recognised body;
- a licensed conveyancer employed by a solicitor, registered European lawyer or recognised body where the office deals solely with conveyancing;
- a registered foreign lawyer who is a partner in the practice, or director of the practice (if it is a company), or member of the practice (if it is a limited liability partnership).

See note (v) to Rule 23 for the position when controlled trustees instruct an outside manager to run the trust or estate on a day-to-day basis.

5.3.10 Minimising the risk of money laundering (Rule 15)

A client account should not be used to provide banking facilities to a client or third party (see Rule 15, note (ix)).

5.4 RECORD-KEEPING REQUIREMENTS (RULE 32)

Solicitors must keep records to show all dealings with client money, controlled trust money and office money relating to any client or controlled trust matter. The dealings must be recorded on a cash account (or record of inter-client transfers) and on a client ledger account for each client or controlled trust. The current balance for each client must be shown or be readily ascertainable.

The records must show all dealings with client money and controlled trust money. It is, therefore, important to record any change in the person(s) for whom money is held.

For example, during or at the end of an administration beneficiaries will become entitled to funds. Normally there will be a cash payment to the beneficiaries which will be recorded as a cash payment from the client account on behalf of the personal representatives. However, the beneficiaries may ask the solicitor to retain funds for them in the client account for a specific reason (but banking facilities must not be provided through the client account – see rule 15, note (ix)). In such a case the solicitor must record – on the client ledger accounts and also on the transfer record – that money is no longer held for the PRs but is now held for the beneficiary. Separate client ledger accounts are necessary.

5.4.1 Relaxation of requirements when acting for both institutional lender and borrower (Rule 32(6))

To regularise the practice of a solicitor opening one ledger account where he or she is acting for both lender and borrower in a conveyancing matter, Rule 32(6) permits the opening of only one ledger account, provided that the funds belonging to each client are clearly identifiable on the ledger. The permission does not extend to private loans.

Rule 32(6) is expressed to apply to mortgage *advances*. There is no mention of mortgage *redemptions*. The normal rules will, therefore apply. If the solicitor holds money for the lender, it will be necessary to show this in the accounts by opening a separate ledger account for the lender. The proceeds of sale can then be shown as held partly for the seller and partly for the lender. Frequently, however, the solicitor acting for the seller will not hold any money after completion for the lender so there will be no need for a separate ledger.

5.4.2 Record keeping when acting for controlled trusts

Solicitors must keep full records of all dealings with controlled trust money unless an outside manager is used to run the trust on a day-to-day basis. In such a case the manager must keep and retain appropriate accounting records which must be available for inspection by the Law Society. See Rule 32, note (ii)(d).

5.4.3 Record-keeping requirements for liquidators, etc. (Rule 9)

Provided liquidators, trustees in bankruptcy, Court of Protection receivers and trustees of occupational pension schemes comply with their own statutory rules and regulations, they will be deemed to have complied sufficiently with the Rules so long as they also comply with the limited record-keeping requirements of Rule 9. They must:

- keep a central record or file of bills;
- retain for at least six years any records kept under the statutory rules;
- keep such records centrally, or maintain a central register of appointments;
- make such records available for monitoring and inspection by the Law Society; and
- produce such records to the reporting accountants to enable them to check compliance.

5.4.4 Record-keeping requirements for joint accounts (Rule 10)

The Rules in general do not apply to solicitors operating joint accounts but various record-keeping requirements do apply (to protect against fraud). Solicitors must:

- keep a central record or file of bills;
- retain statements and passbooks (or duplicates and copy entries) for at least six years;
- keep such statements and passbooks (or duplicates and copy entries as permitted by the Rules) centrally;
- make such records available for monitoring and inspection by the Law Society; and
- produce such records to the reporting accountants to enable them to check compliance.

5.4.5 Record-keeping requirements for client's own account (Rule 11)

The Rules in general do not apply to solicitors operating a client's own account (for example, under a power of attorney) but various record-keeping requirements do (to protect against fraud). Solicitors must:

- receive and keep statements and passbooks (or duplicates and copy entries) for at least six years;
- keep such statements and passbooks (or duplicates and copy entries as permitted by the Rules) centrally;
- make such records available for monitoring and inspection by the Law Society; and
- produce such records to the reporting accountants to enable them to check compliance.

5.4.6 Regular bank reconciliations (Rule 32(7))

Solicitors are required to prepare bank reconciliations for all general client accounts and separate designated client accounts containing client and controlled trust money at least once every five weeks (in effect monthly).

However, where controlled trust money is kept in a passbook-operated separate designated client account, solicitors need only prepare a reconciliation for that money every 14 weeks. There is no requirement to check that interest has been credited since the last statement or entry in the passbook.

5.4.7 Retention of paid cheques and bank statements, etc. (Rule 32(9) and (10))

Paid cheques must be retained for at least two years (see note (xiv) to Rule 32 as to the extent of this requirement). It is not necessary for the bank to return paid cheques, if it is arranged in writing that the bank will keep paid cheques (either the originals or digital images of the front and back of each cheque) for at least two years. Other authorities for withdrawals from the client account must also be kept for at least two years (Rule 32(10)).

Bank statements and all other records must be kept for at least six years (Rule 32(9)). These requirements extend not just to client accounts but to any other account where client or controlled trust money is held.

Notes (xv)–(xvii) to Rule 32 deal more specifically with the retention of digital images of paid cheques in place of the originals. Digital images of paid cheques have been permitted since 17 March 2004.

5.5 RULES ON INTEREST (RULES 24–28)

Solicitors must account to clients for all interest earned on separate designated client accounts (Rule 24(1)). Rule 25(1) requires solicitors to aim for a reasonable rate of interest on such money.

Where money is not held in a separate designated client account, the general rule is that solicitors must account to the client for a sum in lieu of interest (Rule 24(2)). However, there are exceptions (see Rule 24(3)) where there is no need to account. These are as follows:

(a) if the amount calculated is £20 or less;
(b) (i) if the amount held does not exceed the amount, and the time for which it is held does not exceed the period, set out in the table below:

Amount £	Time (weeks)
1,000	8
2,000	4
10,000	2
20,000	1

    (ii) if the amount held exceeds £20,000 but is held for one week or less, unless it is fair and reasonable to account having regard to all the circumstances;

(c) on money held for the payment of counsel's fees, once counsel has requested a delay in settlement;
(d) on money held for the LSC;
(e) on money held in the client account as a result of an advance from the solicitor to the client to cover a payment for which the client had insufficient funds;
(f) if there is an agreement to contract out of the interest provisions of the Rules.

Solicitors are still allowed to retain any interest earned on client money held in a general client account over and above the amount they are required to pay out. It is expressly provided in Rule 13, note (xi)(b) that interest earned in this way is office money. However, there may be a problem if the general client account includes controlled trust money (see Rule 15, note (vi)).

Trustees are subject to the legal duty not to profit from their trust and must obtain the best reasonably obtainable rate of interest. Three options are available in respect of controlled trust money (Rule 15, note (vi)):

1. Place the money in a separate designated client account, in which case all interest earned belongs to the trust.
2. Set up a general client account just for controlled trust money. The interest will be credited to the office bank account in the normal way but it must be allocated promptly to each controlled trust.
3. Continue to mix controlled trust money with client money in a general client account, so long as solicitors are able to comply with their legal duty and ensure that they do not profit from their trust.

A client may fail to present a cheque for payment promptly. Note (vii) to Rule 24 states that whether or not it is reasonable to recalculate the amount due will depend on all the circumstances of the case. Solicitors can make a reasonable charge for any extra work carried out but only if they are legally entitled to make a charge for such work.

When calculating the amount due to a client in lieu of interest, Rule 25(1) requires solicitors to account for a 'fair' sum. It need not necessarily reflect the highest rate of interest available but it is not acceptable to look only at the lowest rate of interest available. Rule 25(2) provides that the sum must be calculated:

- on the balance(s) held over the whole period for which cleared funds are held
- at a rate not less than whichever is the higher of:
  - the rate payable on a separate designated client account for the amount(s) held, or
  - the rate payable on the relevant amount(s) if placed on deposit on similar terms by a member of the business community

at the bank or building society where the money is held.

5.6 ACCOUNTANTS' REPORTS

Accountants' reports are dealt with in the Rules at Part F (Rules 35–49).

Reporting accountants must have registered auditor status together with membership of one of the accountancy bodies listed in the Rules (see Rule 37). To enable the Law Society to maintain accurate records solicitors must inform the Society of any change of reporting accountant (Rule 39).

Solicitors must produce a letter of engagement for accountants incorporating the terms set out in Rule 38(1). The letter (and a copy) must be signed by the solicitor (or a partner, director or member) and by the accountant. The letter must be kept for at least three years after the termination of the retainer and produced to the Law Society on request (Rule 38(2)).

Accountants are also required to report on any substantial departure from the Law Society Guidelines for Accounting Procedures and Systems (see Rules 29, 43 and 44(e), and Appendix 3 to the Rules).

In addition to the requirements for testing already contained in the Rules, reporting accountants have to complete and sign a Law Society checklist which the solicitor must keep for at least three years from the date of signature and produce to the Law Society on request. The checklist is intended to be an assurance to the solicitor and to the Law Society that the work required to be done has indeed been done. It does not impose any additional obligations on accountants. See Appendix 4 to the Rules.

A solicitor who has operated a client's own account as signatory must deliver an accountant's report for the accounting period within six months of the end of the period (Rule 35). The reporting accountant will check compliance with Rule 11.

The reporting accountant will have to check that records, statements and passbooks are being kept as required by the Rules for solicitors acting as liquidators, Court of Protection receivers, trustees in bankruptcy and trustees of certain occupational pension schemes (Rule 9). The reporting accountant will also check the requirements for joint accounts (Rule 10).

From 1 September 2000, the reporting accountant is required to check that the solicitor has a certificate(s) of qualifying insurance for the period covered by the report (Rule 42(1)(p)). The reporting accountant should check that the insurance is issued by a qualifying insurer, a list of whom can be found on the Law Society's website (see **www.indemnity.lawsociety.org.uk**); and that the end date of the certificate(s) is 30 September. The accountant also needs to check the level of cover which, from 1 October 2005, is £2m any one claim for sole practitioners, partnerships, unlimited companies, or companies set up purely as nominees, and £3m any one claim for limited liability partnerships and limited companies. (From 1 September 2000 to 30 September 2005, the minimum sum insured for all practices was £1m any one claim. Limited companies and limited liability partnerships required additional cover of £500,000 any one claim, or £2m in the aggregate.)

5.7   HOW DO THE RULES AFFECT PROBATE WORK?

When solicitors are doing trust and/or probate work they will handle client money and controlled trust money. They will have to pay money into the appropriate bank accounts and follow the rules as to withdrawals. In particular, solicitors will have to classify money correctly as client, controlled trust or office. The rules relating to client money and controlled trust money are very similar, although some differences remain, for example, in relation to interest (see Rule 8 which sets out where controlled trust money is treated differently from client money).

5.7.1   Client money or controlled trust money?

Remember that this is the only choice. There is no longer a category of 'trust' money. Controlled trusts are trusts where a solicitor is the sole trustee or is a trustee with a partner or employee. Rule 2(2)(h) also sets out the circumstances where a controlled trust may arise, where one or more of the trustees are registered European lawyers, registered foreign lawyers or recognised bodies. As the notes to the Rules point out, this definition, which is statutory, gives rise to some anomalies. For example, an assistant solicitor who is a sole trustee is a controlled trustee; two assistant solicitors who are the only co-trustees are not; an assistant and a partner are controlled trustees; a sole solicitor trustee who is a director of a recognised body which is a company is a controlled trustee; two or more directors of a recognised body which is a company are not. Where a trust is not a controlled trust any money received for the trust is client money.

5.7.2 Which bank account?

Client money can go into the general client account or a separate designated client account. It can also be retained in cash or paid into a 'non-client account' if the client so instructs (Rule 16).

Controlled trust money can go into the general client account or a separate designated client account which can be a current, deposit or share account. It can also be paid into a 'non-client account' if the trustees' powers permit it, or be retained in cash in the performance of the trustees' duties (Rule 18).

5.7.3 Reconciliation

Where money is paid into a general client account it will be subject to the requirement for reconciliations at least once every five weeks (Rule 32(7)).

This requirement will apply to controlled trust money in separate designated client accounts unless the account is passbook-operated in which case the requirement is at least once every 14 weeks. Reconciliations are necessary even where the client money or controlled trust money is held in a 'non-client account' under Rules 16 or 18 (see Rule 32(7)(a)).

5.7.4 Records

The record-keeping requirements for controlled trust money are the same as those for client money. However, where controlled trustees instruct an outside manager to run the business or property portfolio of an estate or trust, the manager must maintain, and then produce, appropriate records for inspection by the Law Society (Rule 32, note (ii)(d)).

Remember that if acting as a Court of Protection receiver, operating a joint account or operating the client's own account, solicitors will be required to keep limited records and have them checked by the reporting accountant.

5.7.5 Interest

Remember that if controlled trust money is paid into the general client account, solicitors must be careful not to profit from their trust (as outlined at **5.5** above).

In addition there may be problems for solicitors in calculating how much interest is due to clients. For example, the administration may have been completed and cheques sent to beneficiaries. If the beneficiaries fail to cash those cheques, the solicitor may be under an obligation to pay the beneficiary interest unless the amount falls into one of the exceptions set out in Rule 24(3). The notes to the Rule say that whether or not a solicitor has to recalculate interest will depend on the circumstances of the case.

PART II

Probate, Wills and the Law

This Part includes guidance on certain legal aspects of probate work, and ends with a brief outline of the basics of succession law. The Handbook is not intended to be a legal textbook, however, and details of relevant works can be found in **Further reading**.

CHAPTER 6

Liability for a client's fraud

Alexander Learmonth

6.1 INTRODUCTION

A solicitor may, in good faith, assist a client in a financial transaction which appears at the time to be perfectly proper, but which turns out to involve a fraud on a third party. The solicitor will then want answers to three questions:

- Can I be held liable in any way to the injured third party?
- Can I disclose details of the client's transaction to the third party once I discover (or more likely suspect) the client's wrongdoing?
- Have I committed a criminal offence under POCA 2002?

This chapter gives basic guidance on both of these issues. It does not consider a solicitor's liability for his or her own fraud *per se*, or for actions taken in his or her capacity as a PR under a will, which are considered elsewhere in this book. The first section deals with the extent of liability for a client's fraud in the light of the leading cases. The second section deals with the solicitor's duty of confidentiality. The third section suggests what action solicitors should take when they know or suspect that a client has involved them in a fraudulent transaction. The fourth section considers POCA 2002, and the final section is a summary of the points made.

6.2 EXTENT OF LIABILITY FOR A CLIENT'S FRAUD

6.2.1 How liability can arise

A number of recent cases illustrate the way in which a solicitor (or other professional adviser) can become drawn into a client's improper scheme, and face a claim. In one case, for example, the defendant solicitor acted for several members of the same family in relation to a complex network of family trusts, which included his appointment as trustee. The assets had been acquired by the father of the principal beneficiaries, who was also a trustee and beneficiary under certain of the trusts. The solicitor was asked to exercise his powers as trustee to support the business run by the father, which involved a substantial risk to the assets of the trust. The solicitor was one of the defendants sued by the other members of the family after the business collapsed and the father was declared bankrupt (*Walker* v. *Stones* [2001] QB 902). The court had to decide whether the solicitor was guilty of a breach of his own fiduciary duties, or guilty of assisting others to contravene their own obligations. Though not a probate case, such a situation could equally arise under a will trust.

Another illustration involved a firm of accountants acting for an oil company, which was being defrauded by its in-house accountant. The dishonest accountant had been diverting payments due to the company to a series of shell companies, which the defendant accountants set up and eventually liquidated. The firm took instructions from a French lawyer, and did not discover the nature of the transactions in which they had assisted until the oil company sued them. They thought that they had been involved in a scheme to circumvent exchange controls. Again, the court had to decide whether they were liable for the losses suffered by the company (*Agip (Africa) Ltd* v. *Jackson* [1991] Ch 547).

In both cases, the professional advisers were found to be liable for the losses suffered, although in neither case had they been personally enriched beyond the payment of fees. It is all too easy to imagine solicitors becoming involved in similar transactions.

6.2.2 Liability for receipt and liability for assistance

There are two main ways in which liability can arise:

- for receiving the proceeds of fraud through:

    - unjust enrichment and the common law of restitution;
    - the tort of conversion;
    - a proprietary constructive trust in equity;
    - knowing receipt;

- for assisting in the fraud through:

    - dishonest assistance in a breach of trust or fiduciary duty;
    - breach of contract;
    - the tort of negligence.

Each of these will be examined in turn.

6.2.3   Liability for receiving the proceeds of fraud

Liability for unjust enrichment

In *Lipkin Gorman* v. *Karpnale Ltd* [1991] 2 AC 548 the House of Lords set out the conditions under which a claim for unjust enrichment can succeed:

- the defendant must be enriched;
- the enrichment must be at the claimant's expense;
- the enrichment must be unjust, which means that there must be a factor, such as mistake or duress, which renders the enrichment reversible, not simply that the enrichment is 'unfair'; and
- there must be no defence.

Liability does not depend on fault by the defendant: the fact of enrichment, combined with the lack of a defence (such as *bona fide* purchase or change of position), will justify the court giving judgment for the claimant.

The application of these tests means that, in practice, solicitors and other professional advisers are unlikely to incur liability to make restitution. There will normally be no enrichment beyond the receipt of fees: while substantial sums may pass through a client account, the professional is not enriched by this, and so no liability will arise.

Receipt of fees from the misdirected funds is clearly an enrichment, but *bona fide* purchase should provide a defence. Provided that the advisers have acted in good faith and without notice of the fraud, their services will amount to good consideration for the receipt of the fees, and they will not be liable to return them.

Change of position is also a defence, and so a firm which has relied upon the receipt of fees may be able to show that it is inequitable to be asked to return them. In practice, change of position is unlikely to add anything to the defence of *bona fide* purchase: if the firm cannot show that it acted in good faith and charged no more than a proper fee for the job, it is unlikely to succeed on a defence of change of position.

Liability for conversion

It is easier to incur liability as a result of handling chattels (including cheques and bankers' drafts) on behalf of a client. Liability can arise under the tort of conversion, which applies to any dealings with a chattel inconsistent with the rights of the person entitled to immediate possession. A person who deals with a stolen cheque or bankers' draft will be strictly liable for its face value if there is anyone entitled to immediate possession (*Morison* v. *London County and Westminster Bank* [1914] 3 KB 356; *International Factors Ltd* v. *Rodriguez* [1979] QB 315; *Lipkin Gorman* v. *Karpnale Ltd* (above)). There is no defence of change of position, although the Bills of Exchange Act 1882 provides limited defences based on acting in good faith and for value.

The endorsement of negotiable instruments such as cheques and bankers' drafts is now far less common than it used to be, as a result of the Cheques Act 1992 and the use of 'account payee only' on negotiable instruments, and the increasing use of direct bank transfers. A detailed account of the law of conversion as applied to bills of exchange is therefore unnecessary, and it is enough to warn solicitors not to handle endorsed cheques or bankers' drafts from clients unless they are absolutely sure that the client has good title. The client should be asked to transfer the money in a more conventional way.

Liability under a proprietary constructive trust

A proprietary constructive trust is a trust attaching to property, or its proceeds, which can be traced from the claimant to the defendant under the equitable rules of tracing. Liability arises here because the defendant is in possession of property which belongs, in equity, to the claimant. Defendants will not be liable if they are *bona fide* purchasers for value without notice, and neither will defendants be liable if they no longer have the property or its proceeds.

The greatest risk for a professional in relation to this form of liability is to be faced with competing claims on clients' monies; for example, a third party claiming that funds held in a client account are in fact the traceable proceeds of a fraud which the client has received. In such a situation, a professional faced with a claim which is not obviously hopeless should consider making an application to court for directions: paying the money to the client with notice of the claim attaching to it might lead to liability for knowing assistance in a breach of trust, as described below.

6.2.4   Personal liability to account 'as a constructive trustee'

Personal and proprietary claims distinguished

The use of the term 'constructive trust' to describe two entirely different situations has caused confusion for a long time. In deciding a claim based on a proprietary constructive trust, the court has to ask whether a person takes property subject to or free from an equitable claim. The court looks at whether the defendant had *notice* of the equity, whether the defendant gave value, and whether he or she still has the property or its traceable proceeds.

The phrase 'liable to account as a constructive trustee' is also sometimes also used to describe the situation where the defendant is to have imposed upon him or her the personal burdens and obligations similar to those of a trustee. This usage has been criticised, and is 'no more than a formula for equitable relief' (*Paragon Finance* v. *D. B. Thakerar & Co* [1999] 1 All ER

400, 409). Such liability will arise where the defendant has either received and subsequently disposed of trust property, or become involved in a breach of trust in circumstances in which it is equitable for the defendant to be treated as a trustee. The court therefore looks at the defendant's knowledge, rather than the more technical rules of actual and constructive notice. Liability may extend to the total amount knowingly received by the defendant, or the total foreseeable loss suffered by the claimant as a result of the breach of trust in which the defendant assisted (*Target Holdings Ltd* v. *Redferns* [1995] 3 All ER 785).

Liability for knowing receipt and dealing

To be liable for knowing receipt and dealing, defendants must receive for their own benefit the claimant's property, which had been disposed of in breach of fiduciary duty, or its traceable proceeds. Consequently, a professional who legitimately receives trust property on behalf of a client, and passes it on, cannot be held liable under this head, because there is no beneficial receipt (*Agip (Africa) Ltd* v. *Jackson* (above)). This is why the claimants in *Twinsectra* v. *Yardley* [2002] 2 AC 164 (referred to in detail below) could not claim under knowing receipt.

Again, the difficulty for professionals arises where their fees have been paid out of the property claimed by the claimant. In the earliest case to address this issue, *Carl Zeiss Stiftung* v. *Herbert Smith and Co (No.2)* [1969] 2 Ch 176 the question was whether the solicitors involved could retain the fees which had been paid to them for defending a claim that their client held all of its assets on trust for the claimant. The court held that as the firm acted honestly and provided full consideration, it could not be liable for knowing receipt.

The other, and most difficult, ingredient is what the defendants' state of mind must be. *BCCI* v. *Akindele* [2000] 4 All ER 221 made it clear that dishonesty is not an essential element of a claim for knowing receipt. It is enough that the defendant should receive property in circumstances in which the defendant's state of knowledge makes it unconscionable to retain it. Nourse LJ suggested that this will allow the courts to adopt a commonsense approach, although it could certainly be suggested that in the absence of reported decisions on the application of this test, it will be difficult to predict the nature and degree of knowledge which will give rise to liability in any given case. However, Lord Millett, in his dissenting speech in *Twinsectra* v. *Yardley* [2002] 2 AC 164, has insisted that liability for knowing receipt is restitutionary, and is therefore receipt based, and not fault based. In his view, whilst change of position would be a defence, unconscionability should not be required. It may be that this issue has still not finally been resolved.

In particular, there is now a possibility that professionals may be required to repay fees which were received honestly, but where they had sufficient notice of the claimant's interest to make the receipt 'unconscionable'. In cases of doubt, professionals are likely to be best advised to insist upon payment from another source, or where they already hold the funds when the claim is notified to them, it could well be appropriate to make an application to the court for directions (*Finers* v. *Miro* [1991] 1 All ER 182, and see below as to duties of confidence).

Liability for dishonest assistance

While dishonesty is not an essential element in a claim for receipt of trust property, it remains the most important element in liability for assistance (*Royal Brunei Airlines* v. *Tan* [1995] 3 WLR 64). A person who helps another to misapply trust property will be liable to the beneficiaries if he or she does so dishonestly; no liability arises if the assistance is provided honestly, even if the defendant acted negligently.

If the defendant acts dishonestly, he or she will be liable even if the breach of trust itself is not dishonest. Lord Nicholls in *Royal Brunei Airlines* v. *Tan* (above) gives the example of trustees who innocently wish to deal with the trust funds in their care in such a way as to amount to a breach of trust, who instruct a solicitor to act for them. If the solicitor acts in the knowledge that a breach of trust is being committed, he or she will be liable to the beneficiaries.

The defendant must, of course, assist in the breach of trust. A person who is peripherally involved in a transaction and who does not further the breach of trust in any way will not incur liability, even if that person is aware of the breach. (See *Brinks Ltd* v. *Abu-Saleh and Others* [1995] 1 WLR 1478, where the wife of one of the individuals involved in laundering the proceeds of the Brinks Mat robbery was not liable for knowing assistance simply because she travelled abroad with her husband while he was disposing of the proceeds of the crime.)

The notion of dishonesty is not straightforward. This form of liability was formerly referred to as knowing assistance (in a dishonest breach of trust). A taxonomy of knowledge for these purposes was provided in *Baden* v. *Société Générale* [1993] 1 WLR 509: actual knowledge; wilfully shutting one's eyes to the obvious (very close to actual knowledge); wilfully and recklessly failing to make such inquiries as a reasonable and honest man would; knowledge of circumstances from which a reasonable and honest man would infer the facts; knowledge of circumstances which would put a reasonable and honest man on inquiry (these last two involve a high degree of objectivity).

Since *Tan* (above), it is no longer necessary for the original breach of trust to be dishonest, and the question of the accessory's knowledge of the original breach of trust and its circumstances has been replaced by a straightforward test for 'dishonesty in all the circumstances'. There is therefore no direct application of the *Baden* categories, the defendant's knowledge, and the extent to which the defendant has closed his or her eyes to the obvious, etc., are all relevant to the defendant's probity.

The test is now definitively stated in *Twinsectra* v. *Yardley* [2002] 2 AC 164. Twinsectra lent Yardley £1m, which was paid to Y's solicitor on the undertaking that it would be used to buy a particular property, and was therefore held by him under a trust in those terms. But the first solicitor paid it to another solicitor for Y, on oral assurances that the money would be so applied, but without any undertakings as such. The second solicitor in turn paid it to Y himself, who invested only £650k of the money in the property, and dissipated the remainder. T sued (*inter alia*) the second solicitor for dishonest assistance. The trial judge found that he had considered that he held the money to Y's order, and had shut his eyes to the problems created by the first solicitor's undertakings.

The majority of the House of Lords adopted a test that combined both the objective and subjective tests that Lord Nicholls had referred to in *Tan*:

> before there can be a finding of dishonesty, it must be established that the defendant's conduct was dishonest by the ordinary standards of reasonable and honest people and that he himself realised that by those standards his conduct was dishonest.

Since the second solicitor – due to a mistake as to the law – had not appreciated that his conduct was dishonest by ordinary standards, he was not liable. This is reassuring for solicitors.

However, Lord Millett gave a strong dissenting speech. In his view, merely knowing all the facts that make the conduct wrongful is sufficient to constitute dishonesty in this context; there was no need to be conscious that one is transgressing ordinary standards of honest behaviour. But it seems that the only reason the solicitor did not appreciate the wrongfulness of his actions was that he did not appreciate that the effect of the undertakings given by the first solicitor had been to create a trust of those monies, and that the payment to the second solicitor had been a breach of that trust. The effect of Lord Millett's test, it is submitted, would be to confuse ignorance of the law with dishonesty. That is a question of one's state of mind, and is not the same thing as saying ignorance of the law is no defence.

However, the Privy Council appears to have moved the test in that direction. In *Barlow Clowes International (In Liquidation)* v. *Eurotrust International Ltd* [2005] UKPC 37; [2006] 1 Lloyd's Rep 225 the subjective element of *Twinsectra* test was explained as requiring not an understanding of what the generally accepted standards of honesty were, but a knowledge of those elements of the transaction that made it dishonest by those standards. Like the test in *R.* v. *Ghosh* [1982] QB 1053, it means that one may be dishonest even where one genuinely believes that one's act is morally justified.

Nevertheless, the older cases provide a number of examples of what may or may not be dishonest. So, a defendant who knows that something illegal or improper is being planned will normally be held to be dishonest, even if he does not know the precise details of the fraud itself. For example, in *Agip (Africa) Ltd* v. *Jackson* (above) the defendant accountants thought that they were assisting in a scheme to contravene Tunisian exchange controls, rather than a fraud on the claimant, but were nevertheless held to have acted dishonestly.

Similarly, it will be no defence for a solicitor who fails to question an obviously dubious scheme to say that the client would have produced a convincing answer if asked. Liability depends on whether the defendant acted honestly, which includes consideration of the answers actually received when the scheme is questioned.

Another question of first importance to solicitors is whether a firm is vicariously liable for one partner's dishonest assistance. This was the question considered in *Dubai Aluminium Co Ltd* v. *Salaam* [2002] UKHL 48; [2003] 2 AC 366, where a partner was held to have dishonestly assisted in a complex fraud on the claimant by drafting bogus consultancy agreements. Under these agreements the claimant ended up paying some $50m, although the partner received no personal benefit from so doing save his normal fees. The House of Lords held that the firm *was* vicariously liable for its partner's dishonest assistance. This was because Partnership Act 1890, s.10 is not confined to vicarious liability for torts, but extends to equitable wrongs as well. Further, the drafting of such agreements, even though they were sham agreements, was sufficiently close to the 'ordinary course of the firm's business' to fall within the section.

In *Walker* v. *Stones* (above), however, it was held that the decision by the solicitor trustee to misapply trust property was not within the scope of the firm's practice, with the result that the claim against the other partners in the firm was struck out. The crucial distinction is that the solicitor there was acting in his capacity as professional trustee, rather than in his capacity as solicitor; acting as a trustee is not a 'partnership activity'.

Breach of contract and negligence

Solicitors engaged in financial transactions will clearly owe a contractual duty to safeguard the client's financial interests. Thus, if the client is a company, the solicitor will have a duty to make inquiries and take further action if there is a suspicion that the company is being defrauded by its executives. This is not to say that the solicitor must regard everyone with suspicion: the relationship between a legal adviser and the individuals giving instructions must be one of trust. The solicitor must merely make inquiries if a reasonable person in his or her position would have doubts about the transaction.

The extent of the solicitor's duty of care in tort to third parties is less clear. The recent cases on solicitors' involvement with dishonest clients have indicated that the principal test for liability is dishonesty on the part of the solicitor, and the courts have taken care to emphasise that negligence is an inappropriate test for liability. Thus it is unlikely that the courts would find that a duty of care exists in favour of third parties, and liability will be confined to cases of dishonest assistance rather than careless involvement, except possibly for cases involving closely related parties, such as groups of companies, where a solicitor retained by a subsidiary may owe a duty of care in tort to the parent company.

6.3 FRAUD, PRIVILEGE AND CONFIDENTIALITY

6.3.1 Nature of the problem

Solicitors who fear that they may inadvertently have become involved in a fraudulent transaction are placed in a difficult position with regard to client confidentiality. If the solicitor has acted properly, there should be no liability in relation to past actions. However, the solicitor may incur liability by continuing to act after his or her suspicions have been aroused, and assistance previously provided to the client may allow that client to continue to defraud innocent persons in the future.

Further, the position under the general law as set out below is subject to the radical changes effected by POCA 2002, considered below.

6.3.2 Decision of the Court of Appeal in *Finers* v. *Miro*

The leading case on the options available to an inadvertent participant in a fraud at common law remains the decision of the Court of Appeal in *Finers* v. *Miro* [1991] 1 WLR 35. The solicitors in that case helped their client to set up a complex series of trusts which made his ownership of his assets difficult to detect, and did so in such a way that they found themselves holding the assets as bare trustee for the client. The solicitors honestly believed that the client's aims were simply to prevent foreign states from nationalising his property. They then discovered a report from a committee of the United States House of Representatives which accused the client of defrauding a now-insolvent American insurance company. The solicitors feared that the assets in the trusts were the proceeds of the fraud, and applied to the court for directions under RSC Ord.85 (which has not yet been replaced by the Civil Procedure Rules). In particular, they wanted the court to rule on whether the liquidator of the insurance company should be notified of the application. The Court of Appeal held that the liquidator should be notified.

The solicitors accepted that they did not have conclusive proof that the client was guilty of the fraud: their aim was to have the court determine what they should do as a result of their suspicions. The court held that the liquidator should be notified of the existence of the trusts, because, on the evidence available, there was proof on the balance of probabilities that the alleged fraud had been committed.

The court held that communications between a solicitor and client for the purpose of furthering a client's fraud are not confidential. Committing a fraud is not part of the solicitor–client relationship, and so professional duties do not arise. Professional obligations are regarded as never having arisen if solicitors discover in the course of acting that clients have been using them to commit a fraud, and so disclosure can be made without the client's consent. For these purposes, 'fraud' covers all forms of dishonesty, as long as the conduct in question amounts to real dishonesty and not merely disreputable conduct or a failure to maintain good ethical standards (*Gamlen Chemical Co (UK) Ltd* v. *Rochem* (1980) 124 SJ 276 (CA, 1977, per Goff LJ), followed in *Finers* v. *Miro* (above)).

A solicitor can disclose information if he or she is consulted by a client who wants help to plan, execute or conceal a fraud. However, if the fraud is already complete, and the client is seeking advice which would not further it or conceal it, the solicitor cannot disclose the fraud to the injured party. The solicitor would be in breach of both the legal duty of confidentiality and the rules of professional conduct if any disclosure were to be made without a court order. But that position is now subject to POCA 2002, discussed below.

6.3.3 Privilege and confidentiality

The position of solicitors is complicated by the fact that information may be privileged as well as confidential. The two concepts are distinct: privilege is much narrower than confidentiality, as it relates only to the inadmissibility of solicitor–client correspondence in litigation. *O'Rourke* v. *Darbyshire* [1920] AC 581 is authority that as fraud is outside the solicitor–client relationship, information relating to the solicitor's furtherance of a fraud is not privileged.

6.4 ACTION BY SOLICITORS INVOLVED IN DISHONEST TRANSACTIONS

Having outlined the basic legal position in relation to fraud and confidentiality, the next issue is the appropriate course of action for any solicitors who fear that a client has been using their services to defraud an innocent third party.

6.4.1 Professional rules

The Solicitors' Practice Rules have recently been amended, replacing the guidance found in *The Guide to the Professional Conduct of Solicitors 1999* with a new Rule 16E. However, it is submitted that the guidance formerly in the first paragraph of the commentary to Rule 16.02 ('The duty to keep a client's confidences can be overridden in certain circumstances') remains an accurate summary of the general law:

> The duty of confidentiality does not apply to information acquired by a solicitor where he or she is being used by the client to facilitate the commission of a crime or fraud, because that is not within the scope of a professional retainer. If the solicitor becomes suspicious about a client's activities the solicitor should normally assess the situation in the light of the client's explanations and the solicitor's professional judgment.

The new guidance is lengthier, and published on the Law Society's website and **Appendix A1**. A telephone call to Professional Ethics at the Law Society, or the policy adviser in the Representation and Law Reform directorate (see **Useful addresses** for details) is likely to be the next step. Any such communication would be treated in confidence.

6.4.2 Legal problems

The recommended approach to the legal problems of inadvertent involvement in fraud is as follows. If the solicitor has been honest throughout the transaction, he or she will have incurred no liability for assisting the client, and the worst that could happen would be that the solicitor might be ordered to return any fees received. If suspicions arise, the solicitor can avoid liability for dishonesty simply by refusing to act further.

If a solicitor has strong *prima facie* evidence of fraud, disclosure may be justifiable. In difficult cases, the Law Society or the Solicitors Indemnity Fund may be approached for guidance, but neither can give legal advice, which must be sought from specialist solicitors and/or counsel. The Court of Appeal in *Finers* v. *Miro* (above) has suggested that disclosure may be justified where on the balance of probabilities it appears that the solicitor's services have been used improperly, but it is hard to see how disclosure could be justified without first giving the client the opportunity to explain the situation. In practice, the issues involved in disclosing a transaction against the client's wishes are likely to be so difficult to resolve that an application to the court for directions may provide the only solution.

The greatest problem arises when a firm cannot simply refuse to act because it is still holding some of the proceeds of the suspected fraud. The solution, again, when the client has failed to satisfy the solicitor of the honesty of the transaction, is to apply to the court for directions on how to apply the funds held on trust. This happened in *Finers* v. *Miro*, where the court held that it had jurisdiction to give directions for the administration of a bare trust, even where the apparent beneficiary opposes the application and asks for the funds to be paid direct to him or her. An application to the court is therefore necessary if the client tells the solicitor to pass the money on to someone else.

6.5 PROCEEDS OF CRIME ACT 2002

The relevant parts of POCA 2002 came into force on 24 February 2003. The Act contains a number of parts, of which the most important to solicitors is Part 7, concerning money laundering. However, it is important to be familiar with the other parts too. It is a complicated and lengthy Act, and most of its provisions have yet to be examined by the courts. This book therefore only provides a summary of the relevant law. Further and detailed guidance (although largely speculative) may be found on the Law Society website (see **www.guide-on-line.lawsociety.org.uk**).

6.5.1 Money laundering

For solicitors, the most important part of POCA 2002 is the anti-money laundering provisions in Part 7. Probate practitioners are perhaps particularly likely to encounter danger, because their work will frequently involve their clients disclosing their affairs in great detail, and then managing or distributing their client's property. Solicitors must carefully consider their position as soon as they know or suspect, or have reasonable grounds for suspicion, that the client's property may be 'criminal property' within the meaning of POCA 2002; that is to say, any property which the defendant knows or suspects to represent a benefit from criminal conduct, either directly or indirectly, in whole or in part. This definition is broad indeed, since criminal conduct is defined as any activity constituting an offence in the UK, or which would constitute such an offence if it had taken place in the UK. From a probate practitioner's perspective, it is important to note that it appears that criminal property will continue to be criminal property even after the death of the person guilty of the original criminal conduct.

Money laundering offences under POCA 2002

There are a number of offences to consider:

- concealing, disguising, converting or transferring criminal property, or removing it from the jurisdiction (s.327);
- making arrangements to facilitate the acquisition, retention, use or control of criminal property by or on behalf of another (s.328);
- acquiring, using or having possession of criminal property without having given adequate consideration (s.329).

It is a defence to each of these offences if a person makes an authorised disclosure and has obtained the appropriate consent, or where the defendant intended to make such a disclosure but had a reasonable excuse for not so doing. Authorised disclosures must be made to a constable or customs officer, or to the nominated officer of the disclosing party's employer, who will then pass on the disclosure to the National Criminal Intelligence Service (NCIS). Where an authorised disclosure is made prior to a transaction which would otherwise be an offence, the disclosing party must wait for consent before proceeding with the transaction in question.

The most important offence for solicitors in general is that of making arrangements under s.328. The Court of Appeal in the recent case of *Bowman* v. *Fels* [2005] EWCA Civ 226; [2005] 1 WLR 3083 has provided some welcome guidance on the scope of that offence. It was held that s.328 was not intended to cover the ordinary conduct of litigation, which included any step taken from the issue of proceedings to final judgment, and it is thought that litigation also extends to pre-action steps and the disposal of property in accordance with any judgment or settlement. However, 'sham proceedings' would still be caught, and would probably involve misleading the court in any event.

Section 328 is therefore of more importance in transactional work. Almost all transactions involving criminal property, including its distribution under the terms of a will, might be said to facilitate the retention, use or control thereof. It might also constitute an offence of transferring or removing criminal property from the jurisdiction under s.327. However, accepting suspected criminal property as fees will not be an offence under s.329, provided they are reasonable fees and provided the fees are not paid for services which are known or suspected to help another carry out criminal conduct.

The only safe course is to make an authorised disclosure, and refrain from taking further steps until consent is given, or the time for considering whether to given such consent has expired. However, solicitors may be in breach of their duty of confidentiality and the client's legal professional privilege if they do so, unless they have *prima facie* evidence that they are being used in furtherance of a crime. The Law Society recommends that in such circumstances, solicitors should either obtain a waiver of privilege from the client (subject to tipping-off issues), or withdraw from the case altogether. See the Law Society's guidance arising out of the judgment in *Bowman* v. *Fels* for further assistance, also available on the Law Society website (**www.lawsociety.org.uk**).

Disclosure obligations and tipping off

Moreover, POCA 2002 creates the following additional offences, which are of particular relevance to solicitors who acquire detailed knowledge of their clients' affairs:

- failing to make an authorised disclosure of information received in the course of a business in the 'regulated sector' (for example managing investments) that another person is engaged in one of the above offences (s.330);

- tipping off: disclosing the fact of an authorised or protected disclosure so that any investigation which might follow the disclosure would be prejudiced (s.333).

However, it is not an offence for a professional legal adviser to refuse to disclose information which was received in privileged circumstances, nor is it an offence to 'tip off' a client in the course of giving the client legal advice or in connection with any present or contemplated legal proceedings, provided the 'tip off' is not given with the intention of furthering a criminal purpose.

6.5.2 Confiscation and restraint orders

The power to confiscate the proceeds of crime under Part 2 of POCA 2002 arises only after conviction of an offence, and applies only to assets in which the convict has a beneficial interest or 'tainted gifts'. However, restraint orders under s.41 may be granted even before criminal charges are brought, and have the effect of freezing any realisable assets in the hands of a specified person. That could quite easily be money held on account by a solicitor. The order may, but does not have to, allow payment of reasonable legal expenses, but not in relation to the suspected offence.

6.5.3 Investigatory powers

The investigatory powers granted to the police, HM Revenue and Customs (HMRC) and the Assets Recovery Agency do affect solicitors, however. Solicitors must comply with production orders under POCA 2002, Part 8 save insofar as the material sought falls within the exception provided by s.348: privileged material and excluded material, unless it is held with the intention of furthering a criminal purpose.

Similarly, a solicitor might be guilty of an offence under s.342 of prejudicing an investigation if he or she 'falsifies, conceals, destroys or otherwise disposes of relevant documents, or causes or permits another to do so', provided he or she knows or suspects that an investigation is on foot or imminent. Again, there is an exception for privileged documents, unless held with the intention of furthering a criminal purpose. Accordingly, if a solicitor tells a client that it is likely that the client is the subject of an investigation, after the client has told the solicitor that he or she intends to destroy documents if that is the case, the solicitor may be guilty of an offence.

6.6 SUMMARY

As this area of law is difficult and complicated, a brief summary of the general principles may be useful.

- The starting point is that solicitors who receive any money (including fees) for their own benefit will be liable to return that money if they have acted dishonestly, or if they had sufficient knowledge of the rightful owner's interest to make it inequitable to retain that money.
- A solicitor should therefore consider requiring payment from a third party if there is doubt as to the beneficial ownership of the funds claimed by the client.
- A solicitor is unlikely to owe a duty of care in tort to a person defrauded by the solicitor's client. Duties of care are likely to arise only where there is an extremely close relationship between the client and the third party, such as a parent and subsidiary company.
- If a solicitor dishonestly assists in a fraudulent transaction, the solicitor is likely to be liable for the full extent of the injured party's losses in all cases.
- A dishonest solicitor's partners or employer will be vicariously liable for the solicitor's actions in the course of the partnership business, but not in a trustee capacity.
- Solicitors who have doubts as to the honesty of a client's transactions should always ask the client for an explanation. If the explanation is satisfactory, the solicitor can continue to act: the law does not expect solicitors to distrust their clients and look for evidence of dishonest conduct; neither does it require a solicitor to be given every last detail of a transaction as long as the transaction is *prima facie* lawful.
- Solicitors who have *prima facie* proof on the balance of probabilities that they have been inadvertently involved in the commission of a fraud can disclose this information to the injured party, but it would be wise to consult the Law Society or take independent advice from specialist counsel before doing this, and to consider an application to the court for directions.
- Fraud covers all forms of dishonesty, but not merely disreputable conduct.
- If the solicitor only has suspicions which do not amount to *prima facie* evidence, it would be wrong to make any disclosure. As a matter of professional conduct and self-interest, the solicitor should consider refusing to act any further.
- Significant risks are involved in handling endorsed cheques and bankers' drafts, and the situations in which these are properly used are increasingly rare. Solicitors should consider asking the client to provide funds in a more conventional manner.
- The Proceeds of Crime Act 2002 is of the first importance to all solicitors. Firms should ensure that at least one solicitor has a thorough and up-to-date knowledge of the Act and the decisions on it in order to be able to assist other practitioners with its implications.

CHAPTER 7

Appointing guardians of children

Gillian E. Cockburn and David Hodson

7.1 INTRODUCTION

A guardian of a child is someone who is appointed to take over responsibility for a child in the event of the death of the child's parent or other carer. The appointment is not only necessary if a child has property or money but also to provide day-to-day care for the child, as the guardian will have the right to decide on the child's upbringing, health care, religion and education. It is very important to ensure that the right person or persons are appointed as guardians in accordance with the law. It is unrelated to the appointment of guardians who look after children in public law care proceedings.

The law on the appointment of guardians changed radically as a result of the Children Act 1989 (CA 1989) which came into effect from 14 October 1991. It is essential for the will drafter and probate practitioner to understand the main elements of CA 1989 and in particular the concepts of parental responsibility and residence orders. In some cases it may also be important to liaise with a family law practitioner to find out what court orders have been made concerning a child which may in turn affect the appointment of guardians under the will.

7.2 WHO MAY APPOINT A GUARDIAN?

This is governed by CA 1989, s.5, which provides that guardians may be appointed by:

(a) a parent with parental responsibility for the child (CA 1989, s.5(3)); or
(b) an existing guardian of the child (CA 1989, s.5(4)); or
(c) a court order in family proceedings (CA 1989, s.5(1) and (2)).

Except as set out below, the appointment in (a) and (b) becomes effective when the person who makes the appointment dies. At that time the guardian will acquire parental responsibility for the child.

7.2.1 Parental responsibility

The Children Act 1989 defines parental responsibility for a child as all the rights, duties, powers, responsibilities and authority which by law a parent of a child has in relation to that child and the child's property (CA 1989, s.3(1)).

7.2.2 Who has parental responsibility?

If the child is legitimate (or has been legitimated or is adopted), the parents (or adopting parents) will each have parental responsibility (CA 1989, s.2(1) and (3)) and both may appoint guardians for the child in the event of their respective deaths (CA 1989, s.5(3)).
  If:

- the parents of a child were not married to each other at the time of the birth; and
- the child has not been legitimated by the parents' later marriage or adopted; and
- the father's name is not registered on the birth certificate

the mother alone has parental responsibility for that child (CA 1989, s.2(2) and (3)). The father does not have automatic parental responsibility and so will not be able to appoint a guardian of the child on his death. However, the father may *acquire* parental responsibility (and therefore be able to appoint a guardian) in the following ways:

- through a court order granting him parental responsibility (CA 1989, s.4(1)(c)); or
- by entering into a parental responsibility agreement with the child's mother (CA 1989, s.4(1)(b));
- by being appointed, either by the mother or by the court, to assume parental responsibility after the mother's death; or
- becoming registered as the child's father primarily on the birth certificate (CA 1989, s.4(1)(a)), provided that the child was born after 1 December 2003. If the child was born before that date, the father will not acquire parental responsibility through this method unless the birth was re-registered after that date with the father's name then appearing.

The parental responsibility agreement must be in accordance with Parental Responsibility Agreement Regulations 1991, SI 1991/1478, reg.2 as amended. The agreement must contain the names of the child's parents and of the child to whom the agreement is to relate, and must contain the signature of both parents and be witnessed. It must provide for only one child; not more than one. Both parents must have their signature witnessed at court by a JP or court official and provide evidence of their identity (including a photograph and signature). The mother must also provide the child's full birth certificate.

The agreement will only take effect once it has been received and recorded in Section A at the Principal Registry of the Family Division (see **Useful addresses**). A stamped copy is then given to each parent.

The agreement may be brought to an end only by a court order (CA 1989, s.4(3)). It should be noted that a parental responsibility agreement can only be made with an unmarried father and not with any other family member.

The Adoption and Children Act 2002 introduced a concept of 'special guardians'. They are only appointed by the court; only a limited category of persons connected with the child can apply; they cannot be a natural parent and have to give three months' prior notice of the application to the relevant local authority which then prepares a report. It is a stage short of a full adoption and is a semi-permanent order, lasting until the child attains 18. A special guardian has parental responsibility and is entitled to exercise parental responsibility to the exclusion of any other person with parental responsibility apart from other special guardians. They are therefore in a more powerful position than a natural parent with parental responsibility, in that they can override their wishes. In addition, a parent with parental responsibility has to apply for the court's leave to discharge a special guardianship order, and the court may not make that order unless there has been a 'significant change in circumstances' (CA 1989, s.14D(5)). A special guardian may appoint another individual to be the child's guardian in the event of his or her death. In many ways, the position of the special guardian is the same as the orthodox guardian. Both are substitutes for the parent rather than a substitute parent. Special guardianship is intended to meet the special needs of children who will benefit from a secure placement rather than adoption, e.g. due to cultural or other issues with adoption itself. On parental death, an appointment of an orthodox guardian will invariably be more appropriate than of a special guardian.

The Adoption and Children Act 2002 also allows a parent with parental responsibility to give parental responsibility to their partner if they are married to them (s.112) or by court order. All other persons with parental responsibility must agree. This took effect from 5 December 2005. A step-parent who is the civil partner of a parent with parental responsibility may also be able to obtain parental responsibility by agreement with the parents of the child or by court order.

7.2.3   Who can be a guardian?

Subject to **7.2.4** below, a parent with parental responsibility for a child, or a properly appointed guardian, may appoint another individual to act as guardian for the child on his or her death (CA 1989, s.5(3) and (4)). Although CA 1989 refers to an individual in the singular, more than one individual may be appointed in accordance with Interpretation Act 1978, s.6(c). In addition, CA 1989 also contemplates the subsequent appointment of further guardians

(CA 1989, s.6(1)). However, the term 'individual' would not include a trust corporation, local authority or other non-individual.

7.2.4   Residence orders

A residence order is a court order settling the arrangements to be made about the person with whom a child is to live (CA 1989, s.8(1)). It also affects the testamentary appointment of guardians and so needs to be considered by the will drafter.

Shared (or joint) residence orders are sometimes (and increasingly) made in favour of both parents, or a parent and another carer of the child (CA 1989, s.11(4)). It may not even be the case that the parents and/or carers have the child living with them for approximately equal periods of time.

A residence order may be made in the context of divorce, judicial separation or nullity proceedings. It can be made in freestanding applications under the 1989 Act, for example to unmarried parents, grandparents or others who are given leave of the court to apply (s.10). It is not an automatic replacement of the care and control orders made under the pre-Children Act law; in many respects it is wider and more flexible. Also, unlike parental responsibility which is bestowed by law on all parents except as set out in **7.2.2** above, residence orders can only be granted by a court.

However, residence orders are not automatically granted on or post divorce to, say, the parent who has the child primarily living with him or her. By CA 1989, s.1(5), the court shall not make any order in respect of the arrangements for a child unless it considers that doing so would be better for the child than making no order at all. In practice, most family courts do not make residence orders and other child orders on divorce if the arrangements between the parents for the child are working satisfactorily. Will drafters should therefore enquire of clients whether there is an existing residence order and not presume that there is one simply because a child is living with a particular parent following a divorce or other family law proceedings.

7.3   APPOINTMENT OF A GUARDIAN

If, on the death of the appointor of a guardian (even if the parents are separated or divorced):

- there is a surviving parent with parental responsibility; and
- the deceased did not have a residence order in his or her favour,

the appointment of the guardian *does not take effect until the death of the surviving parent with parental responsibility* (CA 1989, s.5(8)). Then effective appointments by both parents will take effect simultaneously: this can lead to conflicts between the two separately appointed guardians which the court may have to resolve.

A parent of a child can only appoint a guardian to act jointly with the surviving parent if the deceased parent with parental responsibility had a residence order in his or her favour and in force at the date of his or her death and it was not a joint or shared residence order with the surviving parent (CA 1989, s.5(7)) or he or she was the child's only (or last surviving) special guardian. This situation of an appointed guardian acting jointly with a surviving parent can lead to some bitter and contested children proceedings as the surviving parent often resents the interference and involvement of the guardian appointed by the deceased parent, from whom the surviving parent may have been divorced, etc. Great care and sensitivity is needed and the matter is invariably better dealt with by specialist family lawyers. The outcome is determined by the paramountcy of the child's welfare.

If:

- on the death of the appointer the child has no surviving parent with parental responsibility; or
- immediately before the death of the appointor, a court residence order was in existence in the appointor's favour regarding the child; or
- he or she was the child's only (or last surviving) special guardian

then the appointment of the guardian takes immediate effect on the death of the appointor (CA 1989, s.5(7)).

A properly appointed guardian of a child may also appoint another individual to take his or her place as the child's guardian on his or her death (CA 1989, s.5(4)). However, if there is a surviving parent with parental responsibility and the guardian does not have a residence order in his or her favour (or was not the last surviving special guardian) then the appointment by the guardian will only take effect on the death of the surviving parent (CA 1989, s.5(8)).

7.3.1 How is a guardian appointed?

Under CA 1989, the appointment by a parent or guardian will not be effective unless it is made in a written document and dated. It must also be signed by the person appointing the guardian, except in the case of a document signed at the appointor's direction, in his presence and in the presence of two witnesses who each then attest the signature (CA 1989, s.5(5)). An appointment made by will (or other testamentary document) signed at the appointor's direction must be properly witnessed as required under the provisions of Wills Act 1837, s.9.

The court can also appoint a guardian (on specific application or in general family proceedings) if either:

- a child has no parent with parental responsibility; or
- a residence order has been made in favour of a parent or guardian who has died whilst the order was still in force (CA 1989, s.5(1)).

The former applies to orphans or to children of unmarried fathers without parental responsibility. The latter applies even though the child may have a surviving parent, albeit without a residence order. In practice, the court is only likely to appoint a non-parent as sole guardian when the deceased, having a residence order in his or her favour, did not make a lifetime appointment and a third party is likely to be better able to care for the child than the surviving parent. (An account of the full circumstances in which courts appoint guardians is beyond the scope of this Handbook.)

7.3.2 Can the appointment be revoked or refused?

During the lifetime of the person who has made the appointment, he or she may revoke the appointment in the following ways:

- by a further appointment of a guardian unless clearly consistent with the appointment of an additional guardian rather than revoking the first appointment (CA 1989, s.6(1));
- by specifically revoking the appointment in writing, subject to the same conditions for the appointment of guardians as set out in **7.3.1** above (CA 1989, s.6(2));
- if the appointment is made other than in a will or codicil, by destroying the original written document which provided for the appointment of the guardian, with the intention of revoking the appointment (CA 1989, s.6(3));
- by revoking the will or codicil which contains the appointment (CA 1989, s.6(4)); or
- if the person appointed is the spouse of the appointor and their marriage is dissolved or annulled in England or Wales, or abroad and recognised here, unless a contrary intention appears by the appointment (CA 1989, s.6(3A)); or if the person appointed is the civil partner of the appointor and the civil partnership is dissolved or annulled as before.

The court has power to revoke the appointment at any time under CA 1989, s.6(7). In addition, the person who is appointed guardian may refuse the appointment by any document in writing signed by him or her made within a reasonable time of his or her first knowledge that the appointment has taken effect (CA 1989, s.6(5)).

The provision concerning spouses came into effect from 1 January 1996 (and civil partners from 5 December 2005). If such a spouse or civil partner has parental responsibility, his or her right over any children would be unaffected. The result is that, unless there is anything in the will to the contrary, the appointment of a step-parent as guardian in such circumstances would be revoked unless the step-parent had parental responsibility.

7.3.3 Pre-Children Act 1989 orders

As noted at **7.2** above, CA 1989, s.5(3) provides that a parent with parental responsibility may appoint a guardian. What is the position then, in respect of court orders made under pre-Children Act enactments? There are complex transitional provisions contained in CA 1989, Sched.14, para.4. In practice, CA 1989 has now been in force for 15 years and there are few minor children with pre-Children Act orders which have not been replaced by post-Children Act orders.

7.3.4 Effect of the 1989 Act on appointment of guardians by will or codicil

An appointment of a guardian may still be made in a will or codicil as these documents are written instruments under CA 1989, s.5(5). Although an appointment may be made in any written document, there is an advantage in appointing in a testamentary document as such documents are likely, by their nature, to be preserved, easily identifiable and be considered by those dealing with the estate of the appointor on death. However, as substitute or additional guardians may also be appointed in other written documents, the probate practitioner cannot assume that the guardians appointed in the will are the only guardians and enquiries should be made as to any other appointments which might take effect either instead of, or in addition to, the appointment in the testamentary document.

Even if a guardian is appointed in the will or codicil, the appointment may be revoked in any written document in accordance with CA 1989, ss.5 and 6 or may be revoked by a dissolution or annulment of the marriage or civil partnership. Thus a will may be valid, apart from the appointment of guardians which may have been revoked in a later non-testamentary document or by dissolution or annulment of the marriage or civil partnership. The converse situation could never arise, i.e. a revoked will but a valid appointment of guardians due to the provisions of CA 1989, s.6(4), so that if a will or codicil is revoked, the appointment of a guardian contained in the testamentary document will also be revoked.

It is advisable, when dealing with an estate involving minors, to check whether there are any other written documents which may have revoked an appointment of guardians in a will or codicil. Also checks should be made to see whether the marriage or civil partnership was dissolved or annulled after the appointment. However, a contrary intention in a will or other testamentary document would mean that the appointment of the ex-spouse or ex-civil partner as guardian would remain valid.

However, it is possible to have an invalid will (e.g. if the formalities for signing and witnessing the will have not been complied with) containing a valid appointment of guardians. The appointment will be valid provided that the invalid will qualifies under CA 1989, ss.5 and 6 as a document in writing, is signed by the appointor, and is dated.

It has been common in the past for both parents to appoint a guardian or guardians, the appointment to take effect on the death of the second parent. In general, it is no longer necessary that such a specific condition should be included within a will because under the terms of CA 1989, where both parents have parental responsibility (and there is no residence order in force), the appointment will not take effect until the second death. Some parents may however feel happier knowing that the provision is in place were they to be the first to die.

At any one time more than one person may have the right to appoint a guardian for a child but the appointment of guardians on death will not, in general, take effect until the child's last surviving guardian or parent with parental responsibility dies. The situation may then arise of two or more separately appointed guardians acting. This should be taken into account by the probate practitioner.

As noted from **7.3** above, the position will be further complicated if there are any residence orders in force with respect to the child. Will drafters and probate practitioners should also take this into account. If clients are at all unclear as to the existence of residence orders, the prudent will drafter should make enquiries of a specialist family law practitioner to ascertain the correct position.

If the will drafter is acting for the mother of a non-marital minor child, enquiries should be made as to whether the father is registered on the birth certificate (and if so, the date) or the existence of any parental responsibility agreement, as the father of the child may then be able to appoint testamentary guardians. As the significance of parental responsibility is of such importance for the appointment of guardians, and the requirements for parental responsibility agreements are strict, it may be prudent for the will drafter or probate practitioner, in appropriate cases, to check the existence of a valid agreement at the Principal Registry. Enquiries should be directed to the Searches Department, and a fee (currently £25) is payable to include a copy of any agreement found.

There is no provision in CA 1989 for successive appointments by the original appointor (i.e. 'I appoint Jane Smith as guardian of my minor children and when she dies then I appoint her husband William Smith as guardian'). However, there seems to be no prohibition on substitutional appointments taking effect if the first choice as guardian does not survive the appointor (i.e. 'I appoint Jane Smith as guardian of my minor children but if she has pre-deceased me then I appoint her husband William Smith as guardian').

There are often a number of clauses included in wills giving executors, trustees and appointed guardians certain rights and powers in relation to financial provision for minor beneficiaries under the will. If the will refers to provision for the child being made to the child's guardian, care should be taken by executors and trustees as well as those administering estates to ensure that the named guardian is properly and effectively appointed.

CHAPTER 8

Time for probate

Gillian E. Cockburn

Time limits are of crucial importance in probate and estate planning. This chapter considers, in brief, some of the more important time limits that practitioners should bear in mind during the administration of an estate.

8.1   OBTAINING THE GRANT

In general, a grant of probate will not issue from the probate registry within seven days of the date of death and a grant of letters of administration will not issue within 14 days of the date of death. In exceptional cases, a district judge or probate registrar may give leave for the grant to issue earlier but the applicant will first have to explain the need for expedition by way of a letter accompanying the application (Non-Contentious Probate Rules 1987, SI 1987/2024 (NCPR 1987), Rule 6(2)).

8.1.1   Caveats

If a caveat is entered to prevent a grant of representation being issued in an estate it should be remembered that the caveat will only remain in force for a period of six months from the date of entry (NCPR 1987, Rule 44(3)(a)–(c)). It may be extended for further periods of six months but each application for extension must be made in the last month prior to the expiry of the caveat.

8.2   RECTIFICATION OF THE WILL

It is possible to correct errors in wills of testators dying on or after 1 January 1983 provided that the court is satisfied that the will fails to express the testator's intentions as a result of either a clerical error or a failure by the drafter to understand the testator's intentions (Administration of Justice Act 1982, s.20). An application for rectification of a will must be made within six months of the date that representation to the estate is first taken out.

The court does have power to consider applications outside the six-month period but the applicant has to show that there was a very good reason why the application was not made within the time limit. If there is a possibility of rectification the PRs should not distribute the estate within the six-month period referred to above. (See Administration of Justice Act 1982 regarding distributions once the six-month period has expired.)

8.3 FAMILY PROVISION CLAIMS

(See also **Chapter 10**.) Certain individuals have the right to apply for financial provision from the estate of a person who dies domiciled in England and Wales (Inheritance (Provision for Family and Dependants) Act 1975 (IPFDA 1975), s.1). A claim must be made within six months of the date that representation to the estate is first taken out (IPFDA 1975, s.4). If there is a possibility of a claim the PRs should not distribute the estate within this period. (See IPFDA 1975, s.20 for more on distributions.) The court has power to allow a claim to be made outside the six-month period. The basis for exercising its discretion was set out by Megarry V-C in *Re Salmon (Deceased)* [1979] 3 WLR 802 where he identified six guidelines. Examples of cases in which the court has exercised its discretion are *Re Hancock (Deceased)* [1998] 2 FLR 346 and *McNulty* v. *McNulty* [2002] WTLR 737 in which assets of the estate had increased substantially in value. Note that the court can only use its power under s.9 to make an order against the deceased's share of property held as beneficial joint tenants if the application is made within the six-month period. There is no power to extend the time limit.

Note that civil partners now have the right to apply for financial provision under Civil Partnership Act 2004.

8.4 INTEREST AND LEGACIES

(See also **Chapter 16**.) Personal representatives must administer the estate properly and should not unduly delay the payment of legacies. Personal representatives who delay payment without good reason may find themselves personally liable to pay interest to aggrieved beneficiaries. In certain cases, legatees have the right to interest at the basic rate payable for funds in court, at present 4 per cent per annum (para.15, CPR Practice Direction 40 with periods prior to 2 December 2002 at the rate of 6 per cent per annum) on their legacies, if they are paid late, as follows:

- General pecuniary legacies should be paid within one year ('the executors' year') from the date of death. Where they are paid outside that period they must carry interest calculated from the first anniversary of the death (when the right to receive the legacy arose). Any interest paid will come from the residue of the estate (from monies which might otherwise have passed to the residuary beneficiaries).

- Specific legacies do not carry the right to interest but they do carry any income arising from the gift, subject to the wording of the will.
- Immediate legacies will carry interest from the date of death if it is clear from the will that the testator or testatrix intended that the payment should be made immediately on death. Legacies (whether immediate or contingent) provided for the maintenance of the testator's or the testatrix's children will also carry interest from the date of death.
- Future or contingent legacies will in general carry interest from the date the future event or contingency occurs.
- Residuary gifts do not carry interest in accordance with these provisions. However, residuary beneficiaries are entitled to a share in any income the estate generates after payment of estate liabilities and legacies.

8.5 ADVERTISING FOR CREDITORS

Personal representatives should consider advertising for creditors and potential beneficiaries before starting to distribute the estate (Trustee Act 1925, s.27). The point during the administration at which the advertisement is inserted will depend on a number of factors, varying with each estate. The advertisement gives notice of the PRs' intention to distribute to those who may have claims against the estate. A suitably worded advertisement should be inserted in the *London Gazette* and in a newspaper circulating in any area where the deceased owned land. In addition, the PRs should also consider advertising elsewhere if there are any special factors affecting the estate. The advertisements must give claimants at least two months to notify the PRs of their claim. After the advertisements have been inserted, and assuming that no claimants have come forward in the two-month period, the PRs may distribute the estate with reference only to claims known to them at the time of distribution.

8.6 INTESTACY

Under Law Reform (Succession) Act 1995, s.1 and with effect from 1 January 1996, a spouse must survive for 28 days before becoming entitled under the intestacy laws.

The surviving spouse also has the following rights, both of which should be exercised within 12 months of the date that representation to the estate is first taken out:

- to redeem the life interest and instead receive a capital sum (Administration of Estates Act 1925, s.47A as amended by Administration of Justice Act 1977); and/or
- to have the deceased's interest in the matrimonial home appropriated as part of the surviving spouse's interest in the estate (Intestates' Estates Act 1952, Sched.2).

A partner in a civil partnership now has the same rights as a surviving spouse under an intestacy (Civil Partnership Act 2004, Sched.4, paras.7–12, which amends the Administration of Estates Act 1925).

8.7 INHERITANCE TAX

8.7.1 Payment of tax

The due date for payment of inheritance tax (IHT) on death is six months after the end of the month in which the death occurs (Inheritance Tax Act 1984 (IHTA 1984), s.226). Late payment will result in interest charges under ss.233 and 234. However, when the application for the grant of representation is made, any IHT payable on the non-instalment option assets (e.g. money, chattels, quoted shares, etc.), must be paid at that time even if prior to the due date.

IHT on instalment option assets (as set out in IHTA 1984, s.227) may be paid by 10 equal yearly instalments if the personal representatives so elect. If this election is made, the first instalment is due six months after the end of the month in which the death took place and the remaining nine instalments on successive anniversaries of that six-month date. The election is usually made within the HMRC account but it may also be made separately at a later date. In practice there does not appear to be any specific time limit within which this election should be made.

8.7.2 Delivery of accounts

An account must be delivered to HMRC within 12 months of the end of the month in which the death occurs or, if later, three months from the date the personal representatives first act (IHTA 1984, s.216). Regulations may be made under s.256 dispensing with this requirement in certain cases (e.g. excepted estates). Failure to deliver an account within the time limit may render the PRs liable to financial penalties (IHTA 1984, ss.245 and 245A, as amended by Finance Act 1999, s.108).

8.7.3 Reliefs and exemptions

If an estate includes a holding of qualifying investments (usually quoted shares) which are sold within 12 months of the date of death for less than the probate value, the PRs, or other person liable for the tax, may apply to have the lower sale price substituted for the probate value (IHTA 1984, ss.178 and 179). In addition if land or an interest in land is sold within four years of the date of death for less than the probate value, the PRs, or other person liable for the tax, may be able to substitute the lower sale price for the probate value (IHTA 1984, ss.190 and 191).

8.7.4 Variations and disclaimers

It is possible to vary the terms of a will or the provisions applicable to an estate under the intestacy laws so that the varied provisions take effect (for IHT and/or capital gains tax (CGT) purposes) as if those provisions had been included in the deceased's last will (IHTA 1984, s.142 and Taxation of Chargeable Gains Act 1992 (TCGA 1992), s.62(6) and (7), as amended by Finance Act 2002). A variation must be made in writing by the people who would otherwise benefit from the varied assets within a period of two years from the date of the death. For instruments made on or after 1 August 2002, formal elections to the Board of the Inland Revenue are no longer necessary. Instead of elections, a statement must be contained within the instrument made by all the relevant parties that they intend IHTA 1984, s.142(1), and TCGA 1992, s.62(6) to apply to the variation. If more tax is payable as a result of the variation then a copy of the deed must be delivered to HMRC within six months of the date of the deed informing them of the additional tax to be paid.

A disclaimer of an interest under a will or under the intestacy laws must also be made in writing and within two years of the date of death. No elections are necessary for the disclaimer to be treated as though made by the deceased for IHT or CGT purposes.

8.7.5 Property settled by will

Capital distributions or appointments from a discretionary will trust (i.e. from a settlement and before any interest in possession arises) within two years of the date of death (or any shorter period stated in the will) will be treated as having been made under the deceased's will and taking place at the date of death (IHTA 1984, s.144). This provision only applies if the capital distribution or appointment is an event which would otherwise have been chargeable to IHT. Thus a capital distribution or appointment from the property within the first three months after death would not qualify (IHTA 1984, s.65(4)).

8.7.6   Quick succession relief

If the deceased's estate was increased by a chargeable transfer within five years of the date of death then quick succession relief will be available to reduce the IHT payable on the death (IHTA 1984, s.141). The reduction is a percentage of part of the IHT paid on the earlier transfer. The percentage applicable will depend upon the period between the transfer and the date of death.

8.7.7   Overpayments of tax

Claims for repayment of overpaid IHT (including interest) must be made within six years of the payment of the tax (IHTA 1984, s.241). However, if too much tax was paid as a result of a mistake of HMRC then a repayment can be claimed within 20 years.

8.7.8   Underpaid tax

HMRC will not bring any proceedings for underpaid tax once a period of six years has expired from the later of:

- the date when the payment of tax or the last instalment was made and accepted; and
- the due date for payment of the tax or last instalment (IHTA 1984, s.240).

This restriction on HMRC will not apply if there is any fraud, wilful default or neglect on the part of the person liable for the tax when the time limit is six years from the time the fraud, willful default or neglect is made known to HMRC.

8.7.9   Events prior to death

There are a number of important time limits for probate practitioners in relation to pre-death events. For instance, chargeable transfers and potentially exempt transfers made within a period of up to seven years before death must be taken into account by the PRs in the calculation of the IHT due on the transferor's estate at death (IHTA 1984, ss.7 and 3A).

Gifts with reservation may also have to be taken into account when calculating the IHT due on death if the gifts are either still subject to the reserved interest at the date of death or alternatively the reservation was released within seven years before the date of death (Finance Act 1986, s.102 and Sched.20).

There may also be a liability to IHT payable by the transferees of these different types of lifetime transfers following the death of the transferor within the seven-year period. Any additional IHT payable by a transferee as a result of the death will be due for payment six months from the end of the month in which the death occurs, but payment by instalments may be available in certain cases (IHTA 1984, s.226).

However, if the transferee does not pay within 12 months of the end of the month in which the death occurs HMRC may look to the PRs for payment of the tax (IHTA 1984, ss.200, 204: see also **Chapter 15** on PRs and IHT). It is important, therefore, for the PRs to make full enquiries to discover any lifetime transfers. If any are discovered, the estate should not be fully distributed until the tax due on these transfers has been settled and an appropriate certificate of clearance issued by the Capital Taxes Office.

8.8   CAPITAL GAINS TAX

Personal representatives are entitled to the individual's annual CGT exemption for the tax year of death and the following two tax years (TCGA 1992, s.3(7)). After that time an annual CGT allowance will not be available unless the PRs qualify in another capacity, e.g. as trustees. It should be noted that under the self-assessment regime the due date for payment of CGT is 31 January following the end of the tax year in which the gain was made.

8.9   INCOME TAX

8.9.1   Appeals

An appeal against an income tax (or CGT) assessment or an appeal against an amendment to a self-assessment must be made in writing and lodged within 30 days of the issue of the assessment or notice of amendment (Taxes Management Act 1970 (TMA 1970), s.31A). *Inland Revenue* v. *Wilkinson* [1992] STC 454 demonstrates the importance of making a formal appeal against tax assessments. An application for postponement of payment of some or all of the tax assessed may be made at that time. HMRC may allow appeals to be made outside the 30-day period but it is under no obligation to do so.

8.9.2   Returns

During the course of the administration it may be necessary to submit income tax returns. In order to avoid the possibility of automatic penalties and surcharges (see at **8.9.3** below) always make enquiries of HMRC about the deceased's income tax affairs and do so as soon after the death as possible. To avoid interest and penalties under the self-assessment regime completed returns must be submitted to HMRC by 30 September following the end of the tax year (if the taxpayer wishes HMRC to calculate the tax due). If taxpayers calculate the tax themselves then the return should be submitted to HMRC by 31 January following the end of the tax year (or if the return is issued after the end of October, then within three months of the date of service of the return). Taxpayers who do not submit self-assessment returns by the due date will be subject to an automatic penalty of £100 (TMA 1970, s.93). A further penalty of £100 will be charged if the return is still outstanding after a further six months. In cases of more serious delay other penalties will be charged. It should be noted that, in general, a self-assessment return is not considered to have been submitted unless it is complete. Thus 'to be advised' figures are not acceptable (although best estimates may be).

8.9.3   Payment of tax

Under the self-assessment regime, tax must be paid in full by 31 January following the end of the tax year. In addition, payments on account in two equal instalments for the current tax year may be required to be paid by 31 January in the tax year and the following 31 July. A balancing payment may then be required on the following 31 January. Interest will be charged on overdue tax plus a 5 per cent surcharge if the balancing payment is outstanding more than 28 days after the due date (TMA 1970, s.59C). A further 5 per cent surcharge may be payable if the tax is still unpaid more than six months after the due date.

8.10   PREVENTING PROBLEMS

Missing just one time limit could prove to be an expensive error involving an application for extension of the normal time limit, interest charges, and even a claim for damages. It may also spoil a good solicitor–client relationship.

How can a practice guard against missing an important time limit? It is clear that there are too many time limits for it to be safe to rely on memory alone. The use of a central diary (whether handwritten or on computer) operated by a responsible member of the practice may be of considerable benefit. Fee earners could provide the diary keeper with a list of their important dates, perhaps by completing a pro forma list. The diary keeper would then be responsible for reminding each fee earner of the date well in advance of the time limit concerned. If a fee earner was unexpectedly absent, important dates would not be missed as the diary keeper would be able to bring the date to the attention of another member of the practice. Used in this (or a similar) way, a central diary system could prove to be invaluable in the running of an efficient and trouble-free probate practice.

CHAPTER 9

Probate and benefits

Meg Andrews

9.1 INTRODUCTION

Some clients may not be concerned about potential IHT liability or how best to invest their legacy, but more practically how they are going to cope financially without the deceased.

9.2 FUNERAL COSTS

The first problem is often: how is the funeral to be paid for? One does come across the enterprising client who has withdrawn the money for the funeral refreshments and flowers using the deceased's cashpoint card, or paid for the funeral using an enduring power of attorney before the bank is aware of the death, but clearly this should not be encouraged.

For a family used to paying cash on the nail, the prospect of a bill of £2,000 or more hanging over them can be distressing. The suggestion that they take the funeral account to the deceased's bank or building society as soon as it is received may be all that is required. Where someone has a collection of small accounts, closing them all by cheques payable to the funeral director can be cheaper than a collection of statutory declarations in lieu of a grant.

Unfortunately, some financial organisations make a habit of referring the bereaved customer to a solicitor as soon as they find out a will is involved, when the bank's own small estates procedure would be perfectly appropriate. The fairest thing to do in those circumstances (unless there is a pending flotation, when other considerations may apply) is to refer the client back to the institution involved, perhaps having telephoned the branch manager first. On the other hand, where a bank has actual knowledge of the state of the PR's own finances, it may insist on a grant for a very modest estate, in order to protect its position and that of the beneficiaries.

If the deceased was a member of a trade union or hospital fund, it is worth contacting the organisation before the funeral arrangements are made. Some will only pay funeral benefits if the claim is made before the funeral, while others, especially if a funeral bond is involved, may wish to specify a particular funeral director. Many make their cheque payable to the funeral director, rather than the family, which can present problems if the family have already clubbed together to pay the bill.

The Social Fund will pay the costs of a basic funeral, if the person responsible for paying for it is on income support, in receipt of pension credit, income based job-seeker's allowance, council tax benefit, housing benefit, disabled person's tax credit or working families tax credit. The funeral payment will cover the costs of a burial plot and interment or cremation costs, including the doctors' certificates, the cost of a hearse and up to £700 for any other funeral expenses. The claimant's savings are ignored.

The cheque is normally payable to the funeral director and the application can be made immediately or up to three months after the funeral. The application form asks for some detailed information about the relationships between the claimant and the deceased and the deceased and other members of his or her family, to confirm that the applicant is the appropriate person to have responsibility for paying for the funeral. The Social Fund will be able to recover its costs from the estate, if it turns out that there are liquid assets after all. Although some funeral directors keep a stock, the application form can be obtained from the local social security office or downloaded from the website of the Department for Work and Pensions (**www.dwp.gov.uk**).

9.3   BEREAVEMENT

9.3.1   Bereavement payment

Since April 2001, a surviving spouse (and now civil partner) of either sex has been able to claim a tax-free lump sum bereavement payment of £2,000. This is not means-tested, but is conditional on the deceased spouse having paid appropriate national insurance contributions and either not being entitled to state retirement pension when he or she died or the surviving spouse being under retirement age at the date of death. As from December 2005, the surviving partner in a registered civil partnership can also claim on the same basis.

9.3.2   Bereavement allowance

If the surviving spouse or registered civil partner is over 45 years old at the time of death, he or she may be entitled to bereavement allowance, a taxable weekly benefit, for 52 weeks from the date of death. Again, this can be conditional on the deceased having paid appropriate national insurance contributions, but will also be paid if death was caused by their employment. The amount payable (rates correct at April 2006) depends on the age of the surviving spouse or partner, with those aged over 55 getting the full rate of £84.25 per week and those aged between 45 and 54 getting only part of this (£25.28 per week if the surviving spouse or partner was 45 at the time of bereavement). Unfortunately the rate is fixed and does not go up if the claimant crosses an age threshold during the year in question. Current rates and claim forms can be found on the Jobcentre Plus website (**www.jobcentreplus.gov.uk**).

9.4 ORPHANS

If the surviving spouse or registered civil partner has children entitling them to child benefit, or was expecting the deceased's child, then widowed parent's allowance will be paid instead of bereavement allowance. Unlike bereavement allowance, this includes state earnings related pension, if the claimant qualifies, and an allowance for each dependent child, as well as a basic allowance for the claimant at the (April 2006) rate of £84.25 per week. The widowed parent's allowance continues for as long as the claimant meets the conditions, generally until the youngest child leaves school.

A lone parent who was not married to the deceased or in a registered civil partnership may, like a widow or widower, be entitled to income support, help with rent in the form of housing benefit or council tax benefit. Those receiving income support are also eligible for budgeting loans to buy things for the home or Social Fund crisis loans if immediate help is needed in an emergency. If the child is under five, income support also entitles the claimant to cold weather payments. Other triggers for this last benefit are the claimant being disabled or over 60.

Child benefit is not means-tested and is payable to any person bringing up children, while the child is under 16, or under 19 and studying full-time either A level, NVQ level 3 or an equivalent qualification, or under 18 and actively looking for work or a training place while registered for work or training with the Careers Service or Connexion Service. It is paid in respect of each child, at the rate of £17.45 a week for the first child and £11.70 a week for others.

If the carer is not the child's parent, the carer may also be entitled to guardian's allowance, if both parents are dead, or one has died and the other is in prison or cannot be found or the parents were divorced. Guardian's allowance is paid at the rate of £12.50 for each child.

9.5 INCAPACITATED DEPENDANTS

Sadly it is often the ostensibly fitter half of a couple who dies first, and it may only then be apparent how much care the surviving partner has been receiving. If he or she is under pension age, then there may be an entitlement to incapacity benefit, if the right to statutory sick pay has expired. This benefit is dependent on national insurance contributions, unless the claimant became unable to work between 16 and 20 years of age, or the claimant is under 25 and was in education or training when under 20. Rates (at April 2006) vary between £59.20 and £95.00 per week, depending on the age of the claimant, the length of time that the claimant has been incapacitated and the level of incapacity.

Attendance allowance is available to those over 65 who have needed help looking after themselves for at least six months or who have received a terminal diagnosis. The need may be for daytime care, help at night, or both, with the rate payable depending on the need (£62.25 per week for day and night attendance or if there is a terminal diagnosis, or £41.65 per week if day or night care is required). Attendance allowance is not means-tested or taxed and does not count as income for income support assessment purposes.

The claim forms can be completed on behalf of claimants, so that the fact of a terminal diagnosis need not be disclosed to them.

9.6 OTHER SOURCES OF HELP

The right to means-tested benefits may have been lost by cohabitation as man and wife or in a same sex relationship, even if there is no registered civil partnership. The death of one of a couple may mean the survivor can resume claiming in their own right.

Apart from state help, it is worth looking at what pension rights the deceased had or what pensions the deceased was receiving. Most pension schemes make provision for widows or widowers and dependent children of any age and more will now pay pensions to cohabitants. The old-fashioned schemes where a widower was only entitled to a pension from his late wife's pension if he was disabled are no longer found. A spouse should now be interpreted as covering a registered civil partner. If the deceased had not reached retirement age, an employer's pension scheme will generally provide that a lump sum or pension is payable at the discretion of trustees, who will be guided by any letter of wishes signed by the deceased. In the absence of any such expression, trustees generally follow the intestacy rules, but it may be possible to persuade them to pay money into a purpose-built discretionary trust, if this would avoid the beneficiary losing means-tested benefits.

It is always worth checking the death certificate to see what the deceased died of, or what illnesses he or she suffered from at the time of death. The number of industrial diseases for which compensation can be claimed is growing all the time. If the deceased was a miner's widow or child, it is wise to ask if the late miner suffered from emphysema or chronic obstructive airways disease, as his claim for compensation did not necessarily die with him and may not have been recognised at the time of his death.

Many types of employment have their own charities attached, from the

Royal Agricultural Benevolent Association to the Solicitors Benevolent Association. The Civil Service has its own charity, which offers emotional as well as financial support, as do each of the services. Counsel and Care is a charity which specialises in pointing people, including legal advisers, in the direction of appropriate charities who may be able to assist elderly people in financial need or requiring help or advice (see **Useful addresses**).

Benefit advice can be given under the Legal Help scheme or, of course, *pro bono*.

CHAPTER 10

Inheritance (Provision for Family and Dependants) Act 1975 claims

Dawn Goodman and Sue Medder

10.1 INHERITANCE (PROVISION FOR FAMILY AND DEPENDANTS) ACT 1975 AND WILLS

It is not possible to guarantee to exclude the possibility of a claim under the Inheritance (Provision for Family and Dependants) Act 1975 (IPFDA 1975) but there are some simple steps that can be taken when drafting wills which may reduce the likelihood of a claim or, if one is made, reduce its chances of success.

10.1.1 Check background facts

Establish the extent of all the client's family and dependants. There is no point in skating round the issue of a client's secret relationships and non-marital children, only to find that claims are made against the estate after the client is dead.

10.1.2 Ask questions

A client may have dependants who are not immediately obvious to the client as such. Examples are gratuitous payments to a niece or nephew, or accommodation provided for a mother-in-law, companion, or even an elderly nanny or other former member of staff.

10.1.3 Options

Clients may have been providing for people who could claim against the estate as dependants, but who do not fall within any of the other categories of claimant under IPFDA 1975: spouse, former spouse who has not remarried, civil partner or former civil partner, cohabitant, or children (including adopted and non-marital children and those treated as children of the family). If so, the client should be advised that the chance of a claim could be reduced by:

- making provision by will or otherwise for them; or
- ceasing to maintain them.

If the second option is taken, the solicitor should also advise the client to make it clear to any dependants that he or she no longer assumes responsibility for their maintenance. A memorandum can be left with the client's will explaining that maintenance has ceased but it is preferable for the client to send a letter (keeping a copy) to each dependant explaining that maintenance (or the assumption of responsibility) is ceasing.

Some clients will say they are making no or little provision for their wife, husband or civil partner because she or he has adequate personal assets. This may reflect a misunderstanding on the client's part about what would be regarded for these purposes as adequate assets, so make further enquiries and ensure that the client understands the position. It may be prudent to remind the client that one of the criteria the court will use for assessing what is reasonable provision is what the wife or husband would have received if the marriage had been terminated by divorce rather than death. (Note that surviving civil partners are similarly entitled to the more generous provision to which spouses are entitled, and IPFDA 1975, s.1(1)(a) has been amended to include the civil partner of the deceased.) As a result of the ancillary relief decision in *White* v. *White* [2001] 1 AC 596 the 'yardstick of equality' may be referred to when considering the quantum of a surviving spouse's or civil partner's claims in long marriages/relationships. This is having some impact on the level of provision that the court views as appropriate in IPFDA 1975 claims brought by spouses and civil partners, although it is not applied universally in all reported IPFDA 1975 cases. See the favourable decisions for spouses in *Fielden* v. *Cunliffe* [2006] Ch 361 and *P* v. *G, P&P* [2006] 1 FLR 431.

10.1.4   Former spouses

A former spouse or former civil partner (who has not remarried or entered into another civil partnership) may make a claim if he or she is receiving maintenance at the time of the ex-spouse's death. It is best to try to forestall the claim by making some provision. It is sensible to check whether the client is bound by the terms of any ancillary relief orders for transfer of matrimonial assets, ongoing maintenance payments, or obligations to provide by will or life assurance: if the latter, check whether the policy is still valid.

10.1.5   Leaving a memorandum

If the client fears a claim under IPFDA 1975 but does not wish to make provision for the potential claimant, the client should be encouraged to leave a memorandum with the will explaining why no provision was made, unless the reasons for making no provision are unreasonable, in which case the memorandum could do more harm than good. As with a will, a memorandum should be updated as and when the potential claimant's financial circumstances alter from those in place at the date of the memorandum. A memorandum based on outdated financial facts may assist a claimant in securing provision if the reasoning behind the limited provision by the deceased spouse/civil partner no longer reflects the reality of the claimant's financial circumstances.

There appears to be a trend in IPFDA 1975 actions towards the introduction of parallel claims (such as proprietary estoppel, declarations as to beneficial interests, mutual will obligations, and claims based on a contractual relationship with the deceased) to bolster inheritance claims. Such claims are based on a combination of the deceased's intentions and of fact. The claim will only be made after the deceased's death. Often there are no independent witnesses so the surviving claimant is free to give their version of the deceased's intentions, unchallenged by contemporary evidence.

With this in mind, it may well be appropriate for a detailed attendance note of the initial instructions to be copied to the client with the draft will. The client should be asked to confirm the attendance note details are correct when confirming instructions to engross the will. The attendance note should be kept, as with any memorandum, with the will. At least then there is an accurate contemporaneous record of the testator's intention.

10.1.6 People with special needs

If a client has dependants with mental or physical disabilities, and is assuming that the state will support them, the client should be warned that the local social services department can make an application on behalf of the dependants for provision from the estate. Solicitors may wish to consider with their clients the advantage of making provision for such a dependant in the form of a discretionary trust with the possibility (not guaranteed) that this will protect the fund from a claim from the social services department and/or alternatively will not be taken into account when assessing the capital resources of the dependant.

10.1.7 Cohabitees

Clients who are living with someone as a cohabitee should be advised that a will may be necessary to provide for his or her partner. Cohabitees cannot claim under the intestacy rules and will not be able to make a claim under IPFDA 1975, if:

- they were not living together for two years prior to the death; or
- they were not dependent upon the deceased.

They can be severely disadvantaged by their partner's death.

Guidelines which the court should consider when applications are made by cohabitees are given by IPFDA 1975, s.3(2A). These are:

- the age of the applicant and the length of the period during which the applicant lived as the husband or wife of the deceased and in the same household as the deceased; and
- the contribution made by the applicant to the welfare of the family of the deceased, including any contribution made by looking after the home or caring for the family.

10.1.8   Caveats

Sometimes a claimant lodges a caveat against the issue of the grant – this is wrong use of a caveat and it should be possible to have it warned off.

10.2   WHAT SHOULD BE DONE IN THE EVENT OF A CLAIM

If a claim has been issued, PRs should be cautious about how they administer the estate. Broadly speaking, PRs faced with a claim should pay debts and funeral expenses and collect in the assets of the estate; but they should not distribute until the claim has been disposed of.

10.2.1   Small legacies or cases of hardship

If there are small legacies which are unlikely to be affected by the claim, or beneficiaries are experiencing hardship, PRs can seek agreement of the parties affected, including the claimant, to payment of legacies or a distribution to relieve hardship (*Re Ralphs sub nom: Ralphs* v. *District Bank* [1968] 1 WLR 1522). If consent is not forthcoming, an application can be made to the court for directions (CPR Rule 64.2(a)).

If the converse applies and it is the claimant who is suffering hardship, and the beneficiaries will not agree to a distribution, the claimant can apply under IPFDA 1975, s.5 for an interim payment.

10.2.2   Time limit

Claimants have six months from the issue of the grant to put in a claim, so PRs will not be liable if they distribute the estate more than six months after obtaining the grant if no IPFDA 1975 application has been issued. However, claimants can apply for leave to apply out of time. *McNulty* v. *McNulty* [2002] WTLR 737 is a recent example of a successful application.

A Trustee Act 1925, s.27 advertisement does not protect PRs who distribute after two months has expired from the date of advertisement but within six months from the grant of probate.

10.2.3 Personal representatives as claimants

Obviously, as a solicitor for the PRs, you cannot act both for potential claimant and potential defendant(s) in the IPFDA 1975 claim. If a PR or proposed PR is, say, a widow who does not think that her late husband's will or the application of the intestacy rules provides for her adequately, then she must be independently advised by another firm on whether or not to claim.

In this situation your firm can continue to act in the administration with the agreement of all PRs. The PR who is claiming as a claimant and the PRs who are defending the claim as beneficiaries should instruct two firms other than yours, i.e. there will be three firms involved. Any PRs who are not claimants or beneficiaries can be represented by you in the litigation. The PRs as a body should adopt a neutral role and not attempt to defeat the claim. Without this approach being seen to be followed, the administration of the estate is likely to grind to a halt while the claim is pending.

A claimant who is one of the proposed PRs can have power reserved. It is not necessary to renounce if he or she is going to make a claim. A PR who has taken out a grant and proposes to claim need not be removed from office.

10.2.4 Sole personal representatives

If the intending claimant is the sole PR, he or she might prefer not to take out the grant (although power might be reserved). In such a case, the grant may have to be taken out by the person next entitled, or by a nominee of the intending claimant pursuant to Supreme Court Act 1981, s.116.

10.2.5 Personal representatives as beneficiaries

The PRs are also often beneficiaries who are resisting a claim. Although PRs should adopt a neutral stance, leaving it to the claimant and the beneficiaries to fight the matter out, beneficiary PRs are not obliged to be neutral *in their capacity as beneficiaries*. They must not pay the costs of defending the claim out of the estate: such costs are their personal liability.

Difficulties arise where one or more PRs are professionals and another is a beneficiary who wishes to contest the claim. If all PRs are content to accept your advice, or counsel's, on how to handle the claim, and are not causing costs to be incurred unnecessarily, you should not have a conflict of interest in acting for all the PRs.

Nevertheless, it is much better to ensure that the PR with the beneficial interest is separately represented in his or her capacity as beneficiary.

10.3 HOW TO HANDLE A CLAIM

If the solicitor learns about a claim which appears meritorious before proceedings are issued (and the would-be claimant is either in time or likely to get an extension), he or she should consider asking the beneficiaries (assuming they are all adults and competent) if they are willing to enter into a deed of variation. They must be advised to obtain independent advice.

Once the claim is issued, the PRs should promptly provide the information required by CPR Rule 57.16(5) and PD57 para.16 unless all parties agree to freeze the obligation to respond by witness statement in order to save costs.

PRs must comply with their obligations to bring to court matters within their knowledge which may be relevant to the court's exercise of its discretion. Equally, they should maintain a neutral position with regard to the merits of any claim and not usurp the function of the beneficiary defendants.

Although PRs have extensive common law and statutory powers (see Trustee Act 1925, s.15 as substituted by Trustee Act 2000) to compromise claims against the estate, provided that they act in good faith, these powers do not extend to compromising an IPFDA 1975 claim because the claim, instead of being against the estate, is to become a beneficiary in the estate. The PRs ought to leave the claimant and the beneficiaries to negotiate a settlement but should indicate:

- their readiness to assist by providing up-to-date information on the composition and administration of the estate;
- their desire to be involved at the final stage of negotiations to ensure that the agreement reached between the parties is workable from the administrative point of view and that the PRs' own position on costs is protected.

Solicitor PRs should be concerned to ensure the part that they play is as limited as possible. The estate should not be put to unnecessary additional expense. It may be appropriate for PRs to seek directions from the court that the beneficiaries' advocate represent them during proceedings.

10.3.1 Charity beneficiaries and Inheritance (Provision for Family and Dependants) Act 1975

(For more on charity beneficiaries see **Chapter 16**.) A charity can agree to a compromise of proceedings through its duly authorised officer. The charity may need separate advice on whether to agree a compromise and if in doubt can seek an order from the Charity Commissioners or a letter of opinion or advice under Charities Act 1993, ss.26 and 29, although this is not normally necessary.

In some cases, charities may feel a moral obligation to renounce part of their entitlement and under Charities Act 1993, s.27 the Charity Commissioners have powers to authorise charity trustees to give effect to a perceived moral obligation. Charities cannot give effect to a moral obligation without such authority. The Charity Commission has produced a very useful leaflet CC7, *Ex Gratia Payments by Charities* (available from **www.charity-commission.gov.uk**).

10.3.2   Costs

Unless the PRs have acted unreasonably (such as by adopting too proactive a stance) or for their own benefit rather than that of the estate, they should receive their costs out of the estate on the indemnity basis (CPR Rule 48.4). PRs and trustees should be aware of the new provisions in CPR Part 48 Practice Direction, paras.50A.1 to 50A.3, which list the criteria that the court will use in assessing whether the costs were properly incurred. However it is not generally necessary for a PR to obtain the court's consent to adopt a neutral stance when defending an IPFDA 1975 claim.

The PRs will also be expected to act in accordance with the overriding objective of CPR Rule 1.1(2) in dealing with the claim and will be expected to do so in a way which is proportionate to the amount of money involved, the importance of the case, the financial position of each party, and the complexity of the issues. In making costs orders the court will give consideration to whether the parties have complied with the overriding objective.

A successful claimant's costs are usually paid from the estate, commonly on the standard basis; conversely, an unsuccessful claimant's costs are not always borne by him or her. Frequently, an unsuccessful claimant is not ordered to pay the costs of the PRs or other defendants. PRs should be aware of the effect on the estate of costs orders in favour of a number of parties and it may be appropriate to bring this to the attention of the claimant and beneficiaries.

10.3.3   Wasted costs

Solicitors for the PRs should be aware that, if they have acted improperly and unreasonably or have been negligent, and in consequence any party to the proceedings has incurred additional costs, they can be disallowed their costs or asked to meet all or any wasted costs of another party (Supreme Court Act 1981, s.51(6) as amended; CPR Rules 44.14 and 48.7). An example of causing wasted costs would be the negligent provision of incorrect information about the size and nature of the estate when preparing the PR's witness statement under CPR Rule 57.16(5).

The case of *Ridehalgh* v. *Horsefield and Another (No.2)* [1994] 3 WLR 462 provides an analysis of when it would be appropriate to bring an application for a wasted costs order and reference was made to this analysis in *Morris* v. *Roberts (Inspector of Taxes)* [2005] PNLR 41.

CHAPTER 11

Contentious probate

Henry Frydenson

11.1 INTRODUCTION

The proportion of contentious work in private client departments is growing rapidly. The growth is partly the result of an increasingly litigious society and partly the result of the fact that there is more wealth around for people to argue over.

Practitioners who find that more work of this type is coming their way may be interested in joining the Association of Contentious Trusts and Probate Specialists. (More information and application forms are available online from their website **www.actaps.com**.)

The purposes of the Association include raising the standard of contentious work and developing a common approach. Members agree to endeavour to act in accordance with a voluntary Code of Conduct. Under this Code members agree where appropriate to try to use the full range of solutions, in particular alternative dispute resolution.

Alternative dispute resolution is an informal alternative to formal litigation and an attempt to overcome and avoid the acrimony, expense and frustration of litigation, as a way of settling disputes. Increasingly its main method is mediation. In mediation, the parties select an independent third party who will assist the parties in reaching their solution to the problem. The mediator will have experience in this method of problem solving. He will air the problem with both sides initially together and then privately with each party. The private sessions will be blunt and open and the mediator will do his best to get both sides to look at their real interests and priorities. Mediation produces non-binding solutions until the parties reach agreement and then the parties are able to agree between themselves that the new agreement is to be binding. The mediation process is a without prejudice one. See the case of *Dunnett* v. *Railtrack* [2002] EWCA 303, where the court penalised a party in costs for failing to mediate; *Halsey* v. *Milton Keynes General NHS Trust* [2004] EWCA Civ 576, where the court highlighted the importance of mediation before court proceedings were issued, and stated that an unreasonable refusal to mediate would attract cost sanctions; and *Burchell* v. *Bullard and Others* [2005] EWCA Civ 358, where the Court of Appeal added weight to the *Halsey* decision. Lord Justice Ward said '*Halsey* has made plain not only the high rate of a successful outcome being achieved by mediation, but also its established importance as a track to a just result running parallel with that of the Court system'. He continued 'The profession can no longer with impunity shrug aside reasonable requests to mediate. The parties cannot ignore a proper request to mediate simply because it was made before the claim was issued. With Court fees escalating, it may be folly to do so'.

11.2 IDENTIFICATION OF ISSUES

When advising a client it is important to identify the points which are likely to be in issue.

If there is a will there will be two possible questions relating to the will:

- Is the will valid? This may require considering any of the following questions:
  - Have the formal requirements for making a will been complied with? (See Wills Act 1837, s.9.)
  - Did the testator have the capacity to make a will?
  - Do claims of undue influence or lack of knowledge and approval arise?

- How is a particular provision in a will to be construed?

11.3 METHODS OF ATTACK

Where a person is unhappy with the terms of a deceased's will or the provisions which would arise on intestacy, there are various grounds of possible attack. Before considering these grounds in detail, thought should always be given as to what the outcome of a successful attack will be. For example, the overthrow of a will may result in intestacy or in the provisions of an earlier will remaining in effect. There is absolutely no point in overthrowing the later will if your client will have no rights on intestacy or under the earlier will.

Consideration must also be given to the all-important question of costs (see **11.6.5** below).

11.3.1 Lack of due execution of the will

The burden of proving that the will was executed in accordance with Wills Act 1837, s.9 (as substituted by Administration of Justice Act 1982, s.17) is on the party seeking to establish the validity of the will.

109

It may be possible to challenge the will on the following grounds:

- the signature was not made by the testator or testatrix in the presence of two witnesses present at the same time, but see *Couser* v. *Couser* [1996] 1 WLR 1301;
- the two witnesses did not subscribe or acknowledge their signatures to the will in the presence of the testator or testatrix;
- the signature of the testator or testatrix was not intended to give effect to the will; or
- the signature which appears on the will was not in fact made by the testator or testatrix himself or herself, or for him or her, or in his or her presence, or by his or her direction.

11.3.2   Lack of testamentary capacity

The test of testamentary capacity is still that established in 1870 in *Banks* v. *Goodfellow* (1870) LR5QB 549. For a more recent example of the *Banks* v. *Goodfellow* test, see *Brown* v. *Deacy and Others* [2002] WTLR 781. A person may suffer from a mental disorder and yet still be able to fulfil that test.

Mental states are presumed to continue, so if a person is normally mentally capable it will be presumed, provided the will appears rational, that he or she had capacity when the will was made. For examples of the importance of this presumption, see *Vaughan* v. *Vaughan* [2002] EWHC 699 and *Sharp* v. *Adam* [2005] EWHC 1806. However, this presumption is rebuttable by evidence. Where a person lacks general mental capacity, the person putting forward the will has to prove testamentary capacity.

The difficulty in bringing a case where lack of capacity is alleged is to gather together sufficiently convincing evidence. It is very important to try to get together the evidence before advising the client on the likelihood of success.

11.3.3   Lack of knowledge and approval

The burden of proving that a testator or testatrix knew and approved the contents of his or her will rests with the person seeking to prove that will. However, where testators read through a will (or have had the contents read to them) there is normally a presumption that they knew and approved the contents of the will.

There is no presumption if the testator or testatrix was deaf and dumb or blind or if there were suspicious circumstances (such as where a major beneficiary prepares the will or is active in arranging its execution). See *Richards* v. *Allan* [2001] WTLR 1031. The burden of proof is then upon the person attempting to set up the will to remove any such suspicions and to prove positively that the testator or testatrix knew and approved of the contents of the will.

It is usually preferable to plead lack of knowledge and approval rather than to allege undue influence. Once you can show suspicious circumstances the burden of proving knowledge and approval falls on the person putting forward the will. In a case of undue influence, the person alleging it must prove it. There can be adverse costs consequences where an allegation of undue influence fails.

11.3.4   Undue influence

Undue influence is one of the most difficult allegations to sustain, since the primary witness – the deceased – is by definition unavailable to give evidence and not able to assist the court. There is no presumption of undue influence in relation to wills, unlike the position in relation to lifetime gifts (see below).

Where a solicitor makes an allegation of fraud or undue influence and loses, the solicitor will be particularly at risk of a costs order being made against his or her client.

It should be clearly understood that there is nothing inherently wrong with influence by itself; people who make wills are influenced by various factors when deciding on what they will include in their will. What the law will not allow is *undue* influence.

As mentioned above, proving undue influence in relation to a will is extremely difficult whereas sustaining an allegation of lack of knowledge and approval is somewhat easier. However, you are not allowed to disguise what is in reality a plea of fraud or undue influence as a lesser plea of lack of knowledge (*Re Stott (Deceased)* [1980] 1 WLR 246).

There have been an increasing number of cases involving allegations of undue influence in relation to lifetime gifts.

There is a presumption of undue influence where the donee is in a position of trust and confidence in relation to the donor and the transaction is one that requires an explanation – see the House of Lords decision in *Royal Bank of Scotland* v. *Etridge* [2002] AC 773. Recent cases, such as *Watson* v. *Huber* [2005] All ER (D) 156, and *Turkey* v. *Adwadh and Another* [2005] EWCA Civ 382, have applied the principles set out in *Etridge*.

Daniel v. *Drew* [2005] EWCA Civ 507 has clarified the differences between actual and presumptive undue influence, while the other cases have focused on the significance of the relationships, the nature of the transaction, and the rebuttable characteristic of the presumption.

11.3.5   Beneficial interest under resulting or constructive trust

It may be possible to claim a beneficial interest under a resulting or constructive trust.

11.3.6 Claim under Inheritance (Provision for Family and Dependants) Act 1975

If the client falls within one of the categories set out in IPFDA 1975, s.1 it may be possible to make a claim under the Act.

11.4 PRACTITIONER'S TOOLS

11.4.1 Law Society Ruling of September 1959

There is often a need for information about the circumstances in which a will was made. Solicitors are under an obligation to provide information about wills which they have prepared.

In accordance with the Law Society Professional Purposes Committee Ruling of September 1959 there is an obligation on a solicitor who prepares testamentary instruments to state the circumstances relating to the preparation of these instruments. The Law Society's recommendation was considered in *Larke* v. *Nugus* [2000] WTLR 1033 by the Court of Appeal in an appeal from the decision of Browne Wilkinson J.

11.4.2 Caveats

(See NCPR 1987, Rule 44.) A caveat is a notice issued out of the Principal Probate Registry or a district registry or sub-registry preventing a grant from being issued. If a person does not wish to prevent the issue of a grant but wishes to be notified when a grant is made, a standing search is appropriate.

11.4.3 Citations

(See NCPR 1987, Rules 46 and 47.) Where a probate dispute can be seen on the horizon, those named as executors may well feel a natural reticence towards doing anything. In addition, very often if the validity of a last will is called into question, the executors may be unhappy to release earlier wills.

In all these cases it is necessary to seek the assistance of the Principal Probate Registry by way of a citation. A citation is a document issued out of the Principal Probate Registry or a district registry and can be issued for any one of the following reasons:

Citation to accept or refuse a grant

Where there is a delay in obtaining the grant and the person entitled does not renounce his or her entitlement to do so, a citation may be issued.

Citation to take probate

Where the executor has intermeddled in the estate and thereby accepted office but has not applied for a grant within six months of death, the citation is to take the grant. The citor may be any person with an interest in the estate. Non-Contentious Probate Rules 1987, Rule 47 allows a grant to the citor as an alternative to an order directing the executor to take a grant within a specific time.

Citation to propound a will

Where the validity of a will is doubted, a person entitled on intestacy or under an earlier testamentary document may cite the executors and persons interested under the alleged will to propound it. It should be noted that a citation is not appropriate for executors appointed by a will doubting the validity of a codicil.

The procedure with a citation is to lodge it in draft form with the district judge/district probate registrar so that he can settle it.

There are alternatives to the citation procedure which may be more effective. Citations are often used to try to force someone who is being dilatory to do something. However, even if the citation is successful in the short term, future progress may still be slow.

11.4.4   Subpoena procedure

(See NCPR 1987, Rule 50.) If the original will/codicil is in the possession of a person who will not release it and is thus preventing an application for a grant by the person entitled, an application may be made under Supreme Court Act 1981, s.123 for the issue of a subpoena by the district judge/registrar. The application must be supported by an appropriate affidavit. The effect of the subpoena is to require the person in possession of the will to file it in the registry. The subpoena must be served personally and endorsed with the penal notice. Committal is not normally the result of disobedience, and more usually the person is ordered to attend for examination as to possession of the testamentary document.

If a person is not in possession of the will but has knowledge of it, s.122 allows the court to require the attendance of such a person for examination and it is a contempt of court not to comply. This could apply to the witnesses to a will who have declined to swear an affidavit of due execution.

11.4.5   Supreme Court Act 1981, s.116

Where there are appropriate circumstances the court can pass over the persons entitled to a grant and appoint such person or persons as the court feels expedient. This form of application is particularly useful where those entitled to a grant cannot be traced or where it is desired to appoint some person who is not interested in the estate as beneficiary or creditor.

The application is made *ex parte* under NCPR 1987, Rule 52 to a district judge or probate registrar, supported by an affidavit. It is possible to pay a fee of £5 to have the affidavit approved by the registrar.

11.5 TYPES OF PROBATE ACTION

11.5.1 Probate action re validity of a testamentary document

The action is commenced by the executor or someone else with an interest under the document or someone opposing a grant. Persons entitled on intestacy may put executors to proof of the will. The attesting witnesses may be called for examination or to swear an affidavit of due execution.

11.5.2 Action regarding interests

An interest action is one in which a person's interest in opposing a will or claiming the right to letters of administration is disputed. Such an action may involve proof of a person's entitlement, for example by production of a birth certificate. Such actions are often about validity of a marriage or legitimacy. The applicant in an interest action will ask the court for a declaration against the person who is claiming entitlement to a grant and instead to make an order in his favour. If the court can be persuaded to make an order, the person who was not entitled to the grant will have their right 'cleared off' and the grant will issue to the person who is properly entitled to administer the estate.

11.5.3 Action regarding revocation of a grant

Such an action would be appropriate where a grant has been improperly obtained by a person not entitled or where the will is invalid. On an intestacy the action may force a person who has obtained letters of administration to prove his entitlement. If a will is subsequently found the action will be to revoke the earlier grant and pronounce the will's validity. The court will be asked to pronounce against any earlier will and in favour of the later document, which will in turn enable a correct application for a grant to then be made.

Where a grant has been obtained by mistake, e.g. a filing department has produced the wrong will which has then been proved, an application should be made by the person who obtained the grant with an affidavit specifying the error. The district judge/registrar will then make an order revoking the grant and a further correct application may then be made (see NCPR 1987, Rule 41).

In a revocation action the original grant should be filed within seven days of the claim form or within 14 days of service on the defendant of the original grant.

11.5.4 Action for the removal of personal representative

This form of action was introduced by Administration of Justice Act 1985, s.50. If the application by summons does not request the appointment of a substituted PR, the court will not allow the estate to be unrepresented. The applicant will swear an affidavit giving reasons for the removal and as to the suitability of the replacement PR who must consent to act. An example of this would be where a partner in a firm is an executor and then leaves the firm. It would be appropriate for him to be removed and replaced with another partner. The Civil Procedure Rules 1998, Part 57 requires every PR to be joined as a party and for the grant to be lodged in court.

Under Supreme Court Act 1981, s.116, as stated above, the court has discretion to appoint as administrator any person it considers expedient even if the person entitled, for example on intestacy, would thereby be passed over.

A district registrar or district judge may be willing to contemplate revoking a grant where a PR refuses or neglects to participate properly in the administration of an estate. (See **Chapter 15**.)

11.5.5 Appointment of a judicial trustee

Applications are governed by the Judicial Trustees Act 1896 and the Judicial Trustees Rules 1983, SI 1983/370.

This can be a more expensive exercise than the appointment of a new PR under Administration of Justice Act 1985, s.50 but may be the more practical solution where, for example, the sole PR has a beneficial interest in the estate and there has been a substantial breakdown in confidence and/or communications between the PR and the other beneficiaries.

Where an application is made in relation to an estate, the Judicial Trustees Act 1896, s.1(7) provides that the court may, if it sees fit, proceed as if the application were made under Administration of Justice Act 1985, s.50.

The judicial trustee has all the powers and discretions of a properly appointed PR but the court has wide powers to give directions as to the custody of the funds in the estate. Following the appointment of the judicial trustee the trustee or any beneficiary interested can apply to the court for further directions by letter.

11.5.6　Breach of trust or breach of fiduciary duty

Executors who, through negligence and default, have caused loss to an estate will clearly be open to an action by a beneficiary of the estate. Such neglect or default might consist of failures to carry out the provisions of the will; making distributions to persons not named in the will; a failure to maintain neutrality between the beneficiaries on the one hand and the claimants on the other; executors who derive a personal benefit from the estate; or failure to obtain sufficient information regarding the estate.

11.5.7　Claims relating to the administration of estates and trusts

It is possible to apply to court under CPR Part 64 for:

- the court to determine any question arising in the administration of an estate or in the execution of a trust;
- an order for the administration of an estate or the execution of an estate to be carried out under the direction of the court (an 'administration order').

It is unusual for the court to take over the administration of an estate or trust. It will only do so if it considers that the issues between the parties cannot properly be resolved in any other way. It is more likely to give directions on specific points.

The Practice Direction which accompanies Part 64 gives the following examples of the types of claims which may be made for specific directions under Part 64:

- the determination of any question as to who is included in any class of persons having:

  - a claim against an estate;
  - a beneficial interest in an estate;
  - a beneficial interest in any property subject to a trust;

- the determination of the rights or interests of any person claiming:

  - to be a creditor of an estate;
  - to be entitled under a will or intestacy;
  - to be beneficially entitled under a trust;

- a claim for an order requiring a trustee to:

  - provide and, if necessary, verify accounts;
  - pay into court money which he holds in that capacity;
  - do or not to do any particular act;

- a claim for an order approving any sale, purchase, compromise or other transaction by a trustee;

- a claim for an order directing any act to be done which the court could order to be done if the estate or trust in question were being administered under the administration of the court.

Claims under Part 64 can be made by beneficiaries, trustees, PRs or other interested parties. They must use a Part 8 claim form.

11.5.8 Summons to deliver an inventory and account

This is an extremely useful procedure. It is available in the probate registry and is therefore relatively cheap. Every deponent to an oath leading to a grant of administration swears 'to exhibit on oath . . . a full inventory of the estate and when so required render an account of the administration'. (See Administration of Estates Act 1925, s.25, as amended by Administration of Estates Act 1971, s.9.)

This means that anyone with a beneficial interest in the estate can apply by summons at any time for an inventory and account. The summons issues out of the registry from which the grant issued and should be supported by affidavit.

When an inventory is requested, it is a good idea to ask for an order for costs. If an outline of the costs incurred is available when attending the summons, the registrar can assess costs there and then, which avoids the 7.5 per cent taxing fee which would otherwise be payable.

The probate registry's jurisdiction is limited to ordering an inventory and account. For an administration order it will be necessary to go to the Chancery Division under CPR Part 64.

11.5.9 *Beddoes* summons

A problem often faced by PRs is whether in the administration of an estate they should defend a claim brought against them, initiate an action on behalf of the estate, or compromise a claim on behalf of the estate. A PR who brings or defends a claim without obtaining leave of the court may find himself exposed to the costs that arise. A PR can obtain protection by applying to the court for directions. This is often referred to as a *Beddoes* order, from the case of *Re Beddoes* v. *Cottam* [1893] 1 Ch 547. The decision as to the granting of a *Beddoes* order is a matter which the court will decide in its absolute discretion in each case, and a *Beddoes* order is not given as of right by the court.

The case of *Singh* v. *Bhasin and Another* [2000] WTLR 275 is a salutory illustration of the risks of not seeking an order.

In some cases it will also be prudent for executors to seek directions from the court under CPR Part 64.

11.5.10   Rectification under Administration of Justice Act 1982, s.20

Under Administration of Justice Act 1982, s.20, the court may order that a will be rectified so as to give effect to the testator's intention. There are two grounds for such rectification:

- in consequence of a clerical error; or
- in consequence of a failure to understand the testator's or testatrix's instructions.

It is important to appreciate that s.20(1)(b) applies where the testator's or testatrix's instructions are not understood, which is not the same as a failure to carry out those instructions. Thus, rectification will not be available where the testator or testatrix, or his or her solicitor, does not understand the meaning and effect of words used, unless it is unclear what his or her instructions were or he or she had failed to inform the solicitor.

If the person seeking rectification has obtained the grant and has the will in his or her possession, they must be lodged with the court when the claim form is issued. If a defendant has the probate or letters of administration in his or her possession, or under his or her control, the defendant must lodge them in the relevant office within 14 days after the service of the claim form on the defendant.

11.5.11   Claims against solicitors

If rectification is not available due to an error by the solicitor who prepared the will, the disappointed beneficiary may have a claim against the solicitor.

11.6   CPR PART 57

With effect from 15 October 2001, CPR Part 57 and the accompanying Practice Direction deal with probate claims, claims for the rectification of wills and claims to replace or remove a PR. For this purpose a 'probate claim' is:

- a claim for the grant of probate or letters of administration;
- a claim for the revocation of such grant; or
- a claim for a decree pronouncing for or against the validity of an alleged will not being a claim which is non-contentious (or common form) probate business (such matters being dealt with by Supreme Court Act 1981, s.128).

Non-contentious probate business remains outside the scope of the CPR and is still governed by the RSC.

[*Note*: Transitional provisions – contentious probate proceedings for the rectification of wills started before 15 October 2001 continue to be dealt with by the Practice Direction which supplements CPR Part 49. Applications for the removal or substitution of PRs made before that date continue to be dealt with under CPR, Sched.1, Ord.93, Rule 2.]

11.6.1 Commencing a probate claim under CPR Part 57

Probate claims issue from:

- Chancery Chambers at the Royal Courts of Justice; or
- a Chancery District Registry; or
- a county court which has a Chancery District Registry (at present this means Birmingham, Bristol, Cardiff, Leeds, Liverpool, Manchester, Newcastle-upon-Tyne or Preston) if:

    - an application for grant has been made in the Principal Registry of a district probate registry, and
    - the value of the net estate after payment of expenses and debts does not exceed the county court limit (currently £30,000).

The CPR Part 57 procedure must be used for probate claims, and CPR Part 57 Practice Direction, para.2.1 sets out the requirements for the probate claim form (Form N2). It is a standard claim form save that it is headed 'In the estate of X deceased (Probate)'. The notes for the claimant (Form N2A) are helpful and set out most of the special requirements.

11.6.2 Response to probate claim

The defendant must file an acknowledgment of service on the new Form N3. Moreover, if the particulars of claim are served with the claim form, the defendant must file the acknowledgment of service form within 28 days of service of the claim form.

11.6.3 Lodging testamentary documents and filing of evidence of them

Any testamentary documents (previously known as testamentary scripts) in the possession or control of any party must be lodged with the court. Unless the court directs otherwise, these documents must be lodged by the claimant when the claim form is issued and by a defendant when the defendant files his or her acknowledgment of service.

In addition, the claimant and every defendant who acknowledges service must in written evidence describe any testamentary document of which he or she has knowledge or if he or she does not know of any such document, state that fact. Also, if the claimant/defendant has knowledge of any testamentary document which is not in his or her possession or control, the claimant/defendant must give the name and address of the person in whose possession or under whose control it is. If the claimant/defendant does not know the name and address of such persons, he or she must state that fact. There is a prescribed form for written evidence set out in the CPR Part 57 Practice Direction.

In cases of urgent need, the court may permit the claimant to issue the claim form against an undertaking to the court to lodge the documents and file the evidence within such time as the court may specify.

11.6.4   Contents of claim form

The claim form must contain a statement of the nature of the interest of the claimant and each defendant in the estate.

A plea of want of knowledge and approval must be particularised as must a claim that a will was not duly executed, that the testator or testatrix was not of sound mind, memory and understanding or that the execution of the will was obtained by undue influence or fraud.

CPR Part 57 also deals with revocation actions, judgments in default, summary judgment, discontinuance and settlement, rectification of wills, substitution and removal of PRs.

It is important to appreciate that CPR Part 57 and its Practice Direction are not a comprehensive reformulation of procedure and accordingly practitioners must bear in mind the other relevant provisions of the CPR.

11.6.5   Costs

Supreme Court Act 1981, s.51 provides that in contentious probate actions all parties' costs are at the discretion of the court.

It is, however, true to say that a 'wind of change' has been blowing for some time in relation to the old 'rule of thumb' that, if the proceedings were reasonable, costs would usually come out of the estate. The issue of costs is now looked at very carefully, and the parties who lose can often find themselves saddled with *inter partes* standard costs (and on occasion with indemnity costs) particularly if it is found that they have instituted untenable or unreasonable proceedings. A prudent practitioner will therefore always keep the question of costs under review and where appropriate make 'without prejudice' offers in accordance with the *Calderbank* principle. Also as stated at the beginning of this chapter, reasonable requests for mediation must be carefully considered, since failure to do so can attract meaningful costs consequences.

CHAPTER 12

Wills and best practice

Lesley King with Helen Clarke

12.1 DRAFTING POINTS

12.1.1 Appointment of solicitor-executor

Probate registries report frequent problems with the wording of clauses appointing solicitor-executors. An appointment of 'one of' or 'two of' the partners in a firm is void for uncertainty. The appointment should be of 'the partners' in the firm at the date of the deceased's death and express the wish that only two should prove.

The clause included in *Williams on Wills*, 8th edn (Sweet & Maxwell, 2002) (as B3.8 Alternative Form), has the approval of the Principal Registry of the Family Division. The commentary usefully outlines the issues.

Incorporation and conversion into limited liability partnerships (LLPs) have caused problems where there is a will appointing 'partners in the firm of'. The Probate Registrars decided at their annual conference in 2003 that where a firm becomes an LLP an appointment as executors of 'partners in the firm' is void. The basis of their decision was that the members of the successor LLP were not 'partners' in a 'firm'.

In *Re Rogers (Deceased)* [2006] 2 All ER 792 Mr Justice Lightman considered the effect of a standard appointment of 'partners' in relation to a firm which had become an LLP. He said that the wishes of the testatrix should not be frustrated by the decision of the solicitors to alter the legal nature of the vehicle through which they carry on that practice. He, therefore, held that profit-sharing members of the LLP were able to apply for probate.

The decision was welcome. It made no mention of incorporated practices but the spirit of the judgment would suggest that the owners of an incorporated practice ought to be treated as partners for this purpose.

The judgment drew a clear distinction between profit sharing partners/members and others. The judge said:

> even as the 'partner in the partnership' means in the case of a partnership a profit sharing partner and not merely a salaried partner or a person merely held out (but not in fact) a partner, so when transposed to a limited liability partnership the member must mean a profit sharing member.

This distinction causes problems for partnerships where salaried partners have been in the habit of obtaining grants of representation as this will no longer be possible if the appointment is of 'partners'. Going forward, the will can be drafted to define 'partner' as including 'salaried partner'. In the case of existing wills, it would be possible for all the profit sharing partners to grant a power of attorney to the salaried partner to allow the salaried partner to take a grant on their behalf.

Partners applying for a grant under standard appointment clauses should describe themselves as 'profit sharing partners'.

12.1.2 Sole practitioners

Sole practitioners should include in their own wills an appointment of a special executor to deal with the affairs of the practice. Suitable clauses were published in the *Probate Section Journal* (November 2001). They are also available from the Sole Practitioners' Group (see **Useful addresses**).

12.1.3 STEP: standard conditions for wills

On behalf of the Society of Trust and Estate Practitioners (STEP, see **Useful addresses**), barrister James Kessler has prepared a set of standard administrative clauses for wills and settlements (see **Further reading**). STEP's aim in publishing the standard provisions was to enable wills and settlements to be shortened, and to provide 'the necessary standard powers . . . in language which is lucid, contemporary and easily understood' by non-lawyers.

A Practice Direction from the Principal Registry of the Probate Division dated 10 April 1995 allows wills incorporating the STEP provisions by reference to be proved in the normal way without providing the text of the provisions themselves.

If incorporating the STEP provisions it is helpful to place a copy of the current provisions with the will. Testators may not die until many years later, by which time the provisions may have been amended several times. Life will be much simpler for the person dealing with the administration if the relevant provisions are to hand.

12.1.4 Clauses excluding liability for negligence in respect of professional executors/trustees

Many people feel that it is inappropriate to include in wills and settlements clauses which seek to limit the liability of a solicitor or other professional trustee, when acting as an executor or trustee, to loss or damage through fraud or dishonesty and to exclude liability for negligence. Solicitors should in any event be fully insured against their own negligence.

However, in *Armitage* v. *Nurse* [1997] 3 WLR 1046, CA and *Bogg* v. *Raper* (1998) *The Times*, 22 April; [1998] CLY 4592, the Court of Appeal stated that such clauses were not contrary to public policy nor to the nature of a trust. Millett LJ stated that although many people felt such clauses had gone too far, it would require legislation to change their validity.

Bogg v. *Raper* confirmed that a solicitor who prepares a will or settlement which appoints the solicitor or a partner as an executor or trustee and which then restricts or excludes liability for negligence, does not receive a benefit. The clause merely limits liability.

Whatever the correctness of such clauses in general, there are clearly special cases where it would be reasonable for the trust document to exclude or restrict liability for negligence (for example, estates or trusts involving assets held overseas in countries with unreliable legal systems, long-running and serious family or other disputes, or continuing litigation).

On 19 July 2006 the Law Commission published a report (No.301) on trustee exemption clauses favouring a non-legislative solution. It recommends that professional and regulatory bodies should adopt rules or guidance to the effect that any paid trustee, who causes a settlor to include a trustee exemption clause in a trust instrument which has the effect of excluding or limiting liability for negligence, must before the creation of the trust take steps to ensure that the settlor is aware of the meaning and effect of the clause.

The Law Society was consulted by the Law Commission prior to publication of the report and supports this approach. At the time of writing, the Law Society is preparing guidance for the profession.

12.1.5 Mutual wills

For wills to be mutual wills there must be evidence of an agreement between two people that:

- they will each leave their property in a particular way (not necessarily to each other, *Re Dale (Deceased)* [1994] Ch 31); and
- neither party will revoke unilaterally.

The mere fact that the wills are 'mirror-images' does not make them mutual.

In fact the agreement is impossible because wills cannot be made irrevocable. Each party is always free to revoke. Revocation may be out of the hands of the survivor as where a later marriage revokes an earlier will.

However, revocation will not assist the survivor as equity will intervene. If the first party to die has carried out his or her part of the agreement, the law imposes an obligation on the survivor to give effect to the agreement. In effect, assets of the survivor are held under a trust.

Apparently the trust is a floating one during the lifetime of the survivor and crystallises on the survivor's death (*Re Goodchild (Deceased)* [1996] 1 WLR 694 confirmed by the Court of Appeal [1997] 1 WLR 1216). There is some uncertainty as to how the trust works. What if the survivor spends or gives away everything before death? In *Birmingham* v. *Renfrew* (1937) 57 CLR 666 the court said:

> No doubt gifts and settlements, inter vivos, if calculated to defeat the intention of the compact, could not be made by the survivor and his right of disposition, inter vivos is, therefore not unqualified.

This means that the survivor is free to dispose of the assets unless such disposal is made with the object of defeating the interests of the agreed ultimate beneficiary. Mutual wills may provide little protection for the agreed beneficiary as there may be few assets left by the time the surviving testator or testatrix dies.

Birch v. *Curtis* [2002] WTLR 965 illustrates the need for evidence of an agreement that the wills were to be irrevocable. In that case Rimer J accepted that there may well have been an agreement between the husband and wife as to how the husband was to leave his property after the wife's death. However, there was no evidence of an agreement that he would not revoke his will. Therefore, the wills were not mutual and the husband was free to leave his property as he wished. Always include an express statement if there is such an agreement.

Even more importantly, however, consider including a statement that there is no such agreement in other wills. This makes the true position clear to the clients. It will also help deter disgruntled family members from incurring the expense and ill-feeling of challenging the will of the survivor.

If the agreement relates to land it is necessary to comply with the requirements of the Law of Property (Miscellaneous Provisions) Act 1989 which provides that there must be a written agreement signed by both parties. In *Healey* v. *Brown* [2002] All ER (D) 249 a husband and wife had made mutual wills dealing with their respective beneficial interests in the matrimonial home. The wife died first and the husband transferred the house into joint names with his son from a previous marriage. On the husband's death the court held that the agreement was void as there was no writing signed by both parties. If making mutual wills relating to land, it is, therefore, important to have a separate written agreement which both parties sign. It is not sufficient that each party signs his or her own will. Both parties must sign one document.

12.1.6 Making provision for animals

This is often a difficult problem for clients. In an interesting article in the July 2003 issue of the *Probate Section Journal*, Julia Abrey, a principal of the London firm Withers, gave three possible solutions to the problem of caring for animals after the owner's death.

1. The animal and a sum of cash are left to the executors with a note of wishes that a particular person should care for the animal using the money available.
2. The animal and a sum of cash are left to a named legatee with the proviso that the legatee only gets the money if they care for the animal. A substitute legatee can also be named.

Both of these solutions place a burden on the executor in terms of policing the arrangement.

3. The animal and the money are left to an animal charity, such as the RSPCA asking them to find a suitable home. This leaves the money free of IHT, but the gift cannot be conditional.

A spokesperson for the RSPCA confirmed that it comes across problems involving animals and legacies quite regularly.

> We are becoming a more and more litigious society and some people are not happy when they find they have been cut out of a will in favour of an animal. Sometimes they have a good case under the Inheritance Act, but some are try-ons by the family. We look at each case individually and we take legal advice. We will do what we can to avoid going to court. Unfortunately costs usually end up coming out of the estate in these cases. At the same time we will do what is necessary to protect our interests.

The charity confirmed that in every case where it has been left an animal to rehome, it has so far been successful. 'The welfare of the animal is our priority and even if an animal is elderly we have managed to find a home.'

Anyone wanting advice on drawing up specific clauses involving the RSPCA undertaking care of an animal can contact the RSPCA's Legacy Department for further information.

12.1.7 Wills and public funding

The making of wills and matters of trusts law generally are amongst the services that cannot normally be publicly funded as part of the Community Legal Services scheme (Access to Justice Act 1999, Sched.2). However s.6(8) gave the Lord Chancellor power to issue directions authorising the Legal Services Commission (LSC) to fund certain services which would normally be excluded. On 2 April 2001 he issued *Scope of the Community Legal Service Fund – Exceptions to the Exclusions* which authorises the LSC to fund Legal Help where the client is:

(a) aged 70 or over; or
(b) a disabled person within the meaning of the Disability Discrimination Act 1995; or
(c) the parent of a disabled person (as defined in (b) above) who wishes to provide for that person in a will; or

(d)   the parent of a minor who is living with the client but not with the other parent, and where the client wishes to appoint a guardian for the minor in a will.

Applications for funding under this direction must still satisfy all relevant criteria in the Funding Code and regulations.

12.2   CAPACITY

12.2.1   The 'golden rule'

Questions of capacity frequently arise in connection with the validity of a will. In cases where there is room for doubt the solicitor drafting a will should have considered the question of capacity at the time. If capacity is in question the solicitor should consult the client's medical practitioner as to the client's capacity in general and should aim to have the doctor present at the time the will is signed so as to be able to give an opinion on the client's capacity at that point. In *Buckenham* v. *Dickinson* [1997] CLY 661 the court pronounced against a will where the solicitors had not followed the 'golden rule' applied in *Kenward* v. *Adams* [1975] CLY 3591 and followed in *Re Simpson (Deceased)* (1977) 121 SJ 224, that a medical practitioner should be present where there are doubts as to a testator's capacity. Templeman J (as he then was) said in *Kenward* v. *Adams*:

> In the case of an aged testator or a testator who has suffered a serious illness, there is one golden rule which should always be observed, however straightforward matters may appear, and however difficult or tactless it may be to suggest that precautions be taken: the making of a will by such a testator ought to be witnessed or approved by a medical practitioner who satisfies himself of the capacity and understanding of the testator, and records and preserves his examination and findings.
>   There are other precautions which should be taken.
>   If the testator has made an earlier will this should be considered by the legal and medical advisers of the testator and, if appropriate, discussed with the testator.
>   The instructions of the testator should be taken in the absence of anyone who may stand to benefit, or who may have influence over the testator.
>   These are not counsels of perfection. If proper precautions are not taken injustice may result or be imagined, and great expense and misery may be unnecessarily caused.

It is important to take these precautions. Where a will is successfully challenged for lack of capacity, a solicitor who failed to take appropriate steps to check capacity may be made liable for the costs suffered by the estate. See the comments made in *Worby* v. *Rosser* [1999] Lloyd's Rep PN 972 and *Corbett* v. *Bond Pearce* [2001] EWCA Civ 531.

The presence or absence of such precautions will not affect the validity of the will. This will depend on whether or not the testator actually had the appropriate capacity and knew and approved the contents of the will and whether or not there was any force, fraud or undue influence. In *Sharp* v. *Adam* [2006] EWCA Civ 449 May LJ said:

> The golden rule is a rule of solicitors' good practice, not a rule of law giving conclusive status to evidence obtained in compliance with the rule. Nevertheless, where a testator's apparent mental state is observed and recorded at the time when he actually executes the will in complete compliance with the rule and with the care with which it was in the present case; and where professional people concerned reached a properly informed and recorded conclusion that the testator does have testamentary capacity, it will require very persuasive evidence to enable the court to dislodge that conclusion.

12.2.2   Association of Contentious Trusts and Probate Specialists checklist

The Association of Contentious Trusts and Probate Specialists (ACTAPS) has published a checklist on capacity. We have reproduced it below with their kind permission.

RISK ASSESSMENT

Factors to be taken into account in the assessment of mental capacity/undue influence

By Christopher Allen, consultant with Lawrence Graham and Member of the Association of Contentious Trust and Probate Specialists Committee

A 'Golden Rule' was reemphasised by Mr Justice Templeman (as he then was) in *Re Simpson deceased* (*Solicitors Journal*, 1 April 1977). Templeman J there said that the events of this case, which involved the disputed will of an old and infirm testator 'constrained him to repeat the warning he had given in *Kenward v. Adams, The Times*, 29 November 1975, that the making of a will by such a testator ought to be witnessed and approved by a medical practitioner who satisfies himself as to the capacity and understanding of the testator and makes a record of his examination and findings'.

The points in issue were recently reinforced by *Re Morris, Trustees of Great Ormond Street v. Rushin and others* (Lawtel, 15 May 2000). In referring to the rule, Rimer J stated that the rule must always be observed 'however straightforward matters appear and however difficult or tactless it may be to suggest that precautions be taken'. The desirability of review and discussion of earlier wills with testators and for instructions to be taken in the absence of a potentially influential beneficiary were also emphasised.

In the light of these cases and *Killick v. Pountney, The Times*, 30 April 1999, ACTAPS with assistance from Susan Midha of the Probate Section has drawn up a suggested checklist which has now been adopted by the Probate Section.

Possibly there has been diffidence about producing a 'Code of Conduct' lest the already heavy duties placed on practitioners be further increased. It seems to me to make little difference what one calls the following; we have Lord Templeman's 'Golden Rule' and individually we have to decide how to apply it in the many and various situations with which we are faced.

Preliminary notes

1. The test of testamentary capacity remains that established in *Banks v. Goodfellow* (1870) LR5QB 549, namely:

   (a) the testator must not be affected by any disorder of mind or insane delusion. A disorder which operates only in respect of a particular individual may amount to lack of capacity although it must be sufficient to affect the testator's judgment – mere eccentricity or irrationality does not in itself invalidate the will;

   (b) he should appreciate the nature and consequences of making a will, e.g. understanding that the will operates only on death, that it can be changed or revoked and beneficiaries might die before him. He should generally be aware of the purposes of appointing executors;

   (c) he must understand the extent of his property (in general terms). He ought also to realise that his estate may reduce (or increase) over time and know if any assets are jointly owned;

   (d) the testator should consider the moral claims of those persons for whom he ought to make provision.

2. Lack of capacity and vulnerability to undue influence may go hand in hand but equally one may exist without the other. It is felt helpful to separate them because the precautionary measures to be taken by the practitioner (e.g the attendance of a doctor) are not necessarily the same in each case.

3. The following constitute important areas for practitioners to raise with their clients. It should, however, be noted that the list is not exhaustive, nor are all items compulsory (e.g in the case of an elderly and very alert client whom the practitioner has known for many years) but there may well be additional points to be raised in particular cases.

Capacity

Client's name and date of birth	
Have you any reason to doubt your client's testamentary capacity?	
Are you aware of any medical problems of your client? What are they?	
Is your client taking any medication and if so what?	

If in the light of the above, you feel that your client's capacity may be questioned:

Have you advised the client of the importance of having either a medical report or medical witness or both if he/she has any medical or other condition which could invalidate the will?	
Have you kept contemporaneous file notes?	

128

Undue influence

Do you consider there are any issues of vulnerability or suggestibility in the client or do you feel that the client might be subject to undue influence as defined by case law?	
Who contacted you to see the client or to draft the will?	
Who else was present when the instructions were given?	
Has your client made an earlier will or wills?	
What changes is your client making?	
Was the client able/prepared to tell you why the changes were being made?	
Attach a brief family tree.	
What relationship do the main beneficiaries have with your client?	
Has your firm acted for the client (or his or her family) before?	

If there seems to be a problem:

Did you discuss the existence of lifetime gifts with the client? If so, were they made to someone with whom your client had a 'special relationship' as defined in case law? Has that person subsequently benefited under the will?	
Who was present, apart from the witnesses, when the will was executed?	

12.2.3 Mental Capacity Act 2005

The Mental Capacity Act 2005 is due to come into force in 2007. Section 2(1) of the Act states:

(1) For the purposes of this Act, a person lacks capacity in relation to a matter if at the material time he is unable to make a decision for himself in relation to the matter because of an impairment of, or a disturbance in the functioning of, the mind or brain.

In relation to the capacity to make a will, the tests in existing case law will continue to be relevant to the question of whether or not the testator or testatrix was able to make the decision.

12.2.4   Instructing medical practitioners

Denzil Lush in an article in [1996] *Gazette*, 24 January, points out that capacity is not an absolute concept. It is relative to the particular transaction. Thus, the lawyer has a duty to explain to any doctor involved the test relevant to the particular activity. We have set out below a form of letter which may be adapted and used when writing to a client's general medical practitioner for a report as to mental capacity. The letter was published in Gordon R. Ashton, *Elderly Client Handbook*, 2nd edn (Law Society, 2000) and we are most grateful to Gordon Ashton for allowing us to reproduce it. The letter assumes that the solicitor has already attended the client and received preliminary instructions but that there is a doubt as to mental capacity which may need to be resolved.

Dear Dr_____

Our client and your patient: Mrs _____ of _____

We act for your patient and are presently advising her in regard to the preparation of a new will. [We have previously made several wills for her the last one being some ___ years ago.] She has [only a small estate] [a fairly substantial estate] – [*amplify if there are any complications*].

We seek from you a report as to the mental capacity of your patient to sign this will. The legal test of capacity in these circumstances is whether she understands first, that she is giving her property to persons of her choice on her death, second, the extent of that property and third, the nature and extent of her obligations to relatives and others. Your report should relate specifically to these questions and you may if you wish qualify the report by stating that you do not express any further opinion with regard to the mental capacity of your patient. Legal tests of capacity vary according to the nature of the transaction, and there is no universal test of capacity. However, you may form your view on the balance of probabilities and do not need to be satisfied beyond reasonable doubt.

If the capacity of this patient tends to fluctuate please mention this in your report and we may then need to ask you to be one of the witnesses so as to confirm your view of capacity at the time of signature. You will no doubt need to attend on her before preparing your report and we confirm that we shall be pleased to pay your reasonable fee for such attendance and the preparation of the report. She is presently at [her home] and expecting you to contact her there.

Yours sincerely

The Law Society and the British Medical Association joined together to publish *Assessment of Mental Capacity: Guidance for Doctors and Lawyers*, 2nd edn (BMJ Books, 2004) which is extremely useful reading and provides answers to many awkward questions. It sets out the specific legal tests of capacity to make particular decisions or carry out legal transactions, and explains how these relate to the medical practicalities of assessing capacity.

Mind has issued two booklets on wills and trusts to help people with mental health problems gain greater financial control of their lives. *Find Peace of Mind* is a step-by-step guide to wills. *Making Provision* is aimed at parents and carers of people with mental health problems and explains how the carers can make financial provision for such people. Both can be ordered via its website (**www.mind.org.uk**).

12.3   NEGLIGENCE AND WILLS

Clients are much swifter to allege negligence than used to be the case. There are a number of problem areas in connection with taking instructions for a will.

12.3.1   Preparing a will for someone who lacks capacity without making adequate checks

As we saw at **12.2.1** above, solicitors who do not take appropriate steps to satisfy themselves that a client has appropriate capacity may be liable to the estate for the costs of a successful challenge to the validity of the will. See *Worby* v. *Rosser* [1999] Lloyds Rep PN 972.

12.3.2   Failing to take steps necessary to make the will effective

A solicitor may be held liable to a disappointed beneficiary who cannot benefit under a will because the solicitor has not taken steps necessary to ensure that an asset is part of the estate (for example, failing to advise on the possibility of severing a beneficial joint tenancy). In *Carr-Glynn* v. *Frearsons* [1998] 4 All ER 225 the Court of Appeal held that the solicitor was negligent because she had allowed the testatrix to execute a will at a time when neither she nor the testatrix knew whether the testatrix was able to leave her interest in her house to the desired beneficiary. The solicitor should have advised the client that it was possible to serve a notice of severance as a precaution irrespective of whether the property was actually owned as beneficial joint tenants or tenants in common.

12.3.3 Failing to clarify the property owned

Clients do not always remember how they own property. In *Chittock* v. *Stevens* (2000) 1 WTLR 643, the matrimonial home was believed to be in joint names but eight months after the death of the husband (partially intestate) it was discovered that it had been in his sole name.

Property in joint names may be held on a resulting trust for the original purchaser. In *Carlton* v. *Goodman* [2002] 2 FLR 259 the Court of Appeal found that although a property had been conveyed into joint names, it was in fact in the sole beneficial ownership of the deceased.

Proprietary estoppel may mean that someone else can claim an interest in property 'owned' by the client. See *Gillett* v. *Holt* [1998] 3 All ER 917; *Campbell* v. *Griffin* [2001] WTLR 981; *Jennings* v. *Rice* [2002] WTLR 367; *Clark* v. *Clark* [2006] EWHC 275 (Ch).

Does the client have a power of appointment over trust property? If it is a general power of appointment, an ordinary residuary gift will be sufficient to exercise it without any express reference to the power. The client may not realise this and may believe that, because the power has not been expressly exercised, the trust property will pass to the person entitled in default. In *Gibbons* v. *Nelsons* [2000] PNLR 734, the court found that a solicitor was in breach of duty in not clarifying the client's wishes in such circumstances.

Solicitors should always try to resolve any ambiguities or uncertainties when taking instructions. Where there is any doubt, the solicitor should record that the will has been prepared on the basis of the information provided by the client.

Be aware that serving a notice of severance is not the only way of severing a joint tenancy. Law of Property Act 1925, s.36(2) expressly preserved the pre-1925 methods of severance. *Williams* v. *Hensman* (1861) 1 John & H 546 lists three methods:

(a) an act of any one of the persons interested operating upon his or her own share may create a severance as to that share;
(b) mutual agreement; and
(c) any course of dealing sufficient to intimate that the interests of all were mutually treated as constituting a tenancy in common.

This means that although a client may appear to be the sole beneficial owner of property as a result of survivorship, there may have been an earlier severance by conduct. See *Re Woolnough (Deceased)* [2002] WTLR 595.

As in *Re Woolnough* a solicitor may be consulted by two clients who are beneficial joint tenants but who indicate by the instructions they give for their wills that they are treating the joint tenancy as at an end. The solicitor should make sure that there is clarity as to when the severance takes place. Is it when the instructions are given or when the wills are signed? The solicitor should consider preparing a signed statement or notice of severance on the spot.

12.3.4   Failing to prepare a will sufficiently quickly

The speed required depends on circumstances. In *X (A Child)* v. *Woollcombe-Yonge* [2001] WTLR 301 a solicitor was alleged to have been negligent where a testatrix, known to be suffering from terminal cancer, died before he had prepared a will. He had intended to have the will ready for signature one week after taking instructions. Neuberger J held that on these facts the amount of time taken was not unreasonable. It was significant that although the testatrix was terminally ill, she was not expected to die in the near future. Neuberger J went on to say that:

> Where there is a plain and substantial risk of the client's imminent death, anything other than a handwritten rough codicil prepared on the spot for signature may be negligent. It is a question of the solicitor's judgement based on his assessment of the client's age and health.

Note the useful decision of *Atkins* v. *Dunn & Baker (A Firm)* [2004] All ER (D) 324 in which the Court of Appeal held that the retainer to prepare a will normally extends only to the preparation of a will which the client is free to execute or not. There will normally be no obligation to 'chase' a client who does not execute a will.

12.3.5   Failing to keep an appointment

A solicitor who cancelled an appointment to visit a client in hospital for execution of the client's will was held to be negligent in *Hooper* v. *Fynemores (A Firm)* [2001] WTLR 1019:

> there is a positive duty on the solicitor to satisfy himself that the additional delay caused by his (not the client's) request is not to the client's detriment.

12.3.6   Allowing a will to be executed conditionally

In *Corbett* v. *Newey* [1996] 3 WLR 279 solicitors allowed a testatrix to sign a will but not to date it. Her intention was that the will was not to come into effect until she had completed certain lifetime gifts. The will was held to be invalid because executed conditionally. The solicitors therefore were liable to compensate the disappointed beneficiaries.

12.3.7   Failing to offer an opportunity to execute the will under supervision

In *Esterhuizen* v. *Allied Dunbar* [1998] 2 FLR 668 Longmore J said:

> It is in my judgement not enough just to leave written instructions with the testator. In ordinary circumstances just to leave written instructions and to do no more will not only be contrary to good practice but also in my view negligent.

To protect themselves solicitors should have in writing an offer in the following terms:

- the client can visit the solicitor's office for execution;
- if the client prefers, the solicitor will visit the client's house with a member of staff; or
- if the client prefers, the client can make his or her own arrangements.

Although the safest course is clearly to follow *Esterhuizen*, it is worth noting that in the earlier case of *Gray and Others* v. *Richards Butler (Recovery)* [2000] WTLR 625 Lloyd J found that a solicitor who had not offered to oversee execution had not been negligent in the circumstances of the case. He referred to the 'very clear terms of the attestation provision of the will' and went on to say that:

> What steps are appropriate in discharge of these various duties in any given situation may depend on who the client is and the view that the solicitor has formed, or ought to have formed if acting with reasonable competence, as to the ability of the client to understand and follow advice as to the relevant procedures.

12.3.8   Failing to inspect a will returned after execution

In *Ross* v. *Caunters* [1979] 3 All ER 580 Megarry V-C accepted that the solicitors had breached their duty by *inter alia*:

- not checking the will after execution;
- not noticing that one of the witnesses was a spouse of a beneficiary; and
- not bringing that fact to the attention of the testator.

In *Gray* the court accepted that there was nothing about the particular will under consideration which should have aroused suspicion. However, the case proceeds on the basis that solicitors have a duty to inspect a will that has been returned.

In *Humblestone* v. *Martin Tolhurst Partnership* [2004] EWHC 151 (Ch) the court accepted that a solicitor has a duty to inspect a will returned for safe-keeping whether or not asked to do so.

12.3.9 Failing to offer a client advice required for the transaction being carried out

In *Hurlingham Estates Ltd* v. *Wilde & Partners* [1997] STC 627, Lightman J had to consider whether or not a property lawyer had entered into an effective agreement with his client to exclude any obligation to advise on the tax aspects of a property transaction. He concluded that there was insufficient evidence of such an agreement. It ought to have been recorded in a letter to the client so that the client could have considered the implications and discussed them with others, but it had not been. He also held that to be effective such a limitation on liability would require fully informed consent on the part of the clients.

He went on to consider whether, in the absence of an effective retainer limiting liability, a solicitor carrying out a commercial conveyancing transaction for a client has an obligation to advise on tax implications. Obviously this is an issue for probate practitioners too.

Lightman J said that the test was whether, having regard to all the circumstances, the solicitor should reasonably have appreciated that the client 'needed his advice and guidance in respect of the tax liabilities to which entry into the transaction would expose it'.

A solicitor cannot gain protection from liability by claiming to rely on counsel's opinion. In *Estill* v. *Cowling* [2000] WTLR 417 an estate suffered unnecessary IHT because a discretionary trust was established in inappropriate circumstances.

Arden J said that he endorsed the approach taken in *Locke* v. *Camberwell Health Authority* [1991] 2 Med LR 249 that a solicitor does not abdicate his professional responsibility when he seeks the advice of counsel.

The principles to be derived from the relevant authorities were, he said, as follows:

1. In general, a solicitor is entitled to rely upon the advice of counsel properly instructed.
2. For a solicitor without specialist experience in a particular field to rely on counsel's advice is to make normal and proper use of the Bar.
3. However, he must not do so blindly but must exercise his own independent judgment. 'If he reasonably thinks counsel's advice is obviously or glaringly wrong, it is his duty to reject it . . .' (per Taylor LJ, at page 254, with whom Sir George Waller and Parker W agreed).

Arden J went on to consider what in his view a reasonably competent solicitor would do to give himself sufficient general knowledge of the subject:

as respects the tax considerations, he would have read some general outline of the tax implications of setting up a trust, and (having discovered IHT applied to all transfers of value subject to exemption) looked to see what exemptions were available. The point was not some obscure point of tax law. It was a basic principle of IHT which had been discussed in the professional press at the time, particularly when the law was changed to make transfers to IIP trusts PETs. As it was, Mr Anderson did no research of his own . . . His conclusion that a transfer of value to the settlement was a PET was negligent.

12.4 WILLS PROCEDURE CHECKLIST

Some practitioners like to use a checklist with their clients. Others prefer to have one available for their own use as an *aide-mémoire*. The following check-list was compiled by the Law Society after discussions with the various probate registries around the country. It is intended to be used while taking instructions, as an *aide-mémoire* of the topics to cover and record of those instructions.

The checklist draws attention to common mistakes which can lead to delay in obtaining the grant and other points, certain of which are mentioned in this Handbook, which can easily be overlooked. Probate registries report difficulties in relation to the drafting of clauses appointing solicitor-executors (see **12.1.1** above).

Wills procedure checklist

1. Did you obtain full, clear instructions from the client?
2. Was there any reason to suspect a later challenge to the client's testa-mentary capacity? If so, did you ask questions to satisfy yourself? And record them in a full written attendance note?
3. Did you check the client's eligibility for public funding: age; capacity; intention?
4. Did you check that any charity mentioned is really charitable? And the correct charity name, number and address? And that the estate is likely to be solvent and all the legacies can be paid?
5. Have you explained to the client (in no particular order):

   - the pros and cons of appointing members of the family/solicitors/ others as executors?
   - the implications of the clauses extending or varying the executors' general law powers and duties?
   - the impact of the general law on the will (e.g. effect of marriage, formation of civil partnership)?
   - the implications of any charging clause?
   - the need for parents to appoint guardians of minor children?
   - the position of single parents under the Children Act 1989?
   - the law relating to specific, general or demonstrative legacies, where appropriate, e.g. the need to review specific legacies if the property the subject of the gift alters or is sold or destroyed?
   - the terms and effect of any residuary gifts made?
   - whether there will be any secret or half-secret trusts?
   - whether the will is to be mutual, i.e. not to be revoked unilaterally?
   - the effect of mutual wills? (are they appropriate for the client?)
   - whether the will incorporates any document – was that intended?

- the general law concerning the payment of tax, testamentary expenses or other liabilities (especially those items which will not be paid out of residue)?
- the tax planning considerations which affect the terms of the will, e.g. lifetime gifts within seven years of death?
- the likelihood of a claim under the Inheritance (Provision for Family and Dependants) Act 1975 and, if any, what should be done?
- about the position of a cohabitee (with and without an interest in the home)?
- the consequences for the beneficiaries if the residue is much larger (say because of an unexpected windfall) or smaller (say because a property has had to be sold to pay for care) than anticipated?
- the advisability of making an enduring power of attorney and discussed with the client a procedure for making the will available to the attorney (to avoid problems such as accidental ademption)?
- the need to sever a joint tenancy if the client wants to make a gift of property held as beneficial joint tenant?

6. Have you agreed the arrangements for valid execution of the will, and advised the client accordingly? Have you offered to inspect the will after execution?
7. What is to happen to any previous wills or codicils? It is advisable to destroy them so as to avoid any possible confusion; similarly letters of wishes relating to personal chattels.
8. Have you asked the client if there are any other practical or legal steps they want to consider in relation to their financial and other arrangements – writing a life insurance policy in trust, drawing up an enduring power of attorney making an advance directive or living will?
9. Was the will executed within a reasonable time? If not, did you:

- explain to the client the implications of not executing the will, i.e. intestacy or non-revocation of existing will?
- sought instructions about new provisions, if the client is unhappy about the terms or effect of the draft will?
- ensured that existing provisions have not been overtaken by events in the intervening period?

10. After the will has been executed, have you:

- checked it was executed and witnessed properly by people who are neither beneficiaries nor married to beneficiaries?
- kept a copy for your files?
- if you are holding the original, have you given a copy to the client?
- advised on the importance of placing the will where it will be found, and telling executors and family where it is?
- advised on the desirability of the client placing a Personal Assets Log [available from the Law Society] with their papers?
- explained to the client that it is necessary to review a will every two to five years and sooner if there is a major change of financial or personal circumstances?
- agreed the extent of your retainer? Is the client aware that you will/will not be reminding them of the need to review their will in five years' time or in any other situation, and will/will not be notifying them about tax changes affecting provisions made? [The

> *dramatic changes to the taxation of trusts introduced in the Finance Act 2006 were a good illustration of the importance of being clear as to whether or not the solicitor has an obligation to inform clients of changes in the tax rules.*]
> * if partners of the firm have been appointed as executors have you a separate record of this so that the client can be approached if a partner leaves, retires or dies?

12.5 SOLICITOR'S DUTY AFTER WILL EXECUTED

This guidance was approved by the Law Society's Standards and Guidance Committee and Property and Commercial Services Committee in 1991.

1. It is for clients to ensure that their wills are kept up to date and solicitors may help clients to do this by retaining in a manual or computer database (note the requirements of the Data Protection Act 1984 [repealed by DPA 1998] and European legislation in relation to manual records and databases) the names of clients for whom they have drawn up wills in the past. Solicitors may write to these clients from time to time reminding them of the need to review a will regularly and of their firms' services.

2. The preparation of a will for a client is in the ordinary case an entire contract so that when the work is completed and the final bill is submitted, the relationship of solicitor and client may be assumed to have ended as far as will preparation is concerned. Of course, the relationship of solicitor and client may continue with that client on other matters. Where solicitors have a continuing relationship with clients, they may wish to consider agreeing with those clients whether or not the client wishes the firm to maintain a watching brief on legal changes or tax changes which might affect their will; the Society considers that it would be appropriate for a charge to be made for such a service in addition to charges for preparation of a will.

3. Without specific instructions from the client, a retainer for will preparation would not entail the solicitor in maintaining any such 'watching brief', but it is possible for a solicitor by his or her conduct to change a retainer so that a client comes to have a reasonable expectation that such a watching brief will be maintained. Solicitors would be well advised to ensure that these matters are clear between themselves and their clients.

4. Many firms store clients' wills as a free service and a courtesy to their clients. The storage of a will does not of itself create a retainer. Solicitor and client may agree otherwise.

5. In relation to wills stored by firms, should a solicitor or clerk named as executor or executrix in such a will retire, move to another practice, or die, or otherwise become unable or unwilling to act, the firm should consider writing to the testator or testatrix at the client's last known address detailing the changed circumstances. Informing clients of such internal changes to a firm is not considered to be any indication that a watching brief on matters of law has been agreed upon, but is, rather, part of the necessary changes which follow retirement or resignation, etc., of a solicitor from a firm, such as changes to the notepaper.

6. Some firms may retain large numbers of wills for clients from whom they have not heard for many years. Solicitors wishing to clarify the position in relation

to these wills may wish to consider writing to a testator or testatrix at the last known address. However, even if no reply is received, such wills should never be destroyed as they remain the clients' property or the property of the clients' PRs.

In February 2001 the Probate Section obtained counsel's opinion (from Sian Warnock-Smith and Tracey Angus) on client retainers. The opinion deals with a variety of aspects of retainers and contains some useful clauses for inclusion in a client care letter.

It contains the following paragraphs:

A solicitor who is instructed to prepare a Will would not, unless he has expressly agreed to do so, owe any duty to conduct a regular review of the client's Will which he holds (for example, an annual review in the light of the Budget). However, a solicitor who is instructed to prepare a codicil, would usually owe a duty to review the contents of the Will and any earlier codicils.

Firms that provide Will drafting services should certainly review their standard precedents in the light of any important reported authority (such as *Re Benham*) or change in the law. However, once this task is performed, the firm does not, in our opinion, owe any duty to its past clients to review its old Will files and to contact clients for whom it has prepared Wills in the past in order to advise them of the implications of that decision or change in the law unless it had agreed with the clients in question that it would provide this service.

12.6   RETAINERS GENERALLY

Also note the cases of *Cancer Research Campaign* v. *Ernest Brown & Co* [1997] STC 1425; *Gibbons* v. *Nelsons* [2000] PNLR 734 and *Gray* v. *Buss Murton* [1999] PNLR 882, all of which emphasise the importance of clarity in the terms of a solicitor's retainer. In *Gibbons* v. *Nelsons* (above) Blackburne J stressed that a solicitor has a general duty to the client when preparing a will and the burden is on the solicitor to demonstrate any limitation on that retainer:

Although the burden of proof rests with the claimant to establish what the scope was of the solicitor's retainer, once the claimant establishes that the solicitor was retained to prepare a will, the burden must, I think, shift to the solicitor to show, if he can, that his responsibility for the preparation of the will did not extend to advising the client on some aspect of the will relevant to the claim.

In *Gray* v. *Buss Murton* (above) Rougier J said that any ambiguity in the retainer would be determined in favour of the client. It is the solicitor's duty to clarify precisely the terms of any retainer.

Lightman J in *Hurlingham Estates Ltd* v. *Wilde & Partners* [1997] STC 627 emphasised the need for a client to give informed consent to any limitation in the retainer and to the importance of a clear written record of any agreement to limit the retainer.

In *Atkins* v. *Dunn & Baker (A Firm)* [2004] All ER (D) 324 Pill LJ held that the retainer for preparing a will did not normally extend to sending reminders to a client who failed to execute it.

> The evidence was that the instructions were that a draft Will should be prepared and submitted to the client. That was done promptly in accordance with instructions. The solicitor had completed the task which he had been asked to perform. It does not necessarily follow from the retainer rules, which cover a variety of situations, that in this situation there was inevitably a duty upon a solicitor to send a reminder.

The Probate Section opinion referred to above contains useful precedent clauses setting out the extent of the retainer. The following is included by way of illustration:

1975 Act Advice

The Inheritance (Provision for Family and Dependants) Act 1975 may enable certain persons to seek additional provision out of your estate after your death. If an application is made under this Act it is likely to involve your estate in expense and may result in a variation of the dispositions made in your Will.

   If the information which you provide to us for the purposes of preparing your Will suggests that there is a real risk of such an application being made in respect of your estate, we will advise you that this is the case. However we will not offer more detailed advice in relation to the 1975 Act unless you ask us to do so and, in those circumstances, an additional fee will be charged.

12.7   ADVANCE DIRECTIVES AND 'LIVING WILLS'

12.7.1   Introduction

'Advance directives or statements' and 'living wills' are different terms for the same thing. They are documents intended to allow individuals to specify the extent and nature of the medical treatment they would or would not find acceptable should they lose capacity in the future. The term 'living will' can be confusing since such documents have no connection with ordinary wills but this term is probably too well established to change.

   Competent patients can authorise or refuse consent to treatments, both contemporaneously and in advance. They cannot make legally enforceable demands about specific treatments they wish to receive. *R. (on the application of Burke)* v. *General Medical Council* [2005] EWCA Civ 1003 confirmed that medical practitioners are under no obligation to provide a specific treatment requested by the patient if in their view it is clinically inappropriate. The case of *Re B (Consent to Treatment: Capacity)* [2002] 2 All ER 449 reviewed the authorities and states very clearly that a mentally competent patient has an absolute right to refuse consent to medical treatment for any reason, rational or irrational, or for no reason at all.

The difficulty with advance directives is that they are normally in issue in cases where patients are unable to speak to make their wishes known.

The following cases support advance directives: *Re T (Adult: Refusal of Treatment)* [1992] 3 WLR 782; *Airedale NHS Trust* v. *Bland* [1993] 2 WLR 316, HL; *Re C (Adult: Refusal of Medical Treatment)* [1994] 1 All ER 819 and *HE* v. *A Hospital NHS Trust and AE* [2003] EWHC 1017 (Fam). In *Re T* (above) the Court of Appeal said that an anticipatory choice will bind a medical practitioner if it is:

- clearly established, and
- applicable in the circumstances.

The British Medical Association (BMA) published a statement in 1992 on advance directives. It stated that the BMA 'strongly supports the principle of an advance directive' and points out that 'patients have a legal right to decline specific treatment, including life prolonging treatment'. It stresses 'the significant ethical and legal difference between the concept of an advance statement and the issue of euthanasia . . . [which] is illegal' and emphasises that its conclusion on advance directives should not be seen as supporting euthanasia.

This distinction was supported by the House of Lords Select Committee on Medical Ethics, HL Paper 21–I (HMSO, 1994), which commended the development of advance directives, but recommended no change in the law to permit euthanasia. Its recommendations led to a Code of Practice from the professions entitled Advance Statements about Medical Treatment, (BMA, 1995). The Code restates the law with explanatory notes and gives health professionals the protection of guidance and an accepted body of professional opinion.

The Law Commission published a report *Mental Incapacity*, Law Com. No.231 (1995), which also supported the use of advance directives, and called for legislation in order to clarify the current common law position that an advance refusal of treatment made with capacity survives any supervening incapacity.

In its report *Withholding and Withdrawing Life-prolonging Medical Treatment*, 2nd edn (BMA, 2001) the BMA claimed that:

A valid advance refusal of treatment has the same legal authority as a contemporaneous refusal and legal action could be taken against a doctor who provides treatment in the face of a valid refusal.

Living will documents are not like normal testamentary documents. Their validity is determined by the patient's capacity, not the document. There are obviously strong reasons for using a written document but an oral living will could be just as binding.

Information on the assessment of capacity to consent to or refuse medical treatment is contained in Nicola Greaney, Fenella Morris and Beverley Taylor, *Mental Capacity Act 2005: A Guide to the New Law* (Law Society, 2005) and BMA and Law Society, *Assessment of Mental Capacity: Guidance for Doctors and Lawyers*, 2nd edn (BMJ Books, 2004).

One of the difficulties with advance directives is the requirement that they be 'applicable to the circumstances'. In *Re B* (above), Ms B had executed a living will in 1999 after she had first become ill. It said that if she was unable to give instructions, she wished treatment to be withdrawn if she was suffering from 'a life-threatening condition, permanent mental impairment or permanent unconsciousness'. When she became paralysed from the neck down and needed ventilation, the doctors concluded that the terms of the directive were not specific enough to authorise withdrawal of ventilation. Although she was able to make her wishes known, the doctors argued that she had lost her mental capacity to make decisions as to her treatment. The Court of Appeal did not agree and Ms B was allowed to reject ventilation.

An alternative to consider is a health care proxy document. In this a competent patient appoints an agent to make health care decisions for him or her, should the patient become incompetent. There is a common misconception that the next of kin are normally responsible for making treatment decisions. This is not so. In *Re T*, Lord Donaldson pointed out that the responsibility lies with the doctor:

> There seems to be a view in the medical profession that in emergency circum-stances the next of kin should be asked to consent on behalf of the patient and that, if possible, treatment should be postponed until that consent has been obtained. This is a misconception because the next of kin has no legal right either to consent or to refuse consent. This is not to say that it is an undesirable practice if the interests of the patient will not be adversely affected by any consequential delay. I say this . . . because contact with a next of kin may reveal that the patient has made an anticipatory choice which, if clearly established and applicable to the circumstances . . . would bind the practitioner.

12.7.2   Specimen living wills

There are numerous precedents for living wills and advance directives in exis-tence, particularly those available through charities, such as the Terence Higgins Trust and the Alzheimer's Society.

In an article in [1999] *Trusts and Estates Law Journal*, September, Chris Docker discusses three options which exist when preparing a living will. We are grateful to the *Trusts and Estates Law Journal* and to Chris Docker for permission to reproduce this section of the article.

Some options include:

- drawing up a living will from scratch;

- using a simple standard text;
- using a more sophisticated document.

The first option is desirable in some ways, but the practical pitfalls mean that it is inadvisable without very extensive research. One of the most common errors is to draw up a complicated document with extensive checklists. These might look very impressive to the lay person, but the medical pitfalls mean that they are unconvincing in practice – the exact details of medical exigencies can rarely be predicted in such accurate detail.

The second option could mean simply photocopying the form apppearing with this article, or using the text from it as a basis for a document on the firm's notepaper. The form includes all the minimum requirements recommended by the BMA. Usually, when people first think of making a living will, they want to make a very simple statement.

Later on, clients may wish to put effort into completing a more sophisticated document (the third option) which enables them to state their wishes more precisely, and probably gives them greater protection. These documents can be obtained at relatively low cost from The Scottish Voluntary Euthanasia Society or the Terence Higgins Trust [see **Useful addresses** for contact details]. Both of these sources provide well-researched documents which apply anywhere in the UK. The one from VESS comes as part of a pack with medical stickers, a carrying wallet, an emergency medical card and an advice booklet.

If solicitors draw up their own version of a living will, then, like all legally binding forms for use by lay people, it should be well designed, clear and straight-forward. Lord Donaldson in *Re T* commented on the desirability of using different sizes of typeface, underlining, and colour print.

The BMA says that the minimum information to be included is as follows:

- the person's full name;
- their address;
- the name and address of their GP;
- whether advice was sought from health professionals;
- their signature;
- the date the will was drafted and reviewed;
- the signature of a witness;
- a clear statement of wishes, either general or specific;
- the name, address and telephone number of the person's nominated contact, if they have one.

Within the Law Society these matters are the responsibility of the Mental Health and Disability Committee, in the Regulation and Law Reform Directorate.

There is also a useful section by Chris Docker in *Finance and Law for the Older Client* (Tolley's, looseleaf). The website **www.euthanasia.com** is also useful.

12.7.3 Mental Capacity Act 2005

The Mental Capacity Act 2005 is expected to come into force during 2007. Sections 24–26 provide for advance decisions to refuse medical treatment. The Act will allow people to make 'advance decisions' that a specified treatment is not to be carried out after they have lost capacity. Sections 25(5) and (6) state when advance decisions are not applicable to life-sustaining treatement:

(5) An advance decision is not applicable to life-sustaining treatment unless –

(a) the decision is verified by a statement by P to the effect that it is to apply to that treatment even if life is at risk, and

(b) the decision and statement comply with subsection (6).

(6) A decision or statement complies with this subsection only if –

(a) it is in writing,

(b) it is signed by P or by another person in P's presence and by P's direction,

(c) the signature is made or acknowledged by P in the presence of a witness, and

(d) the witness signs it, or acknowledges his signature, in P's presence.

Lasting Powers of Attorney dealing with personal welfare decisions can authorise an attorney to give or refuse consent to life-sustaining treatment on behalf of the donor.

12.8   ISLAMIC WILLS

There is a lot of interest in Islamic wills, and useful articles by Hajj Ahmad Thomson, head of chambers at Wynne Chambers, London, have been published in [2005] *Probate Section Journal*, April and in (2006) 156 *New Law Journal*, 24 March.

Muslims are normally free to leave a portion of their estates to whomever they wish, but the balance must be divided amongst surviving relatives in prescribed shares. They can leave the whole estate to be divided amongst the surviving relatives but may not allocate an extra portion from the one-third to a relative who is already going to receive a fixed share out of the two-thirds. Such a gift will be void. Not all of the deceased's surviving relatives will necessarily be entitled to a fixed share. The closer relatives exclude the more distant relatives who will only be entitled to shares if the closer relatives have predeceased the testator.

At the time the will is prepared, it will be impossible to know which relatives will survive the testator so a discretionary trust and letter of wishes is likely to be the most appropriate solution. Some testators will be willing to consider a life interest to the surviving spouse with power for the trustees to appoint capital elsewhere.

A software package called IRTH: the Islamic Inheritance Programme, which can calculate who would be entitled to what share if the client had just died – and who would not – is available on the internet free of charge (**www.IslamicSoftware.org/irth.html**). Bequests to those not entitled can then be included in the will. If when the testator dies such a relative is, in fact, entitled to a fixed share, the bequest is automatically nullified and the fixed share is given instead. Note that the Islamic Inheritance Programme offers a choice of which Sunni school of jurisprudence to follow as there are variations between them as to the fixed shares. The programme is not suitable for a Shi'a client.

12.9   HOW LONG SHOULD WILL FILES BE RETAINED?

Ideally, all documentation should be retained until after any possibility of dispute is over: hence, not just until the testators' death but at least until a grant of representation is obtained.

12.10   INTERNET WILLS

12.10.1   Using the internet

The increasing number of solicitors' firms who promote their legal services through their own websites continues to rise and so does the variety of legal services including will drafting via the internet. The delivery of legal services via the internet raises important issues in respect of the use of this modern technology when taking instructions and preparing wills, including the solicitor's duty of care in relation to e-commerce.

Some solicitors are keen to use the internet to its full potential and have readily embraced the e-commerce age, whilst others are more cautious and some are openly hostile to the idea of preparing wills via the internet. As the legal and technical difficulties surrounding electronic signatures are resolved it will become possible for wills and other documents to be completed and executed online. The possibility of wills executed electronically has serious implications, so it is worth reviewing the advantages and disadvantages of using the internet for the preparation of wills.

The type of legal services offered by legal firms via the internet varies, although e-mail communication with clients, companies and government departments is increasingly the norm. However at present most firms who do private client work use their websites merely to promote their services to existing and new clients and to provide legal knowledge. There are some firms which offer a more interactive site, enabling the client to download forms and to complete and return questionnaires and information to the firm. Relatively few legal firms at present return the will electronically for the client to print and sign.

12.10.2 Advantages of using the internet for wills

The internet provides easy access for computer literate clients possibly on a 24-hour basis and is heavily used by the younger generation who consider it to be an essential part of their life. Giving instructions via an interactive site is likely to appeal to the under 35s who, overall, tend to resist making wills. Some firms may regard a sophisticated IT set-up as a marketing tool promoting a modern image of solicitors and may use it specifically to target a younger generation and to encourage them to make wills.

It *should* be possible to offer a less expensive service as overheads and reduction in staffing could cut costs in the long term; however, the start-up costs of setting up a truly interactive site would not be insignificant and it can require a considerable amount of time and effort to develop an accurate and responsive system.

The internet knows no boundaries, therefore the actual drafting of wills can be carried out at a different location where the overheads may be cheaper. This may result in more flexible working practices for staff, as if the instructions are received via the internet there is no need for the staff to be located in a central office. Accessibility problems may be overcome for disabled clients or staff if they choose to use the internet instead of attending at the solicitor's office. A considerable amount of information can be presented to clients via the website, which they can access in the privacy of their home and at their own speed.

If regularly updated a firm's website can provide clients with useful information about recent legislative changes which affect the client, for example the introduction of the Civil Partnership Act 2004 and the now infamous BN25 HMRC statement regarding the Finance Bill 2006, Sched.20.

If the appropriate prior consent has been obtained from clients, newsletters, mail alerts and marketing information can be distributed to clients via e-mail in a quick, cost-effective manner. Remember that overuse of the e-mail format to send newsletters and or other information can be very annoying and counter-productive – most private clients are unlikely to want a weekly or even a monthly newsletter from their solicitor.

Face-to-face access should continue to be made available, as a significant proportion of clients for the foreseeable future are likely to choose to have a meeting in person at the solicitor's office when discussing complex issues.

12.10.3 Disadvantages of using the internet

A will is not a commercial contract; it is a unilateral document which may not become operative for many years. To create a valid will the statutory requirements of Wills Act 1837, s.9 and an adequate level of testamentary capacity must be satisfied. What sets a will apart from other forms of commercial transactions is the fact that by the time the will is challenged the testator or testatrix (and possibly the witnesses) will be dead and unable to verify the will.

Without a personal interview with the client it would be difficult to spot underlying problems or the 'hidden agenda'. There is a potential risk of fraud or coercion of clients, particularly if they are vulnerable or elderly.

It can be very time-consuming for the client to access the appropriate information on the taxation system, information concerning claims under IPFDA 1975 or complexities which can occur where second marriages are involved. There is a real risk that the clients may lack the ability to use the software properly or to understand key explanations and definitions in the computer software. For example, 'children' includes illegitimate and adopted children but not step-children, and clients may not appreciate this distinction.

It is essential that any website is regularly maintained and upgraded. Regrettably some existing sites run by solicitors (both small and larger firms) include out-of-date tax information and sometimes even misleading advice.

Issues of mental capacity cannot be easily resolved. If you have not had a meeting with your client when taking the instructions and discussing the same, how would you be able to confirm to any court in the event of a dispute that the client did actually have the necessary mental capacity to make a will?

If the final will is downloaded and printed out by the client, it will be impossible for the solicitor to ensure that the pages have in fact been printed correctly on suitable quality paper.

Some databases recorded in old computer formats are already obsolete and it is now impossible to retrieve the data. There is also evidence that floppy disks and CDs degrade after a relatively short period. An electronic will should be capable of being stored for at least 75–80 years and easily retrievable, but at present there is no technical standard or guarantee that data can be stored for any long-term period, i.e. 50 years or more.

12.10.4 Confidentiality

The client, understandably, will expect confidentiality but *this cannot and should not be guaranteed.* Many large global organisations have set up complex security systems, which have then been compromised by computer hackers. Nevertheless solicitors will be keen to try and emphasise that efforts have been made to make the website as secure as possible. Possible means of doing this will be by using a guaranteed encrypted system, or software, which includes other security devices to protect the information from being intercepted.

Protecting personal information and privacy are likely to be key issues for most clients. Fear of their credit card being misused and invasion of their privacy are likely to be factors which will cause clients to resist purchasing products online. Therefore any solicitors' firm wishing to encourage clients will need to consider confidentiality and security very seriously. Some firms have had their information systems independently audited and arranged for an attempted penetration to check the levels of security. An American security company challenged hackers to break into its security system which it described as the 'Fort Knox' of computer security. It took the hackers one day to access the main server and claim their prize of £35,000.

Verifying the authenticity of the message and the sender/recipient is important. Cameras linked into the computer are likely to become increasingly important in the future alongside electronic keys and electronic signatures as a means of confirming the identity of the client. The cost of creating and, in particular, maintaining the computer software to support security systems will have cost implications for solicitors.

12.11   E-COMMERCE: STATUTORY FRAMEWORK

12.11.1   Introduction

The UK Government, as a member of the European Union, is required to implement the Electronic Commerce Directive 2001/31/EC (the E-Commerce Directive), which requires all Member States to ensure that their legal systems permit contracts to be executed by electronic means. The Directive was adopted by the EU on 8 June 2000 but has not yet been fully implemented by the United Kingdom.

The Electronic Communication Act 2000 (ECA 2000), which partly came into force on 25 May 2000, seeks to create public confidence in e-commerce by:

- confirming the legal status of electronic signatures;
- creating a statutory framework for the approval of cryptography providers; and
- providing a system to facilitate the removal of any legal barriers against the use of electronic communications.

12.11.2   What is an electronic or digital signature?

ECA 2000, s.7(2) defines an 'electronic signature' as something which incorporates or is linked to electronic data or an electronic communication with the purpose of establishing the authenticity or the integrity of the communication or data.

ECA 2000 did not attempt to define the basis on which an electronic signature would be treated as valid. ECA 2000, s.7(1) states that electronic signature and the certification by any person of the signature are deemed to be admissible in any legal proceedings, but it is left to the courts to decide what evidential weight to give to an electronic signature.

148

A paper signature can be treated as a record of the intention of the signatory to be committed to a course of action. An electronic 'signature' can be used to verify the identity of the person and to bind them in the same manner as a manual signature. An electronic signature is not a scanned image of the individual's normal signature.

The Electronic Signature Regulations 2002, SI 2002/318 came into effect on 8 March 2002 with the purpose of implementing the provisions of the Electronic Signatures Directive 1999/93/EC. The regulations include a definition of an 'advanced electronic signature' by reference to certain specific requirements and are intended to encourage their legal recognition throughout the EU. The electronic signature is treated as an 'advanced electronic signature' if the signature:

(a)   is uniquely linked to the signatory;
(b)   is capable of identifying the signatory;
(c)   is created using means that the signatory can maintain under his or her sole control; and
(d)   is linked to the data to which it relates in such a manner that any subsequent change of the data is detectable.

The term 'digital signature' is somewhat misleading as the 'signature' consists of complex information which is encrypted. The system relies on the signature having been approved by way of a digital certificate issued by a certification authority. The system relies on 'keys' which are in fact complex mathematical algorithms; the complexity of the algorithms means that only the specific individual should be able to sign the e-mail or other electronic document. There are public and private keys, which when matched together enable encrypted information to be decrypted and read. So the keys enable information to be encrypted with a public key which can then be simply sent via the internet and only be decrypted with a private key.

The Government, financial institutions and commerce are all trying to create secure systems which will enable fully integrated electronic business to be conducted via the internet. The whole area of digital and electronic signatures is likely to continue to change dramatically in the next few years. At the moment there is no specific legislation which prohibits the use of an electronic signature to effect the creation of a will, although it still has to satisfy the requirements of the Wills Act 1837, as amended.

12.11.3   Privacy and Data Protection Act 1998

Solicitors when they collect and store personal information are required to comply with the obligations set out in the Data Protection Act 1998 (DPA 1998). These include the eight principles of good information handling, which are set out on the Information Commissioner's Office (ICO) website (**www.ico.gov.uk**).

The eight principles state that the data must be:

- fairly and lawfully processed;
- processed for limited purposes;
- adequate, relevant and not excessive;
- accurate and up to date;
- not kept longer than necessary;
- processed in accordance with the individual's rights;
- secure;
- not transferred to countries outside the European Economic area, unless there is adequate protection.

Personal data includes information such as lists of names and addresses. Most solicitors' firms are likely to handle personal data and will need to notify (register) under DPA 1998.

It is possible to check online whether a firm or company is registered by searching the Data Protection Public Register held by the ICO.

The Seventh Principle contained in DPA 1998, Sched.1, Pt.II requires appropriate technical and organisational measures to be taken against unauthorised or unlawful processing of personal data and against accidental loss or destruction of or damage to the personal data. This means that if solicitors are in receipt of personal information about a person they will have an obligation to ensure the reliability of all the employees that have access to that personal data to ensure that it is not misused. Non-compliance is an offence and directors/officers of a company can be held personally liable.

The Law Society E-mail Guidelines for Solicitors (revised 2005) contain useful information and guidance about data protection issues which may arise from personal information contained in e-mails whether sent or received. For a detailed analysis of what is meant by 'personal data' see *Durant* v. *Financial Services Authority* [2003] EWCA Civ 1746.

If a firm fails to comply with the provisions of DPA 1998, it may be liable to claims for compensation from the party providing the data as well as to criminal proceedings (DPA 1998, s.13).

12.11.4 Consumer Protection (Distance Selling) Regulations 2000

Firms intending to develop a website which is more than an information portal will need to comply with the Consumer Protection (Distance Selling) Regulations 2000, SI 2000/2334 (as amended) which became operative from 31 October 2000. These regulations were primarily aimed at mail order catalogues, telephone sales and other types of 'distance selling', but the regulations also affect faxes, newspaper advertisements, the internet and contracts that are not made face to face. The regulations only apply to transactions involving consumers; they do not apply where the services are being offered to a business.

The regulations set out the minimum requirements concerning the information which must be supplied to the client/customer by the supplier. A solicitor or legal firm which is offering to sell legal services or legal knowledge to a consumer or lay client over the internet is deemed to be a supplier of legal services.

The regulations include an automatic seven-day cooling-off period (unless agreed between the parties that the contract will commence at an earlier point) and unless the time is specifically extended, all contracts must be completed within 30 days.

The right to return 'goods' to the supplier after they have been received by the consumer does not apply if the goods that are supplied are customised for that particular client (reg.13(1)(c)). Most wills should be capable of being treated as specific to the client and therefore should not be caught by the right of return.

A cooling-off period should, however, be incorporated into the firm's terms and conditions of business regardless of whether the transaction is over the internet or in written form.

In addition to the firm's business terms and conditions, the E-Commerce Directive requires solicitors who either provide services electronically or advertise electronically to inform their clients or customers that the service is provided by solicitors of England and Wales, that they are regulated by the Law Society and information on how to access the Law Society's rules (the easiest way to do this is to provide a link to **www.guide-on-line.lawsociety.org.uk**). The name, address, e-mail address and VAT number of the firm must also be provided. If there is electronic trading, such as the purchase of legal forms or the purchase of a will online for a specific fee, additional information about the steps required to enter into the contract have to be displayed on the website.

12.11.5   Contractual implications of wills via the internet

The internet may not recognise geographical boundaries but anyone providing services via the internet needs to define in which country or legal jurisdiction any contractual disputes are to be to be decided. It is also necessary to define the place of performance of the contract or the provision of services. Failure to define the terms clearly could result in the case being heard in another country and the legislation of that country being applied. Although this problem is less likely to apply to wills than to the purchase of other goods, such as books or videos, it is obviously preferable to avoid uncertainty wherever possible. An EU Council Regulation 44/2001 on jurisdiction and the recognition and enforcement of judgments in civil and commercial matters imposes additional restrictions if there is a consumer contract.

12.11.6 Duty of care limiting liability

Using e-mail, a website or other internet facilities to provide legal services does not negate the basic duty of care which a solicitor owes to a client. E-commerce is simply a different modern method of delivering solicitor's services.

E-mail and the internet may increase the pressure for an immediate response to the client, but it does not reduce the professional standard of care to which a solicitor is expected to adhere.

Different levels of information may be agreed or may be appropriate for different clients. Ideally, the client should normally be told in appropriate language at the *outset of a matter or as soon as possible thereafter* the issues in the case and how they will be dealt with. In particular, the immediate steps to be taken in a transaction must be clearly explained.

It may be helpful to provide linked specialist text for the client to access explaining particularly complex issues, i.e. parental responsibility if the parents are unmarried, or when and why including a life interest trust would normally be recommended.

Drafting questionnaires

The emphasis therefore is on *informing* the client. So, if clients will be asked to complete an online questionnaire they need to understand the legal language used. For example, it might contain a statement such as:

> This questionnaire is only appropriate if your assets and possessions do not exceed the inheritance tax threshold – £285,000 for tax year 2006/2007.

This statement assumes that the client understands what is meant by the term 'assets'. Many clients and members of the public might query what from a legal perspective appears to be a straightforward question. The client might want to ask the following questions:

- Does that include my half share in the house I own jointly with my wife – I thought that was tax-free and did not count?
- What about my life policies – I think they go to my children if I die – are they included?
- I also have a timeshare in Grand Canaria – I wonder if that is included?

The example given above demonstrates that even a simple statement concerning the client's assets may require a considerable amount of further knowledge and information to be available in order for the client to make a reasoned judgement. If such information is to be gathered electronically, detailed additional information and checks need to be included and this can make the process time-consuming and off-putting to the client.

Very few wills are straightforward, and in fact more and more wills are becoming complex. Second or third marriages, children from different partners and a variety of pension schemes and investments mean solicitors must take a detailed profile in order to prepare a suitable will.

It is unlikely that the internet is going to be the appropriate method for preparing complex wills which involve tax planning. This is already recognised by some of the unregulated will writer websites, which suggest the customer seeks 'independent advice' where the assets include business or farming interests, foreign domicile, or complex trusts.

12.11.7 Can you limit your liability?

Some solicitors who are already using the internet to provide will services have tried to limit their liability to the information provided in the will questionnaire:

> We will prepare your will strictly on the basis of the information provided in the will questionnaire and cannot be held responsible for an incorrectly drafted will based on inaccurate information provided.

It is understandable that a solicitor does not want to be held liable if the client has provided inaccurate or inadequate information which the solicitor has then relied upon to draft the will. However, if the solicitor has failed to provide an adequate level of information to assist the client in completing the questionnaire, the clauses attempting to limit liability are unlikely to be given effect by the courts. Furthermore if the questionnaire is completed electronically how does the solicitor know that *the client* actually completed it? (Even if the completed questionnaire is handed to the solicitor, specific confirmation should be obtained that the client completed the form – see *Clancy* v. *Clancy* [2003] EWHC 1885.)

Hurlingham Estates Ltd v. *Wilde & Partners* [1997] STC 627 suggests that the obligations of the solicitor to the client appear to be widening, and *Hurlingham* cannot be viewed as an isolated case as it has since been followed in *Estill* v. *Cowling* [2000] WTLR 417. It should be noted that both the cases of *Hurlingham* and *Estill* refer to express agreements with the client. This would seem to indicate that simply sending terms of engagement or a retainer letter, whether through the post or via e-mail, may not always be enough.

There are also certain implied duties, which a solicitor cannot exclude. The problem for the draftsperson is ascertaining which tasks should be included or excluded.

Some IT experts argue that if a basic 'no frills' service is offered it is unreasonable for the client to expect a high level of information or service. However, by holding themselves out as a solicitor, a standard of care of a competent solicitor will be expected irrespective of the standards offered by other internet sites which may be offering a will-making service. An interesting question will be whether the courts when dealing with other internet sites offering will-drafting services will be willing to follow the principles formulated in the case of *Esterhuizen* v. *Allied Dunbar* [1998] 2 FLR 668, where the court stated that a commercial company, Allied Dunbar, had to apply the same standards of care as a solicitor when carrying out a will-making service.

Where a retainer has been agreed, the status of the parties may be significant. An elderly client who does not have detailed knowledge of tax or trust law is unlikely to be expected to understand the significance of clauses which seek to limit the solicitor's areas of responsibility under a retainer unless it can clearly be shown that the client understood the consequences of the clauses, as was identified in the Jersey Court of Appeal decision *Pickersgill* v. *Riley* [2004] UKPC 14. In *Pickersgill* the court recognised that the duty of care was variable (at para.8):

> the scope of the duty may vary depending on the characteristics of the client, in so far as they are apparent to the solicitor. A youthful client, unversed in business affairs, might need explanation and advice from his solicitor before entering into a commercial transaction that it would be pointless, even sometimes an impertinence, for the solicitor to offer to an obviously experienced businessman.

It is arguable that in these circumstances the duty towards the client will widen and solicitors should take additional time and effort if necessary to explain the terms of the retainer to their client. If the only communication is by e-mail, how can solicitors assess the situation?

12.12   INTERNET SERVICES OFFERED BY FIRMS

12.12.1   Larger firms

Although private client work has been eschewed by many of the large commercial firms in the city of London and elsewhere as not being cost effective, some commercial firms have focused only on established commercial clients and individuals with a high net worth and aim to offer a bespoke service. There are also other large firms which have developed highly sophisticated IT case management systems (usually for property transactions), capable of carrying out a high volume of legal work via the internet. It is likely that having gained the expertise in providing volume legal services in one area they will seek to expand this expertise into other areas, such as will writing. There are also indications that if the Legal Services Bill is enacted, non-legal companies such as AA law intend to offer legal services including will-writing services, and it is likely that many of the services will be delivered electronically.

It is also anticipated that some large legal firms will develop will-drafting packages for their institutional clients, which the clients can then market through their individual high street shop or premises. Instructions will be taken in the commercial premises of the company or institution from the individual and then e-mailed back to the legal firm to implement. The legal firm does not actually deal with the individual client directly. The legal firms acting on behalf of the institutions are hopefully aware of the potential risks in drafting wills via the internet but they are likely to make a commercial judgement based on risk assessment. If the volume of business generated is sufficiently large, they will be prepared to take the commercial risk of having to deal with some potential problems/claims.

However as the threats from computer viruses, computer hackers and criminals continues to increase the level of technical expertise and knowledge needed to maintain a fully interactive website will also rise. Certainly the level of financial investment available to the largest firms enable sophisticated security systems and rigorous quality checks to be undertaken which would not be realistically cost effective for smaller firms to undertake.

12.12.2   Small firms' potential use of the internet

Some small firms have viewed the internet as a possible way of widening their client base without the need to purchase costly additional premises. An increasing number of smaller firms have readily seized on the opportunity to set up a low cost website and already offer wills on the internet.

Potential problems that may occur will be the failure to maintain and to upgrade the website at regular intervals; out-of-date or inaccurate information on which a client relied could result in a negligence claim. A general disclaimer from liability on the website may not be enforceable, the court is likely to consider that a firm of solicitors should be able to provide up-to-date information on the basic UK tax regime. It is relatively easy to set up a simple website and to claim an expertise in will drafting; the question is whether or not some of the solicitors' firms have the necessary levels of competence actually to draft the documentation.

There is an expectation by courts when considering negligence claims against solicitors and by clients themselves (perhaps even more so because they are using the internet) that the work will be completed quickly and this may place considerable pressure on a small firm with limited resources.

There will be an ongoing need to update and upgrade security systems including contingency plans in case a security incident compromises data. The website will need to be protected by a firewall and intrusion detection software, which will have resource implications for small firms.

12.12.3 Areas to define and limit when using the internet

Foreign assets

Foreign assets such as a holiday home in France or Spain require careful thought and specialist advice. In most circumstances, therefore, the retainer should explain that such specialist advice is not provided as part of the will-making service offered through this particular internet service. The internet has no geographical boundaries and the issues concerning domicile and residence may be relevant. A client's e-mail address will not necessarily give any indication of where the client is resident, although this could affect the legal advice that should be offered.

Solicitors may, if appropriate, suggest that they meet the client in person to discuss the matter further, but they should make it clear that an additional charge will be made.

Inheritance tax advice

In most circumstances solicitors will be expected to ascertain the extent and the nature of the estate. If the estate is well below the nil-rate band for tax purposes is it reasonable to try and exclude tax advice?

Some solicitors' firms who are already offering legal services over the internet have sought to restrict their liability to give tax advice by excluding such advice in the terms of their retainer. If the *Hurlingham* and *Estill* decisions (above) are followed such a clause may not be enough as it is necessary to establish that the client had informed consent. So if a solicitor is seeking to try to limit liability for tax advice, at least a résumé of tax principles should still be provided and this information must be up to date.

It may be prudent to include a clause within the terms of the agreed retainer with the client defining clearly that the advice given and the prepared will are based on the law at a definite moment in time and that the firm does not accept responsibility to notify the client of any future changes in the law or any legal decisions which might affect the terms of the will.

Due execution of the will

Clients using the internet for will drafting are perhaps less likely to be willing to attend in person at the solicitor's office to execute the will. Provided the client is willing and able to understand instructions on how to execute the will and a clear set of written instructions has been provided, the solicitor in normal circumstances should have discharged his duty of care. The danger lies in the fact that having taken instructions via the internet, the solicitor may not have identified possible complications and if there are unusual circumstances any exclusion in the retainer is unlikely to be effective.

As problems concerning the correct execution of the will have been a fertile area of litigation in recent years with cases such as *Esterhuizen* v. *Allied Dunbar* [1998] 2 FLR 668, the risk of failing to provide adequate instructions should not be underestimated.

Printed documentation

Where the will-drafting service is via the internet an additional issue may arise concerning the printing of the will as well as the execution of the will.

In these circumstances any retainer should very clearly state the potential risks and seek to define whether or not the solicitor is responsible for checking the will if it is returned to the firm. However, there is still the risk that the courts would not accept the retainer as being reasonable in all circumstances: see *Humblestone* v. *Martin Tolhurst Partnership* [2004] EWHC 151 (Ch).

12.12.4   Is it worth the risk?

Many solicitors are already carrying out an increasing amount of their legal work via the internet and this is likely to increase further. However, wills by their nature are very specialist documents, which require specific procedures, i.e. careful drafting and correct execution in order to be valid. There is real danger that firms that do not have specialist knowledge will simply set up websites offering services without considering the relevant dangers and risks and this in turn will lead to negligence claims at a later date.

Even for the experienced practitioner, the time required to provide the essential detailed information for the client should not be underestimated. Furthermore such information will still not negate the obligation to explain (in person, if necessary), complex issues to clients who are vulnerable or have special needs.

It is inevitable that the internet increasingly will be used to deliver a wide range of legal information, knowledge and services to the public. Although cost is undoubtedly a factor for some individuals, superstition and a reluctance to make decisions are also key inhibitors which cause people to delay making a will and these are likely to remain the same whether the will is created via the internet or made in person.

The speed with which consumers are embracing new opportunities to purchase goods and services on line should not be underestimated – online banking services and electronic ticketing for airline tickets are now the preferred options for many consumers, and this demonstrates that further change is inevitable. However, while electronic signatures may be appropriate for contracting to purchase the weekly shopping online, the creation of a will is quite different. In addition to satisfying the legal formalities of the Wills Act 1837 (as amended), ensuring that there are adequate safeguards against abuse or exploitation of the vulnerable will continue to provide a considerable challenge to those seeking to offer a fully automated will-writing service. However, a clear advantage offered by the use of IT is the ability to store and then easily retrieve specific information about the client, which enables the firm to provide a more client-focused service. For example, the client database can be programmed automatically to generate a reminder letter to clients of the need to review a will/enduring/lasting power of attorney after a given period of time. Such a system may, however, be counter-productive if there is insufficient staff available to respond to the work generated.

Whilst the use of the internet to prepare and send draft wills inevitably will increase, the creation and recognition of totally electronic wills using electronic signatures is a more complex matter and is unlikely to be widely implemented in the near future.

12.12.5   Further advice and information

- The Wills and Equity Committee published guidance in connection with the preparation of wills on the internet, which was published by the Law Society in May 2000 and appeared in (2000) 14 *Probate Section Newsletter* (June).
- The Law Society has also prepared guidelines for best practice in respect of electronic mail, originally published in 2000. A revised and expanded guide was published in November 2005 and can be accessed on the Law Society's website (**www.lawsociety.org.uk**).
- The Department of Trade and Industry website (**www.dti.gov.uk**) contains useful information concerning electronic signatures and other e-commerce issues.
- Susan Singleton, *E-commerce – A Practical Guide to the Law* (Gower Publishing, 2003) is a useful reference book including practical advice and precedent clauses written by a solicitor specialising in e-commerce.

Points and actions that solicitors should consider regarding wills prepared via the internet include the following.

- You could choose to ignore the internet and continue with traditional service.
- Consider your market carefully – do you prepare a lot of simple wills or are they complex?
- Litigation involving wills has increased dramatically in recent years – do you have the necessary expertise and the IT knowledge to provide the service?
- You could create a website of services offered by the firm, plus information for clients and a checklist that the client can download to use to collate information before a face-to-face meeting (this could be an effective marketing tool).

- You could create an interactive website enabling clients to complete a questionnaire to send to the firm but then still post the will to the client.
- You could set up a totally electronic system, with payment by credit card and the will dispatched electronically.
- Any information on the website must be accurate and regularly updated.
- Insurance-loading may become an issue in the future.
- Be careful about relying on retainers and make sure you have written agreement from clients and that they understand the terms of the agreement.
- Any website should be protected by a firewall and up-to-date intrusion detection software.

CHAPTER 13

The law on probate and succession: a review

Lesley King

There are many excellent works covering the law relating to probate and succession already available (see **Further reading**). This Handbook is not intended to be a legal textbook. However, a brief summary of the principal legal issues is included here on the basis that this may be helpful generally, and also may act as a pointer to some of the grounds on which the validity of a will, or parts of it, may be challenged.

13.1 IS THE WILL VALID?

Check the following matters.

13.1.1 Age

Was the testator or testatrix over 18 (or, if a minor, a soldier on actual military service or a mariner or seaman at sea) at the time the will was made?

13.1.2 Formalities

Wills Act 1837, s.9 states:
No will shall be valid unless:

(a) it is in writing and signed by the testator, or by some other person in his presence and by his direction; and
(b) it appears that the testator intended by his signature to give effect to the will; and
(c) the signature is made or acknowledged by the testator in the presence of two or more witnesses present at the same time; and
(d) each witness either:

   (i) attests and signs the will; or
   (ii) acknowledges his signature, in the presence of the testator (but not necessarily in the presence of any other witness).

Whereas previously the signature had to be at the foot or end of the will, the rule now is that in (b) above. The emphasis is on giving effect to the will as far as possible whilst not opening the door to fraud.

Signature is given a wide meaning: a mark, an initial, and even a thumb print have all been held to suffice, but not a seal. Even an incomplete signature will do: *Re Chalcraft* [1948] P 222; *In the Estate of Cook* [1960] 1 All ER 689. See also *Weatherhill* v. *Pearce* [1995] 1 WLR 592. Presence is also given a wide meaning: see *Couser* v. *Couser* [1996] 1 WLR 1301.

Attestation clause

Whilst an attestation clause is not required by Wills Act 1837, s.9, if such a clause is included and recites that the formalities of s.9 were observed, it will raise the presumption of due execution. Further, the inclusion of such a clause will normally avoid the necessity of providing the registrar with an affidavit of due execution.

The presence of an attestation clause reciting that the formalities have been complied has been held to create a powerful presumption which requires the strongest evidence to rebut. See the Court of Appeal decision in *Sherrington* v. *Sherrington* [2005] EWCA Civ 326.

13.1.3 Mental capacity

Requirements

Did the testator or testatrix understand:

- the nature of his or her act and its effects;
- the extent of his or her property; and
- the moral claims which ought to be considered?

For the classic statement of the test of testamentary capacity, see *Banks* v. *Goodfellow* (1870) LR5QB 549.

The testator or testatrix must understand:

- the nature of the act;
- the claims he or she ought to consider;
- the extent of the property he or she has to dispose.

In addition the testator or testatrix must:

- not be subject to any disorder of the mind as shall 'poison his affections, pervert his sense of right or prevent the exercise of his natural faculties' i.e. he or she must not be suffering from an insane delusion.

Proof of capacity

Capacity is presumed unless the contrary is shown. There is a presumption in favour of a duly executed will if it is rational on the face of it, i.e. those opposing it must produce evidence to suggest lack of capacity. It will then be for those putting forward the will to establish capacity. A will fails if the person putting it forward cannot discharge the burden of proof (see *Vaughan* v. *Vaughan* [2002] EWHC 699). If the testator or testatrix generally lacked mental capacity (e.g. he or she was mentally ill), lack of capacity is presumed; this can be rebutted. A person alleging that a will was made in a lucid interval will have to prove this (see *Brown* v. *Deacy* [2002] WTLR 781).

The time for testing capacity is normally when the will is executed. However, if the testator or testatrix was competent when giving instructions, but not at actual execution, the will is nonetheless valid if he or she recalls giving the instructions and believes the will to accord with them: *Parker* v. *Felgate* (1883) 8 PD 171. For a recent example of the principle being applied to save a will see *Clancy* v. *Clancy* [2003] EWHC 1885.

13.1.4   Intention

Requirements

The testator or testatrix must intend:

* to make a will; and
* to make the particular will executed. He or she must, therefore, know and approve its contents: *Guardhouse* v. *Blackburn* (1886) LR1P&D 109.

Where a capable testator or testatrix has signed the will, there will normally be a presumption of knowledge and approval. There may be suspicious circumstances which rebut the presumption so that the burden falls on the beneficiary to dispel suspicion that the will was not the product of the testator's or testatrix's free will: *Barry* v. *Butlin* (1838) 2 Moo. PC 480.

Proof of intention

Knowledge and approval of the particular will are presumed from the fact that the testator or testatrix had capacity and executed the will, unless:

* he or she was blind or illiterate or the will has been signed by someone else on his or her behalf (e.g. in the case of someone totally paralysed). Here the registrar must be satisfied that the testator or testatrix had knowledge of the will's contents and execution;

162

- suspicious circumstances are present (e.g. the will substantially benefits the person who prepared it). Here, the greater the degree of suspicion, the stronger must be the affirmative proof to remove it: *Fulton* v. *Andrew* (1875) LR7HL 448; *Wintle* v. *Nye* [1959] 1 WLR 284. If there is a question of suspicious circumstances, is there a careful and full record of events? In some cases the burden of proof may be so heavy as to be impossible to discharge, as in *Wintle* v. *Nye* itself.

Cases such as *Fuller* v. *Strum* [2002] 1 WLR 1097 and *Hart* v. *Dabbs* [2001] 1 WLR 527 suggest that where a will is simple and straightforward and the testator or testatrix had an opportunity to read it, the court may well accept that he or she knew and approved the contents even where a beneficiary was concerned in the preparation of the will. See also *Shuck* v. *Loveridge* [2005] EWHC 72, Ch.

Rebutting the presumption of knowledge and approval

If knowledge and approval are presumed, those opposing the will must prove that such knowledge and approval were absent by establishing that:

- the testator or testatrix was induced to make the will by force, fear or fraud; or
- he or she was subjected to undue influence and so did not make the will voluntarily. In the case of a will, undue influence must be tantamount to coercion, i.e. the testator or testatrix being driven to make the will against his or her wishes, e.g. by physical threats or actual violence, or incessant nagging may suffice: *Wingrove* v. *Wingrove* (1885) 11 PD 81. However, persuasion (appeals to sentiment, ties of kindred, etc.) is permissible.

Motives are irrelevant.

13.1.5 Mistake

Mistake will invalidate a will, or that part of it included by mistake, but only if the relevant words are present without the testator's or testatrix's knowledge: it will not save a disposition where the testator or testatrix was mistaken as to the effect or meaning of the words used. Thus, he or she is deemed to know and approve the technical language used by the person drafting the will: even though that person was mistaken as to its legal effects, such language must be admitted to probate: *Re Horrocks (Deceased)* [1939] P 168.

Conversely, a mere clerical slip or error (such as a typing mistake) will generally be omitted from probate unless it has been brought to the testator's or testatrix's notice: *Re Morris* [1971] P 62.

13.2 HAS A DOCUMENT BEEN INCORPORATED?

To be incorporated as part of a will an unexecuted document must be:

- in existence at the date of execution of the will;
- referred to in the will as already existing; and
- clearly identified in or identifiable from the will.

Care should be taken to avoid reference in a will to an existing document if incorporation is not intended. The registrar may require production of any such document, with evidence of possible incorporation.

The consequence of incorporation is that the document incorporated will be open to public scrutiny, as it will be admitted to probate with the will.

13.3 ARE TWO WILLS MUTUAL?

See **12.1.5** for a discussion of the requirements for mutual wills.

Be aware that once one testator or testatrix dies with a will in the agreed terms, the property of the survivor becomes subject to a trust. The property will pass to the agreed beneficiary even if the surviving testator or testatrix makes a new will purporting to leave the property elsewhere.

Re Hobley Deceased (1997) *The Times*, 16 July (reported at [2006] WTLR 467) shows that there can be difficulties in deciding whether or not the first testator has died with a will in the agreed terms where there has been any kind of alteration to the agreed will.

There is a useful article on cases on mutual wills in [1997] *Trusts and Estates*, November, 83.

13.4 TYPES OF LEGACY

Legacies may be categorised as follows.

13.4.1 Specific

This is a gift of property forming part of the testator's or testatrix's estate at death and distinguished in the will from other property of the same kind, e.g. 'my race horse Red Rum', 'my dwelling-house Blackacre, or such other dwelling-house in which I shall reside at the date of my death'.

Even a gift of money may be a specific legacy (*Re Wedmore* [1907] 2 Ch 277) although this is relatively rare.

13.4.2   General

This is a gift of property not distinguished in the will from other property of the same kind, e.g. 'to X the sum of £5,000; to Y £5,000 shares in ICI'. Whilst most general legacies are of money, it is not essential that they be so – although clearly an attempt to give a general legacy of some types of property would create problems and might well be void for uncertainty (e.g. 'to X a horse' – how does one define a horse, what value, etc?).

13.4.3   Demonstrative

This is a general legacy payable out of a specific designated fund, e.g. '£1,000 payable out of my paid-up share account with X Building Society'. Here, in so far as the fund is still in existence at the testator's or testatrix's death, it will be treated as a specific legacy. In so far as it is not, it will be treated as a general legacy and abate accordingly should there be insufficient in the estate to discharge debts without recourse to the other general legacies.

The distinction between specific, demonstrative and general legacies is particularly important because:

- a specific legacy is subject to ademption; a general one is not, e.g. if Red Rum (see above) has been sold, given away, or has died during the testator's or testatrix's lifetime, the legatee will get nothing unless there is a substitutional provision (as in the case of the gift of Blackacre (again, see above));
- a general legacy must be applied for payment of debts before a specific one;
- a demonstrative legacy is only treated as a specific legacy in so far as the designated fund remains at the testator's or testatrix's death.

13.4.4   Pecuniary

This is a gift of money which may be specific, general or demonstrative. Administration of Estates Act 1925, s.55(i)(ix) defines a pecuniary legacy as including:

> an annuity, a general legacy, a demonstrative legacy, so far as ... not discharged out of the designated property, and any other general direction by a testator for the payment of money, including all death duties free from which any devise, bequest or payment is made to take effect.

Thus a legacy specified to be free of tax or free of expenses will be treated as a legacy conferring an extra benefit, the amount of which would be equivalent to the tax or expenses being paid out of the estate.

13.4.5 Residuary

The residue is what is left after all debts, liabilities, legacies and other expenses have been paid.

Where residue is left to be divided between an exempt and a non-exempt beneficiary (e.g. a charity and a member of the deceased's family) problems arise as to how the burden of tax should fall. See the discussion of *Re Benham* in para.16.9.

With regard to legacies to institutions (including charities), the solicitor will need to know whether or not the institution is charitable, as the *cy-près* doctrine only applies to charities, and charities are not bound by the rule against perpetuities. This means that a charity can generally take an interest under a will, no matter how distantly in the future it vests.

The Charity Commission (see **Useful addresses**) may be able to advise if problems arise. More information on charitable beneficiaries is included at **16.8** onwards.

13.5   IS INTEREST PAYABLE?

Legacies should be paid with due diligence and usually within the executors' year. Even where the will directs earlier payment, this cannot be compelled.

Interest (payable from residue) normally runs from the time when payment is due (or otherwise if so provided by the will, e.g. 'and I direct that the said legacy shall carry the interim income').

Exceptionally, interest runs from death where the legacy is:

* charged on realty;
* in satisfaction of a debt charged on unconverted realty;
* to the testator's or testatrix's minor child(ren); or
* to any other minor if the will shows an intention that the income is to be used for maintenance or education.

At what rate is interest paid?

Unless the will provides otherwise, interest is paid at the same rate that it would be payable if the court ordered an account of legacies. CPR, Practice Direction 40 provides that this is normally at the basic rate payable for the time being on funds in court.

13.6   LOST WILLS

Where a will is lost it is possible to apply for proof of a draft, copy or reconstruction under NCPR 1987, Rule 54. The application has to be accompanied by an affidavit setting out the grounds of the application and such evidence as is available as to:

- the due execution of the will;
- its existence after the death of the testator or testatrix;
- the accuracy of the copy or other evidence of the contents of the will;

together with the consents in writing of any person, not under a disability, who would be prejudiced by the grant.

If a will known to have been in the possession of the deceased cannot be found after his or her death, there is a presumption that the deceased destroyed it with the intention of revoking it. The presumption can, of course, be rebutted by appropriate evidence.

In *Rowe* v. *Clarke* [2006] WTLR 347 the court had to consider the presumption where it was unclear whether or not the will had been in existence after the deceased's death. The court held that there is no requirement on the party relying on the presumption to prove the non-existence of the will at the time of death (see *Sykes* v. *Sykes* (1907) 23 TLR 747). Therefore the presumption did arise. However, the strength of the presumption in any given case depends on the character of the custody which the testator had over the will, and the character of that custody in the present case was exceptionally weak. The deceased was not careful or well organised with his papers.

13.7   PROVISION ON INTESTACY

Note: The statutory legacies quoted are applicable for deaths on and after 1 December 1993. At the time of writing there are proposals to make substantial increases to the amount of the statutory legacy payable to surviving spouses and civil partners.

13.7.1   Deceased married or in a civil partnership at death

The Law Reform (Succession) Act 1995 introduced a survivorship period of 28 days in respect of deaths occurring on or after 1 January 1996 for spouses (and civil partners).

(a)   If the intestate leaves issue (e.g. children and/or grandchildren) the spouse or civil partner takes:

    (i)   personal chattels absolutely (as defined by Administration of Estates Act 1925, s.55(1)(x)); and

    (ii) £125,000 plus interest at the rate of 6 per cent from death until payment (free of tax, with costs and interest coming from the residue); and

(iii) a life interest in half the residue, the remainder and the other half going to the children on the statutory trusts.

(b) If the intestate leaves no issue, but does leave a parent or brother or sister of the whole blood or their issue, the spouse or civil partner takes:

(i) the personal chattels absolutely; and
(ii) £200,000 plus interest as above; and
(iii) half the residue absolutely.

(c) If the intestate leaves no issue, no parents, no brothers or sisters of the whole blood or their issue, the spouse or civil partner takes the whole estate absolutely.

13.7.2 Deceased dies without a spouse or civil partner

The estate goes to the intestate's:

(a) issue on the statutory trusts; if none,
(b) parents; if none,
(c) brothers and sisters of the whole blood on the statutory trusts, failing whom to remoter relations and, if none, to the Crown or the Duchy of Cornwall. The Treasury Solicitor will deal with the estate in these cases (see **15.3** below). The Treasury Solicitor has a discretion to make payments from the estate to anyone unrelated but close to the deceased during his or her lifetime.

'Personal chattels' excludes any which are used for business purposes. It also excludes money or securities for money, but has been held to include, for example, valuable collections.

Under the statutory trusts (Administration of Estates Act 1925, s.47), a child of the intestate has a contingent interest in the estate. This is satisfied if the child reaches 18 or marries or forms a civil partnership before that. A child dying under 18, unmarried and without having formed a civil partnership, is treated as never having existed.

If a child of the intestate does not survive the intestate, but he or she leaves a child or children, then that child or those children will take his, her or their deceased parent's share (in equal shares if more than one), again contingently on attaining 18 or marrying or forming a civil partnership before that.

13.7.3 Spouses and civil partners: special rights

A surviving spouse or civil partner may elect (generally within 12 months of the grant) to do the following.

• Redeem any life interest in the estate in return for a lump sum (Administration of Estates Act 1925, s.47). If the spouse or civil partner so elects, this does not count as a transfer of value for IHT purposes. He or she is treated as if, instead of being entitled to the life interest, he or she had been entitled to the lump sum from the outset.

- Take the matrimonial home, or the deceased's share in it, in or towards satisfaction of any absolute or capitalised interest in the estate (Intestates' Estates Act 1952, Sched.2). The value of the house is taken at the date of appropriation, not of death: *Re Collins* [1925] 1 WLR 309. To qualify, the surviving spouse or civil partner must be living in the house concerned at the intestate's death.

Exceptions to the right of the surviving spouse or civil partner to take the matrimonial home include cases where the intestate's interest in the property was a tenancy expirable (by notice or otherwise) within two years of death and where the house forms part of a commercial unit, such as a farmhouse on a working farm or a flat in a family hotel.

If the value of the matrimonial home is more than the statutory legacy, the spouse or civil partner may make up the shortfall.

Under this provision the surviving spouse or civil partner is able to *require* PRs to make this appropriation. This is in direct contrast to the position under Administration of Estates Act 1925, s.41, under which PRs have the power (whether the deceased died testate or intestate) to appropriate his or her property in (or towards) satisfaction of interests in the estate. Such an appropriation will require the consent of the beneficiary unless the will has removed the need for consent.

13.7.4   Hotchpot

The Law Reform (Succession) Act 1995 abolished the rules as to hotchpot in their entirety for deaths occurring on or after 1 January 1996.

13.8   JOINT PROPERTY

Joint property can cause a number of problems for solicitors.

In *Carr-Glynn* v. *Frearson* [1998] 4 All ER 225, the testatrix wished to leave her interest in a house to her niece. She was uncertain whether her interest was held as joint tenant or as tenant in common with her nephew. The solicitor explained to her that the will would be ineffective if the house was held as joint tenants and that it would be necessary to sever the joint tenancy. The solicitor offered to obtain the title deeds to check. The client said that she would do it herself but did not do so. When she died, it was discovered that the house had been held as joint tenants so the will was ineffective.

The Court of Appeal found the solicitor negligent: the service of a notice of severance was part of the will-making process. The niece was as much an intended beneficiary of the severance as she was of the new will. The solicitor should have explained that it was possible to serve the notice of severance as a precaution without any need to check the title deeds:

> She did not tell the testatrix that the doubt, identified in her letter of 6 February 1989, could and should be laid to rest by the service of a notice of severance before or at the same time as the will was executed; that there was no need to obtain the deeds before serving the notice; and that there was nothing to be gained, and potentially much to be lost, by delay.

It is important to check the basis of ownership and, if there is any doubt, advise service of a notice of severance.

Re Woolnough (Deceased) [2002] WTLR 595 confirms that it is possible to sever a joint tenancy in any of the ways possible before the Law of Property Act 1925 (see **12.3.3**).

In *Re Woolnough* a brother and sister had made wills leaving their interest in a house owned as joint tenants to the other for life with a gift over to a third party. After the sister's death the brother left the house to charity. If the joint tenancy had already been severed, only half of the value of the house was in his estate. If it had not, the whole value of the house was his.

The fact that the two had made wills giving each other a mere life interest in the property was sufficient to amount to an agreement to sever:

> It is not a case of one of them acting behind the back of the other. The reference in the Will to a half share makes it clear that they were treating their share as disposed of by their Wills.

It would not, of course, have amounted to severance had one joint tenant alone made a will dealing with the half share.

When administering an estate there may be cases where it is necessary to investigate whether or not there was an earlier severance by consent. Although an estate may appear to have acquired the entire interest in a property by survivorship, there may have been severance by consent at an earlier stage.

13.9 RELEVANT STATUTES

13.9.1 Law of Property (Miscellaneous Provisions) Act 1994

The Law of Property (Miscellaneous Provisions) Act 1994 came into effect on 1 July 1995. Helpful articles on this, by Philip Rossdale and Robin Towns, appeared in [1995] *Solicitors Journal*, 28 July and [1995] *New Law Journal*, Probate Supplement, 29 September. The 1994 Act affects sales of land by PRs and also vests intestates' property pre-grant in the Public Trustee (instead of the President of the Family Division).

13.9.2   Trusts of Land and Appointment of Trustees Act 1996

The Trusts of Land and Appointment of Trustees Act 1996 (TLATA 1996) came into force on 1 January 1997. It prevents the creation of new trusts for sale and strict settlements in respect of land and introduces the 'trust of land'. Trustees of land have all the powers of an absolute beneficial owner including the power of sale. Property of an intestate is no longer held on a trust for sale.

Where a will creates a continuing trust, s.11 imposes an obligation on trustees of land to consult beneficiaries of full age with an interest in possession when exercising any function in respect of land.

Section 12 gives a beneficiary with an interest in possession a right to occupy land in certain circumstances.

Section 13 allows trustees to regulate the respective rights of beneficiaries where more than one has an interest in possession.

Section 19 allows beneficiaries of full age and capacity entitled to the whole beneficial interest to compel the existing trustees to retire in favour of new trustees of their choice. See **13.10.3** below.

All of these provisions can be varied by the will.

Helpful articles appear in [1996] *Solicitors Journal*, 1154 on the will-drafting implications of TLATA 1996, in [1996] *Family Law*, December, 736 on the provisions of the Act relating to joint ownership, expansion of trustees' powers and beneficiaries' right of occupation and in [1997] *Conveyancing*, July/August, 263 on drafting to restrict trustees' powers.

13.9.3   Trustee Delegation Act 1999

The Trustee Delegation Act 1999 came into force on 1 March 2000. It prescribed a new short form of power of attorney, amended Trustee Act 1925, s.25 and repealed Enduring Powers of Attorney Act 1985, s.3(3).

In *Inland Revenue Commissioners* v. *Eversden and Another (Executors of Greenstock, Deceased)* [2002] EWHC 1360 (Ch); [2002] STC 1109, Lightman J suggested that TLATA 1996, ss.12 and 13 had affected the legal position of co-owners.

Trustee Act 1925, s.25, as amended, allows trustees to delegate all powers and discretions but subject to various restrictions. The appointment cannot be an enduring power; cannot exceed 12 months (although the appointment can be renewed); cannot be to a sole trustee; the donor remains liable for the acts of the attorney; and notice of the delegation must be given to all co-trustees.

Enduring Powers of Attorney Act 1985, s.3(3) allowed trustees to delegate all trustee functions and contained none of the Trustee Act 1925, s.25 safe-guards. In particular it allowed a sole co-trustee to be appointed as attorney despite the rule that two trustees are required to give a good receipt for capital money. There was a feeling that Enduring Powers of Attorney Act 1985, s.3(3) had gone too far in removing the safeguards of the Trustee Act 1925, s.25, hence the changes introduced by the 1999 Act.

The main effects of the Trustee Delegation Act 1999 are as follows:

- Section 7 confirms and strengthens the rules that capital money must be paid to, and a valid receipt for capital money must be given by, at least two trustees, and that a conveyance or deed must be made by at least two trustees to overreach any interests affecting a legal interest. In effect two individuals must always act. So, for this purpose a trustee acting on his or her own behalf and as attorney for all the other trustees only counts as one person. The provisions relating to delegation must be read subject to this.
- Prior to the 1999 Act co-owners could not delegate by using a general power of attorney. They had to use a Trustee Act 1925, s.25 trustee power of appointment or an enduring power. Section 1 of the 1999 Act allows trustees with a beneficial interest in the trust property (for example, co-owners) after 1 January 2000 to use a general power of attorney to delegate their trustee functions in relation to land, the proceeds of sale of land and income arising from it. The effect is that they are freed from the restrictions of s.25 so there is no limit on the length of time the delegation can last, it can be to a sole co-trustee and notice need not be given to co-trustees. In a typical husband and wife co-ownership, one could delegate to the other. However, under s.7 of the 2000 Act there will still need to be two individuals to give a good receipt for capital money. If the attorney wanted to sell, there would have to be another trustee appointed.
- Section 8 gives an attorney who cannot sell because there is no other trustee, power under an amended Trustee Act 1925, s.36 to appoint a further trustee. However, s.8 is a complicated section and only applies where there is a registered enduring power under which the attorney is authorised to exercise the donor's trustee functions.
- Enduring Powers of Attorney Act 1985, s.3(3) is repealed so that from 1 March 2000 onwards trustees who do not have a beneficial interest in the trust property can now only delegate their powers and discretions by complying with the requirements of Trustee Act 1925, s.25. The delegation can be by an ordinary s.25 trustee power or it can be by enduring power. However, whichever route is used s.25 limits the delegation to 12 months. The only advantage to using an enduring power is that the incapacity of the trustee will not revoke it. The attorney will also be able to appoint an additional trustee under s.8 of the 1999 Act.

Helpful summaries of the Trustee Delegation Act 1999 appear in [2000] *Solicitors Journal*, 3 March, (2000) 64 *Conveyancer* and [2000] *Gazette*, 2 March. An interesting letter published in (2002) 33 *Trusts and Estates Law*

Journal, 13 suggests including in wills and trusts a wider power for specified persons to remove trustees who are becoming mentally incapable and, in appropriate cases, to appoint a replacement.

13.9.4 Mental Capacity Act 2005

At the time of writing the Mental Capacity Act is not yet in force. When it does come into force it will no longer be possible to create new enduring powers of attorney although existing powers will continue to be effective. Instead, it will be possible to create lasting powers of attorney.

Lasting powers will have to be registered before they can be used. The donor must get an appropriate person to certify that the donor understood the purpose of the power and the scope of the authority that it confers and also that the donor was not subject to any fraud or undue pressure. The donor will be able to make a separate lasting power, if desired, to authorise attorney(s) to make decisions about health and welfare on behalf of the donor.

13.9.5 Trustee Act 2000

The Trustee Act 2000 came into force on 1 February 2001. It implies a set of default powers into trusts unless the trust document specifies differently by exclusion, modification or widening and irrespective of whether the trust was created before or after 1 February 2001. The powers implied are a general investment power, power to use agents, nominees and custodians and a general power to insure. These are dealt with at **13.11** below.

The Trustee Act 2000 makes various changes to the law on charging clauses. Under s.28:

- a trustee of a non-charitable trust who acts in a professional capacity (defined as one providing services in connection with the management and administration of trusts) can charge for work that a lay person could do without express authorisation in the charging clause;
- a charging clause is no longer treated as a legacy so:
  - a partner in a firm with the benefit of a charging clause can witness the will without losing the benefit of the clause;
  - the charges will not abate with other pecuniary legacies where there are insufficient funds (so it is no longer necessary to provide for this expressly in the clause).

Under s.29 a trustee of a non-charitable trust who is acting in a professional capacity can charge reasonable remuneration for his or her services without a charging clause, provided a majority of co-trustees authorises it. This does not apply to a sole trustee (other than trust corporations).

The Act also imposes a general duty of care. Whenever the duty applies, the trustee must exercise such care and skill as is reasonable in the circumstances, having regard in particular:

- to any special knowledge or experience that the trustee has or holds himself out as having, and
- in the case of a professional trustee, to any special knowledge or experience it is reasonable to expect that person to have.

13.9.6 Proceeds of Crime Act 2002

The relevant provisions of POCA 2002 were outlined at **4.3.8**.

There are three main offences which a probate solicitor could commit under the Act. They are:

- concealing, disguising, converting, transferring or removing criminal property from the UK (s.327);
- entering into or becoming concerned in an arrangement which the solicitor knows or suspects facilitates (by whatever means) the acquisition, retention, use or control of criminal property by or on behalf of another person (s.328);
- being in the regulated sector and failing to disclose knowledge or suspicion that another person is engaged in money laundering (s.330).

The subject is too large to address adequately in a book of this nature. Practitioners should refer to the Law Society's website where up-to-date information is available, in particular the Anti-Money Laundering Guidance for Solicitors Conducting Private Client Work (see **Appendix A1**).

Note the following key points:

1. Solicitors can be at risk of an offence if their work involves assisting with the distribution of assets which include suspected 'criminal property'.
2. A defence may be available if a report is made to the Serious and Organised Crime Agency (SOCA), and if relevant, 'appropriate consent' is obtained or can be deemed through lapse of time (see paras.2.23–2.27 of the Law Society's Money Laundering Guidance – Pilot January 2004 (the Guidance)).
3. However, because of the judgment in *Bowman* v. *Fels*, before a solicitor reports to NCIS/SOCA a key consideration will be whether the solicitor's knowledge or suspicion of money laundering is based on information received in legally professionally privileged circumstances.
4. Whenever solicitors are conducting any 'relevant business' for a client, they will need to comply with the Money Laundering Regulations 2003, SI 2003/3075 (see paras.3.6–3.15 of the Guidance). Suggested identification methods for individuals, estates and trusts are also covered in Chapter 3 of the Guidance.

5.   Although will writing is not 'relevant business' for the purposes of the Money Laundering Regulations 2003, ancillary services provided by solicitors when drafting wills may be. For example, tax advice and trust services are within the definition and administration of estates is likely to be. However, obtaining a grant of probate may fall outside the definitions.

Risk areas

ADMINISTRATION OF ESTATES

Since the administration of estates is likely to be relevant business, solicitors could be guilty of the s.330 (regulated sector) offence of failure to report as well as offences under ss.328 and 329. Solicitors should be alive to factors which can increase the money laundering risk of the work they are undertaking and act accordingly.

An extreme example of when administration of an estate may constitute a money laundering offence would be where a solicitor dealing with administration knows or suspects that the deceased was accused or convicted of acquisitive criminal conduct during his or her lifetime, perhaps because the solicitor's firm acted in the relevant criminal litigation.

Where a solicitor forms knowledge or suspicion that the deceased improperly claimed welfare benefits during his or her lifetime, for example because the capital of the deceased took them over the financial threshold for the relevant benefit claimed, there will be 'criminal property' included in the estate, and so usually a money laundering report may be required.

Whilst administering an estate a solicitor may form knowledge or suspicion that beneficiaries are not intending to pay the correct amount of tax, or are avoiding some other financial penalty, e.g. creditors, or the Assets Recovery Agency. For example, beneficiaries may be reluctant to disclose gifts that they have received from the deceased less than seven years before death. Depending on the circumstances these types of matters may not in fact constitute money laundering because no criminal conduct has yet occurred, and therefore there is no 'criminal property', but solicitors should carefully consider their position in conduct terms under Principle 12.02 because they may be in breach of the law or professional conduct rules.

TRUSTS

Although trusts are most commonly used for legitimate reasons, they can also be used as money laundering vehicles. Discretionary trusts and complex offshore trusts are most vulnerable to money laundering. When setting up trusts, solicitors should remain alive to the warning signs of money laundering, and consider whether the purpose of the trust could be money laundering. Information about the purpose of the trust, including why any unusual structure or jurisdiction has been used, can help allay concerns. Similarly, information about the provider of the funds, and those who have control over the funds, may also assist.

CHARITIES

Whether the Money Laundering Regulations 2003 apply to work undertaken for charities depends upon whether 'relevant business' is being undertaken. Where the work will constitute 'relevant business' the charity will need to be identified. In common with trusts, whilst the majority of charities are used for legitimate reasons, they can also be used as money laundering/terrorist financing vehicles. Solicitors who act for charities may need to consider the purpose of the charity itself. Remaining alert to the warning signs of money laundering may assist with this. An extreme example of the misuse of charities may be terrorist purposes, and where there is concern, reference should be made to the Bank of England terrorist lists.

Where a solicitor is acting for a charity and is due to receive money on behalf of the charity from an individual or company donor, the solicitor needs to be alert to unusual circumstances including significant sums. Where the charity is due to receive a bequest from an estate similar considerations apply.

POWERS OF ATTORNEY/RECEIVERSHIP

Execution of a power of attorney for clients does not itself constitute a 'financial transaction' for the purposes of the Money Laundering Regulations 2003. However, solicitors acting for an attorney, or as an attorney themselves, are likely to be undertaking 'relevant business'. Similarly, solicitors acting for receivers appointed by the Court of Protection, or who are appointed as receivers themselves, are likely to be undertaking 'relevant business'.

All these areas of work can give rise to money laundering issues. For example, a solicitor acting as an attorney may learn financial information about the donor, such as non-payment of tax or wrongful receipt of welfare benefits. Whether this is a matter which is reportable to NCIS/SOCA as money laundering will depend upon a detailed analysis of the *Bowman* v. *Fels* guidance, especially where the knowledge or suspicion has been formed from information received in legally professionally privileged circumstances. Where the Court of Protection has an interest because of a receivership or registered enduring power of attorney, consideration will need to be given as to whether the Master needs to be informed. Informing the Master is unlikely to be tipping off because it is unlikely to prejudice an investigation, which is a necessary criterion for either of the tipping-off offences.

If a solicitor forms knowledge or suspicion that a donee has already completed an improper financial transaction this may amount to a money laundering suspicion, and a money laundering report to NCIS/SOCA may be required, depending on whether legal professional privilege applies. However, solicitors may find it hard to decide whether they have a suspicion if the background is a family dispute, and it can help to discuss matters with Professional Ethics.

Legal professional privilege

The case of *Bowman* v. *Fels* has drastically altered the approach private client solicitors undertaking private client work should take to their reporting obligations because of the increased importance of legal professional privilege. Administration of estates or other types of private client work should lead solicitors to consider in detail the *Bowman* v. *Fels* guidance (available on the Law Society's website, **www.lawsociety.org.uk**).

Legal professional privilege is a key consideration and recent case law has defined privilege in transactional work widely. Instructions to prepare wills are likely to be covered by legal professional privilege (unless there is a criminal intention behind the instructions), and after death but before publication of wills, rights to legal professional privilege vest in the PRs.

Warning signs

The Money Laundering Guidance (referred to above) sets out the following warning signs (with a reminder that money laundering techniques change over time). These are general warning signs but many will be relevant to private client practitioners.

The secretive client

6.15   Although it is not always necessary for solicitors to have face to face contact with their clients, dependent upon the circumstances, excessively obstructive or secretive clients might cause solicitors to be suspicious.

Unusual instructions

6.16   Unusual instructions can give rise to concerns because they are unusual in themselves, or because they are unusual in the light of the work usually undertaken by the firm.

6.17   Taking on work which is outside the firm's normal range of expertise can be risky, not only in terms of potential negligence claims, but also because money launderers might decide to use such firms to avoid answering too many questions. An inexperienced solicitor might be more easily influenced into taking steps which a more experienced practitioner would not contemplate. Solicitors should be particularly wary of instructions in niche areas of work in which the firm has no background, but in which the client purports to be an expert. Solicitors should advise their clients about how cases develop, not vice versa.

6.18   If your client is based a long way from your offices think about why you have been instructed. For example have your services have been recommended by another client, or is the matter based near your firm, e.g. a client relocating to a property near your offices. Making these types of enquiries makes good business sense as well as being a sensible anti money laundering check.

6.19   Clients whose instructions, or cases, change in unexpected ways might also be suspicious, especially if the changes are inexplicable. . . . For example, if a client deposits funds in your client account, but then aborts the transaction for no discernible reason, this might be cause for concern. Again, a client may tell you that funds are coming from one source, and at the last minute the source may change, Why?

Unusual settlement requests

6.20   Disputes which are settled too easily could give cause for concern, as can loss making transactions where the loss is avoidable.

6.21   Solicitors should also be wary about dealing with money or property where there is a suspicion that money or property is being transferred in order to avoid the attention of a Trustee in Bankruptcy, Inland Revenue, or a law enforcement agency.

6.22   Settlements paid in cash, or paid direct between parties, might also be suspicious. For example, cash being passed between vendors and purchasers, perhaps at a property auction, might lead to concerns about mortgage fraud or tax evasion if inadequate explanations are given.

Use of client account

6.23   Putting dirty money through a solicitor's client accounts can clean it, whether the money is sent back to the client, on to a third party, or invested in some way. Introducing cash into a banking system can be part of the 'placement' stage of money laundering. Therefore cash can be a warning sign. It can be helpful to think about how the client account could be misused. Client account should only be used for holding client money when necessary to effect legitimate transactions for clients, or for a proper underlying legal purpose.

. . .

6.25   Proceeds of crime can arrive through the banking system. Accounts staff have their part to play in monitoring whether the funds they receive on behalf of a client come from an unusual source. For example, if monies are received from a company, the client might be a director of the company which is a reasonable explanation so long as they have the authority to use the money in this way. However, other sources of finance might lead to further enquiries, especially if the client has not mentioned what they intend to do in advance. If a decision is made to accept funds from a third party, perhaps because time is short, enquiries might properly be made of how and why the third party is helping with funding.

6.26   Solicitors should think carefully before disclosing their bank account details as these allow money to be deposited into client accounts without prior knowledge.

. . .

Suspect territory

6.31   Some jurisdictions have not brought their anti money laundering procedures into line with the international community, and for that reason they can pose a greater risk of money laundering. Reference can be made to the Financial Action Task Force (**www.oecd.org/fatf** . . .) which produces up to date information about different countries. In particularly high risk situations special consideration might be whether the client appears on the Terrorist list, or whether funds are going to be sent to somebody on the Terrorist list, . . .

13.9.7   Civil Partnership Act 2004

The Civil Partnership Act 2004 received Royal Assent on 18 November 2004 and came into force on 5 December 2005. It deals separately with changes to the law in England and Wales, Scotland and Northern Ireland. The aim is to put civil partners on the same statutory footing as spouses within each of the three jurisdictions. The relevant property provisions in relation to succession to property are found in ss.71–72 and Sched.4. Enactments relating to wills, administration of estates, claims under IPFDA 1975 and the provisions of Married Women's Property Act 1882, s.11 are amended to apply in relation to civil partnerships as they do to marriages.

The Act does not contain any general statement that the word 'spouse' is to be construed as including civil partners in private documents. In wills and trusts if the intention is to include a civil partner in a class of beneficiaries it is necessary to say so.

The Act has some implications when it comes to the wording of oaths. If a deceased dies intestate without ever marrying or forming a civil partnership, he or she will be described as a spinster or bachelor. If there is a surviving civil partner, the civil partner must be described as the 'lawful [male] [female] civil partner and [the only person now entitled to] [one of the persons entitled to share in] the estate of the said intestate'. If the intestate had a civil partner who predeceased, it will be necessary to declare that the intestate died 'without a surviving lawful [male] [female] civil partner'.

13.9.8   Gender Recognition Act 2004

The Gender Recognition Act 2004 came into force on 4 April 2005. Its purpose is to provide transsexuals with legal recognition in their acquired gender. Legal recognition will follow from the issue of a full gender recognition certificate by a Gender Recognition Panel.

Before issuing a certificate, the Panel must be satisfied that the applicant:

- has, or has had, gender dysphoria;
- has lived in the acquired gender throughout the preceding two years; and
- intends to continue to live in the acquired gender until death.

Where applicants have been recognised under the law of another country or territory as having changed gender, the Panel need only be satisfied that the country or territory in question has been approved by the Secretary of State.

The effect of legal recognition is that, for example, a male-to-female trans-sexual person will be legally recognised as a woman in English law for all purposes (s.9(1)). The transsexual will receive a new birth certificate in the new gender. There will be no link between the original certificate and the new one, which will presumably make life difficult for genealogists.

Section 15 provides that a change of gender does not affect the distribution of property under a will or other instrument made before the day on which the Act comes into force. For wills or other instruments made after that day, the general principle stated in s.9(1) will apply. For example, if a will refers to the 'eldest daughter', and a person who was previously a son becomes the 'eldest daughter' following recognition in the acquired gender, that person (subject to s.18) will inherit as the 'eldest daughter'.

There is protection for PRs under s.17. They are relieved from any fiduciary duty to inquire whether a gender recognition certificate has been issued to any person or revoked, even if that fact could affect entitlement to property which the PR is responsible for distributing.

The beneficiary will nevertheless retain his or her claim to the property and may enforce this claim, for example, by following the property into the hands of another person who has received it instead.

Under s.18 the court has power to make orders to deal with the situation where the devolution of property under a will or other instrument is different from what it would be but for the change of gender. If, for example, a will left property to 'eldest daughter' of X, and there is an older brother whose gender becomes female under the Act, then the person who was previously the 'eldest daughter' will cease to enjoy that position. A person who is adversely affected by the different disposition can apply to the court and the court, if it is satisfied that it is just to do so, may make such order as it considers appropriate in relation to the person benefiting from the different disposition of the property. There is no guidance as to how the court should exercise its powers.

Neither the Act nor the explanatory notes deal with the situation of a legacy leaving property to 'my son, John' and by the date of death there is no son, John but instead a daughter, Joanna. There is no one who fulfils the description. Will the use of the name be sufficient to identify the person intended?

Obviously, testators who know of the change can review their wills. From a general drafting point of view, it is probably advisable to refer to the desired beneficiaries by name or by a non-gender related description rather than to use a description such as 'the son/daughter of X'. An alternative approach is to include a clause stating that the will is to be construed as if the Act had not been enacted and that gifts are to pass to those who fulfil the relevant description at the date the will was made.

13.9.9   Finance Act 2006

The Finance Act 2006 made fundamental changes to the treatment of trusts for IHT purposes whether the trusts are created by will or in the lifetime of the settlor. Many more trusts will be subject to the regime formerly applying only to discretionary trusts.

After 22 March 2006 it is no longer possible to create new accumulation and maintenance trusts attracting privileged treatment for IHT purposes. However, a trust created for a child of the testator where the child will obtain a vested interest in capital at or before 18 will have the same IHT advantages as an accumulation and maintenance trust. There is special provision for bereaved children who become entitled at or before 25.

A person with an interest in possession created after 22 March 2006 will only be treated as entitled to the underlying capital if it is an immediate post-death interest. This means it must be created on death. Interest in possession trusts created in the settlor's lifetime will be subject to the tax regime previously applied to discretionary trusts. Such trusts will be subject to an immediate charge to IHT to the extent that the value transferred exceeds the nil rate band and to anniversary and exit charges.

13.10   APPOINTMENT AND REMOVAL OF TRUSTEES AND PERSONAL REPRESENTATIVES

13.10.1   Retirement

There is no power for a PR who has taken a grant simply to retire from the office of executor in favour of another person. However, where a will appoints a person to act as executor *and* trustee, it will be possible for that person to retire from the office of trustee.

When does a personal representative become a trustee?

This can be a difficult question. Once the PR has ascertained the amount of residue available to the residuary beneficiary and, if appropriate, obtained approval of the estate accounts it is likely that the PR then holds the remaining assets as trustee. If, however, other assets or liabilities were discovered, the PR would have to deal with these assets or liabilities as PR since that office is never lost.

In what circumstances can a trustee retire and/or appoint new trustees?

The circumstances may be covered by the will. If not, the provisions of Trustee Act 1925, ss.36 and 39 will apply. These sections allow a trustee to retire provided this does not result in there being a sole remaining trustee and provided the continuing trustees consent. Continuing trustees can appoint replacement or additional trustees. The PRs of a sole trustee who has died can appoint replacements.

13.10.2 Removal of personal representatives by the court

Under Administration of Justice Act 1985, s.50 the court has a discretion to appoint a new PR or PRs in the place of existing PRs or any of them, or to terminate the appointment of one but not all of the PRs (unless appointing at least one substituted PR).

The court's jurisdiction under s.50 is not limited to cases of conflict between PRs. It can be used where a PR wishes to retire.

Where the court has ordered the administration of the estate under its supervision (a comparatively rare event) it has power to appoint PR(s).

The court has power to remove PRs and appoint new ones under Trustee Act 1925, s.41 where without an order it is 'inexpedient, difficult or impracticable' to appoint a new trustee or new trustees (including PRs). Such appointees may be 'in substitution for or in addition to any existing trustee or trustees'. The wording of s.41 is sufficiently wide to enable the court to remove PRs and trustees from office for other than the common causes – residing permanently abroad, becoming mentally disordered, becoming bankrupt or being convicted of serious crime. In *Probate Disputes and Remedies* (Sweet & Maxwell, 1997), Dawn Goodman and Brendan Hall state that:

> The court will not exercise this jurisdiction lightly and will generally do so only:
>
> (a) when there has been a breach of duty and the court thinks that the estate will not be safe, or will not be administered in accordance with the will or the intestacy rules;
> (b) where it is in the interests of the beneficiaries that the personal representatives be removed; or
> (c) where there is considerable friction between the personal representatives.

In *Letterstedt* v. *Broers* (1884) 9 App Cas 371 the court was at pains to point out that there are no hard and fast rules and that the main guide in these cases must be the welfare of the beneficiaries. In the majority of cases an application is made under Administration of Justice Act 1985, s.50 rather than under Trustee Act 1925, s.41.

There is power under Judicial Trustees Act 1896, s.1 for the court to appoint a judicial trustee but this is rarely used.

The Law Society has power under Solicitors Act 1974 to apply to court for the appointment of a new trustee in substitution for a solicitor who is a controlled trustee. This would be a step of last resort.

13.10.3   Trusts of Land and Appointment of Trustees Act 1996, s.19

It is worth noting that under TLATA 1996, s.19, beneficiaries who are of full age and capacity and between them entitled to the whole beneficial interest can compel the retirement of the existing trustees and the appointment of trustees of their choice.

In the past, beneficiaries who were at odds with their trustees could not simply change the trustees (*Re Brockbank* [1948] Ch 206). In such circumstances they had to bring the trust to an end and then resettle the property with trustees of their choice, but this would frequently have had adverse capital gains tax (CGT) consequences. The new provision is subject to contrary intention in the will or trust instrument. However, for most people the CGT advantage will outweigh the concern over arbitrary replacement of trustees, so only rarely will it be appropriate to exclude the s.19 power.

It is important to note that because of the requirement for full age and capacity and absolute entitlement to the whole beneficial interest there will be comparatively few occasions where s.19 will be relevant.

13.11   POWERS AND DUTIES OF EXECUTORS AND TRUSTEES: A SUMMARY

13.11.1   Powers

Unless the powers of executors and trustees are extended or varied by the will, they are limited to the powers given to them by statute. The main statutory powers are set out below.

Trustee Act 2000, s.3 gives a general power to invest in anything other than land as if the trustees were absolute owners. The power is in addition to any express power but subject to any restrictions contained in the trust instrument. However, nothing in a trust instrument made before 3 August 1961 will be treated as restricting or excluding the general power of investment (s.7(2)). While this power will make little difference to modern, professionally drafted trusts, it makes an enormous difference to trusts arising on intestacy and to older or home-made trusts.

The Act does have important implications for all trustees even those acting under express investment clauses as it imposes additional duties.

Section 4(1) provides that when exercising *any* power of investment trustees must take into account the statutory investment criteria which are:

- the suitability to the trust of investments of the type proposed and of that particular investment as an investment of that type; and
- the need for diversification of investments of the trust, in so far as is appropriate to the circumstances of the trust.

Section 4(2) provides that trustees must review investments from time to time and consider whether they should change investments.

Unless the trustees reasonably conclude that it is unnecessary or inappropriate in all the circumstances to do so, they must obtain and consider proper advice before investing and when reviewing (s.5).

Trustee Act 2000, s.8 gives power to acquire freehold or leasehold land in the UK. This can be for investment or residence by a beneficiary. It does not provide power to buy land abroad or an interest in land.

Trustee Act 2000, ss.11–27 authorise the appointment of agents, nominees and custodians subject to certain safeguards. Trustees will not be liable for the acts of their appointees unless they fail to exercise reasonable care and skill in the appointment or in keeping the arrangements for employment under review.

Section 14 provides that where trustees wish to delegate their asset management function, they must do so in writing and must prepare a policy statement giving guidance as to how the agent is to carry out its functions. The statement should deal with such matters as:

- attitude to risk;
- the balance to be maintained between income and capital;
- level of liquidity;
- attitude to capital gains (undesirable if the life tenant is very elderly and there is a possibility of tax-free uplift on death in the relatively near future);
- willingness to be exposed to foreign currency.

There is a helpful article on the relationship between trustees and investment managers by Robert Smeath in [2001] *Private Client Business*, Nov/Dec, 371 and one by Toby Harris outlining the main provisions in [2002] *New Law Journal, Wills and Probate Supplement*, 21 June, 945.

Administration of Estates Act 1925, s.19 as substituted by Trustee Act 2000, s.30, gives trustees a general power to insure any trust property against all risks and to pay the premiums out of income or capital.

Administration of Estates Act 1925, s.39 gives PRs all the powers of trustees of land (generally the powers of an absolute owner).

Administration of Estates Act 1925, s.41 gives power to appropriate assets.

Administration of Estates Act 1925, s.42 enables payment of a minor's gift to be made to a trust corporation or at least two trustees, if the minor is absolutely entitled. The section is less important since the Children Act 1989, which provides that all parents with parental responsibility have the same rights, powers and duties as guardians appointed under the Children Act. These rights are set out in s.3 and include the right to receive property in their own name for the *benefit of the child*.

Trustee Act 1925, s.31 gives power of maintenance in relation to income.

Trustee Act 1925, s.32 gives power of advancement in relation to capital.

13.11.2 Exercise of powers

These powers are fiduciary. A sole, or sole surviving, executor or executrix may act alone in all cases. Where there is more than one executor or executrix, authority is joint for land (i.e. all must execute any deed) and joint and several for some personalty (i.e. just one may deliver an asset (e.g. jewellery) to a beneficiary and get a good receipt and discharge).

The Law of Property (Miscellaneous Provisions) Act 1994 covers aspects of sales of land by PRs, including the contract for sale: see at **13.9.1** above.

13.11.3 Duties

The executors must safeguard the estate and, with due diligence:

- collect and realise the assets;
- pay the debts and legacies; and
- distribute the residue of the estate among the beneficiaries.

13.12 FOREIGN ASSETS AND DOMICILES

13.12.1 Foreign assets

Some clients may own property abroad because of a family connection; others because they have bought second homes or businesses. Potentially disastrous consequences can ensue if those clients are not fully advised about local laws regulating the inheritance of land and other property. In certain civil law jurisdictions, for example, children are automatically entitled to a fixed share of the estate regardless of any will to the contrary.

Solicitors need to be aware of the possibility both when preparing wills and when dealing with estates, and solicitors may need to instruct a solicitor in the UK with the necessary knowledge and experience or a local lawyer in the jurisdiction. The Law Society can help with the names of appropriately qualified lawyers (contact the International division, see Law Society under **Useful addresses**).

13.12.2 Wills for clients with foreign assets

Sometimes an English will dealing with foreign property can put the testator's or testatrix's wishes into effect, but it is often helpful for the client to make a will in accordance with the requirements of the other jurisdiction to deal separately with those assets. Once a client has a foreign will, it is important to ensure that any new English or foreign will does not start with a standard revocation clause revoking *all* other wills.

13.12.3 Dealing with the estates of clients with foreign assets

If the deceased died domiciled in England and Wales, but with assets in another country, a foreign will may have been made. A lawyer of that country may have to be instructed. Usually it is necessary to extract the grant in England and Wales first and then send it accompanied by a sealed and certified copy of the will to a local practitioner. This does not apply in a country where the Colonial Probates Act 1892 applies, or in Scotland or Northern Ireland. There are many publications dealing with buying property abroad which often contain helpful sections on wills and probate.

13.12.4 Foreign domiciles

If the deceased died domiciled outside England and Wales, but left assets in England and Wales (unless the Colonial Probates Act 1892 applies, or the deceased was domiciled in Scotland or Northern Ireland) it will be necessary to obtain a grant in England and Wales: see NCPR 1987, Rule 30.

Questions of domicile arise with increasing frequency. Probate practitioners may be involved with the question of domicile either in relation to IPFDA 1975 (claims can be brought only if the deceased died domiciled in England and Wales) or in relation to liability to IHT. The following cases are useful: *Morgan* v. *Cilento* [2004] EWHC 188 (Ch); *Allen* v. *HMRC* [2005] WTLR 937; *Agulian & Another* v. *Cyganik* [2006] EWCA Civ 129; *Mark* v. *Mark* [2005] UKHL 42.

13.13 LIFETIME GIFTS AND UNDUE INFLUENCE

Probate practitioners may find that after death, there are allegations that lifetime gifts made by the deceased are void on the basis of undue influence. There have been cases where virtually no assets remain to pass under the terms of the will. See, for example *Special Trustees for Great Ormond Street Hospital for Children* v. *Rushin* [2001] WTLR 1137. Such allegations can be very distressing for all concerned and will inevitably prolong and complicate the administration of the estate. However, the law is relatively well established.

The decision of the House of Lords in *Royal Bank of Scotland* v. *Etridge* [2002] AC 773 made the following points:

1. There are two forms of unacceptable conduct which will cause the courts to find a transaction void for undue influence.
2. The first consists of overt acts of improper pressure or coercion such as unlawful threats.

3. The second arises from a relationship where one person has acquired a measure of influence or ascendancy over another a person of which the ascendant person takes advantage. There is an irrebuttable presumption that one person has influence over another in the case of certain relationships (parent/child, lawyer/client, doctor/patient). In other cases the complainant must prove that there was a relationship of trust and confidence.

Once such a relationship is proved, it is sufficient for the complainant to show that there was a transaction requiring an explanation. There is no need to prove that the transaction was the result of undue influence.

A presumption of undue influence arises and the court will infer that the transaction was the result of undue influence unless sufficient evidence is produced to show that this was not the case.

In *Hammond* v. *Osborn* [2002] EWCA Civ 885 the Court of Appeal emphasised that in cases of presumed undue influence the court intervenes not on the ground that any wrongful act has actually been committed by the donee but on grounds of public policy to prevent any abuse of the relationship of trust and confidence.

In *Niersmans* v. *Pesticcio* [2004] EWCA Civ 372 the Court of Appeal emphasised that the submission that the donee had 'done nothing wrong' was an instance of the 'continuing misconceptions' as to the law of presumed undue influence mentioned by Sir Martin Nourse in *Hammond* (above). The basis of the court's intervention is not the commission of a dishonest or wrongful act by the defendant, but that, as a matter of public policy, the presumed influence arising from the relationship of trust and confidence should not operate to the disadvantage of the victim, if the transaction is not satisfactorily explained by ordinary motives.

In *Aldridge* v. *Turner* [2004] EWHC 2768 (Ch) the court accepted the proposition that gifts of individually modest amounts could give rise to the presumption of undue influence when added together.

There were 62 transactions which depleted the deceased's resources by £25,000 at a time when his regular monthly income was less than £2,000. On the facts, some of the transactions were legitimate but others were wholly unauthorised or the result of undue influence. The defendant, the deceased's son, had to account to the estate for the unauthorised withdrawals and also for some loans made in the 1990s which he had never repaid.

See also *Randall* v. *Randall* [2004] All ER (D) 570; *Macklin* v. *Dowsett* [2004] EWCA Civ 904; *Vale* v. *Armstrong* [2004] EWHC 1160 Ch; *Stevens* v. *Newey* [2005] EWCA Civ 50; *Watson* v. *Huber* [2005] All ER (D) 156; *Wright* v. *Hodgkinson* [2004] EWHC 3091; *Turkey* v. *Awadh & Another* [2005] EWCA Civ 382 and *Hughes* v. *Hughes* [2005] EWHC 469.

13.14 ARTIST'S RESALE RIGHT REGULATIONS 2006

The Artist's Resale Right Regulations 2006, SI 2006/346, were made under European Communities Act 1972, s.2(2) and implement Directive 2001/84/EC of the European Parliament and Council. They came into force on 14 February 2006.

The regulations provide for a royalty to be paid to an artist:

- on any sale of 'any work of graphic or plastic art such as a picture, a collage, a painting, a drawing, an engraving, a print, a lithograph, a sculpture, a tapestry, a ceramic, an item of glassware or a photograph';
- during the copyright period (usually 70 years) that is subsequent to the artist's first disposal;
- where the price exceeds 1,000 euros (but it does not apply to any sale made less than three years after acquisition from the author where the price is less than 10,000 euros);
- but only where the buyer or the seller, or (where the sale takes place through an agent) the agent of the buyer or the seller, is acting in the course of a business of dealing in works of art.

These regulations apply to all types of resale, both public and private sales, auctions and private treaty.

The seller is jointly and severally liable for the royalty with his agent, or if there is no seller's agent, the buyer's agent, or if there no buyer's agent then the buyer.

Schedule 1 sets out the percentage of the sale price payable as a royalty on each sale (the price used is net of any sales tax, but not commission and the euro conversion rate will be at a reference rate set by the European Central Bank). There is a maximum on any single sale of 12,500 euros.

0–50,000 euros	4%
50,001–200,000 euros	3%
200,001–350,000 euros	1%
350,001–500,000 euros	0.5%
over 500,000 euros	0.25%

This right is capable of passing on death as personal or moveable property to a natural person or charity (reg.9).

Where an author died before the introduction of the regulations and would have been a qualifying person, the regulations provide for the author's royalty under these regulations to be inherited by:

(a) the person inheriting the copyright from the author if he or she owned it;
(b) the person inheriting the work if the author owned the work but not the copyright to it;

(c)   otherwise, the person(s) inheriting the personal estate.

Management and collection of the royalty will be through a mutual collecting society.

There are two ways in which PRs may be affected by the regulations.

1.   Liability for the royalty is a factor in the valuation of an affected object owned by an estate or trust.
2.   An artist's right to royalties under these regulations will be an asset of his or her estate and will need to be investigated and valued.

13.15   STATUTORY ORDER FOR PAYMENT OF DEBTS

13.15.1   Solvent estates

Where an estate is solvent, all the creditors will be paid but some beneficiaries will have their share of the assets reduced. Administration of Estates Act 1925, s.34 and Sched.1, Part II set out the order in which legacies are reduced to provide assets to pay debts (residue, retained pecuniary legacy fund, specific gifts). Where there are insufficient funds to pay all the pecuniary legacies in full, they abate proportionally unless the will provides otherwise.

Personal representatives who choose to distribute assets before paying all the debts should follow the statutory order. Paying pecuniary legacies too early may mean that there are insufficient assets to meet the debts without recourse to items specifically given. Personal representatives would then be personally liable to the disappointed beneficiaries. (See *Mitchell and Others* v. *Halliwell and Others* [2005] EWHC 937 (Ch).)

13.15.2   Insolvent estates

An estate is insolvent if, when realised, it will be insufficient to meet in full all its debts and other liabilities. No beneficiaries will receive anything and some creditors will not be paid in full.

The relevant statutory instrument is the Administration of Insolvent Estates of Deceased Persons Order 1986, SI 1986/1999, as amended by Administration of Insolvent Estates of Deceased Persons (Amendment) Order 2002, SI 2002/1309.

An insolvent estate can be administered under the directions of the court (CPR Part 50) but this is rare. It will normally be done by the deceased's PRs out of court following the relevant regulations or in bankruptcy following an insolvency administration order made by the bankruptcy court. Whichever option is adopted, the priority for payment of debts is the same: funeral and testamentary expenses first, followed by the bankruptcy order. Personal representatives will be personally liable if they pay an inferior debt before a superior one and there are insufficient funds for the superior one.

If the PRs or creditors decide that a trustee in bankruptcy is required, perhaps to set aside voidable lifetime transactions, they can apply at any stage for an administration order to be made. The form of the petition is set out in the Administration of Insolvent Estates of Deceased Persons Order 1986, SI 1986/1999, Sched.3.

An insolvency administration order can be made at any time during the administration of the estate. If such an order is made, any disposition made by the personal representatives in the period between death and the vesting of the estate in the trustee in bankruptcy is void, unless made with the consent of the court or subsequently ratified by the court. This means that a solicitor who has charged for acting may have to repay sums received. The court will only ratify payments made for the benefit of the estate at a time when there was no reason to suppose that the estate was insolvent. See *Dick v. Kendall Freeman* [2005] WTLR 1619.

PART III

Practical Probate

This Part deals with some of the practical aspects of probate work which often cause problems. It starts by covering IHT, then deals with problem solving, preparation of the accounts and some of the issues arising from distribution, and it ends with a series of checklists covering all stages from the beginning of the administration right through to the closing of the file.

CHAPTER 14

Inheritance tax

Lesley King

14.1 CONTACTING HM REVENUE AND CUSTOMS (CAPITAL TAXES)

For details on contacting HM Revenue and Customs (Capital Taxes), see
Useful addresses.

14.2 INHERITANCE TAX RATES 1999–2009

(For transfers to non-exempt beneficiaries.)

14.2.1 Transfers on deaths occurring on or after 6 April 1999 and lifetime transfers taking place within three years of death

The table gives the IHT threshold limits, beyond which the 40 per cent rate
applies.

For deaths after 5 April	IHT threshold £
1999	231,000
2000	234,000
2001	242,000
2002	250,000
2003	255,000
2004	263,000
2005	275,000
2006	285,000
2007	300,000
2008	312,000
2009	325,000

14.2.2 Lifetime transfers taking place between three and seven years of death

There is a tapering relief available on such gifts but it takes the form of a
reduction in the tax which would otherwise be payable. Thus, it only becomes
effective if the total of the lifetime transfers made between three and seven
years of death exceeds the limit of the nil rate band.

Years before death in which transfer made	Percentage of death rate tax payable
3–4	80%
4–5	60%
5–6	40%
6–7	20%

Note: Lifetime chargeable transfers made between seven and 14 years before the death, although themselves not liable to tax, may affect the rate of IHT applicable to gifts within the seven-year period.

14.2.3   Annual exemption

£3,000 (plus £3,000 for the previous tax year if unused).

14.2.4   Reliefs

Business property relief/agricultural property relief

Each at 100 per cent or 50 per cent of the value of the property transferred, depending on the nature of the assets and subject to minimum ownership requirements.

Woodlands relief

The value of trees or underwood growing in non-agricultural woodlands can be left out of account by election and the tax deferred until disposal of the timber.

National Heritage property

Exempt from IHT if so designated by HMRC and undertakings regarding the property are given and complied with. The notes to IHT200 explain in detail how to deal with Heritage property. More information can be obtained by writing to the Heritage team at the Nottingham office or by telephoning the Heritage team helpline (see **Useful addresses**).

Quick succession relief

Available on a sliding scale when a transfer on death takes place within five years of an earlier transfer on which tax was paid, the point on the scale depending on date of the second death.

14.3   ACCOUNTING FOR INHERITANCE TAX

14.3.1   Is an account necessary? Excepted estates

As from 1 November 2004 an account of some sort is required for all estates.

If the estate fulfils the requirements for an excepted estate, the application for a grant of representation must be accompanied by a return of estate information on form IHT205 (or IHT207 for those domiciled abroad).

In other cases a full IHT200 (or 201 for those domiciled abroad) is required.

Which estates are excepted?

For deaths on or after 6 April 2004 there are three types of excepted estate. The first two apply where the deceased died domiciled in the UK at death (the Channel Islands and Isle of Man are not in the UK); the third applies where the deceased was never domiciled in the UK. None of the anti-avoidance provisions dealing with alternatively secured pensions (IHTA 1984, s.151A–C) can apply if the estate is to be excepted.

CATEGORY 1

An estate is excepted where:

- the estate consists only of property passing by will or intestacy, nomination, survivorship or under a single settlement in which the deceased had an interest in possession; and
- if the estate includes assets held in trust, their gross value does not exceed £150,000*; and
- if the estate includes foreign assets, their gross value does not exceed £100,000*; and
- if there are any 'specified transfers', their chargeable value does not exceed £150,000*; and
- the gross value of the estate and any 'specified transfers' or specified exempt transfers does not exceed the threshold for IHT.

* Note that different figures apply for deaths occurring before 1 September 2006.

CATEGORY 2

An estate is excepted where:

- the estate consists only of property passing by will or intestacy, nomination, survivorship or under a single settlement in which the deceased had an interest in possession; and

- if the estate includes assets held in trust, their gross value does not exceed £100,000; and
- the deceased died without having made any chargeable transfers in the seven years before death other than specified transfers not exceeding £100,000; and
- the gross value of the estate and any 'specified transfers' or specified exempt transfers does not exceed £1m; and
- the net estate after deducting debts and the spouse and charity exemption does not exceed the threshold for IHT.

CATEGORY 3

An estate is excepted where:

- the deceased was never domiciled nor treated as domiciled in the UK at death; and
- the deceased's UK estate consists *only* of cash or quoted shares or securities passing under a will or intestacy or by survivorship in a beneficial joint tenancy and the gross value does not exceed £100,000.

'Specified transfers' are chargeable transfers of cash, personal chattels or corporeal moveable property, quoted shares or securities or an interest in or over land save to the extent that the property became settled on the transfer or was subject to a reservation of benefit.

In working out the value of any 'specified transfers', business and agricultural property relief must be ignored. This means that an estate where £500,000 of property attracting 100 per cent business property relief is left to issue and the remaining £200,000 to the spouse, the estate is not excepted even though no tax is payable.

When can HMRC insist on delivery of a full account?

If you have taken out an excepted estate grant, HMRC can still insist on delivery of a full IHT account. There will be automatic discharge after 35 days (60 in Scotland) unless HMRC has asked for a full account. It will do so on a random basis across the whole population but will also use information available to identify cases near the threshold where tax may be at risk. The regulations require that notice requiring an account is given to the legal personal representatives rather than any solicitor acting for them.

What if additional assets are discovered which mean that the estate is not excepted?

If an excepted estate grant has been taken out before you find out that the estate did not meet the conditions, you have six months from discovery to deliver a corrective account containing details of the changes. The same applies should the beneficiaries execute a variation which changes the devolution of assets so that the estate no longer qualifies.

Different rules apply to deaths before 6 April 2004. HMRC provides a helpline (see **Useful addresses**).

14.4   WHERE AN ESTATE IS NOT EXCEPTED

Practitioners must complete IHT200 Inheritance Tax Account together with the relevant supplementary pages, the probate summary (D18) and worksheet. HMRC publishes a helpful *Practitioners' Guide* (IHT215) which can be found on the website (**www.hmrc.gov.uk**).

14.5   HMRC LEAFLETS

HMRC has produced a series of leaflets about IHT, as follows.

IHT2	Inheritance tax on lifetime gifts
IHT3	An introduction
IHT4	Notes on informal calculations of IHT
IHT8	Alterations to an inheritance following a death
IHT11	Payment of inheritance tax from National Savings or from British Government stock on the Bank of England Register
IHT12	When Excepted Estate grant is appropriate in the case of deaths before 6 April 2004
IHT12(2004)	When Excepted Estate grant is appropriate in the case of deaths on or after 6 April 2004
IHT13	Inheritance tax and penalties
IHT14	The personal representatives' responsibilities
IHT15	How to calculate the liability
IHT16	Settled property
IHT17	Businesses, farms and woodlands
IHT18	Foreign aspects
IHT19	Delivery of a reduced Inland Revenue Account
RI 55	A Revenue Interpretation setting out examples of gifts where they consider a reservation of benefit arises

14.6   ADDITIONAL REMINDERS

14.6.1   Calculation of the tax and interest

Practitioners should note the following.

- Personal representatives have a duty to complete their IHT account properly. They have a legal responsibility to pay the full amount of tax for which they are liable, before they send the account to the probate registry with their application for a grant of representation. Practitioners acting as, or on behalf of, PRs are expected themselves to calculate the correct amount of tax due.
- Finance Act 1989, s.178(1) provides that the rate of interest on unpaid tax shall be increased or decreased automatically in line with general changes in market interest rates.

Recent rates are as follows.

From	To	Rate(%)
6 December 1992	5 January 1994	5
6 January 1994	5 October 1994	4
6 October 1994	5 March 1999	5
6 March 1999	5 February 2000	4
6 February 2000	5 May 2001	5
6 May 2001	5 November 2001	4
6 November 2001	5 August 2003	3
6 August 2003	5 December 2003	2
6 December 2003 onwards		3

- There may be circumstances where it is necessary to apply for a grant quickly and there is not time to obtain final valuations, in which case solicitors should phone the Capital Taxes Helpline and explain the problem. In *Robertson* v. *Inland Revenue Commissioners (No. 1)* [2002] STC (SCD) 182 a solicitor who submitted an account containing estimated values which turned out to be substantially below the true values was ordered to pay a penalty by the Revenue. Eventually the Special Commissioner found that he had acted properly because he had disclosed that his values were estimates and had paid the extra tax required within six months from the end of the month of death. However, it is clearly preferable to avoid the possibility of any argument with HMRC by making arrangements in advance.
- Practitioners should supply HMRC with as much information as possible with the account to enable more focused enquiries to be raised after the grant has been issued. Both HMRC and practitioners want to provide an efficient and speedy service to their respective customers. It will save time

if the IHT200 contains a statement of the basis of an ownership claim rather than waiting for Capital Taxes to raise enquiries.

- Care should be taken when valuing household and personal goods. In the December 2004 Newsletter the Revenue stated that it was anxious to establish whether the value of such goods had been ascertained in accordance with correct statutory principles as set out in IHTA 1984, s.160, i.e. 'the price which the property might reasonably be expected to fetch if sold in the open market'. The Newsletter sets out circumstances which might lead the Revenue to make further enquiries as to the basis of valuation. In the April 2006 Newsletter HMRC reported that there were still problems with the valuation of household and personal goods. Practitioners should be particularly careful of the following:

  - if there are such goods but the PRs consider that they are valueless, it is still necessary to report that such goods exist;
  - where items are valueless, complete Form D10 to explain why they are considered to have no value;
  - do not simply give a value without explanation; attach a valuer's report if one was obtained; if the valuation was a PRs' estimate, explain how the estimate was arrived at and what comparisons were made;
  - a valuer's report must state that it was made on an open market basis;
  - if there is a car, state its value separately on form D10 and give details of its make, model, year of registration and registration number;
  - if the deceased owned a holiday home, separate details of the contents must be provided even if the PRs consider them to be valueless;
  - when taking an inventory, be sure not to overlook items which are not in the house; check garden sheds and garages; ascertain whether there is a car parked in the street and whether any items have been placed with friends or relatives for safekeeping.

- Where an estate includes land or buildings, the IHT Newsletter for April 2006 states that it is necessary to include any development or hope value. When valuing PRs must take appropriate steps to ascertain the value that the land or building may expect to achieve if sold on the open market. This means that the PRs must take into account any feature that may make the property attractive to builders or developers such as a large garden or access to other property. The Newsletter concludes 'Where it is evident that reasonable and adequate steps have not been taken to ascertain the open market value, based on all information that was available, penalties may be sought'.

- Where land is sold within three years of death for less than the probate value, loss relief under IHTA 1984, s.191 may be available. HMRC requires claims to be on form IHT38. Claims by letter or on a C4 corrective account are not acceptable.

- When valuing gilts or other fixed interest stocks that are taxed under the accrued income scheme, the Revenue has accepted (see IHT Newsletter, May 2003) that, when valuing for IHT, interest on securities quoted cum-div should be added net of basic rate income tax. Similarly, where securities are quoted ex-div, the allowance in the IHT calculation for interest accruing after the death should also be net of basic rate tax.

14.7 DEATH OF A LIFE TENANT: APPROVED STANDARD LETTER

A life tenant may be treated as the beneficial owner of the trust capital under IHTA 1984, s.49.

Finance Act 2006 made changes to the taxation of trusts but many life interests will still qualify under IHTA 1984, s.49.

In the case of trusts created before 22 March 2006 a life tenant will continue to be treated as the owner of the underlying trust capital. In the case of trusts created after 22 March 2006 this will only be the case if the interest is an immediate post-death interest created on death or a transitional serial interest.

Where a life tenant is treated as entitled to the underlying trust capital, the IHT payable as a result of the life tenant's death will be apportioned between the life tenant's own estate and the trust fund. It is necessary to inform HMRC of the life tenant's death. HMRC approves the notification letter below, and adds that applications for clearance on IHT30 should not be made until these can be issued. There is no point in submitting the IHT30 with, for example, the IHT100.

As a result of the changes to the excepted estates rules, some estates that include assets held in trust may still qualify as excepted estates (see **14.3**). HMRC Capital Taxes will return any Accounts IHT100 in connection with trust assets the gross value of which does not exceed £100,000, if it is not clear whether the estate as a whole may qualify as an excepted estate.

The Director

HMRC Capital Taxes
DX 701201
Nottingham 4

[Date]

Dear Sir

The Trust of Mr Fred Bloggs (Settlement 1953/Will dated 10/4/55)

Date of Death: 1/5/58
Your Reference: F/123456/53
Life Tenant: Mrs Freda Payne
Date of Death: 25/10/06

The Life Tenant of this Trust has died. We enclose a copy of the Trust Instrument.

We also enclose a completed form IHT 100 with supporting schedules. Please acknowledge receipt.

The Life Tenant's Estate will be dealt with by: Morse & Co, Solicitors, Lewis House, 22 Burt St, Oxford OX1 20X

*[We have not yet been able to ascertain the value of the Life Tenant's free estate.]

OR

*[We understand that the value of the deceased's free estate is about £X.]

We look forward to receiving an assessment or, in due course, confirmation that we may lodge form IHT 30.

Yours faithfully

(Jaguar & Co)

---

* Include as necessary: this will help Capital Taxes decide whether to issue a provisional assessment immediately. It can only do this if it knows the value of the free estate.

14.8   PRODUCING YOUR OWN IHT ACCOUNT FORMS

The forms are available in various formats to complete electronically or to print and complete by hand from the HMRC website.

For firms who wish to generate IHT account forms using their own computers, Capital Taxes produced a booklet 10/02 *Guidelines for Producing Substitute Inheritance Tax Forms,* and an extract from that booklet is shown below. For contact details for the Forms Adviser, see **Useful addresses**.

1.   Introduction

On 13 January 1993, the Board of the Inland Revenue issued a Press Release and Statement of Practice. This allowed professional agents to produce their own versions of inheritance tax (IHT) forms.

This leaflet explains what you have to do to obtain approval for substitute forms. Individual firms can obtain approval to use substitutes 'in-house'.

Software companies can obtain a licence from the Inland Revenue (Capital Taxes) to sell a package of forms commercially.

2. Legislation

Section 257(1) of the Inheritance Tax Act 1984 explains the legal provisions for submitting accounts (inventories in Scotland). Basically, you must complete the correct form as prescribed by the Board of the Inland Revenue.

Inland Revenue (Capital Taxes) acts on behalf of the Board. We will accept an accurate facsimile of the prescribed form in order to satisfy this section of the Act. In the rest of this leaflet, we will use the word 'original' to indicate the 'prescribed form'.

What must the substitute form show?

To satisfy the Act, the substitute form must show all the information that appears on the original. This is so that the taxpayer(s) who sign(s) the declaration read all the information that the Inland Revenue intended them to read.

By this, we mean that you must reproduce all the text that appears on the original. You should not reproduce the Inland Revenue logo.

What about layout and style?

You **must** reproduce the same layout and style as on the original. *See section B for more detailed instructions.*

How will our staff know that the form is acceptable?

You will need to obtain official approval for each different type of inheritance tax form you intend to use.

We will give you an approval reference. You should make sure that this appears in the bottom right-hand corner of the first page of each form you complete. This is an example of the format: 'CT approval ref. A1/01'.

Is there anything else that must appear on the form?

You must show the correct identifier in the bottom left-hand corner of the first page. A version of IHT 200 could show 'IHT 200 (substitute)(S&J)'. *The 'S&J' represents an abbreviation of a firm's name (e.g. Smith and Jones).*

DESIGN NOTES

1. Colour

Your substitute should not be colour-printed. Also, you do not need to print it onto coloured paper.

Where the original form has different tints of colour, you should use differing degrees of monochrome shading.

2. Logo

You **must not** reproduce the Inland Revenue logo on any substitute that you produce. You should, however, include the text part of the header (i.e. the 'Inland Revenue Capital Taxes' part).

3. Paper

You should use the same size paper as the original (A4).

202

You should print on paper of a reasonable standard as the forms will need to survive for many years. You may print either single or double-sided.

4. Text

You **must** reproduce **all** of the text that appears on the original. Your text must also follow the same patterns of bold and italic as on the original.

Our standard font for forms is Stone Sans. You should use a similar sans-serif alternative, such as Helvetica or Arial.

You should use all the same font sizes as the original and any other special styles (e.g. IHT 200 uses some white text on a dark background in its headings).

5. Page content

Each page on your substitute must contain the same information in the same order as the original. You should show page numbers clearly in the same place the originals show them.

6. Lines and boxes

You should try to achieve the same size and positioning of boxes as on the original.

It is important that your version keeps to the same proportional layout as those on the original. You should try to make sure that any boxes and lines are the same length and thickness.

I am happy with my form, what happens next?

You should print out two blank copies of your form and send them to us at the address shown at Section C, note 5, overleaf.

The Forms Adviser will tell you about any changes you must make. When you reach the required standard, the Forms Adviser will give you a unique reference. You must show the reference on each form that you send to us.

PROCEDURAL NOTES

1. Completing the forms for a 'real' case

Enter your details clearly on the form using no less than 9 point type size. You should make sure that our staff can easily distinguish your data from background text.

2. Assembling the forms

When you have filled in your approved form, assemble the pages in the correct order, include any schedules and staple together in the top left-hand corner. Please avoid using paper-clips, bulldog clips or treasury tags. Also, you should not use binders of any type as they can be hard for us to remove.

You should make sure that your stapling does not obscure any important information. You must **print** out your form and make sure that the legal personal representatives sign it. You can then deal with it in the same way as an ordinary IHT form.

3. Copyright

Her Majesty's Stationery Office have changed their Copyright practices as part of a drive to make it easier for people to access and re-use government information.

The Inland Revenue are no longer required to issue Copyright licences to people who wish to market our forms commercially and we will therefore no longer be sending these to producers of substitute forms.

Copyright permission to reproduce substitute forms appearing on the Inland Revenue website is given on our Copyright webpage **www.inlandrevenue.gov.uk/ copyright/index.htm**.

Forms not appearing on our website are normally covered by the new 'Click-use Copyright licence, which you can obtain from HMSO's website **www.hmso.gov.uk**.

These changes do not affect the Inland Revenue approval process. We still need to see drafts of your proposed substitute Inheritance tax forms for approval before they are brought into use. We will notify design approval by letter in the normal way.

Crown Copyright applies to Inland Revenue Inheritance tax forms. HMSO do not intend to seek payment from producers of substitute versions, but the Crown copyright should be acknowledged when these are released to the end-users.

What forms are appropriate for substitutes?

ACCOUNTS AND INVENTORIES
IHT 200
IHT 100
C1
C2
C5/C5(SE)/C5(OUK)
IHT205/IHT207

OTHER FORMS
C4
IHT 30
IHT 35
IHT 38

Where should I send my proposals?

[HMRC] (Capital Taxes)
Forms Adviser
PO Box 38
Ferrers House
Castle Meadow Road
Nottingham NG2 1BB
or
DX 701201
Nottingham 4
Tel: 0115 974 2706

I want to use computerised forms but do not want to do all the work myself

Ask our Forms Adviser to send you a list of the Software firms who operate under licence. You can then contact them yourself and choose the package that suits your needs.

14.9   PAYING PRE-GRANT IHT

Inheritance tax on property which does not attract the instalment option has to be paid with the IHT200 before obtaining the grant. The PRs are, therefore, unable to access the deceased's assets to produce funds. It is always worth asking the deceased's bank whether it is prepared to pay funds directly to HMRC to meet the pre-grant IHT. Many banks will do this and it is normally the quickest and cheapest method of dealing with the payment.

14.9.1   Interest on loans

The interest payable on qualifying loans taken out by the PRs to pay IHT pre-grant is deductible for income tax purposes from income in the PRs' hands in respect of a period of one year from the making of the loan.

14.9.2   Sources of funding

It is advisable to consider options other than borrowing from the deceased's bank first.

Many banks and building societies will make funds available direct to HMRC on an informal basis. However, there is also a more formal scheme called the Direct Payment Scheme to which many banks and building societies belong. The procedure for using the Direct Payment Scheme is as follows:

1. Fill in form D20 'Application to transfer funds to pay inheritance tax'. Use a separate form for each bank or building society that will be making the transfer of funds. Form D20 is a supplementary page to IHT200.
2. Then you should:

   (a) apply to Capital Taxes for a reference number for the deceased by ringing the IHT and Probate Helpline;
   (b) write the reference number on form D20;
   (c) when you have filled in IHT200, complete the rest of the form D20 by following the instructions in D20 (notes);
   (d) when you have completed the form D20 and you are ready to apply for a grant, send:

   - form D20 to the banks or building societies that will be making the transfers;
   - form IHT200, the relevant supplementary pages, form D18 and any other supporting documents to Capital Taxes.

The bank or building society will transfer the money to HMRC and should be able to give an indication of how long it would normally take them to make the transfer.

It is possible to pay IHT by encashing National Savings certificates or British Government stock (no grant being needed for this); however the process is not quick. After Capital Taxes receives the request it takes at least four weeks for the cash to be transferred and so this can slow down the obtaining of a grant quite substantially. HMRC's booklet IHT11 gives guidance on paying IHT from National Savings.

Also consider encashing investments in nominee names, approaching the deceased's building society or asking family members.

Below are two specimen letters which solicitors in private practice may adapt or adopt for the purpose set out on **page iv** of this Handbook, but not for any other purpose. The first letter is to a bank seeking a global loan facility; the second letter is to a building society seeking the early release of funds.

14.9.3   'Global' loans facility – letter to bank

This is an edited version of a letter used by one practice to obtain special favourable facilities. If such an arrangement is established, consider in each case whether there are any issues which would make it advisable to suggest that clients seek separate independent advice on the arrangements for the loan on to them: for example, is this the cheapest arrangement currently available? Also, explain the details the bank will want, and obtain the client's consent to passing on the information shown in item 6 of the specimen letter.

The Manager   Your Ref [   ]

[   ] Bank [etc.]   Our Ref [   ]

Date [   ]

Dear

GLOBAL PROBATE LOANS FACILITY

I should like to discuss a new facility to enable us to arrange short-term bridging loans for clients to meet inheritance tax and probate registry fees.

As you will be aware, personal representatives have to pay inheritance tax and probate registry fees when they apply for a grant of representation (whether of probate or letters of administration) to a deceased's estate. In a typical situation, no funds will be available from the estate until the grant has been issued, which means a loan has to be arranged, usually from the deceased's bank.

The personal representatives may well not be familiar with the deceased's bank, and may therefore instruct us to make the necessary arrangements. In such cases, it would save my firm time and paperwork if we were able to arrange the necessary loan through your bank on an agreed basis.

I would estimate that, on average, the loans would be repaid after approximately six to eight weeks, or nine to 11 weeks if quoted securities have to be sold, allowing for the settlement period and registration with the company registrars.

May I suggest that the basis on which your bank may agree the provision of this facility might be along the following lines:

1. **'In principle' agreement**. I accept that the bank will need to treat the provision of this facility as being an 'in principle' agreement because each loan, for reasons including taxation, branch monitoring and the liabilities of the borrowers, will be set up separately but taken within the 'umbrella' limit. I would hope that the advantage of having this agreement in place would be that the setting up of such accounts could be negotiated with you locally on an immediate basis, rather than suffering delays while negotiating and setting up relevant arrangements with the deceased's bank in each instance.

2. **Global limit**. Having regard to the normal volume of estate administration conducted by this firm, I would suggest that this should be £[100,000].

3. **Availability**. I anticipate that the bank would wish the facility to be expressed to be available for 12 months and that it will be described by you as being technically 'repayable on demand'. If this be the case, I should appreciate your confirmation that the only likely circumstances under which such a demand might be made would be if for some reason the lending had become 'unsatisfactory'.

4. **To whom available**. The facility would be available to the personal representatives of deceased persons where this firm is acting for them.

5. **Purpose**. To enable the personal representatives to deal with the estate's liability to inheritance tax and probate registry fees.

6. **Account arrangements**. I anticipate that you will wish the firm to complete the bank's form of application to open an account on each occasion and it would be helpful if we could be supplied with a stock of these. If you wish, having obtained the agreement of the personal representatives, the firm can provide the bank with the application form, the appropriate HMRC forms (IHT 200, IHT 201, IHT 202) confirming the amount due by way of inheritance tax and the details of the estate assets.

7. **Drawdown**. Each facility will be drawn as a separate loan, although partial drawings against that loan would need to be permitted.

8. **Interest**. I suggest that the rate of interest payable on the amount of each facility outstanding from time to time might be [2 per cent] per annum above the bank's base rate from time to time in force. Presumably interest will be calculated on a daily basis and charged at quarterly intervals to each separate loan facility.

    Please confirm that it will be possible, on request, for the bank to apportion the interest between the amount of loan drawn for payment of inheritance tax (on which tax relief can be claimed) and any part of the loan taken up for other outgoings such as the Probate Registry fees – which do not attract income tax relief.

9. **Arrangement fee**. I would hope that in view of this firm's connection with your bank no arrangement fee will be charged in respect either of the setting up of this facility or the taking up of each individual loan within it.

10. **Repayment and security**. Repayment would normally be made either from liquid assets, e.g. cash accounts, building society accounts,

stocks and shares, etc., or from the sale proceeds of assets of the estate. As regards security, if each account is opened in the name of the firm and designated with the name of the estate, the firm will be responsible to the bank for the payment of each loan facility. We will, of course, secure our own position with the personal representatives in the context of this liability.

11. **Discretionary arrangements**. There will be occasions when the size of the estate is such that the amount required by way of loan would be too large to take under the global 'umbrella' facility. In such circumstances I would expect that we would approach you on behalf of the personal representatives to negotiate terms for a similar facility for the estate and which might involve a discounted rate of interest. I appreciate that you would not necessarily be able to provide as quick a response in this case.

If this facility is provided, my firm will be able to offer an improved service to its clients and the bank will derive benefit as well. I hope that I have covered everything which is relevant in this letter but please let me know if there is any further information you require.

Yours sincerely [etc.]

14.9.4 Release of funds – specimen letter to building society

The Manager   Your Ref [   ]

[   ] Bank [etc.]   Our Ref [   ]

Date [   ]

Dear

THE LATE MRS VICTORIA JONES

Mrs Jones' personal representatives would like to arrange for a withdrawal from her account[s] no[s] _____ [to pay] [the funeral expenses] [the inheritance tax] [Probate Court fees] [so the grant of representation can be obtained].
The payments needed are:

[Funeral expenses: £____, payable to _____]
[Inheritance tax: £ ____, payable to HMRC.]
[Probate Court fee: £____, payable to HM Paymaster-General.]

We hope that you will be able to agree the personal representatives' requests. If so please send the forms they must sign.
We will register the grant with you when we have it.

Yours faithfully [etc.]

14.10 IHT NEWSLETTER

HMRC Capital Taxes produces a quarterly newsletter for its customers, and in order to receive this contact the Customer Services Team at the address given in **Useful addresses**. It is also available to download from the HMRC website (**www.hmrc.gov.uk/cto/newsletter.htm**).

14.11 FOREIGN ASSETS

The IHT Newsletter for August 2006 said:

> For the remainder of 2006 we will be paying particularly close attention to foreign assets. In appropriate cases we will open an enquiry and ask you for further information to satisfy ourselves that all of the foreign assets have been valued on the statutory basis. We will tell you if the estate is one that has been selected for enquiry in this way. Where it appears that the accountable people have been negligent we will consider whether a penalty is appropriate.

CHAPTER 15

Probate problems

Lesley King

15.1 MISSING BENEFICIARIES

If beneficiaries cannot initially be traced, the following can be tried.

- If a date of birth is known, it may be possible for the Office for National Statistics on payment of a fee to forward a letter to the beneficiary at the last address it holds. Address the letter to him or her, care of Traceline in Southport (see **Useful addresses**).
- Trustee Act 1925, s.27 advertisements and searches should be made as early as possible in case they reveal helpful information.
- Instruct genealogists to trace the beneficiaries. Firms divide into those that charge on a time-costing basis and those that charge the beneficiaries a share of their inheritance. Improvements in research technologies and techniques make establishing the existence of entitled kin much more straightforward now than it was even a few years ago. See below for reasons why it may be more appropriate to use a firm which charges on a time basis rather than charging a contingency fee.

In the case of a gift to a wide class of relatives, for example 'my nieces and nephews', PRs should be very cautious about accepting an assurance from one part of a family that 'X died without any children'. It is necessary to check or risk distributing assets wrongly.

The question of where the cost of tracing a beneficiary should fall often concerns practitioners. In the case of a residuary beneficiary *Shuttleworth* v. *Howarth* (1841) CR & PH 227 states that the cost should be paid from the residuary estate before division into shares. There are no modern cases on the cost of tracing a specific or pecuniary legatee. RSC Order 65, Rule 14B (no longer in force) provided that the cost should fall on the specific legatee and it would seem likely that a modern court would take this view. However, if the PRs are doubtful, they should seek directions from the court.

If there is no success in locating a beneficiary, the following options should be considered.

- Take personal indemnities from the other beneficiaries (but from a risk management point of view, these are of doubtful value).
- Apply to court for a *Benjamin* order which will allow the estate to be distributed on the basis of certain assumptions, usually that a particular person died without issue.
- Apply to court for permission to make payment without reservation to meet costs.
- Take out missing beneficiary insurance; but as the case of *Evans v. Westcombe* [1999] 2 All ER 777 shows, it is necessary to insure for an amount large enough to cover the capital entitlement *and* the payment of interest should the missing beneficiary appear. Only a limited number of firms now offer this insurance and, before providing it, they will normally require that genealogists attempt to trace the beneficiaries.
- The entitlements may be paid into court under Trustee Act 1925, s.63 if appropriate: see Hayton, *Underhill and Hayton: Law Relating to Trustees*, 16th edn (LexisNexis, 2002).

Solicitors may be consulted by a beneficiary who has been approached by an heir locator who is offering to inform them of an entitlement in return for a substantial part of the inheritance. In such cases, it is worth looking at the list of recent *bona vacantia* estates published by the Treasury Solicitor to see if the client can recognise a name.

It is also worth pointing out to the beneficiary that the agreement may not be enforceable on any of the following grounds.

- The information provided to the beneficiary by the heir locator may be misleading, in which case the agreement can be rescinded by the beneficiary.
- It may be possible to have the agreement set aside as an unconscionable bargain.
- The particular agreement entered into may be champertous. There are a number of cases where agreements have been set aside on this basis. An agreement to provide information, in itself, is not champertous. However any agreement to provide information and evidence to support legal proceedings will be void for champerty.

In *Rees* v. *De Bernardy* [1896] 2 Ch 437 Romer J set aside a contingency fee agreement on the basis that it was champertous and an improvident bargain on the part of the beneficiaries, obtained as a result of the defendant taking an unfair advantage of the beneficiaries. There are two Irish cases: *McElroy* v. *Flynn* [1991] ILRM 294 and *Fraser* v. *Buckle* [1996] 2 ILRM 34 in which arrangements were set aside. See, however, an interesting article by David Capper in [1997] *Modern Law Review*, 286 in which he regrets the failure of the Irish Supreme Court to examine whether public policy requires heir locator agreements to be void for public policy in the present day and considers the arguments for and against.

There are reasons for solicitors and PRs to be cautious about the use of employing heir locaters on the contingency fee basis:

1. Many firms of genealogists will offer a fee structure based on their recorded time and the necessary disbursements (certificates of birth, marriage and death, etc.) and this will normally represent significantly better value to the estate.

2. If the PR is also a residuary beneficiary, there is a clear conflict of interest in that the PR will benefit from the use of the contingency fee. The PR's share of the residue will be bigger because it will be untouched by the cost of tracing the missing beneficiary.

3. A trustee is not allowed to profit from his trust and must not take advantage of confidential information. Query whether an employee, agent or adviser can do so either. If a PR knows that an heir locater is proposing to demand payment from a legatee, can the PR properly authorise the heir locater to do that? A PR who has instructed an heir locater on such a basis may have breached his or her duty as a PR to preserve assets for the beneficiary.

15.2   UNCLAIMED CLIENT ACCOUNT MONEY

If money has been unclaimed for a long time, the Professional Ethics division of the Law Society (see **Useful addresses**) can advise.

15.3   DECEASED WITH NO KNOWN RELATIVES

Is there a will appointing the solicitor as executor? If so, he or she can take the steps set out at **15.1** above to trace claimants.

Where the deceased is intestate, the usual action is to refer the matter to the Treasury Solicitor's Bona Vacantia Division (see **Useful addresses**) (or in the Duchies of Cornwall and Lancaster to the corresponding Crown Agent, Farrer & Co). However, this is likely to mean that the solicitor will lose the opportunity to deal with the administration.

If the solicitor wishes to investigate the existence of entitled kin who could instruct the solicitor in the administration of an apparently *bona vacantia* estate, he or she should beware of incurring unrecoverable costs, unless prepared to write them off if the exercise is fruitless. However, the breadth of our intestacy provisions and the national demographic mean that the overwhelming majority of estates which appear to be *bona vacantia* do, in fact, yield heirs in priority to the Crown. In this situation, a solicitor might consider asking a firm of professional genealogists if it is willing to establish the position, without committing the solicitor to fees. Some firms will do this by deferring their fee (which should be agreed with them in advance) for locating a person entitled to the grant until after the solicitor has been instructed and the grant extracted, and agreeing that if the estate proves to be *bona vacantia*, or if the solicitor does not ultimately take instructions for whatever reason, the genealogist will waive the fee.

An alternative approach is to apply for a grant of representation under Supreme Court Act 1981, s.116, which gives the court a discretionary power. The solicitor would again need to contact a firm of genealogists and ask if it is willing to carry out a no-cost initial assessment of the likelihood of tracing next of kin. If the results of the initial assessment are good, the solicitor can then apply for leave to be appointed as administrator while the next of kin are traced and then apply for the grant himself or herself.

The Treasury Solicitor must be informed of the application for a grant although it does not need to be informed of the s.116 application. The registrar will require to see the evidence relating to the likelihood of tracing the next of kin, showing that it is appropriate in the circumstances to make such a grant.

In the *Probate Section Journal*, May 2004, Richard Grosberg reported that a member of the Probate Section executive had obtained a grant of representation under s.116 on such a basis despite initial opposition from the Treasury Solicitor. The member then employed a firm of genealogists on a normal fee-paying basis to trace the next of kin. Before embarking on this course it is important to ensure that the assets are protected so as to prevent undue liability. It is also possible that no next of kin will be traced, in which case the estate will have to be passed to the Treasury Solicitor.

There may be cases where there is an immediate danger to the assets of the estate. If so, consider applying to the court for a limited grant *ad colligenda bona*. This is a limited grant issued where there is a pressing need for a grant and it is not possible to wait for the issue of a full grant. It can issue to anyone irrespective of whether or not that person has any right to take out a general grant to the estate. It is not necessary to say whether there is a will or an intestacy nor to do any of the usual clearing off. A caveat does not prevent the issue of an *ad colligenda* grant. However, it is normally limited to 'collecting and getting in and receiving the estate and doing such acts as may be necessary for the preservation of the estate' and ends when a full grant issues.

If applying for an *ad colligenda* grant, the grounds justifying the application must be set out (for example, land which needs to be made secure against vandals or squatters, debts which need to be paid to avoid interest or penalties, volatile assets such as shares which need to be dealt with). The difficulty with an application on this basis is that the Probate Registry may ask why the matter is not being referred to the Treasury Solicitor.

Ex gratia *payments*

It is possible to apply for *ex gratia* payments in exercise of the Royal Bounty to redress hardship or for some other good cause. The Bona Vacantia Division of the Treasury Solicitor will consider claims against an estate by persons who are not kin on grounds such as:

- services rendered;
- a testamentary document invalid as a will;
- an unmarried partner; or
- a factual relationship such as a step-child brought up by the deceased.

If the Treasury Solicitor succeeds in identifying a member of the deceased's family, the estate is no longer *bona vacantia*. The Treasury Solicitor will not adjudicate between claims nor become involved in subsequent disputes between kin.

15.4 CLIENTS AND BENEFICIARIES LACKING MENTAL CAPACITY

The Guide to the Professional Conduct of Solicitors 1999 (the Guide), Principle 24.04 and Commentary 1–3 cover the position if a client lacks capacity. A solicitor's retainer is terminated when a client loses capacity.

The Guidance Notes accompanying the draft Code of Conduct, Rule 2 make the point that although the retainer ends with the loss of capacity, it is important that the client, who is in a very vulnerable situation, is not left without legal representation. It suggests that the solicitor should notify the Court of Protection or look for someone legally entitled to provide the solicitor with instructions, such as an attorney under an enduring power of attorney, or take steps for such a person to be appointed.

If a beneficiary is mentally incapacitated (and cannot therefore give a good receipt) it may be appropriate to consider the appointment of a receiver through the Court of Protection, or payment into court under Trustee Act 1925, s.63.

On very difficult points, guidance may be obtained from the Practice Advice Service and the Professional Ethics Division (see **Useful addresses**). *The Elderly Client Handbook*, 3rd edn (Law Society, 2004) may also assist.

15.5 DISABILITY

One of the most difficult disabilities for wills and probate solicitors to deal with is visual impairment. The RNIB offers a visual awareness course which gives guidance on best practice for helping clients with impaired vision. A benefit of attending the course is that the RNIB's Wills and Legacies Advisory Service is then able to recommend your firm to the visually impaired.

As a result of the Disability Discrimination Act 1995, solicitors must ensure that they do not discriminate against disabled people by, for example, refusing to provide a service or providing one at a lower standard. All service providers, including solicitors, must ensure that their services are provided in a way that makes them accessible to disabled people.

15.6   COPY DEATH CERTIFICATES UNACCEPTABLE

Probate practitioners were concerned when HMSO issued Guidance Notes (No.7, dated 27 October 1999, revised 4 January 2001) stating that because of the potential for photocopy documents to assist in the perpetration of fraud, their use was no longer acceptable. This obviously meant an increase in the cost of administering estates.

However, the Law Society agreed a protocol with the British Bankers Association, the Building Societies Association and the Association of British Insurers. The agreement means that, instead of having to send original certificates to asset holders, solicitors can send a death certificate verification form giving a guarantee that they have in their possession and inspected an original. The protocol letter and form are set out in **Appendix A5**. Solicitors can reproduce the letter and form electronically; the form must remain unaltered although the letter can be modified.

Not all banks and building societies will accept the protocol letters and some solicitors have experienced difficulty even with those that allegedly do so.

15.7   EXTRACTING A GRANT FOR NON-SOLICITOR PRACTITIONERS

Solicitors may be asked to make an application for a grant on behalf of a bank or will and administration company. Be cautious about accepting unsubstantiated figures. A company called Legacies (Will and Probate Services) Ltd was wound up in 2002 after an investigation by the DTI into its financial affairs. The company had instructed solicitors to obtain grants on its behalf on the basis that the estates involved were excepted (they were frequently not excepted). The company had then siphoned off £4.8 million due to beneficiaries of the estates to cover its own losses.

Solicitors who prepare an oath swearing that an estate does not exceed a stated figure when they have not made sufficient enquiries may find that they have themselves committed an offence and/or that they are implicated in the offences committed by others.

215

15.8   PERSONAL REPRESENTATIVES AND PERSONAL LIABILITY

15.8.1   Personal representatives' liability for unpaid IHT on PETs and lifetime chargeable transfers

The primary liability for IHT on lifetime gifts is on the transferee. However, PRs have a secondary liability where tax on lifetime transfers and property included in the estate as a result of the reservation of benefit provisions is unpaid 12 months after the month of death.

The PR's liability to tax is limited to the value of the estate but is not affected by a certificate of discharge.

There is no statutory right to recover from those who were primarily liable except in the case of a reservation of benefit (IHTA 1984, s.211(3)) although such a right may exist as a matter of general law (see *Private Client Business 1998* (Sweet & Maxwell), p.58).

To clarify the position, the following edited note was published in [1989] *Gazette*, 22 November:

> Personal representatives are liable for:
>
> - the inheritance tax payable on potentially exempt transfers (PETs) where the transferor dies within seven years of the transfer, if the tax has remained unpaid by the transferee for 12 months after the end of the month in which the death of the transferor occurs (Inheritance Tax Act 1984, s.199(2)); and
> - any additional tax on inter vivos chargeable transfers payable as a result of the death.
>
> A similar problem for personal representatives exists where property is treated as part of the death estate by virtue of the reservation of benefit rules. Such property will be treated as part of the donor's estate on death (Finance Act 1986, s.102(3)).
>
> The Solicitors Indemnity Fund Ltd (SIF) confirmed that where a solicitor incurred a civil liability in the course of his or her private practice then, subject to the provisions of the indemnity rules currently in force, that liability would be indemnified by the Indemnity Fund but only to the extent that otherwise funds are unavailable.
>
> Further enquiries should be referred to your insurers.

Subsequently, following representations from the Law Society, the Revenue confirmed in a letter of 11 February 1991 that, without prejudice to the application in an appropriate case of IHTA 1984, s.199(2):

> The Capital Taxes Office will not usually pursue for inheritance tax personal representatives who:
>
> - after making the fullest inquiries that are reasonably practicable in the circumstances to discover lifetime transfers; and so
> - having done all in their power to make full disclosure of them to the Board of Inland Revenue,
>
> have obtained a certificate of discharge and distributed the estate before a chargeable lifetime transfer comes to light.

The problem for PRs is determining what HMRC will regard as 'the fullest inquiries that are reasonably practicable in the circumstances'.

15.8.2　PRs and the pre-owned assets charge

Taxpayers who derive a benefit from property which they have disposed of or to the purchase price of which they have contributed are subject to an income tax charge on the value of the benefits received, as from 6 April 2005. It is possible for taxpayers who are liable to pay the pre-owned assets income tax charge to opt out of the regime and into the IHT reservation of benefit provisions within the relevant time limit. The election is made (using Form IHT500) on or before the relevant filing date which is 31 January of the year of assessment that immediately follows the first year in which the taxpayer would otherwise be chargeable (unless the taxpayer can show a reasonable excuse – Finance Act 2004, Sched.15, para.23(3)). For existing schemes the date is, therefore, 31 January 2007.

There will then be no charge to income tax. However, the property will be treated as part of the taxpayer's estate for IHT purposes under the reservation of benefit provisions. The donee who is the person primarily liable for the IHT on the gifted property has no say in the matter.

In the case of a couple who are married or in a civil partnership who jointly owned a property and who are both caught by the pre-owned assets rules, if they both wish to have it treated as property subject to a reservation, they must both make an election. An election by one cannot affect the other. Hence one of them may choose to pay the income tax charge in respect of their share, whilst the other may elect for the gift with reservation of benefit provisions.

Once made, the election can be withdrawn or amended by the taxpayer *but only before* the relevant filing date (FA 2004, Sched.15, para.23(5)). It cannot be withdrawn by the taxpayer's PRs. (Taxpayers with existing schemes are, therefore, advised not to make an election until the last possible moment in case they die before that date. If they do, the pre-owned assets charge saved will be negligible (the tax on the benefit from April 6 2005 to the date of death) whereas the IHT charge under the reservation of benefit provisions may be considerable.)

Points for PRs

The election is sent not to the local Inspector of Taxes but to the Pre-Owned Assets Section, Capital Taxes, Nottingham (see **Useful addresses**). Capital Taxes will inform the local tax office and record the election. There will be a check on death for any elections made by the taxpayer with a view to the collection of IHT.

Before applying for a grant, PRs should make enquiries to see whether or not the taxpayer made any elections. Capital Taxes will want to see reservation of benefit reported on the IHT200 and, where an election exists but no mention is made on the IHT200, Capital Taxes will ask why. (Professional advisers should clearly impress on clients the importance of keeping copies of elections safe and easy to locate.)

The PRs should, as soon as possible, make sure that the donee knows of the election. It is the donee who is primarily liable for the IHT. The election is likely to increase the IHT payable on the rest of the death estate as the property subject to the reservation will benefit from a proportion of any available nil-rate band.

The PRs must remember their secondary liability for IHT on the reservation of benefit property.

15.8.3 Personal representatives' liability for unpaid tax on the death estate

PRs are liable for IHT on the deceased's death estate (excluding settled property). Liability is limited to the extent of assets which the PRs have received or should have received.

Note that PRs remain liable to the extent of assets which they received and handed on to the beneficiaries. The case of *Howarth's Executors* v. *CIR* [1997] STI 640 (and discussed in [1997] *Trusts and Estates*, June, 71) illustrates the danger to PRs. An employee of a firm of solicitors acted as co-executor in an estate. One of the assets of the estate was land on which the instalment option was exercised. The land was transferred to one of the beneficiaries on the undertaking that he would be responsible for the payment of the instalments. Before the end of the 10-year period, the beneficiary became bankrupt, leaving tax unpaid. The land was sold and, as the Inland Revenue had not registered the charge over the land, the purchaser took free of the charge. The solicitors' employee was held personally liable.

The moral is clear: be very careful about distributing assets where there is an outstanding tax liability. Indemnities from beneficiaries will be worthless where a beneficiary has no assets. PRs may wish to consider charging assets before transferring them to beneficiaries, for IHT.

15.8.4 Personal representatives' liability to creditors

PRs are always in danger of a claim from unsatisfied creditors arising after assets have been distributed to beneficiaries. They can protect themselves from unknown claims by advertising for claimants under Trustee Act 1925, s.27. However, sometimes they may know that a possible liability exists but be uncertain as to the amount. Section 27 is then of no help since it protects PRs only against unknown claims.

Unquantifiable liabilities may arise perhaps under leases where the deceased was a tenant or as a result of the deceased being a member of Lloyd's. Limited protection is available in respect of leases under Trustee Act

1925, s.26. For a discussion of possible liability for trustees arising from the ownership of leasehold property see [1997] *Trusts and Estates*, 94.

In many cases the only solution may be to apply to the courts for guidance. This is obviously an expensive option and PRs may wonder if the cost can be justified. In the case of *Re Yorke (Deceased), sub nom: Stone* v. *Chataway* [1997] 4 All ER 907, Lindsay J gave guidance on this subject in the context of possible liability in the estates of deceased Lloyd's Names. He stated that as only a court order can give complete protection, it cannot be wrong for executors of Lloyd's Names to insist upon the protection of a court order.

15.8.5 Personal representatives' liability for unpaid tax of the deceased

PRs may have the misfortune to face a demand from HMRC for arrears of lifetime tax due from the deceased. How far back can HMRC go and can it impose a penalty on the PRs?

Time limits

Taxes Management Act 1970, s.40(1) provides that no assessment in respect of the income or gains which arose to a deceased person during his or her lifetime can be made later than three years from 31 January next following the year of assessment in which he or she died.

Taxes Management Act 1970, s.40(2) provides that assessments on the PRs of a deceased person for the purpose of making good to the Crown a loss of tax or national insurance contributions due to fraudulent or negligent conduct may only be made within the time limit allowed, for any year ending not earlier than six years before his or her death.

Example

If a taxpayer died on 15 May 2003 all assessments would have to be made by 30 January 2008. On that date assessments could be made for years 2001/02 to 2003/04 under s.40(1) and for years 1997/98 to 2000/01 under s.40(2).

HMRC may request the PRs to make what it refers to in its Enquiry Manual (EM 3980) as 'voluntary restitution'. The Manual refers to the fact that HMRC is not entitled to tax due in respect of periods outside the statutory limits (or interest or penalties relating to that tax) but goes on to say:

Nevertheless, it is considered that HMRC is justified in inviting voluntary restitution on equitable grounds. You would then seek from the taxpayer or personal

representative the amount of the expected offer and the irrecoverable tax and NIC with simple interest but without any penalty.

This invitation should however be made only after the maximum that could be charged and the Board's policy of abatement has been fully explained. Where the suggestion of voluntary restitution is not accepted, it should not be pressed, any subsequent negotiations being conducted without reference to the irrecoverable sums. It will be appreciated that any offer in excess of the expected offer will be acceptable.

PRs are under an obligation to act in the best interests of the estate as a whole. It is difficult to see any reason for consenting to make voluntary restitution.

Note that different time limits exist in relation to EU taxes. The Recovery of Duties and Taxes etc. due in Other Member States (Corresponding UK Claims, Procedure and Supplementary) Regulations 2004, SI 2004/674, came into force on 1 April 2004. These regulations require the UK to provide effective enforcement and recovery of unpaid taxes in other EU Member States. A certificate signed by appropriate local fiscal officials stating that certain taxes (and interest) remain unpaid will provide sufficient evidence for UK purposes to enable recovery procedures to be taken in the UK. The relevant time limits applicable for the enforcement and collection of taxes due in other EU Member States will be the time limits applicable in that local jurisdiction. PRs may not therefore be able to rest comfortably on the UK time limits in relation to deceased persons. For a full discussion of this and the position in relation to non-EU foreign taxes, see a very informative article by Stephen Arthur in the May 2005 issue of the *Probate Section Journal*.

Penalties

Taxes Management Act 1970, s.95 provides that where a person fraudulently or negligently:

(a) delivers an incorrect account
(b) makes any incorrect return, statement or declaration in connection with any claim for any allowance, deduction or relief in respect of income tax or capital gains tax, or
(c) submits any incorrect accounts in connection with the ascertainment of his liability to income tax or capital gains tax,

he shall be liable to a penalty . . .

Taxes Management Act 1970, s.100A provides that where a person who has incurred a penalty has died a determination which could have been made on that person may be made in relation to his or her PRs and any penalty imposed on PRs shall be a debt due from and payable out of the estate.

There is substantial case law to suggest that the imposition of penalties for unpaid tax is a criminal charge falling within Art.6 of the European Convention on Human Rights. See *King* v. *Walden* [2001] STC 822; *King* v.

United Kingdom [2003] 5 ITLR 963 and *Georgiou* v. *United Kingdom* [2001] STC 80. In *AP* v. *Switzerland* [1998] 26 EHRR 541 and *EL and Others* v. *Switzerland* [2000] WTLR 873 the European Court of Human Rights held that tax penalties were criminal charges and that the liability of the deceased to a criminal penalty ended with his death and could not be imposed on his heirs. In a persuasive article in the May 2005 issue of *Trusts and Estates Law and Tax Journal*, Nigel Hollinshead argues that any attempt by the Revenue to impose a penalty on PRs should be resisted.

15.9 BANKRUPTCY

More and more firms are handling insolvent estates, which were once a rarity. An estate is only insolvent if the debts and liabilities cannot be paid, and is not insolvent if these can be settled, even if none of the legacies can be paid.

15.9.1 Sources of information

The legislation governing the administration of an estate which is insolvent is the Administration of Insolvent Estates of Deceased Persons Order 1986, SI 1986/1999. Totty and Moss, *Insolvency* (Sweet & Maxwell, 1986) and Berry, Bailey and Schaw-Miller, *Personal Insolvency – Law and Practice*, 3rd edn (LexisNexis, 2001) deal with this issue. A useful outline of the law can be found in *Williams, Mortimer and Sunnucks – Executors, Administrators and Probate*, 18th edn (Sweet & Maxwell, 2004). There is also a useful article by Ian Burman in *Trusts and Estates Law and Tax Journal*, June 2006.

15.9.2 A brief outline of procedure

When conducting the administration of an insolvent estate, there are three possibilities:

(a) Administration by the PRs under the directions of the court pursuant to an administration order (CPR Part 64). This means that the administration is dealt with by the PRs under the direction of the court. The courts are not anxious to undertake such a role and professional advisers rarely consider this route.

(b) Administration in bankruptcy following an insolvency administration order made by the bankruptcy court. Creditors or PRs can petition. In either case the order vests the estate in the Official Receiver. Subsequently a trustee in bankruptcy will be appointed.

(c) Administration by the PRs out of court. This is the most common method of administration. It is generally the most economic and straightforward method. Remember that creditors are entitled to take a grant. PRs do not need to be qualified insolvency practitioners (Administration of Insolvent Estates of Deceased Persons Order 1986, art.4(3)).

Whether the estate is administered by a trustee in bankruptcy or by the PRs out of court, AIEDPO 1986 provides that the same rules apply to the respective rights of creditors, to provable debts, to the valuation of future and contingent liabilities and to the priority of debts.

PRs must be careful to pay debts in the order of priority set out in the Insolvency Act 1986. This is:

- bankruptcy expenses followed by funeral, testamentary and administration expenses;
- preferential debts (e.g. VAT arrears in the six months before death);
- ordinary debts;
- interest;
- deferred debts (e.g. a loan from a person who is the deceased's spouse at the date of death).

PRs will be personally liable if they pay an inferior debt before a superior one and there are insufficient funds for the superior one. They also incur personal liability if they pay one creditor in full when there are insufficient assets to pay all creditors in that class. However, in this case there is a defence if payment was made in good faith at a time when they had no reason to believe that the estate was insolvent.

Although PRs and trustees in bankruptcy follow the same rules when administering an insolvent estate, a trustee in bankruptcy does have certain additional powers. A trustee can:

- challenge transactions made at an undervalue and transactions made to prefer some creditors at the expense of others;
- disclaim onerous property;
- apply for an order for sale of an asset in which third parties have an interest (typically the matrimonial home). Where the application is first made by the trustee in bankruptcy more than 12 months after the deceased's property vested in him, the court will assume, unless there are exceptional circumstances, that the interests of the creditors outweigh all other considerations (Insolvency Act 1986, s.335A(3)). PRs can also apply for such an order but there is no such assumption so they may have more difficulty.

PRs can petition for the appointment of a trustee in bankruptcy if they decide they do not wish to administer the estate themselves. PRs should follow this course if it becomes clear that there are assets which can be recovered only by a trustee in bankruptcy. Alternatively any creditor who could have petitioned for bankruptcy during the deceased's lifetime may petition for an administration order. The PRs will be required to deliver to the Official Receiver the deceased's books of account and records.

Once a trustee in bankruptcy is appointed, the appointment relates back to the date of death. Any disposition made by the PRs in the period between death and the vesting of the estate in the trustee in bankruptcy is void unless made with the consent of the court or subsequently ratified by the court. (Insolvency Act 1986, s.284). This is to give effect to the policy that unsecured creditors should be paid rateably.

PRs may be in difficulties as a result of the relation back. They may have started the administration unaware of the existence of liabilities which mean the estate is insolvent. In *Dick* v. *Kendall Freeman* [2005] WTLR 1619 the executor asked the court to ratify payments covering a nine-year period from death to the appointment of a trustee in bankruptcy, many of which were to the executor's own firm. The court ratified payments made in the two years following death but refused to ratify subsequent payments on the basis that after that date it was clear that the estate was insolvent and it should, therefore, have been administered on that basis. The executor should have followed the insolvency order from that point and only made payments for the benefit of the estate as a whole, not for the benefit of individual creditors. He had not done so and, as a result, the court would not ratify the payments.

It is, therefore, important for PRs to be careful when administering estates to follow the insolvency order as soon as there is any possibility that an estate may be insolvent. Provided they do so, the court should be willing to ratify payments made by them even if a trustee in bankruptcy is appointed.

15.9.3 Will you be paid for acting in relation to an insolvent estate?

The rules on solicitor-executors charging for administering estates have changed as a result of the Trustee Act 2000. Solicitors' charges are no longer regarded as a legacy but instead s.35(3)(b) provides that charges are to be regarded as 'administration expenses'.

As such they are treated in the same way as the charges of a trustee in bankruptcy and have priority over the preferential debts listed in the Insolvency Act 1986.

There are, however, problems.

1. Bear in mind that, although administration expenses have priority, the estate may be too small to cover them. Therefore, if there is a chance that an estate will be insolvent, try to assess the risk before committing a substantial amount of time to the estate. It may help if potential PRs complete a client questionnaire detailing assets and liabilities early in the administration process. The Questionnaire for Personal Representative Clients (available in packs of 25) is published by the Law Society (see

Useful addresses). Solicitor-executors and, indeed, other executors, may want to renounce. It is important not to intermeddle in an estate which may be insolvent.

2. Terms of business letters (see **Chapter 3** on client care) for solicitors employed by PRs may incorporate a clause governing the position in relation to costs incurred if the estate turns out to be insolvent, say Professional Ethics at the Law Society. Even though they are entitled to an indemnity from the estate, PRs are personally liable for the solicitor's costs.

15.9.4   Joint property

A Court of Appeal decision (*Re Palmer (Deceased) (A Debtor)* [1994] 3 WLR 420, CA) held that jointly held property passed to the co-owner on death as usual and was not available to the administrator of the estate.

The effect of this decision has been reversed by a new s.421A inserted into the Insolvency Act 1986 by the Insolvency Act 2000, s.12. The trustee of a deceased insolvent can now apply to the court to recover the value of the deceased's former interest in joint property from the survivor for the benefit of the estate. The trustee can only make the application where the petition for the insolvency order is presented after 2 April 2001 and within five years from the date of death. When deciding whether or not to make the order the court must have regard to all the circumstances of the case including the interests of the creditors and the surviving joint tenant but, unless the circumstances are exceptional, the court must assume that the interests of the creditors outweigh all other considerations.

In practice, there are problems with this provision.

1. Given that the application can be made up to five years after the death, the asset may have increased or decreased in value since death. What will the court do if the asset has changed in value? In the case of increases in value, it is clear from the wording that the court can only order a payment equal to the value at the date of the death. If the asset has decreased in value, the court will presumably take that decrease into account when deciding on the terms of the order.
2. The surviving joint tenant may have died before the order is made. If the survivor's estate is above the IHT threshold, IHT will have been paid and will have been calculated on the whole value of the joint property. There is no obvious procedure for recovering that tax.

15.9.5   Deceased Lloyd's Names

The well-publicised problems at Lloyd's meant that many Names were faced with unquantifiable losses, and to solve the problems Equitas was created.

Names waived their claims against Lloyd's and in return received debt and litigation credits and reinsurance of outstanding open years into Equitas. All business for 1992 and prior years of account was reinsured to close with Equitas upon payment of the appropriate premium.

There is a possibility of claims being made against the Names (or their estates) if the resources of Equitas prove inadequate and it fails. This presents a problem for PRs who face the possibility of personal liability if they distribute the estate without providing for this contingent liability. The Society of Trust and Estate Practitioners (STEP) brought the test case referred to at **15.8.4** above (*Re Yorke Deceased, Stone* v. *Chataway* [1997] 4 All ER 907) hoping that the judgment would remove the need for individual applications to be made for all estates in a similar position. Unfortunately the judgment did not achieve this. It approved the use of Equitas but said that PRs would face different levels of risk depending on the circumstances of the case and that they could only obtain full indemnity by applying to court for directions. He accepted that in appropriate cases, judged to be low risk, PRs could take indemnities or rely on insurance.

There is a streamlined form of application available which will be heard by a Master rather than a judge. This is dealt with in *Practice Statement: Chancery Division: Estates of Deceased Lloyd's Names* [2001] 3 All ER 765.

The procedure applies to cases where the only, or only substantial, reason for delaying distribution of the estate is the possibility of personal liability to Lloyd's creditors and:

- all liabilities of the estate in respect of syndicates of which the Name was a member for the years of account 1992 and earlier have been reinsured into the Equitas Group; and
- all liabilities of the estate in respect of syndicates of which the Name was a member for the years of account 1993 and later:
  - are in respect of syndicates which have closed by reinsurance in the usual way;
  - are protected by an Estate Protection Plan issued by Centrewrite Ltd; or
  - are protected by EXEAT insurance cover provided by Centrewrite Ltd.

The Practice Direction contains a specimen witness statement to support the claim form and a specimen draft order, although both are likely to need adapting to suit the circumstances of the case.

15.9.6 Bankrupt beneficiaries

There is a risk of personal liability for a PR who pays a legacy direct to a bankrupt beneficiary rather than to the trustee in bankruptcy. An article in [1993] *Gazette*, 24 February deals fully with this ('Personal representatives and bankrupt beneficiaries').

There is no specific statutory protection for a PR who transfers assets to a beneficiary who turns out to be bankrupt. This might suggest that a PR should as a matter of routine carry out a bankruptcy search. However, it seems unlikely that a court would impose liability on a PR who paid in good faith, without notice of the bankruptcy and without any reason to suspect a bankruptcy.

It is a different matter if PRs have notice that there may be a query about a particular beneficiary. A bankruptcy-only search under the Land Charges Act 1925 could be made (against any name a beneficiary might use) or the PRs could contact the Insolvency Service (see **Useful addresses**).

Bankrupts must give notice to their trustee in bankruptcy of any after-acquired property (Insolvency Act 1986, s.333). The trustee can then serve a notice in writing on the bankrupt under s.307 claiming the property. It seems, therefore, that PRs could safely hand over money to a bankrupt beneficiary on proof that the bankrupt has complied with his or her duties under the Insolvency Act 1986 under s.333. A PR would be justified in refusing to hand over property until such proof was available.

Be alert to potential problems if a bankrupt beneficiary suggests that the money should be paid over in a way which is at all unusual. If concerned, consider seeking the assistance of the court under CPR, Part 64 (or, as a last resort, paying money into court under Trustee Act 1925, s.63).

Testators who have left property to beneficiaries who have become bankrupt may wish to consider revoking absolute legacies and substituting discretionary trusts.

Rooney v. *Cardona* [1999] 1 WLR 1388 was an interesting case on bankruptcy and life policies under Married Women's Property Act 1882, s.11. A life insurance company paid the proceeds of a joint life insurance policy to a bankrupt husband on the death of his wife. The husband was one of the two executors of the estate and the question was whether he had given a good receipt to the life insurance company. If he had not, the company would have to pay again to the trustee in bankruptcy. (The husband had effectively dissipated the money by the time the trustee heard of it.) The Court of Appeal held that the company had to pay again as the husband's signature was not a good receipt. The policy was a Married Women's Property Act policy and, as such, was not an asset of the estate. The executors held it as trustees for the beneficiaries. Trustees have joint authority and, therefore, the signatures of both trustees were required to provide a valid discharge.

15.10   PERSONAL REPRESENTATIVES SEPARATELY REPRESENTED

The following opinion was originally published in [1986] *Gazette*, 3 September, 2561–2 and may be of assistance if one PR wishes to seek separate advice from the other(s). (Text in italic has been superseded by the

Solicitors' (Non-Contentious Business) Remuneration Order 1994, see **Appendix B4**.)

Costs: Personal representatives separately represented

The following notes are issued by the Law Society's Non-Contentious Business Committee. Since the Joint Agreed Case was reported in [1985] *Gazette*, 24 October, 2987, the number of enquiries which the Society has received from practitioners indicates a need to publish more detailed guidelines. The following guidelines have been settled by counsel but practitioners should note that the Society has no power to determine matters of law, and that matters of dispute may ultimately fall to be determined by the court.

1. The basic principle is that a personal representative is entitled to an indemnity from the estate in respect of costs and expenses properly incurred in the course of his office. Trustee Act 1925, s.23 expressly empowers personal representatives to employ and pay a solicitor to transact any business or to do any act required to be transacted or done in the administration of the estate.

2. The indemnity will not, however, be available (where there is more than one personal representative) to each personal representative who chooses to instruct his own separate solicitor, as the right to instruct a solicitor is limited by the overriding principle that personal representatives must act properly in exercising their rights and powers. In particular they must not make, or cause there to be made, any wasteful or unnecessary payments out of the estate.

3. Thus it is considered that in a normal case it is incumbent upon personal representatives to agree upon the joint instructions of solicitors.

4. In certain cases it may be proper for more than one firm to be instructed, where, for example, in the case of a large landed estate, different skills are required; in such a case it is unlikely that more costs would be incurred than if one firm dealt with all the work.

5. It is, of course, always open to a personal representative to seek independent legal advice separately from the advice given by the firm instructed on behalf of all the personal representatives, but in such circumstances he will normally not be entitled to an indemnity from the estate for the cost of doing so, and will have to pay such costs personally.

6. Mere personal animosity between personal representatives does not justify the appointment of a separate firm so as to increase the costs payable by the estate.

7. Exceptional circumstances justifying the instruction of a separate solicitor at the expense of the estate might include a case where a personal representative became aware of a devastavit or breach of trust by his fellow personal representative and required independent legal advice as to his position; or when the instructed solicitor refused or failed properly to carry out his instructions, thus necessitating the instruction of another firm (although here, strictly, no additional costs should be incurred, as the defaulting solicitor would not be entitled to recover his costs).

8. It is also open to personal representatives to agree that they should be separately represented provided that the estate does not thereby bear any additional costs. As the instruction of two firms in respect of the same work will inevitably involve extra work, it will avoid subsequent dispute if the personal representatives also agree in advance to bear personally the extra costs involved (and agree the proportions in which they will do so).

9. Any personal liability incurred by personal representatives may, of course, be charged to the estate with the concurrence of all the beneficiaries, provided that they are all *sui juris* and are properly advised.

10. Where a personal representative instructs a practitioner in circumstances where he knows that another firm is already acting for the estate he should be made aware of the likelihood that he will be personally responsible for his costs.

11. A distinction may need to be made between the fees charged to the personal representatives by the appointed firm of solicitors on the one hand and fees charged by a solicitor-executor on the other hand. Provided that the 'professional charging clause' expressly so provided a professional executor may properly charge for his time and trouble in acting as an executor, as distinct from his firm's charges for legal work transacted. More than one professional person may be appointed executor and may be entitled so to charge, but such charges will in both cases be of a different nature from the fees of the firm jointly instructed by the personal representatives to do legal work.

12. Beneficiaries who take legal advice in connection with the administration of an estate will rarely be entitled to recover from the estate their costs so incurred, but they may be entitled to recover such costs from a defaulting personal representative who will not in such circumstances be entitled to recover them from the estate.

13. The Society is also asked from time to time to advise as to how the legal fees should be calculated in cases where more than one firm is involved in the administration of an estate. Opinions published in the Society's Digest in the past indicated a split of two-thirds/one-third; these were however published at a time when solicitors' fees were charged on a straight percentage of the value of the estate. *Since the Solicitors' Remuneration Order 1972 this element is only one of the factors to be taken into account in assessing what is fair and reasonable in each case; the two-thirds/one-third split is therefore no longer appropriate. The value element does still have to be taken into account, and will be recognised in the fair and reasonable charges of the respective firms, bearing in mind the amount of work carried out by each firm, the degree of responsibility involved and other factors set out in Article 2 of the Solicitors' Remuneration Order 1972.* This is subject to the overriding principle expressed in para. 8 above that the estate itself should not normally bear the additional expense occasioned by the employment of more than one firm.

15.11 UNSUITABLE PERSONAL REPRESENTATIVES

PRs may be passed over under Supreme Court Act 1981, s.116: an application to the High Court may be made if it appears that the person apparently entitled to take the grant is unsuitable. The person next entitled to the grant will not necessarily be appointed.

An application for the removal of a PR may be made under Administration of Justice Act 1985, s.50. This section also gives the High Court power to appoint someone else to act. (See also at **13.10.2** above.) In *Loftus Deceased* [2005] EWHC 406 (Ch) the court held that removal under s.50 is a matter for the discretion of the court, and it is reasonable for the court to take a pragmatic approach, to consider the views of the beneficiaries and the interests of the estate as a whole. It will often be appropriate for the court will often appoint an independent expert in place of the original PR.

The Family Division has power to revoke grants under NCPR 1987, Rule 41. Normally the consent of the grantee is required before revocation can take place. However, 'in exceptional circumstances' a district judge or registrar can revoke a grant without the grantee's consent. Where an executor or administrator refuses or neglects to participate properly in the administration of the estate, it may be possible to get the grant revoked. It is worth contacting the registry to see whether or not the circumstances of the case would justify such an application. Where they do, it represents a simpler and cheaper solution than a s.50 application.

15.12   PROBLEMS FROM CLIENTS

15.12.1   Distressed clients

Clients coming for help and advice on probate may be suffering grief and distress. Bereavement can generate many and conflicting emotions, which are not always expressed as one might expect. Sometimes clients' feelings spill over, so that the conduct of the administration is affected, for example by a family quarrel.

Helping bereaved clients, and coping with clients' feelings and emotions, can be difficult for practitioners. This is an added (and often unrecognised) source of stress for many practitioners, who may feel ambivalent about how to respond to clients and how to deal with their feelings.

Christopher Clulow, Director of the Tavistock Institute for Marital Studies in London, considered some of these issues in a number of short articles in the series 'Only Connect' in the journal *Family Law* during 1992 and 1993. Although directed mainly to solicitors working with divorce, the articles would be of great value and interest to all private client practitioners. There is a helpful article by Elizabeth McManus in the 2006 issue of the *Probate Section Journal* on the difficulties of working with emotional clients.

It may be worthwhile ensuring that your office holds an up-to-date list of local voluntary and other sources of help and support for distressed and bereaved clients.

Solicitors may be approached by a client involved in a major tragedy. The Law Society's Multi-Party Action Information Service exists to link the solicitors' firms instructed by those involved and their families and friends. The Multi-Party Actions Information Service has two related objectives:

1. To provide the public and their solicitors with basic information about current or recent actions, giving key dates and the names of either local or all participating firms as provided by those participating firms.

The public should telephone the Law Society's public enquiry line and solicitors who want to refer clients should telephone Practice Advice (see **Useful addresses**).

2. To maintain contact with participating firms in order to market them to potential clients and their solicitors and to communicate relevant information.

Firms already participating in or contemplating participating in an action should telephone Practice Advice at the Law Society.

15.12.2 Dealing with sudden deaths abroad

After the Tsunami in December 2004 there was a great deal of media confusion over the distinction between the presumption of death and leave to swear death and whether or not a seven-year period was required.

If there is evidence that a person is dead, it is possible to take a grant at any point by applying to the probate registry under NCPR 1987, Rule 53 for leave to swear death.

The application must be supported by an affidavit setting out the facts. It should deal with the following:

*   when the person was last heard of;
*   whether there have been advertisements;
*   whether there was any relevant communication before the disappearance;
*   whether there is a will and, if not, who is entitled on intestacy;
*   the value of the estate;
*   a statement that the person is dead;
*   anything else of relevance.

If there is an insurance policy which will pay out on death, the company must be told of the application and sent a copy of the affidavit. It can oppose the application.

In cases where there is no evidence, a person can be presumed dead after a continuous period of seven years or more. This requires an application to court. It is necessary to prove that:

(a) there are persons who would be likely to have heard of him over that period;

(b) those persons have not heard of him; and

(c) all due inquiries have been made appropriate to the circumstances, without result, then the presumption of law is that the person died within the period.

Richard Bark-Jones, Partner at Morecroft Urquart, Liverpool and former chairman of the Law Society's Wills and Equity Committee wrote the following guidance on dealing with sudden deaths abroad for the

Probate Section Journal shortly after the tragic events in New York of 11 September 2001:

> The recent appalling events in the United States may mean that some of you have to help clients deal with the sudden death of a relative abroad. Here are some general pointers to help you handle the situation.

If the body is found

Follow the usual procedure ie arrange the issuing of the death certificate in the country of death. The British Embassy/Consulate is invariably helpful and can give some advice on local procedures.

The application for the grant will follow normal procedures.

If the body is not found, but its whereabouts are known

The first port of call will be the deceased's employers (if not self-employed or on holiday) who should be able to provide evidence as to the whereabouts of the deceased.

The second port of call will be the British Embassy/Consulate, which with the benefit of the information supplied by the deceased's employers, will advise on local procedures.

Assuming a death certificate is issued, the application for the grant should be straightforward as there is no difficulty in asserting death.

If no body is found and the whereabouts are not known

Steps 1 and 2 as above.

If no death certificate can be obtained in order to obtain the grant, the applicant can apply for leave to swear to the death on an ex parte application supported by a sworn Statement of Facts. This should set out all the known circumstances relevant to the disappearance and should list the deceased's assets and particularly any life policies (for obvious reasons).

On obtaining leave to swear to death, the application for a grant should be straightforward although the wording of the oath will be different.

15.12.3 Arranging funerals

Solicitors may be asked a variety of questions about funerals. Whose responsibility is it to arrange and pay for the funeral? Do PRs have to carry out the deceased's wishes? What if there is a dispute between surviving relatives? Waterworth and Bedworth, *Rossdale: Probate and the Administration of Estates*, 3rd edn (Legalease, 2006) has an excellent section on the subject. The following may be helpful.

Who is responsible for arranging the funeral?

Nobody owns a dead body (*R. v. Sharpe* (1857) 26 LJMC 47). This is presumably on the grounds of public health and public policy. However, there is a common law duty on an executor to arrange for the proper disposal of the deceased's remains.

As an executor's authority derives from the will and not from the grant, they are entitled to obtain possession of the body for the purposes of burial prior to the grant (by injunction under Supreme Court Act 1981, s.37 if necessary). Philip Rossdale said:

> In a case coming to my notice the threat of an application for an ex parte injunction resulted in the prompt release of the body to the executor. It is true that there is no property in a dead body to support a claim for damages . . . but that is no obstacle to an injunction for the delivery of the body: injunctions are awarded on different principles from damages.

An administrator also has a common law duty to dispose of the body but, as their authority derives from the grant, they may not be able to obtain an injunction for delivery of the body until they have obtained the grant.

A householder has a common law duty to dispose of a body. When the deceased lived alone the duty passes to the local authority (Public Health (Control of Disease) Act 1984, s.46(1)). Local authorities will not pay if there are assets and may instruct solicitors (through their bereavement services department) to trace relatives to authorise the cost of the funeral. If the deceased died in hospital, the duty of disposal falls on the hospital authorities.

In *Lewisham NHS Hospital Trust* v. *Hamuth* [2006] All ER (D) 145 there was a dispute as to the validity of the will and, therefore, as to the validity of the executor appointed in it. The deceased had died in hospital. The executor wished to carry out the deceased's instructions and cremate the body. The family wanted to have the body buried in the family plot. The court held that an executor in general had the right to make arrangements for the disposal of the body but that there was also a common law duty for a householder under whose roof a person had died to make arrangements for a dignified and decent burial. The hospital, being in lawful possession of the body and there being no way of resolving the dispute as to whether executor was validly appointed within an acceptable time period, had the authority to decide the appropriate means for the disposal of the body.

Are the deceased's wishes binding?

No. It was held in *Williams* v. *Williams* (1882) 20 Ch D 659 that a person has no property in their body after their death. Thus, a testator cannot dispose of his body by will and any wishes expressed in the will are not binding on the executors. Directions for a lavish funeral can thus be ignored with impunity. However this is an issue which should be taken seriously when appointing executors. Many religious groups have strong views about burial or cremation

(Judaism and Islam require burial whereas Hinduism requires cremation) while some environmentalists regard cremation as an improper use of fuel. It is, therefore, important to appoint executors who will respect the deceased's wishes.

When are organs available?

A person can give written consent at any time or oral consent during his or her last illness to the use of organs for therapeutic purposes or for the purposes of medical education or research. The persons lawfully in possession of the body can then authorise the use of organs so long as they have no reason to believe the request was withdrawn.

If a solicitor is taking instructions for a will and the client expresses a wish to leave organs for donation, it is important for the solicitor to check whether the client wishes organs to be used only for therapeutic purposes or whether the client is happy for organs to be taken for research or education purposes.

The clause in the will should be worded appropriately. Speed is of the essence in such cases, so clients should be encouraged to carry an organ donor card and to tell close relatives of their wishes.

If there is no evidence of the deceased's wishes, the person who has lawful possession of the body can authorise its use for organ donation or for research or education. However, they have to show that they made reasonable enquiries, have no reason to believe the deceased had expressed any objection and have no reason to believe that any surviving spouse or surviving relative will object.

Carrying a donor card is obviously helpful and people can register with the NHS Organ Donor Register online or by telephone (see UK Transplant contact details under **Useful addresses**). There is a helpful article by Jonathan Smith, a family law solicitor and mediator based in Litchfield, in [2002] *Solicitors Journal*, 4 September, 781. UK Transplant (since October 2005 part of NHS Blood and Transplant) will send registration forms to solicitors which clients can complete and return.

Inquests and post-mortems

Fairly obviously, if there is reason to believe that there will be an inquest, no one can authorise the use of organs without the consent of a coroner. The same applies if a post-mortem is likely.

Alternative burials

Many people now consider burials in woods, fields or gardens. They can arrange for this but will have to obtain the consent of the relevant local authority. This is because a body is treated as clinical waste and can, therefore, only be disposed of by a licensed operator in accordance with the Control of Pollution Act 1974 and the Environmental Protection Act 1990. If relatives want to bury the body in the garden, they will have to take advice from the Environment Agency which has a list of minimum distances from the site of a grave to water, cabling and wells or boreholes. The Department of the Environment confirmed in a letter to the Natural Death Centre in 1994 that it is not necessary to apply for planning permission to bury up to two people in a back garden. Permission would be required to bury any more. It is possible to apply for a certificate of lawfulness as regards planning law, and the result of the application is recorded on a public register. If the application is refused, there is a right of free appeal.

Turning to the even more esoteric it is also possible to have a burial at sea. Readers wishing to know the details are referred to Mathew Knight's article in [2000] *Trusts and Estates*, October, 8.

Cremation of body parts after post-mortem

Under the Cremation Regulations 1930, SR&O 1930/1016, there was a problem where body parts had been removed during post-mortem and not returned at the time of burial. When the body parts were returned, relatives were not allowed to cremate them if the body had been buried, and the parts had to be buried with the body. Separate cremation of body parts was only permitted when the body itself had been cremated. Under the Cremation (Amendment) Regulations 2000, SI 2000/58 it is now irrelevant whether the body was buried or cremated. However, the new regulations do not require cremation, and it will still be possible to bury the parts with the body or to have them disposed of as clinical waste.

Disputes between parents over child's funeral arrangements

In *Fessi* v. *Whitmore* [1999] 1 FLR 767, divorced parents were unable to agree on the funeral arrangements for their 12-year-old son. The boy lived with his mother in the Midlands but had contact with his father who lived in Wales. The boy was killed in an accident while visiting his father in Wales. The father had the boy cremated and wanted to scatter his ashes in the sea off the Welsh coast. The mother wanted to have the ashes interred in the Midlands with a service arranged in conjunction with the boy's school. The parties were unable to agree and an application was made to court. The court concluded that parents with parental responsibility both have an equal right and duty to arrange the child's funeral. Judge Boggis QC said that he was considering an issue where the parties had equal entitlement but conflicting proposals. This was akin to a dispute between trustees and he was, therefore, entitled to consider the issue and come to a conclusion 'which does justice and fairness to both sides'. He ordered that the remains should be disposed of in accordance with the proposals of the mother, in the Midlands. This was because there was a connection there with both sides of the family and this would provide a focus for all the family. For a fuller discussion of the case see the article by David Hershman in [1999] *Trusts and Estates Law Journal*, November.

15.12.4   Difficult clients

Sometimes solicitors will encounter clients who are hard to please. It may just have to be accepted, but in a proportion of cases there may be some misunderstanding which could be discussed and perhaps removed. Asking such a client what the problem is, if appropriate, may be worthwhile, or a colleague may be able to assist. Prompt action may help to avert a complaint.

15.12.5   Are you being misled?

Not all clients are honest. If solicitors suspect a client is misleading them or others involved, these concerns must be discussed with the client, no matter how difficult this seems. There may, of course, be a completely reasonable explanation. The risks of involvement in another's dishonesty are analysed in **Chapter 6**.

The Professional Ethics division may be able to help (see **Useful addresses**).

Solicitors should be aware of the dangers of money laundering. The Law Society has issued guidance which is available on its website. The guidance sets out warning signs to watch for, albeit with the caveat that money laundering techniques change over time. The Law Society's Anti-Money Laundering Guidance for Solicitors Conducting Private Client Work is reproduced in **Appendix A1**. See also **13.9.6**.

15.13   CONSUMER COMPLAINTS SERVICE

15.13.1   Request for another firm to handle the work involved

This request is a variation on the request to renounce. If a solicitor has refused to renounce, there may be a request that the beneficiaries' chosen firm undertake the actual work instead of the solicitor's firm. This may be on a variety of grounds, but cost (the other firm is cheaper), convenience (the other firm is nearer) or familiarity (the other firm is the residuary beneficiary's own solicitors) are the most common.

The Consumer Complaints Service (CCS) suggests that the presumption would be that the original solicitor, having been appointed executor or executrix by the deceased, would undertake the winding up of the estate. That solicitor is free to agree differently, but if so, he or she will need to consider what, if anything, the charging clause in the will allows him or her. If the solicitor wishes to insist on handling the administration, this may lead to a great deal of difficulty and ill-will in the future.

15.14 CHARGING CLAUSES

15.14.1 No charging clause

If a will does not contain a charging clause, Trustee Act 2000, s.29 allows a trustee who acts in a professional capacity in relation to the management or administration of the estate to charge reasonable remuneration for services provided, no matter when the trust was created, provided that the co-trustees consent in writing. The provision is of no assistance to sole executors or administrators who will have to arrange the appointment of co-trustees.

Professional executors can charge for their time if the beneficiaries are all adult and *sui juris* and give their approval. According to Barlow, King and King, *Wills Administration and Taxation: A Practical Guide*, 8th edn (Sweet & Maxwell, 2003), it is possible for a solicitor appointed executor or executrix to employ and pay individual partners in the firm, provided there is an express agreement that the solicitor-PR shall not participate in the profits nor derive any benefit from the charges: *Re Gates* [1933] Ch 913. However, it is better practice in such a situation to inform clients that this problem has arisen and seek their consent to a charge being made. If legal advice is to be taken by lay PRs, they will incur costs in any event.

15.14.2 Inappropriate charging clause

It is important to look carefully at a charging clause to check exactly who is entitled to charge and for what. Lay executors can charge if there is an appropriate charging clause but not otherwise. Charities complain that there is an increasing tendency for lay executors to seek to charge in circumstances where they are not able to do so.

A common form of clause is 'Any trustee engaged in a profession or business may charge for all work done and time spent'. This will allow any professional or business person to charge for any work done. The following clause is more limited: 'Any trustee who acts in a professional capacity may charge'. This will only allow a trustee to charge for professional services rendered. Thus, an accountant could charge for accountancy services rendered and an estate agent could charge for valuations provided.

Also be careful if a company director is to be appointed. The usual wording of a person 'engaged in a profession or business' does not clearly apply to an employee. The Encyclopedia of Forms and Precedents suggests the following:

Any trustee, whether he is engaged in a profession or business, or merely acts in a personal capacity shall be entitled to charge . . .

Even if a trustee is authorised to charge, the clause will normally authorise 'reasonable' charges. A solicitor should check to see whether the charges made are reasonable.

15.15 SOLICITOR-EXECUTOR WITNESSES THE WILL

Trustee Act 2000, s.28 provides that a charging clause is no longer regarded as a gift for the purposes of Wills Act, s.15. Solicitors who witness a will which allows them to charge for their services will no longer forfeit the benefit of the charging clause.

15.16 CHARGING CLAUSE IN INVALID WILL

If a will proves to be invalid (for example, as a result of faulty execution) all legacies fail and naturally a solicitors' charging clause (being analogous to a legacy) also fails.

In *Gray* v. *Richards Butler* [2000] WTLR 625, solicitors who had paid themselves under a charging clause contained in a will which proved to be invalid for want of due execution had to repay the residuary beneficiary of an earlier will. The court did exercise its inherent jurisdiction to order reasonable remuneration for work done by the firm which could have been undertaken for the earlier valid will.

15.17 TWO-YEAR DISCRETIONARY TRUSTS AND THE THREE-MONTH TRAP

Most practitioners are aware that if appointments are made out of a discretionary trust within three months of the testator's or testatrix's death, there will be no reading back for IHT purposes. This was highlighted in the case of *Frankland* v. *Inland Revenue Commissioners* [1996] STC 735 where, as a result the spouse exemption was unavailable and £2m of tax was irrecoverable. See articles in [1996] *Solicitors Journal*, 4 October by Julie Evans and 25 October by Catherine Sanders. The wording of IHTA 1984, s.144 means that an appointment made within the first three months after death is not read back. Appointments to a spouse or charity will not qualify for exemption.

There is no three-month trap if appointments are made to create an immediate post-death interest or a trust for bereaved minors under IHTA 1984, s.71A or D.

15.18   DEALING WITH MISTAKES

See *The Guide to the Professional Conduct of Solicitors 1999* (the Guide), ch.29. How mistakes should be handled depends on the nature and significance of the error, and the applicability of the relevant principles in the Guide, but the following comments may also be of interest.

According to the CCS, relatively minor errors are usually best dealt with promptly by being frank with the client. Most clients will appreciate openness at an early stage and an explanation. It seems that clients find a lack of frankness (or an impression of it, from an absence of explanation, or failure to answer questions or reply to letters, etc.) more irritating, and more likely to found a complaint, than a prompt apology and explanation of the problem.

More serious mistakes create different issues. First, these should be discussed with your insurers. Second, clients may have to be advised to obtain independent advice (see Principle 29.09 and commentaries).

In either case, Professional Ethics and the Practice Advice Service (see **Useful addresses**) may be able to assist.

If solicitors acting for the other side have made an error which they refuse to deal with, or they do not reply to correspondence, it is open to solicitors and/or their client to use the Rule 15 complaints procedure. If this does not resolve the matter, either the solicitors or their client may consider making a complaint to the CCS. Only the client, however, can ask for the complaint to be conciliated.

Conciliation can be an effective means of resolving less serious disputes – more information is available from the CCS.

A booklet entitled Handling Complaints Effectively, 4th edn (Law Society, 2006) can be downloaded from the Law Society's website (**www.lawsociety.org.uk/professional/monitoring/complaintsresolution.law**). Complaints and Complainants in Probate Matters (2004) is also available on the Law Society's main website and reproduced here in **Appendix A2**.

15.19   SOURCES OF HELP

15.19.1   The court

The court can assist in a number of ways: an application under CPR Part 64 may be made for help on a particular point, or for the court's assistance in the administration generally; a PR may be removed by the court under Administration of Justice Act 1985, s.50; and Trustee Act 1925, s.63 provides for payment into court, in appropriate circumstances, if trustees are unable otherwise to obtain good discharge. The court can also assist if it is impossible to trace missing beneficiaries (see **15.1** above) and Administration of

Justice Act 1985, s.49 allows the court to pronounce on the validity of wills if the consent of the beneficiaries has been obtained. Clearly, the cost of such an application means that approaching the court is not one's first recourse, but there may be in the end no other alternative. Personal representatives' costs would usually be met from the estate (but see **15.10** above for counsel's opinion on the costs of PRs separately represented). An excellent series of articles by Dawn Goodman of Withers appeared in [1994] *Solicitors Journal*, August and September, on how to avoid problems and how the court can help.

In *Re Barton (Deceased)* [2002] EWHC 264 (Ch) (20 March 2002) an executor failed to recover his cost incurred in challenging a deed made between the residuary beneficiary (the Society) and an annuitant commuting the annuity to a lump sum. The Society had made it clear before the commencement of proceedings that it and the annuitant accepted the validity of the deed and that there was, therefore, no need to refer the matter to court. The case is an illustration of how careful executors and trustees should be to avoid unnecessary cost. The courts are not prepared to order costs from the estate where the application was misconceived.

15.19.2 Official

The Official Solicitor (see **Useful addresses**) deals with personal injury work for children and adults without mental capacity, and also acts for children in other cases, as next friend or guardian ad litem where appropriate. The Official Solicitor also acts as trustee, obtains grants of representation for the use and benefit of those without mental capacity, and is asked to administer estates of certain intestates to allow IPFDA 1975 claims to be made. The website of the Official Solicitor (**www.officialsolicitor.gov.uk**) has several useful publications and includes various Practice Directions.

15.19.3 Court of Protection

The financial affairs of people lacking mental capacity to handle these personally are the responsibility of the Court of Protection. The Court publishes useful booklets for receivers and enduring attorneys (see address in **Useful addresses**). The Public Guardianship Office is the administrative arm of the Court of Protection and produces many publications which are all available from its website (**www.guardianship.gov.uk**).

15.19.4 Probate registries

The Principal Registry is encouraging registrars to make contact with practices in their catchment areas, for example by meeting local law societies, which were asked to appoint a liaison officer to further this link.

The probate registry offers a very reasonably priced oath-settling service in cases of difficulty. Kevin Donnelly, Probate Department Manager at the Principal Probate Registry wrote, a little hopefully, in [2002] *Probate Section Journal*, February:

> We are becoming equipped with the basis of a communication system which will in a relatively short time encompass all Probate Registries. I hope it should not be too long before you can contact Registries electronically, receive an electronic reply and (who knows) even have your documents settled that way. This will enhance the service to a considerable extent and perhaps even provide the basis for a different way of delivering the goods altogether.
>
> I talk of the future but I can offer these facilities in London now. I confess we have not settled a document electronically but it should be possible although I would ask that as the email facility is a little limited at present, this be used for urgent or complex cases.
>
> You will say you do not know the number: perhaps this is just as well as you might then try to get in touch. But if you really want to know, try **kevin.donnelly@courtservice.gsi.gov.uk**. You never know, I might even be able to help.

15.19.5 Mediation

Seemingly intractable disputes can often be settled with the help of a trained mediator.

15.19.6 Lawyer Line

The following article about the work of Lawyer Line appeared in [2001] *Probate Section Journal*, July. We have edited it and are grateful for permission to reproduce it:

> About five years ago the Office for the Supervision of Solicitors decided to offer a service to the profession whereby solicitors could obtain good advice over the telephone about how to deal with complaints they might receive about the standards of service afforded their clients. Since then the service has been operated with great success and appreciation by those who have made use of the facility.
>
> As far as service complaints in probate matters are concerned, these are mainly of three types. The first, and by far the most common, are concerned with delay – and what seems to be the main cause of the problem is simply failing to do the estate accounts and get the estate administered. It is as if, having done all the donkey work, the file is often put to one side, presumably on the basis that it is just a matter of routine to draw the estate accounts, and it is just forgotten about – or perhaps the solicitor just does not realise how time is passing!.
>
> The second source of complaints is estate accounts that are drawn incorrectly, not infrequently because of simple arithmetical error. In these cases it frequently

transpires that had the Client Account been checked before the final accounts were drawn and the distribution made, the error would have been avoided altogether. The moral is obvious.

The third cause of complaints is the overlooking of liabilities that need to be cleared or specific legacies, payment of which is overlooked. Either way, the result is that residuary beneficiaries are overpaid and the solicitor then has the embarrassing task of writing to them asking for monies to be repaid.

A problem that, from the evidence of the numbers of calls on the subject made to Lawyer Line, is a constant worry to solicitors, is whether and when they need to deal with complaints from residuary beneficiaries. There is no room here to deal with that matter, but readers can refer to the article written by Mike Frith on the subject in the February 2000 edition of the Gazette.

The Lawyer Line service is available by calling 0870 606 2588.

There is a very useful book by Mike Frith dealing with this whole subject, entitled *Complaints Avoidance and Complaints Handling* (EMIS Professional Publishing, 2001), which also deals in much greater detail with the advice referred to above.

15.19.7 The Law Society

The Probate Section caters for solicitors who have an interest in wills and trusts, tax planning, investment advice as part of financial planning, Court of Protection, care planning for elderly clients and estate administration.

The Practice Advice Service answers solicitors' questions on legal practice problems in all areas of law.

The Professional Ethics department offers confidential advice on the application and interpretation of the rules and principles of professional conduct. This advice encompasses such issues as how the rules affect solicitors' plans to develop their practices, or their relationships with clients, the court and others with whom they have dealings. Professional Ethics can be contacted by letter, or by telephone during office hours.

15.19.8 Insurers

Problems which may involve claims against solicitors need to be referred to their insurers. Policies are likely to provide that the solicitor has a discretion whether to inform the insurers of circumstances which the solicitor believes may result in a claim, and a duty to notify them of claims which have been made against the solicitor or which the solicitor learns will be made.

15.19.9 Specialist solicitors and counsel

Counsel's opinion may be necessary on a variety of matters. If the question is one of construction, Administration of Justice Act 1985, s.48 allows a barrister of 10 years' standing to give an opinion to the PRs on which the court may, without hearing argument, allow them to act.

Rather than approaching counsel, some practitioners may like to consider consulting another firm of solicitors. This is a practice which is becoming established in certain specialist fields such as pensions and contentious probate.

It may be particularly useful to approach a professional colleague if a difficulty also raises conduct or practice issues, since another solicitor will be more aware than counsel of the impact of the Practice Rules and issues relating to practice as a solicitor.

15.19.10 Institute of Legacy Management and legacy officers

Where charities are beneficiaries, solicitors should be aware that charities are in a sense 'professional beneficiaries'. The legacy officers of the larger charities have a wealth of specialist knowledge, and it is well worth discussing with them problems arising from the administration of estates in which they are interested, as they may well have had previous experience of that very problem. The website of the Institute of Legacy Management has a number of fact sheets for solicitors (see **www.ilmnet.org**).

15.19.11 Within the office

All solicitors, from time to time, have files which they feel have become bogged down or which are a constant headache. One option is to try to make a deal with a colleague to exchange 'headache' files once a month. A different solicitor may be able to skip through something which has stalled a colleague for days – and vice versa.

15.19.12 Personal

Stress is a major cause of illness. Many solicitors face huge pressures and a heavy burden of others' expectations and responsibility at work. There are now numerous books on stress available which help to identify the symptoms and suggest solutions. There are helpful articles in the *Probate Section Journal* (available on the website, **www.probatesection.org.uk**) entitled 'Stress and legal practice' September 1999; 'A new look at workplace counselling' December 1999; and 'Stress out!' June 2003.

15.19.13 The Solicitors Assistance Scheme

The Solicitors Assistance Scheme (SAS) aims to serve the solicitors' profession by providing solicitors and their staff with initial independent and confidential advice and assistance in respect of professional, business or personal problems. In doing so it seeks to enable individuals requiring help to resolve their problems, such as:

- stress;
- professional problems;
- bereavement;
- illness (including alcoholism and drugs);
- financial worries (including insolvency and intervention);
- employment problems; and
- disciplinary problems.

See **www.solicitorsassistancescheme.org.uk** or call the helpline (see **Useful addresses**).

15.19.14   LawCare

To assist lawyers, the Law Societies of England and Wales, Scotland, and Northern Ireland, the Bar Council and ILEX have funded LawCare, a confidential advisory service to help lawyers, their staff and their immediate families to deal with the health issues and related emotional difficulties that can result from a stressful career as a lawyer. There is a free helpline (see **Useful addresses**) or visit **www.lawcare.org.uk**.

15.20   PARTING COMPANY

Sometimes, solicitors and clients have to part company. Clients may terminate retainers on any grounds they wish. Solicitors may terminate retainers in more limited circumstances, which are set out in the Guide, Principle 12.10 and commentaries. They include a client's supervening incapacity and the breakdown of trust and confidence.

Lay and professional executors, or two or more lay executors, may disagree about a number of issues. Where executors cannot agree, one may seek independent advice. An opinion given by counsel in 1986 on costs issues arising out of such a step is included at **15.10** above. It is clear from this opinion that PRs seeking independent advice may not in every case find that their costs would be paid from the estate.

Other problems arise where it is clear, or feared, that a client intends to act dishonestly, for example, by saying outstanding tax is to remain unpaid. In certain cases, solicitors may decline to act. It is rare, but does sometimes arise, that a third party should be informed. Principle 16.07 of the Guide refers to such problems and in difficult cases the assistance of Professional Ethics (see **Useful addresses**) is always available. Some of the issues are considered in **Chapter 6**. Solicitors should also be aware of the warnings given by the Law Society in relation to mortgage fraud and money laundering.

CHAPTER 16

Accounting and distributing

Lesley King

16.1   INTRODUCTION

Paragraphs 16.2–16.4, the specimen accounts for Victoria Thomas (at **16.3.1** below) and the explanatory notes which follow (at **16.3.2** below) are based on materials prepared by the College of Law for trainee solicitors. We are most grateful to the College for its help in allowing us to reproduce these edited sections.

An increasing number of firms are turning to computerised packages to produce their accounts (see **Chapter 18**). Even so, we have set out the essential elements of the accounts in this chapter.

STEP has recently published an excellent booklet (Jonathan Cooke, *STEP Accounting Guidelines*) which gives fuller guidance and is available from STEP (see **Useful addresses**).

16.2   ESTATE ACCOUNTS

16.2.1   The duty to account

Personal representatives are reminded of their obligation to keep accounts by the wording of all the oaths leading to grants of representation (giving effect to Administration of Estates Act 1925, s.25).

The accounts should give a clear and accurate statement of the estate property and income, and contain full details of all receipts and payments (for which the appropriate corresponding documentation should be available). Solicitor PRs are subject to the Accounts Rules (see **Chapter 5**) as well as the general law.

16.2.2   Form of accounts

The form of estate accounts varies. Some firms use the traditional 'side-by-side' format showing income and outgoings. Others, as here, use a 'vertical' layout. The aim is always to give the PRs and residuary beneficiaries an explanation of the administration of the estate in an easily understandable form.

There is no prescribed layout or form for estate accounts, so whatever format best suits the estate in hand may be used, but the simpler and easier the accounts are, the better. They must, of course, give enough detail to allow a proper appreciation of all the transactions which have taken place.

The following elements are standard.

- *Introduction*: this is a narrative setting out:
  - the date of death, the date and place of issue of the grant of representation, and the PRs' names;
  - if there was a will, a summary of the gifts made; otherwise, an outline of the effect in the estate of the intestacy rules;
  - the value of the gross and net estates and the amount of any IHT paid;
  - details of any joint property passing by survivorship, variations made, elections under IHTA 1984, s.142, funds held back in respect of future tax liability and other relevant information.

- *Balance sheet*: this shows the amount due to residuary beneficiaries at the date of preparation and the remaining assets less any outstanding liabilities.

- *Estate capital account*: this shows the value of the estate for probate and IHT purposes, any transactions and matters taking place during the administration period which affect those values and the balance remaining.

- This account can be drawn up in two parts: (1) the estate at death based on the IHT and any corrective accounts submitted and (2) the transactions and events taking place during the administration period. The first part would show the gross and net estates at death, as agreed for probate and IHT purposes, exactly as they appear on the IHT accounts and probate papers. The second would record transactions which took place during the administration period affecting the probate value of the estate – for example, sales for more or less than book value and administration expenses.

- Alternatively, if the estate is simple, it is possible to combine the two parts to focus on the amount available for beneficiaries. Assets are shown at their probate value with an immediate adjustment for gains/losses in value of assets sold and adjustments for administration expenses.

  - It is important to show the value of assets at the date of death both to allow the beneficiaries to understand what has happened during the administration and because the beneficiaries will use the value at death as their acquisition cost (for CGT purposes) in relation to future disposals of the assets.

- Sometimes there will be differences between the IHT account(s) and the estate capital account, arising from the different tax treatment and legal nature of certain kinds of property (for example, reversionary interests, being 'excluded property', are left out of IHT accounts but appear, as assets, in the estate accounts; conversely, the deceased's share of jointly owned property passing by survivorship will be included in the IHT account but, as far as the estate accounts are concerned, will only be mentioned for information in the introductory narrative).
- Apportionments cause problems. Show income accrued up to the date of death as an asset for IHT purposes and include it in the net estate. However, for income tax and for distribution purposes (if the Apportionment Act 1970 has been varied) such amounts must be treated as income receivable after death. As such, they are credited to the income account. To avoid double counting, they must, therefore, be deducted from the net estate on the capital account.

- *Estate income account*: this shows all the income received during the administration period. When tax is deducted at source (for example, company dividends) only the net amounts of income received need to be shown; otherwise put in gross receipts, with an entry showing the basic rate tax which the PRs have paid.

  - If equitable apportionments have been made, or if any income is apportioned to capital under the Apportionment Act 1870, show the full amount of the income that the PRs receive, with the amount apportioned to capital being shown as an appropriation of part of the total.
  - This account should also show individually any interim payments of income to beneficiaries so that they can check these against the annual certificates of deduction of income tax the solicitor has given them (form R185E). It is helpful to divide the income account into tax years and to show the income received for each tax year and the payments made for each tax year.
  - Show any interest paid on general legacies, and any income produced by property which was given specifically in the will, as deductions from the total income received. Expenses attributable to income can be dealt with in a similar way.
  - This account can be made up to each 5 April.

- *Beneficiaries' or distribution accounts*: carry forward the balances on the capital and income accounts to beneficiaries' accounts. If the beneficiaries are absolutely entitled, add the two figures together to show the total due and then deduct any amounts that have already been paid. If the state is passing to a mixture of exempt and non-exempt beneficiaries, deduct any IHT attributable to the share of the non-exempt beneficiaries.

- *Schedules or annexes*: more detailed information can conveniently be put here, to keep the main accounts uncluttered. Schedules may cover:
  - debts at death;
  - dividends received during the administration;
  - investments owned at death – this will usually be in two parts: (1) showing investments retained and appropriated to, or divided between, the beneficiaries, and (2) showing the investments which were sold, along with gains and losses.
- *Notes*: these may be helpful to draw attention to any aspects of the accounts which might otherwise be overlooked or unclear.

16.2.3   Planning for the end of the administration period

Solicitors should consider early on in the administration the discharge that the PRs will eventually seek from the beneficiaries and whether any special arrangements need to be made, e.g. if any beneficiary lacks capacity. A discharge from residuary beneficiaries will only be valid if there has been full disclosure of the estate assets, the dealings with them and of the balances available for distribution. Solicitors should also anticipate the end of the administration period by, for example, settling all tax liabilities and arranging to withdraw funds from banks and building societies in good time.

PRs will want approval of the accounts from the residuary beneficiaries and may consider withholding some of the assets until this is forthcoming. Receipts for cheques or assets should be obtained and filed with the estate papers. (See **16.7** below for guidance on obtaining receipts.)

16.3   SPECIMEN ACCOUNTS

The following specimen accounts for Victoria Thomas deceased illustrate the points made above, and are followed by notes, beginning at **16.3.2** below, explaining how these accounts were made up.

16.3.1   Victoria Thomas deceased

Miss Thomas died on 3 May 2006. Lowe Snow & Co of Hixley held her will which was dated 15 August 1990 and (in summary) provided:

- revocation clause;
- executors: (1) Miss Emily Thomas and (2) Miss Amy Thomas both of 'Hillview', Hixley, Cheshire;
- charitable legacies (all registered charities):

  (1)   £1,000 to Cheshire Home of Rest for Horses,

    (2) £250 to Hixley Dogs Home,
    (3) £250 to Cheshire Donkey Sanctuary;

- receipts clause;
- residue, after debts, legacies, testamentary expenses – 'to such of them my said sisters Emily Thomas and Amy Thomas as shall survive me and if both equally between them' (gift over to RSPCA in event of both sisters predeceasing: both survived);
- clause dispensing with consents to appropriation.

It was duly executed and attested.

Victoria Thomas: estate for probate and IHT purposes

	£	£
Spring Cottage	300,000.00	
Investments	39,512.00	
Northern Rock plc	4,100.00	
Cash in house	21.00	
Lloyds TSB Bank plc	5,828.00	
Arrears of retirement pension	442.00	
Contents:		
sold gross	500.00	
other: valued	2,500.00	
GROSS ESTATE		352,903.00
Less		
Electricity	31.00	
Gas	52.00	
Income tax	295.00	
Funeral	1,025.00	(1,403.00)
NET ESTATE FOR PROBATE		351,500.00
Less		
Charitable legacies (exempt)	1,500.00	
ESTATE FOR IHT PURPOSES		350,000.00
IHT PAYABLE		
on first £285,000	NIL	
on £65,000 at 40 per cent		(26,000.00)
on delivery of account, on		
net non-instalment property		
(£50,000)	3,714.29	
on Spring Cottage	22,285.71	

The solicitors sent a covering letter with the accounts to the two PRs:

Dear Miss Thomas,

YOUR LATE SISTER'S ESTATE

I enclose the estate accounts which include an outline of your sister's will, and the amount of the estate and of tax and other payments paid and so on. We have not deducted income tax from the £150 this firm has allowed you as interest. You should, therefore, include it in your tax return for the tax year 200–/–. Yours sincerely [etc.]

These are the accounts which were sent.

Accounts: Estate of Miss Victoria Thomas deceased

Included in these accounts are the following:

1. Introduction
2. Capital account
3. Estate income account
4. Beneficiary's account – Miss Emily Thomas
5. Beneficiary's account – Miss Amy Thomas
6. Schedule of investments showing probate values

Introduction

Miss Victoria Thomas, late of Spring Cottage, Tottenhall Road, Hixley, Cheshire died on 3 May 2006, aged 82. Probate of her will dated 15 August 1990 was granted on _____ to Miss Emily Thomas and Miss Amy Thomas, the executors named in the will.

In her will Miss Thomas left these charitable legacies:

(1) £1,000 to the Cheshire Home of Rest for Horses,
(2) £250 to the Hixley Dogs Home,
(3) £250 to the Cheshire Donkey Sanctuary.

The estate remaining after payment of these legacies, and after payment of Miss Thomas's debts and funeral and testamentary expenses, was given to Miss Emily Thomas and Miss Amy Thomas equally.

The net estate for probate purposes amounted to £351,500.00. For inheritance tax (IHT) purposes the taxable estate amounted to £350,000.00, the legacies to the charities being exempt. IHT amounted to £26,000.00. This has been paid and a certificate of discharge obtained.

The residue has been divided between the beneficiaries (Miss Emily and Miss Amy Thomas) and this is shown in the accounts. Miss Thomas's investments have been divided equally between the beneficiaries. The values stated in the beneficiaries' accounts form the acquisition value for the purposes of capital gains tax.

Part of the contents of Spring Cottage was divided between the Misses Thomas as they agreed, and the remainder was sold. Spring Cottage was sold at the agreed probate value. The estate's liability to income tax was met by deduction of tax at source.

Lowe, Snow & Co

Balance sheet as at [date of accounts]

	£	£
Balance due to residuary beneficiaries *(see beneficiaries' accounts)*		
Miss Emily Thomas	47,617.98	
Miss Amy Thomas	47,617.99	
		95,235.97
Represented by		
Cash balances		
Bank money market account	23,478.00	
Lowe, Snow & Co client bank account	71,757.97	
		95,235.97

Capital account

	£	£
Spring Cottage, Hixley		
Probate value	300,000.00	
Net proceeds of sale		290,000.00
Investments per schedule at probate value		39,512.00
Northern Rock plc account	4,039.64	
– Interest to date of death	60.36	
		4,100.00
Cash – in house		21.00
Bank A/c – Lloyds TSB plc, Hixley		
Current a/c	721.50	
Deposit a/c	5,000.00	
– Interest to date of death	106.50	
		5,828.00
Arrears of retirement pension		442.00
Contents of house and personal effects		
Distribution *in specie* (estimated value)	2,500.00	
Proceeds of sale of rest	443.25	
		2,943.25
GROSS ESTATE		342,846.25
Less		
Debts due at death		
Eastern Electricity Co – electricity a/c	31.00	
British Gas – gas a/c	52.00	
Income tax due at death	295.00	
Funeral expenses		
G. Smith & Co	1,025.00	
Administration expenses		
Commissioner's fees	9.00	
Probate court fees	60.00	
Stockbroker Co – valuation fees	517.50	
Lowe, Snow & Co – charges for administering the estate	1650.00	
VAT	288.75	
Inheritance tax	26,000.00	
		(29,928.25)
NET ESTATE		312,918.00

	£	£
Less		
LEGACIES		
Cheshire Home of Rest for Horses	1,000.00	
Hixley Dogs Home	250.00	
Cheshire Donkey Sanctuary	250.00	
		1,500.00
RESIDUE		311,418.00
Divisible		
Miss Emily Thomas – one half	155,709.00	
Miss Amy Thomas – one half	155,709.00	
		311,418.00

Estate income account

Income tax year 2006 to 2007

	£	£
Dividends received		
1.9.2006	255.00	
Interest received		
Northern Rock		
Interest to close a/c on 26.08.2006	76.02	
Lloyds TSB Bank, Hixley		
Interest to close deposit a/c 30.8.2006	45.60	
Refund of income tax	15.55	
		392.17
Less loan interest		
Lloyds TSB Bank, Hixley		
Interest on loan to pay IHT		(62.20)
		329.97
Divisible		
Miss Emily Thomas – one half	164.98	
Miss Amy Thomas – one half	164.99	
		329.97

Beneficiary's account

MISS EMILY THOMAS

	£	£
Share of residue due to you per capital account		155,709.00
Share of residue due to you per income account		164.98
Total due to you		155,873.98
Represented by –		
Transferred to you		
Shares at probate value		
650 Marks & Spencer ord. shares	3,795.00	
500 Tesco Stores ord. shares	1,620.00	
489 Royal Dutch Shell ord. reg. shares	8,316.00	
115 Schroders ord. shares	1,175.00	
865 Tate & Lyle ord. shares	4,850.00	
		19,756.00
Retained by you		
Share of furniture at agreed value		1,250.00
Interim payments to you		
10.7.2006	12,250.00	
13.11.2006	75,000.00	
		87,250.00
Balance now due to you		47,617.98
		155,873.98

Beneficiary's account	£	£
MISS AMY THOMAS		
Share of residue due to you per capital account		155,709.00
Share of residue due to you per income account		164.99
Total due to you		155,873.99
Represented by –		
Transferred to you		
Shares at probate value		
650 Marks & Spencer ord. shares	3,795.00	
500 Tesco Stores ord. shares	1,620.00	
489 Royal Dutch Shell ord. reg. shares	8,316.00	
115 Schroders ord. shares	1,175.00	
865 Tate & Lyle ord. shares	4,850.00	
		19,756.00
Retained by you		
Share of furniture at agreed value		1,250.00
Interim payments to you		
10.7.2006	12,250.00	
13.11.2006	75,000.00	
		87,250.00
Balance now due to you		47,617.99
		155,873.99

Schedule of investments

PROBATE VALUES						
Amount	Stock	Probate value £	Miss Emily Thomas No.	Value	Miss Amy Thomas No.	Value
1,260	Marks & Spencer ord. shares	7,590.00	1,650	3,795	1,650	3,795
1,000	Tesco Stores (Hldings) ord. shares	3,240.00	900	1,620	900	1,620
978	Royal Dutch Shell ord.	16,632.00	640	8,316	640	8,316
230	Schroders ord. shares	2,350.00	400	1,175	400	1,175
1,730	Tate & Lyle shares	9,700.00	600	4,850	600	4,850

16.3.2 Notes on the specimen estate accounts

The accounts start with the narrative Introduction, giving details of the grant and explaining the distribution of the estate.

In this estate, apart from three pecuniary legacies, the entire net estate was divided between two beneficiaries. Thus all that is required is a *capital account*, showing assets and liabilities and the net residue, an *income account* showing income received during the administration, and *beneficiaries' accounts* showing the division of their entitlements and how these were met between the beneficiaries, and a *schedule* showing details of the investments.

16.3.3 Capital account

In preparing the capital account there is a choice: the account can be produced in two parts or in one:

- If the account is in two parts, the first part will mirror exactly the estate as disclosed in the HMRC account (amended by any corrective account). The probate value of all assets, whether or not sold, will be listed together with deductions permitted for IHT purposes, e.g. debts due at death, funeral expenses. The figure produced will therefore be the same as that agreed with HMRC, but of course it will not be the amount available for distribution to the beneficiaries: for example, administration costs may have been incurred which cannot be deducted for IHT purposes (e.g. IHT itself, solicitors' costs, probate court fees, etc.). These costs will have to be deducted in the second part of a two-part capital account, to produce a sum which does represent the net estate available for the beneficiaries.
- If the account is in one part (as here) it shows the net estate available for the beneficiaries. This method produces a different sum from the one shown in the IHT200, and shows the amount the beneficiaries are actually receiving after tax and administration expenses.

A one-part account is used in this example. Accordingly, for any items sold, e.g. Spring Cottage, the net proceeds of sale are used.

Some or all of the investments may have been sold. If so, the probate value of all the holdings will be included, plus or minus the gain or loss on sale as appropriate. (Details of the transactions would be shown in the schedule of investments.)

In this estate, and others where the investments are divided equally between the beneficiaries, the value included in the accounts is the probate value, i.e. value at the deceased's death. This is unlikely to be the same as the market value at the point when the shares are vested in the beneficiaries. However, any increase or decrease in value will be shared equally between the beneficiaries, so this produces no unfairness. The probate value is also the beneficiaries' acquisition value for CGT purposes.

All the assets, then, are listed at the probate value or actual realised value.

In relation to bank and building society accounts, etc., the probate value includes interest accrued to the date of death. For IHT purposes, this interest forms part of the deceased's estate and so is shown in the capital account. (Interest earned after death and before the closing of the account will be shown in the estate income account.) For income tax purposes, however, the accrued interest before death, and any interest received between death and the closing of the account are regarded as income of the PRs and should be included by them in their income tax return. Accordingly, the income shown in the income account is not the amount of income on which PRs actually pay income tax.

The contents of the house have been valued at an estimated £2,500. Some items have been sold and turned into cash. The actual amount received, i.e. the net proceeds of sale, is shown.

Once the gross estate is established, all the debts and liabilities are then deducted from the gross estate figure, including debts not permitted as deductions for IHT purposes.

A sum representing the net estate results. In this estate, of course, there are legacies to be paid before the net estate is distributed between the residuary beneficiaries. So, non-residuary gifts are deducted from the net estate figure, and then the division of residue is shown. These figures are transferred to the individual beneficiaries' accounts.

16.3.4   Income account

This deals with income received during the administration of the estate. In this estate, all the income is received in one tax year. If the administration straddled more than one tax year, two or more separate sets of figures would be shown.

If income is received net of tax, show the net figure. If income is received gross, the PRs will have to pay income tax at basic rate. This payment will be shown as a deduction from income. Also deducted here will be any payments out of income, such as interest on loans, interest on IHT, any solicitors' or accountants' charges related to post-death tax returns.

In this estate, income and capital are received by the same beneficiaries, and no such distinction has been made in the solicitors' charges. If different beneficiaries were entitled to income and capital, e.g. in a life interest, a proportion of the solicitors' charges, referable to income, would be deducted here.

Again, the net entitlement to income is shown, and the balances are taken to the beneficiaries' accounts.

16.3.5   Beneficiaries' accounts

The entitlements have been brought forward and listed. In this estate the beneficiaries are due capital and income.

Once the total due to a beneficiary has been ascertained, the account shows how this has been satisfied. There may be, as with Miss Emily Thomas, three elements:

- assets transferred *in specie*. Here, the shares were divided equally. As these were entered in the capital account at probate value, again probate values are used. Some furniture was also transferred *in specie* at values agreed between the beneficiaries;
- assets which were retained by the beneficiaries. This is regarded as an 'advance' of part of their respective entitlements, and brought into account;
- payments of cash on account, or interim distributions.

Balancing the books

The balance after these calculations represents the amount due to the beneficiary and all together should add up to the amount left in the client ledger, after costs and disbursements.

If these figures do not agree, something has gone wrong. It can sometimes be a trying process to find the mistake, but it must be found.

Note: It could happen that a balance appears to be due from a beneficiary to the estate. This will usually mean that interim distributions were too big – interim payments should only be made after considering all future liabilities, such as tax and costs. A situation like this often causes great difficulty, as the beneficiary will, at the very least, be disappointed.

16.3.6 Schedule of investments

Rather than include on the capital account details of the investments, these can be listed in a schedule or annex. As no items have been sold this schedule is simple, giving capital values and showing the division of the shares between the beneficiaries. If numerous dividends had been received these could also have been recorded in a schedule.

If items had been sold, the sale price and any gain or loss could be shown. This information would be included in the capital account.

16.3.7 Release for personal representatives

Unless the PRs and residuary beneficiaries are one and the same, the beneficiaries should provide written approval of the accounts and a release from liability. Even when they are the same, a note of the beneficiaries' approval of the accounts might be advisable as far as the solicitors are concerned. This could take the form of a simple statement on the accounts indicating their approval.

16.4 CAPITAL GAINS TAX

Death is not a disposal. PRs acquire assets at their market value at the date of death. PRs are chargeable to CGT in respect of gains made in the course of the administration on or after 6 April 2004 at the uniform trusts rate of 40 per cent. The fact that some or all of the beneficiaries are charities and, as such, exempt from CGT does not mean that there is any exemption from CGT for gains made by the PRs during the administration. To obtain exemption the sale must be made on behalf of the beneficiary. See **16.9.7** below.

As with individuals an indexation allowance will be given for periods up to 6 April 1998 but not thereafter. So, for assets held at 17 March 1998 and disposed of after that date an indexation allowance will be calculated for the period from acquisition to 6 April 1998. For assets acquired after that date no indexation allowance will be available.

Taper relief will be available to PRs and trustees who hold assets for an appropriate period (one year for business assets, three years for non-business assets).

PRs continue to receive the same annual exemption as an individual for the tax year of death and the two subsequent tax years. Thereafter, there is no exemption. There is, therefore, an incentive to make disposals in the initial three years.

PRs will be able to treat as allowable acquisition costs a proportion of the costs of obtaining the grant: details are set out in Statement of Practice SP2/04. Costs of transferring the asset to the beneficiaries are also allowable (see Taxation of Chargeable Gains Act 1992, s.6(1)).

When PRs transfer assets to legatees there is no disposal and the legatees acquire the assets at the value at the date of death for CGT purposes. It is advisable for the solicitor to inform specific legatees (or pecuniary or residuary legatees to whom assets are appropriated) of the value at the date of death of assets transferred to them; the legatees can then calculate their liability for CGT without having to refer back to the solicitor, perhaps many years after a file has been closed.

There are particular problems in relation to CGT where charities are entitled to assets. See **16.8**.

16.5 INCOME TAX

PRs pay basic or lower rate tax on income of the estate. They will pay the net income to beneficiaries together with an appropriate tax credit.

Up until 6 April 1995 beneficiaries were assessed to income tax on income of the estate in the tax year in which it was paid to them but at the end of the administration the total of income paid out was apportioned evenly over the whole administration period on a daily basis. This led to recalculation of the beneficiary's tax liability for each tax year of the administration. In cases where a beneficiary was close to the limit of a tax band the apportioning of income could take the beneficiaries into or out of a particular band.

Since 6 April 1995 income paid to a beneficiary is treated as income of the tax year in which it is paid and there is no apportioning of income at the end of the administration. This can result in a beneficiary paying an unnecessarily high rate of tax. For example, if PRs make no interim income payments and pay out all the income at the end of the administration period to a beneficiary, that beneficiary may be pushed into higher rate tax for that year. Had the payments been made in two tax years the beneficiary might have remained a basic rate taxpayer. PRs must provide residuary beneficiaries with form R185E.

The provisions relating to the taxation of income have been rewritten in Income Tax (Trading and Other Income) Act 2005.

16.5.1 Administration of the deceased's estate

We have set out below a helpful article by Mary Hase, formerly partner in charge of executorship at chartered accountants, Hereward Phillips. This article first appeared in [1997] *Solicitors Journal*, 20 June and we are most grateful to Mary Hase and to the *Solicitors Journal* for allowing us to reproduce it.

ADDITIONAL TAX RESPONSIBILITIES FOR SOLICITORS

The introduction of self-assessment puts increased responsibilities on solicitors acting as or advising executors. Tax matters can no longer be left until an estate is fully administered. Put simply, good management of an estate is essential. It saves time, money and – above all – professional reputation.

As a result of self-assessment, solicitors are responsible for ensuring that an estate is administered in a tax efficient manner, with tax returns completed on time and payments made in stages for the current year according to the dates laid down by the new tax regulations.

In the past, it has been common practice for solicitors to leave sorting out the tax on an estate until the estate has been substantially completed. Such practice would now lead to a series of mounting fines for the executor and beneficiaries.

Tax planning

This is the key to success. Consider at the outset when the estate's income is likely to be received and plan the distributions accordingly.

Also consider the financial position of the beneficiaries at the beginning. For wealthy beneficiaries looking to minimise their tax liability it may be best to delay distributions and thereby postpone the impact of higher rate tax until a more convenient time. For those in the middle range the payments might be spread to avoid hitting the higher rate tax threshold. Needy beneficiaries may desire a speedy settlement but again spreading their entitlement over a number of tax years may be more likely to help them utilise allowances and fall beneath tax thresholds.

Remember too that a large income distribution in one year may affect the beneficiaries' tax payments on account in the next.

If in doubt, call in the accountants/tax advisers early to assist with the planning.

The solicitor, acting as executor, must advise the Inland Revenue of the estate's untaxed income and capital gains. The normal deadlines apply – 30 September if the Revenue are to calculate the tax, 31 January if not. However, the Revenue will not work out the income and chargeable gains for you. Beneficiaries who have an absolute interest must also be advised of the income element included in their distributions to enable them to include these figures on their personal tax forms. It is the executor's responsibility to ensure that beneficiaries can meet their deadlines, which may be 30 September if the beneficiaries do not wish to calculate their own tax.

Payments on account

Payments on account underline the importance of good management. Plan the date of cessation and work out how the resulting accounting will be done, so that the beneficiaries are provided with the necessary information in good time to complete their own tax returns and assess their own payments on account.

The basic rule is that a payment on account should be half the previous year's tax liability, excluding capital gains. This is fine when income flow is regular, but distributions from an estate may involve payments over the short term only. It can be particularly difficult for executors and beneficiaries with unreliable income sources to deal with the tax payments. Once assets are realised, and the ensuing untaxed income sources cease, the executor may seek to reduce the payment on account.

Executors should also beware of placing any cash sums received from the estate in investments which pay income gross, such as the money markets, even if this is on a temporary basis. If the liability turns out to be greater than that anticipated when the payment on account was assessed, the executors will be liable for interest and possibly penalties.

For smaller estates it is advisable to avoid these complications by selecting investments which deduct tax at source, even if it means sacrificing one or two interest points and the cash flow advantage of gross income.

For beneficiaries the problem is worse. They may be looking at total income, taxed and untaxed, and can have no idea what their payment on account should be unless the executors give them guidance on how much and when the income distributions are likely to be. Remember that for absolute interest beneficiaries, their distributions will be part income, part capital so merely telling them how much in total to expect is not sufficient.

For life interest beneficiaries, their whole distribution is income so the amounts and dates will suffice for them during the period of administration. Any balance unpaid will be taxable at the date the administration ceases so the date(s) should be planned and made known to the beneficiaries.

Trustees' responsibilities for tax returns start on the death of the person in question, though there may be nothing to report until the estate's assets are vested in them. If a discretionary trust is set up, the payment of income to the trustees or direct to the trust beneficiaries will trigger a liability at the trust rate. So the responsibility for submission of trust returns may start before the closure of the administration.

Even if no formal trust is set up under the will, often it is convenient to leave the estate's assets in the hands of the executors after completion of the administration. This becomes a bare trust and under self-assessment bare trustees are not liable to make returns or to calculate and pay basic rate tax on behalf of the beneficiaries.

Tax liabilities of the deceased

When someone dies, their tax liabilities become the responsibility of the personal representatives, who must then try to keep to the dates above. This may be difficult if the deceased's tax affairs were in arrears, or if there is a delay in obtaining letters of administration.

Problems would occur simply by a death occurring, say, in December. This is because the tax return for the previous year, with up to three tax payments, must all be paid by the following 31 January. These tax payments would be for (a) any outstanding income tax for the previous financial year, (b) capital gains tax for the previous year, and (c) the first tax payment for the current year. As yet, there appears to be no legislation giving the executor more time to assess the tax situation, or to wait until probate is granted, or, indeed for the penalties to be mitigated in these circumstances.

If delay is unavoidable, it would be advisable to write to the Revenue at the earliest opportunity (and before the relevant deadline has passed) explaining the situation, giving an indication of when matters could be dealt with and requesting no penalties.

Delays may be considerable where a will is contested and it may not be clear which beneficiary gets which assets if applications are to be made under the Inheritance (Provision for Family and Dependants) Act 1975. The rigidity of the self-assessment regime cannot cope with such uncertainties.

Early clearance of income and capital gains tax

It has, however, been announced that procedures will be introduced to facilitate the speedy completion of trusts and estates. This will include early issue of tax returns and early written confirmation that the Revenue do not propose to enquire into the return. This will assist both executors and trustees who would otherwise have to wait for a year following the next 31 January to know if the deceased's and the estate's income and capital gains tax liabilities are settled and that they are in the clear.

In summary

It is likely that further legislation will be passed or concessions granted to simplify some of these matters. Until that time, early tax planning for the entire administration of the estate is the best approach.

16.6 TOP 10 TAX TIPS

In an article in [2000] *Solicitors Journal*, 21 January, Mary Hase gave her top 10 tips for making the preparation of key tax reports relatively straightforward whether solicitors are preparing them themselves or instructing accountants. We are grateful to *Solicitors Journal* for allowing us to provide an updated list of tips.

As a preliminary two general tax planning tips:

If the beneficiaries have unused CGT exemptions and/or pay tax at the standard rate, PRs may consider transferring assets to them for sale especially if the administration has exceeded three tax years.

If the beneficiaries are non-UK residents or if they have capital losses against which they could offset any gains, transfer assets to them prior to sale in order to avoid a tax liability.

Date the accounts

Show the starting date (the date of death) and the end date (the date the administration ends or the date of interim accounts). This will clarify which tax year you are dealing with.

List all assets

It is important to itemise all assets (not just those which are encashed) and what happens to them. This is because assets transferred to a beneficiary count as a distribution to that beneficiary when calculating the amounts to be shown on their tax return.

Keep a note of sub-totals

Make sure that you keep a record of income received each tax year and within each year, work out a sub-total for each income source. Even if you don't show this information directly in the accounts, it will help you to fill in the Statement of Residuary Income Forms 922 and also the tax certificates R185 (Estate Income).

Highlight gross income and the date received

It is the date of receipt which determines the fiscal year for which you complete the tax return. Bear in mind that if you do not receive a return, the onus is on you to ask the Revenue for the relevant tax return under Self Assessment.

If you do not receive a tax return and there are capital gains or untaxed income to report:

–   Advise the Revenue before the 5 October after the end of the tax year (eg before 5 October 2007 for the tax year 2006/2007).
–   Submit the tax return by 31 January following the end of the tax year in order to avoid the automatic penalty (e.g. by 31 January 2008 for 2006/2007).

However:

–   If you miss the 5 October deadline but subsequently ask for the tax return and submit it with the tax by 31 January, you will avoid any penalties or interest.
–   If you don't know which tax office deals with the estate's affairs, contact the tax office which dealt with the deceased during his lifetime and explain the position.

Keep running totals of any capital gains

Calculate the capital gains as they arise and keep running totals for each fiscal year. If the gains exceed the losses at the end of year, a tax return should be submitted. (Also be aware that if the gains exceed the annual exemptions at the end of the first three fiscal years, a tax return should be completed.) The procedure is as above. But do remember to retain enough cash to pay the tax due on the following 31 January.

Record distributions to beneficiaries

Note the date of all distributions to the residuary beneficiaries as they occur. Remember that any transfer of assets counts as a distribution, so list these transfers as well as cash payments. The dates will tell you the tax years for which R185s are needed. Remember the R185s must be given to the beneficiaries in good time for them to meet the deadlines on their personal tax returns ie 30 September or 31 January following the end of the tax year.

General tips

Interest on TESSA or ISA accounts is taxable after the date of death. PEPs lose their tax exemption on death. Thereafter income and gains are taxable. The sale of the deceased's main residence may not be exempt from CGT – check to see whether the concession applies.

Income accrued and not paid at the date of death, but which is shown on the IHT 200 should be included as part of the estate income when it is received. Relief from double taxation can be claimed on form 922 by noting the relevant amounts. (However, it is only worth doing this calculation if a beneficiary pays higher rate tax.)

Deduct administration costs for R185 (Estate Income) calculations

When you work out income less deductions for the R185 calculations, you can deduct part of the administration expenses relating to income. Unless bills are rendered separately, you will have to estimate the amount which can be deducted, but it is important to reduce the tax liability for beneficiaries who are higher rate taxpayers. Deductions can be made for the 'management of assets of the estate properly chargeable to income'. This includes the cost of completing the income tax part of the tax return and completion of the Statements of Residuary Income and preparing the relevant figures for forms 922 in addition to the R185s.

Interest on loans for IHT

Record the dates on which you pay interest on any loans taken out to pay IHT. The interest is tax deductible so include it on the tax return. However, if you would not otherwise submit a tax return because there is no untaxed income or capital gain, you can claim a tax repayment against the estate's income which is taxed at source.

Interest on tax

Although interest on a loan to pay IHT can be deducted against estate income, any interest on IHT or other tax is only deductible against the beneficiaries' higher rate tax – and then only if they have limited interests in residue. No relief is given if the beneficiaries have absolute interests. All other income management expenses will reduce the beneficiary's higher rate tax whether limited or absolute interest.

Keep specific legacy income separate

Keep a separate record of income from assets which are specific legacies and advise the relevant legatee so that he can put the appropriate amounts on his annual tax return.

16.7   RECEIPTS FOR LEGACIES

The following article first appeared in [1992] *Gazette*, 14 October. It is reproduced here, edited and with a revised draft of the recommended receipt and discharge wording approved by the Law Society's Land Law and Succession Committee. Mr Richard Oerton revised the original wording of the receipt and discharge for the journal *Clarity*. This version is identical to Mr Oerton's with one minor change.

Receipts for payment of legacies

Periodically the Law Society receives complaints from beneficiaries who have been asked by solicitors administering an estate to sign receipts for their legacies before payment is made. This has been considered by the Land Law and Succession Committee (now the Wills and Equity Committee).

It should now be standard practice for all solicitors to write to legatees and beneficiaries early in the administration of an estate to inform them of their legacies and entitlements and then, when funds are available, to pay legatees and beneficiaries direct by cheque, unless other arrangements have been made.

The Committee (except as stated below) considers that it is no longer reasonable or necessary for legatees and beneficiaries to be asked to sign receipts in advance of payment and that such a practice is bound to generate additional correspondence and thus to add unnecessarily to the cost of the administration of the estate.

Precedents for simple forms of receipt for the payment of pecuniary, specific and residuary legacies are available. However, solicitors may find it more convenient to ask the legatee or beneficiary to acknowledge receipt by signing and returning a duplicate copy of the letter accompanying the cheque. In any case, Cheques Act 1957, s.3 provides that: 'An unindorsed cheque which appears to have been paid by the banker on whom it is drawn is evidence of the receipt by the payee of the sum payable by the cheque.'

Solicitors are also reminded of the protection for cheques which is afforded by the 'account payee' crossing under the Cheques Act 1992.

With regard to residuary beneficiaries, the estate accounts will first have to be approved by the personal representatives. When that has been done, solicitors should then, in most cases, proceed with the final distribution by sending the residuary beneficiaries copies of the approved accounts, and cheques in payment, with a request that the beneficiaries acknowledge payment by signing a receipt either endorsed on the accounts or supplied separately; the receipt to include, if needed, a discharge to the personal representatives.

If difficulties have arisen during the administration, there may be occasions when solicitors, before making final distributions, wish to make sure that the residuary beneficiaries are not going to object to the amounts. In such cases the residuary beneficiaries should be sent, in advance, copies of the approved accounts and be asked to sign a form of receipt and discharge to the personal representatives on the basis that they will be sent a cheque immediately upon the solicitors receiving back the signed form.

It is recommended that the receipt and discharge should be in the following form:

THE LATE_____
The estate accounts show the final sum due to me as £_____

I approve the accounts and will accept that sum in full satisfaction of all my claims against the estate. Please pay it by a crossed cheque in my favour and send it to me by post.

Finally, it must be remembered that a discharge will only be fully effective if the beneficiaries have been given full details of all the assets and liabilities of and all dealings with the estate.

16.7.1   Problems with legacies to minors

PRs need to consider who can give a good receipt on behalf of a minor. First, look at the will to see whether it authorises parents or guardians to give a good receipt on behalf of the minor or whether it authorises the minor to give a good receipt at a specified age (usually 16).

Even in the absence of such authority PRs do not need to hold the legacy until the minor is 18. If the legacy is contingent, there will usually be trustees appointed who can hold the legacy. If it is absolute, the PRs can appoint trustees under Administration of Estates Act 1925, s.42 to hold the legacy.

There is a further alternative. In an interesting article in (1997) 1 *Private Client Business*, 37, Michael Waterworth of 8 Gray's Inn suggests that there is not (and has not been for some time) any problem with receipts for legacies to minors. As a result of the Children Act 1989 all parents with parental responsibility have the same rights, powers and duties as guardians appointed under Children Act 1989, s.5. These rights are set out in s.3 and include (emphasis added):

> the right to receive or recover in his own name *for the benefit* of the child, property of whatever description and wherever situated, which the child is entitled to receive or recover.

The words in italic indicate that the parent or guardian will hold the property in a fiduciary capacity.

16.8   CHARITABLE BENEFICIARIES

There are a number of special factors to bear in mind if a charity is left a substantial gift. The rest of this chapter highlights the important issues. We are grateful to the Charity Commissioners for their advice, and the help of the Institute of Legacy Management and Brian Walsh of Hempsons in revising those parts of the Handbook covering charities, has been invaluable.

An excellent 40-page booklet entitled *Charities as Beneficiaries* is available on the Institute of Legacy Management website (**www.ilmnet.org.uk**). It is a joint ILM and Law Society publication and provides practical advice for practitioners.

The ILM website has a number of fact sheets available for solicitors and a database of former names and addresses for identifying the successors to organisations named in elderly wills.

16.8.1   Charities and wills

Charities now work very hard to maximise their legacy income. Because of the importance of legacies for charitable funding, the larger charities in particular are very knowledgeable about their rights and entitlements and are very experienced beneficiaries. They can be expected to be well organised and efficient. Remember that charities have a responsibility to protect their trustees against any claim that the charity has not sought its full entitlement.

Where a charity is a residuary beneficiary, solicitors are not *obliged* to inform them that they have been named in the will. Harman J reviewed the relevant case law in *Cancer Research Campaign* v. *Ernest Brown & Co* [1997] STC 1425 and said:

> Until an executor is fully satisfied that there has been a complete payment of all debts, he cannot be under any obligation whatever to pay any legacy or, to my mind, to give notice to legatees of their prospective gain.

However, although there is no obligation to inform a charity (or any other legatee), it is good practice to do so. The charity may be in contact anyway as many charities subscribe to a notification service, so it is better to take the initiative. The charity will appreciate being sent a copy of the will and if possible a schedule of assets and liabilities to give an idea of their possible entitlement. It will usually be helpful to agree with the charity the basis on which they will be kept informed of the progress of the administration. Charities do not wish to increase the cost of the administration unnecessarily, but legacy officers need to know the likely timescale. Charities comment that they often receive fuller information when banks are acting as executors than they do when solicitors are handling the administration.

Certain charitable and other residuary beneficiaries are entitled to obtain a remuneration certificate, see **Chapter 2**.

16.8.2   Checklist: charitable beneficiaries

The following reminders should help avoid problems:

1. *Changed circumstances.* A charity may feel a moral obligation to renounce part of its entitlement under a will (or even make a payment from the estate) if there are grounds for believing that, in the events which have happened, the will does not in fact carry out its maker's intentions. The charity will need full details of the circumstances justifying the payment.

A charity normally needs authority from the Charity Commissioners to make an *ex gratia* payment. They have a discretion to refer individual cases to the Attorney-General for a decision. Applicants can have their cases considered afresh by the Attorney-General if the Commissioners refuse authority. The Charity Commission's leaflet CC7 explains the procedure. In [2001] *Probate Section Journal*, March, Michael Carpenter, Legal Commissioner at the Charity Commission made three points:

(a) The application to the Commissioners must come from the trustees of the charity who must regard themselves as under a moral obligation. The Commissioners will not entertain an application from executors, members of the family, disappointed beneficiaries or their advisers.

(b) Where there is a genuine dispute, for example an IPFDA 1975 claim, the *ex gratia* regime is irrelevant. The charity has a power to compromise claims.

(c) A disappointed beneficiary may allege that a solicitor prepared a will negligently. A negligence action against the solicitor would not involve the charity so the charity would have no power to compromise it. However, *Walker* v. *Medlicott & Son* [1999] 1 WLR 727 determined that in appropriate circumstances a disappointed beneficiary might be expected to bring a rectification action. The charity would be affected by a rectification action and, therefore, might use its power to compromise. It would only consider compromise 'where there is a genuine case which is likely to be successful'. There may be cases where a rectification claim might fail for technical reasons unconnected with the substantive merits. The Commissioners will consider an *ex gratia* application from the charity in such a case provided the charity considers that it would be morally unacceptable not to carry out the deceased's wishes.

Changes do not always work to a charity's advantage – a gift may be adeemed, for example, and clients should be warned about this possibility when making a will.

2. *Wrong descriptions.* Problems of a different kind are caused by wrongly describing the intended charity in a will. It is quite common for wills to refer to charities that have never existed and it is then necessary to determine what happens to the gift.

Responsibility for correctly reproducing the institution's current name rests with the draftsman. Brightman J said in *Re Recher's Will Trust* [1972] Ch 526 that it was the draftsman's 'elementary duty' not only to get the name right but to ensure that the institution was in existence at the date of the will. It is possible to check registered charities on the Charity Commission's website (**www.charity-commission.gov.uk**). If a charity is not registered, check its details with its treasurer.

Where the name is wrong, solicitors would expect to have to apply to court for a direction on how to apply the legacy. However, in a very useful article in [2001] *Solicitors Journal*, 22 June, Victoria Forwood of the Government Legal Service Charities Team explained the procedure for applying to the Attorney-General for a direction under the Royal Sign Manual. Such a direction identifies the charitable beneficiary whose identity was previously uncertain. The PRs then administer the gift in accordance with the direction. Examples of such gifts are to 'the Cancer Research Trust', 'the association for the preservation of tropical rain forests', 'the Ethiopa Fund'. The procedure is quick (weeks unless there is a dispute) and cheap – the Attorney-General does not charge.

3. *Charity dissolved.* A different problem arises when a charity did exist at the date of the will but has ceased to do so by the date of death.

It may have amalgamated with another charity, in which case there will be no problem if the will includes a standard provision dealing with amalgamation. Well-drawn wills normally include a provision allowing the PRs to give effect to a charitable gift which fails by paying the money to the institution which most closely resembles it. If the will does not include such a clause, the gift fails but the *cy-pres* rule may allow effect to be given to the gift if the will shows a generable charitable intention.

4. *Incorporated charities going into liquidation after the date of death.* The case of *Re ARMS (Multiple Sclerosis Research) Ltd* [1997] 2 All ER 679 highlights a particular problem in relation to incorporated charities. In that case a charitable company overspent and went into liquidation. The court had to decide whether legacies to the charity taking effect after the date of the winding up order but before dissolution were payable to the liquidator – so as to be available to the company's creditors – or whether, as the Attorney-General argued, the legacies were given and should be applied for the charity's purposes. The court directed that all the legacies were payable to the liquidator.

This case is significant for the probate practitioner when administering an estate and also when drafting wills including legacies to incorporated charities. The draftsman should consider adapting the standard amalgamation/dissolution clause to create a substitution or to give executors a discretion where a legatee is in liquidation at the date of death but not yet formally dissolved.

This decision also illustrates the clear distinction between incorporated charities, which take legacies beneficially in their own right, as opposed to unincorporated charities which take for their charitable purposes. Gifts to incorporated charities are much more likely to fail if the charity no longer exists at death than gifts to unincorporated charities which are more likely to take effect as gifts for the purposes of the defunct charity. It is, therefore, particularly important when drafting gifts to incorporated charities to include substitutional gifts or to give the executors a power to apply funds to similar charities. It made no difference that one of the legacies in the *ARMS* case was expressed to be 'for the general purposes' of the charity.

5. *Conditional gifts.* If your client wants to give a gift on condition, find out from the charity whether the terms of the gift will be acceptable or feasible; alternatively, provide in the will for what is to happen if the charity declines the gift.

It is also important to make clear what is to happen if it is impossible to carry out the condition at the time of the testator's death (e.g. a gift which is conditional on a charity caring for the testator's pets and at the time of the testator's death there are no pets). Failure to do so will result in uncertainty and possible litigation (see *Watson* v. *National Children's Home* [2001] WTLR 1375). There is a useful article in [2001] *New Law Journal*, Christmas Appeals Supplement, 3 December by Lucy Hickman summarising points to bear in mind when drafting gifts to charities.

6. *Delayed distribution.* If your client wants to enable the PRs and trustees to be able to distribute a gift over an extended period of time, you need to draft this carefully. The Commissioners' Annual Report for the year 1990 highlights the decision in *Re Muller's Estate* (unreported) which concerns a gift using a precedent in *Williams on Wills* 6th edn (Butterworths) vol.2, p.1185. It was held that the gift implied that distribution would be made within a reasonable time, and hence this formulation may not be suitable if the client wishes to provide otherwise.

7. *R185E.* Form R185E (annual certificate of tax deduction) is especially important to charities. They need these certificates for each tax year of the administration, as evidence that tax – which they can reclaim – has been deducted. The amounts may be small in each individual estate but the total is a significant addition to charities' income. There is a statutory obligation (ICTA 1988, s.700(5)) to provide beneficiaries with details of income and tax deducted if they make a written request. However, the joint Law Society and ILM booklet *Charities as Beneficiaries* advises that it is good practice to produce such documents as a matter of course. Provided full accounts have been prepared, it should be possible to lift all information required direct from the accounts without further work. It is suggested that the accounts be structured to include estate income (whether gross or net) in a separate income account, broken down into years. These figures can then be easily entered on the form 922 which will form the basis for the production of the tax certificates.

In some estates, the amount of tax that can be reclaimed by the charity is minimal and the cost of the production of the certificates may outweigh any benefits. Charities will be unlikely to pursue tax certificates where their reclaim value is less than £20 and will often take a view on those between £20–£40.

The Institute of Legacy Management reports that firms sometimes say that there is no need for form R185E because their client account pays gross. However, it is important to remember that charities can reclaim not only tax on income which has arisen during the administration period, but also tax which has accrued prior to the date of death and not been paid (e.g. building society interest) – but not without form R185E.

Solicitors' failure to issue these forms is a complaint frequently made to the Law Society and it is the responsibility of the firm undertaking the administration, and not the bank or building society, to prepare them and send them to beneficiaries. Having to produce these forms is a chore but as the charities will continue to ask for them, producing them early will allow the file to be closed more quickly.

Complete form R185E with the tax district reference number. Without this number, charities cannot reclaim the tax shown on the certificate.

If the deceased was a non-taxpayer, and the tax district reference number is not known, the problem can be solved by writing to the local tax office. Send a copy of the estate accounts and ask HM Revenue & Customs to waive the need for tax returns for the administration period. The local tax district reference number can then be quoted on form R185E. (See also **16.10.4** below.)

8. *CGT*. Charities are exempt from CGT. Where they have been left assets, they will normally want the assets sold. It is important for PRs to follow the correct procedure to save the estate suffering an unnecessary CGT bill. (See **16.9.7** below.)

9. *Land: Charities Act 1993, s.36.* Section 36 provides that no land held by or in trust for a charity can be sold without an order of the court or of the Charity Commissioners unless certain conditions are satisfied. PRs may have to comply with the requirements of s.36 if they make a sale on behalf of a charity. (See **16.9.8** below.)

10. *Interest.* Interest will be due on legacies not paid at the end of the executors' year and may be due beforehand.

11. *Form of gift.* Discuss with the charity the best way for them to receive the gift: in some cases an appropriation *in specie* may allow the charity to sell an asset and thus save CGT. The charity may customarily use a particular auction house or estate agency, with which they may have a special arrangement relating to fees, which may also be able to assist. Appropriation of assets can be done on paper, that is, without any necessity physically to transfer securities. The sale is then made as bare trustee on behalf of the charity. It is, however, important to have a written record of the appropriation. See point 14 and **16.9.7** below.

12. *Deeds of variation.* Consider deeds of variation to make the gift in the most effective way (see the points set out at **16.10** below).

13. *Exempt and non-exempt beneficiaries.* If the residuary gift is to both exempt and non-exempt beneficiaries, the problem of how to distribute the estate in the light of *Re Benham* arises. See **16.9** below.

14. *Early notice.* Sending a copy of the will at an early stage alerts a charitable residuary beneficiary to its entitlement and enables it to put forward its own wishes for the PRs' consideration. Obtaining the PRs' consent to briefing the charity on progress can also be worthwhile. However, PRs remain, of course, obliged to act in the interests of the estate as a whole, not just those of one particular beneficiary.

15. *Interim distributions.* Consider whether one or more interim distributions can be made. The Institute of Legacy Management comments that some firms only write to charities when the administration is complete, sending their first letter, estate accounts and cheque all together. The justification is that it saves costs. Crispin Ellison, formerly of the Institute of Legacy Management, says that most charities would agree to a little more in costs in return for more information during the administration and some interim distributions. He also comments that while banks charge more, their level of service in providing regular information and in their accounting is superior.

16. *VAT.* Charities are no longer able to recover VAT on costs associated with sales made in relation to land or buildings.

17. *Indemnities.* Do not ask for indemnities which are too sweeping as a charity will not be able to give an indemnity which goes beyond its share of the estate; it will normally want its indemnity to be conditional on the PRs not accepting, compromising or otherwise admitting any claim without the previous written consent of the charity.

16.9   THE PROBLEM OF *RE BENHAM* AND *RE RATCLIFFE*

The case of *Re Benham's Will Trusts*, [1995] STC 210 caused great problems for PRs. To some extent they have been alleviated by the later case of *Re Ratcliffe (Deceased)* [1999] STC 262. (The notes at **16.9.1** *et seq* have been written specially for us by Chris Whitehouse, Barrister of 2 Stone Buildings and we are most grateful to him for doing so.)

As a general rule a testator or testatrix is free to decide where the burden of IHT is to fall. Specific gifts are, in the absence of any direction to the contrary, tax free with the tax being paid out of residue. To preserve the value of exempt transfers, however, and notably of gifts to spouses and charities, IHTA 1984, s.41 provides that:

Notwithstanding the terms of any disposition:

(a)   none of the tax on the value transferred shall fall on any specific gift if or to the extent that the transfer is exempt with respect to the gift; and

269

(b) none of the tax attributable to the value of the property comprised in residue shall fall on any gift of a share of residue if or to the extent that the transfer is exempt with respect to the gift.

In a simple case where residue is split between chargeable and exempt beneficiaries (for instance, between a testator's son and his wife) any tax attributable to the son's share must be borne out of that share; no part of that tax can come out of the portion of residue passing to the surviving spouse.

16.9.1   When is it necessary to consider *Re Benham* and *Re Ratcliffe?*

In practice, difficulties only arise if residue is split between chargeable and exempt beneficiaries. Commonly this occurs when part of the residue is left to charity with the rest passing to the relatives of the testator. A will leaving a specific legacy to charity with residue to the testator's or testatrix's family does not, therefore, give rise to problems. A second point to bear in mind is that *Benham* is concerned with the calculation of IHT on the chargeable portion of an estate. Accordingly, if that portion falls within the testator's or testatrix's nil rate band, no computational difficulties can arise.

16.9.2   Grossing up a chargeable share of residue

Given that IHTA 1984, s.41 prevents tax on a chargeable share of residue from being borne by an exempt share, how can the wishes of a testator that the net residue after payment of all expenses and IHT is to be divided equally between (say) his wife and daughter be satisfied? Only, it is thought, if the will provides for the chargeable share (in this example the daughter's share) to be grossed up to include the tax which is charged on it.

Illustration

Assume net residue of £100,000 to be divided equally between surviving spouse and daughter, estate rate 40 per cent.

- Option 1: deduct tax on £50,000 and divide balance (£80,000) equally: prohibited by s.41.
- Option 2: divide equally so that spouse gets £50,000 and daughter gets £50,000 but then bears tax so that she ends up with £30,000.
- Option 3: gross up daughter's share (X) so that both end up with the same, i.e.:

$X + (100X/60) = £100,000$; therefore $X = £37,500$
Both receive £37,500; gross value of daughter's share is £62,500.

	Spouse (£)	Daughter(£)	Tax Man (£)
Option 1	40,000	40,000	20,000
Option 2	50,000	30,000	20,000
Option 3	37,500	37,500	25,000

The facts of Re Benham's Will Trust

In this case, under clause 3 of the will residue was left as follows:

- upon trust to pay debts, funeral and testamentary expenses;
- after such payment 'to pay the same to those beneficiaries as are living at my death and who are listed in List A and List B hereunder written in such proportions as will bring about the result that the aforesaid beneficiaries named in List A shall receive 3.2 times as much as the aforesaid beneficiaries named in List B and in each case for their own absolute and beneficial use and disposal'.

List A contained one charity and a number of non-charitable beneficiaries; and List B contained a number of charities and non-charitable beneficiaries. By an originating summons, the executor sought, *inter alia*, the opinion of the court on the following questions:

- whether the wording in clause 3(b) meant that each qualifying beneficiary in List A should receive 3.2 times the sum taken by each beneficiary in List B, or whether the List A beneficiaries should between them receive 3.2 times the total sum taken by the List B beneficiaries;
- whether, in view of IHTA 1984, s.41 and the terms of the will, the non-charitable beneficiaries should receive their shares subject to IHT, or whether their shares should be grossed up; and
- whether the shares of legatees who predeceased the testatrix accrued by survivorship to the other legatees or became applicable for the payment of funeral and testamentary expenses and debts.

The deputy judge agreed that the choice between the two interpretations of clause 3(b) was not so clear that it could be said that there was no real doubt or ambiguity and he admitted extrinsic evidence under Administration of Justice Act 1982, s.21(1)(b). He then concluded that clause 3(b) directed payment of the residue to two groups of beneficiaries and, whilst the persons named in Lists A and B, respectively, took as between themselves in equal shares provided that they survived the testatrix, the part of the residue available to List A beneficiaries to share equally between them was a fund 3.2 times as large as the fund available for the List B beneficiaries.

On the second question, there were three possibilities:

- the non-charitable beneficiaries received their respective shares subject to IHT, which would mean that they would receive less than the charities;

271

- the non-charitable beneficiaries should have their respective shares grossed up, so that they received the same net sum as the charities; or
- the IHT was paid as part of the testamentary expenses under clause 3(a), and the balance was distributed equally between the non-charitable beneficiaries and the charities.

The deputy judge agreed that the third possibility was precluded by IHTA 1983, s.41. However, he did not agree that the charities should receive more than the non-charitable beneficiaries. The plain intention of the testatrix was that each beneficiary, whether charitable or non-charitable, should receive the same as the other beneficiaries on the relevant list. That result, he concluded, was consistent with the express terms of the will and s.41. Thus, he considered that the non-charitable beneficiaries' shares should be grossed up.

Finally, clause 3(b) made it a condition that any named beneficiary should be living when the testatrix died. Thus, the deputy judge said, the two funds should be divided between the beneficiaries in the two lists, after deleting those who had died.

16.9.3   Difficulties arising from *Re Benham*

The main difficulty posed by *Re Benham* lies not in the actual facts of the case (which were obviously somewhat unusual!), but in the assertion of the judge that 'the plain intention of the testatrix is that at the end of the day each beneficiary, whether charitable or non-charitable, should receive the same as the other beneficiaries'.

This view, if correct, would appear to result in the implication (as a matter of construction) of a grossing up clause in all cases where:

(a) the residue is left to be divided between exempt and non-exempt beneficiaries;
(b) the will provides for them to take in equal shares and there is no evidence that the testator did not intend *Benham* to apply; and
(c) the value of the estate is such that IHT is payable on the chargeable portion of residue.

This approach goes against the existing practice which had been to apply s.41 in such cases.

16.9.4   Attitude of HMRC (Capital Taxes)

The attitude of the former Inland Revenue to the *Benham* case and the consequent problems of construing and drafting wills can be gleaned from the following exchange of correspondence.

The British Heart Foundation wrote to Inland Revenue Capital Taxes in the following terms:

Re: Benhams Will Trusts

The British Heart Foundation, like many other charities, is alarmed at the potential threat to its income if, as has been widely propounded in the legal press, the decision in the above case is applied in cases where the will is drawn not in the terms of the *Benham* will but in the very much more common terms usually applied.

The cases I refer to are of course those involving gifts of residue to exempt and non-exempt beneficiaries, where the will directs the executors to pay IHT and legacies and then divide the residue. Our concern is that if the *Re Benham* judgment is applied then non-exempt beneficiaries wrongly benefit from the exempt status of organisations such as ourselves, contrary to s.41(b) of the IHT Act 1984; that is that charities as a whole could lose a great deal of money, part of which will effectively go towards paying the IHT of non-exempt beneficiaries, contrary to our charitable objects.

We at the Foundation believe that *Re Benham* really turns on the rather unusual terms of the will and has no general application to bequests of shares of residue between exempt and non-exempt beneficiaries as expressed in the common cases outlined above. We and other charities are currently considering two cases to be put to the court, but clearly a decision may take some time. Whilst this information may hold off executors from distributing estates along the lines of *Benham*, we would be obliged however if you would confirm the following: that the CTO's view is also that the *Re Benham* decision is inapplicable for this more common type of provision and that in such cases no IHT will arise that will deplete charitable shares of residue as a result of the *Benham* decision.

The response of the Capital Taxes Office indicates that they will abide by a proper construction of the will (so that the fact that extra tax is payable if grossing up applies is not a factor to be taken into account):

We consider the decision to be primarily concerned with ascertaining the intention of the testatrix and hence as not directly involving the Inland Revenue. In an attempt to be helpful, however, we would comment as follows.

Like you, our view is that the decision followed from the particular facts of the case with the court deciding that the plain intention of the testatrix was that at the end of the day and therefore after the payment of tax each beneficiary whether charitable or non-charitable on the respective lists should receive the same amount as the other beneficiaries in that list.

Generally speaking the court is concerned in such cases to establish the intention of the testator or testatrix from the wording of the will and admissible extrinsic evidence. If the will is drafted in common form with a direction to ascertain residue after payment of funeral and testamentary expenses and debts followed by a bequest of that residue then it is focusing on the ascertainment and division of disposable residue rather than on what each residuary beneficiary is to receive. Accordingly wills so drafted would not appear to involve *Benham* style grossing up computations.

P. Twiddy

16.9.5 *Re Ratcliffe*

The testatrix gave her residuary estate to her trustees (the claimants) on trust, after payment of her debts and funeral and testamentary expenses, to hold one half for the two sons of her cousin ('the cousins') in equal shares absolutely, and the other half for four charities ('the charities') in equal shares.

The charities contended that the two half shares of residue were to be calculated after providing for the debts and funeral and testamentary expenses (and three legacies) but before payment of the IHT due on the cousins' half share. The cousins would thus receive less because of the deduction of tax. The cousins contended that there were to be equal half shares of net residue after payment of the appropriate amount of IHT, which was to be treated as a testamentary expense. They argued that this equality was to be achieved, as in *Benham*, by grossing up their beneficial share of residue to produce an initial unequal division of residue which would leave equal amounts once the tax was paid.

Blackburne J held that it was a question of construing the will to decide what the testatrix had intended. The wording used was a common form trust for sale. Blackburne J found that while the testatrix could have left her residue to be divided unequally as the cousins contended, there was nothing in the wording used to indicate that this was her intention.

Of *Re Benham* he said this:

> The difficulty that I feel about that decision is that, with all due respect to the deputy judge who decided it, it is not at all clear why he came to the conclusion that the testatrix's plain intention was that 'at the end of the day each beneficiary, whether charitable or non-charitable, should receive the same as the other beneficiaries in the relevant list'.

He went on to say that had he thought that *Benham* laid down some principle, then, unless convinced that it was wrong, he would have followed it. However, he did not consider that it did and, accordingly, was not bound to follow it.

16.9.6 Practical advice on the distribution of residue

(a) Whenever an estate which exceeds the nil rate band is to be divided between exempt and non-exempt beneficiaries, it is necessary to consider the wording of the will to determine whether or not the basis of division is clear.

If the will clearly provides for the beneficiaries to receive equal amounts (*Benham* division) or unequal amounts (*Ratcliffe* division), that is the end of the matter. For practitioners who find themselves in the unenviable position of having to perform a *Benham* calculation there is an interesting article on software available to do the job in [1997] *Private Client Business*, April, 197–202.

(b) If not, everything turns on a correct construction of the document. A relevant exercise is to calculate the IHT that would be payable on the alternative bases of:

(i) applying IHTA 1984, s.41; and

(ii) grossing up.

It will normally be the case that, if grossing up occurs, the tax take is increased; chargeable beneficiaries get a greater slice of the estate and the loser will be the exempt beneficiary (i.e. either spouse or charity).

(c) When the only beneficiaries of the residue are family members (typically therefore the surviving spouse and children) it is often possible to agree an approach which will resolve the difficulties. Commonly, the children will be prepared to accept that *Benham* should not apply thereby ensuring that more is received by their mother than would otherwise would be the case (and, of course, that less is received by HMRC!).

(d) If a 'deal' is not possible, then counsel's advice may be taken and the executors may then act in accordance with his opinion. Executors should always be warned that it does not prevent them from being sued by disappointed beneficiaries and in reality the absolutely safe course is to go to the court for directions. (Note, in this connection, that the court's general power to excuse executors and trustees under Trustee Act 1925, s.61 depends on the executors satisfactorily showing that a failure to obtain the court's directions before carrying out the relevant distribution was not culpable.)

(e) If full agreement cannot be reached between the beneficiaries as to what is to be done then the executors may decide to apply s.41 if an indemnity is given either by the charity or by the surviving spouse. Given the uncertain value of such indemnities and the difficulties of enforcement, this approach cannot be wholeheartedly recommended.

Note: When drafting a will where residue is to be divided between exempt and non-exempt beneficiaries, make it clear whether the division is to be equal before consideration of IHT (*Ratcliffe* division) or whether the beneficiaries are to receive equal amounts after consideration of IHT (*Benham* division). The following are examples of suitable precedents.

Benham division

I declare that the shares of my estate of any beneficiaries who do not qualify for exemption from inheritance tax shall be deemed to be of amounts such that the amounts received, after payment of inheritance tax due, shall be the same for all the beneficiaries named in clause –.

Ratcliffe division

I declare that if the share in my estate of any beneficiary named in clause – does not qualify for exemption from inheritance tax, that share shall bear its own tax so that the amount received by each beneficiary named in that clause is the same before the payment of inheritance tax.

16.9.7 Importance of assent or appropriation of assets to charity entitled to residue

Charities benefit from CGT exemption in respect of gains realised on the disposal of assets if the gains are applicable and applied for charitable purposes (see Taxation of Chargeable Gains Act 1992 (TCGA 1992), s.256). However, the exemption will only apply if the relevant property is beneficially owned by the charity. If, during the administration of an estate, an asset, which has increased significantly in value since the date of death, is to be sold, it will be important either for the assets to be vested in the name of the charity prior to the sale, or for the executors to execute an assent declaring that they hold the asset for the charity absolutely. Failure to take these elementary steps will mean that the gain will be realised by the executors and not by the charity and HMRC may claim CGT on the gain realised, even if the benefit of the sale proceeds will ultimately pass to the charity. The need to consider appropriation before sale is a good reason for consulting charities early in the administration.

Many of the major charities have very helpful notes advising executors on the correct procedure. We print by way of example the note issued by the Guide Dogs for the Blind Association:

May we please draw the attention of the executors and their advisers to the fact that as a national charity we are exempt, under the provisions of TCGA 1992, s.256(1), from payment of capital gains tax on the sale of any securities made on our behalf.

The exemption relates to any sale made on our behalf in respect of the residue or shares of the residue of the estate to which we are entitled.

The procedure to be followed to comply with Inland Revenue requirements is that the securities should be appropriated to our account by a simple but clear designation in your books, or by a memorandum or resolution signed by the personal representatives in your files. Any sales subsequently made by you are made as bare trustee on our behalf under TCGA 1992, s.60.

Executors should be careful if they require an indemnity from the charity for the payment of administration expenses in return for the transfer of assets to the charity. HMRC may argue that such an indemnity is to be construed as a payment for the asset and accordingly a sale by the executors, or alternatively that the gain realised by the charity is not fully applicable and applied for charitable purposes.

A specimen memorandum of appropriation is available on the solicitors section of the ILM website (**www.ilmnet.org**) and is set out below for convenience.

Specimen Memorandum of Appropriation

Miss A N Other deceased

Miss Alicia Nora Other (The Testatrix) late of 1 Fairlawn Road, Leeds, LS12 9DW, died on 1 January 2000.

The Will dated 1 January 1993 was proved by Robert Scott and Titus Oates at the Leeds Probate Registry on 1st April 2000.

Under the terms of the Will, the ABC Charity of The Lodge, 25 High Street, Anytown is entitled to a one-third share of the residuary estate.

We, Robert Scott and Titus Oates, as Personal Representatives of Alicia Nora Other hereby give notice to ABC Charity that we have today together appropriated the stocks and shares set out in the Schedule hereto in part satisfaction of the said Charity's one-third share of the residuary estate of the Testatrix.

As from the date hereof, we the Executors declare that we shall hold the shares set out in the Schedule hereto as 'bare' Trustees for ABC Charity and not as Personal Representatives of Alicia Nora Other.

Suggested format for a schedule of investments appropriated to ABC Charity and referred to above

Name of Company	Number of shares appropriated (i.e. ABC Charity share)
XYZ plc	1234
ZZZ plc	4321
etc.	

Dated this _____ day of _____ 20–.

Signed

Robert Scott

Titus Oates

We hereby acknowledge that we have received a Notice of which the above is a duplicate

Signed   Date

For and on behalf of ABC Charity

For CGT purposes, the assets are deemed to have been appropriated at probate value. For the purposes of the estate accounts, investment values are usually taken to be the middle market price at the close of trading on the day of appropriation.

Where some of the investments need to be sold for administration costs or payment of legacies, the balance can still be appropriated to reduce the CGT burden. If the firm does not take these simple steps, then it may be in breach of its responsibilities to maximise the benefit to the estate. It might be worth noting that the major bank executorship departments now appropriate investments by default.

Some charities will choose to take investments *in specie*. Most of the larger charities are also companies limited by guarantee or are incorporated under Royal Charter, and have the appropriate investment powers.

16.9.8   Charities Act 1993, s.36

Charities Act 1993, s.36 was enacted in order to ensure that charities are dealing properly with the disposition of real property in which they have an interest. Unfortunately, it has led to some confusion over the correct procedure where land is bequeathed to charities by will. The ILM instructed Christopher McCall QC to provide an opinion and settle a fact sheet, both of which are available on the ILM website (**www.ilmnet.org**). The following is a brief summary of the fact sheet.

Section 36 will have to be complied with when land in England and Wales held by or in trust for registered charities is sold, leased or otherwise disposed of.

The requirements of s.36

In order for a charity to effect a disposition of land, an order of the court or the Charity Commissioners is required, unless the following three requirements are complied with:

1.   the disposition is not to a connected person;
2.   the disposition is preceded by an agreement to effect the disposition;
3.   before entering into such an agreement, the trustees comply with the procedure set out in s.36(3) or (5) which involves obtaining advice from a suitably qualified person on the merits of the proposed disposition.

The trustees must obtain and consider a written report on the proposed disposition from a qualified surveyor acting exclusively for the charity. Once the report has been obtained, the trustees should advertise the proposed disposition as advised by the surveyor. Once an offer has been made, they should consider whether the terms on which the disposition is to be made are the best which are reasonably obtainable by the charity. The requirements of the report are laid down by the Charities (Qualified Surveyors' Reports) Regulations 1992, 1992/2980.

When are personal representatives affected?

If land is disposed of by the PRs during the administration of an estate as part of the ordinary administration process the land is not charity land and s.36 will not need to be complied with. This applies even if a charity is acting as PR.

By contrast, where an appropriation has taken place, the PRs have no further power of sale other than at the instruction of the entitled beneficiary. Where a single charity is the beneficiary of the interest in land, and there has been an appropriation, trusteeship of the land for s.36 purposes automatically transfers from the PRs to the charity's trustees, who then have power of sale even though the legal title stays with the PRs; i.e. the PRs must do with the land what the charity tells them. Where there are two or more charities, the power of sale will remain with the PRs or nominated trustees if not the PRs themselves. They are therefore the 'charity trustees' for the purposes of s.36 and not the trustees of the individual charities.

Section 36 will need to be complied with in the following circumstances.

- The land is, prior to entry into an agreement to effect a disposition of that land, appropriated by the PRs wholly to a charitable institution (the charity's trustees must comply) or wholly between two or more charitable institutions (the PRs must comply).
- The land is held in a trust of land, the life tenant of which has died, and the remainderman is a charitable institution (the charity's trustees must comply) or the remaindermen are all charitable institutions (the will trust trustees must comply).
- Land has been assented to the charity.

Section 36 will not need to be complied with wherever there is a mix of charities and non-charities. Thus s.36 will not apply where:

- Appropriation has the effect of creating a trust of land in which some of the beneficiaries are not charities.
- Land is held in a trust of land and is sold during the life of the life tenant even though the remainderman is a charitable institution.
- On the death of the life tenant, the remaindermen are not all charities.

Note that the requirements of the section must be complied with before entering into any *agreement* to effect a disposition of charity land. Failure to do so prior to exchange of contracts will mean that the contract is not enforceable, and can only be completed with the sanction of an order under s.36(1). See *Bayoumi* v. *Womens Total Abstinence Union Ltd* [2003] EWCA Civ 1548.

16.10 ADMINISTRATION EXPENSES

The notes below are based on an article originally published in [1991] *Gazette*, 15 February by Alan Jarvis, a partner in Wilde Sapte & Co. We are most grateful to him for allowing us to adapt and update it.

16.10.1 Administration expenses and IHT

Most administration expenses are not deductible for IHT purposes. Careful planning at the time of the preparation of the will can, however, achieve an additional benefit whereby the administration expenses will, in effect, be deductible for IHT purposes.

For example, a testator leaves an estate of £685,000 with a gift to charity of £200,000 and the balance of the estate passing to a nephew absolutely.

The IHT position will be as follows:

	£
Value of estate	685,000
Legacy to charity	200,000
Residue to nephew	485,000
Less	
Inheritance tax on residue (£485,000 – £285,000) × 40%	(80,000)
Administration expenses	(6,000)
Net amount received by nephew	399,000

An alternative approach might be to give the nephew a specific legacy which after the payment of IHT, would leave him a net sum of £399,000. The residue of the estate would then pass to the charity. The revised IHT position will be:

		£
Gross legacy to nephew		475,000
Less inheritance tax on legacy	(£475,000 – £285,000) × 40%	(76,000)
Net legacy sum due to nephew		399,000
Residue	£685,000 – £475,000	210,000
Less administration expenses		(6,000)
Net residue payable to charity		204,000

Similarly, a benefit can be given to charity where none previously existed at no extra cost to a beneficiary:

Intended disposition	£
Gross estate due to beneficiary	685,000
Less inheritance tax	(160,000)
Net estate	525,000
Less administration expenses	(6,000)
Net amount received by beneficiary	519,000
Alternative disposition: legacy to beneficiary equal to £519,000 after payment of tax, residue to charity	
Legacy to beneficiary (£519,000 grossed up)	675,000

Less inheritance tax	(156,000)
Net amount received by beneficiary	519,000
Residue to charity (£685,000 – £675,000)	10,000
Less administration expenses	(6,000)
Net amount received by charity	4,000

16.10.2 Use of discretionary wills

Fine tuning to the degree mentioned in the above examples is not normally possible at the time of preparing the will since the estate is likely to alter in nature or value before death. Consideration might be given to two alternative approaches.

First, testators may wish to consider the establishment of a two-year no-interest in possession trust established under the will (see IHTA 1984, s.144). If a trust without a qualifying immediate post-death interest is established by will, any distributions or appointment from the trust within two years of death will be treated for IHT purposes as a disposition under the will occurring on death. The advantage, as demonstrated in either of the above examples, can be achieved with full knowledge of the value of the deceased's estate. The disadvantage of such a trust is that IHT will be charged in full on the application for the grant of representation, even if the intention is to make subsequent appointments from the trust that will attract the spouse or charitable exemptions. This problem may be avoided if the executors exercise their discretionary powers before making the application for the grant. They can do this since, unlike administrators, executors' powers commence upon death. (Do be careful not to make a distribution from the trust within three months of the death or the advantages of s.144 will be lost. This trap is pretty well known but *Frankland* v. *IRC* [1996] STC 735 shows the cost of getting caught out.)

Secondly, it is possible to effect a post-death variation of the will of the deceased under IHTA 1984, s.142.

16.10.3 Administration expenses and income tax

As most expenses of administration are not deductible for income tax, they will be paid out of the income of the administration which has borne tax at the basic rate. This will reduce the income which is distributed to the charity and, therefore, the scope for a repayment claim as the charity cannot reclaim the tax deducted from the income used to pay income expenses. The fewer expenses which are attributable to income, the greater will be the tax repayment to the charity. However, without specific power to pay income expenses out of capital, the level of expenses which are attributable to income will not be determined according to the executors' discretion but according to the law.

It may be appropriate to include in a will a direction that the executors shall have the power to pay administration expenses out of capital or income

281

at their discretion, thereby enabling the executors to attribute all expenses to capital and allowing the charity to effect a full recovery of all basic rate tax paid.

In the absence of this power, it is important for the executors to ensure that no more than the correct amount of expenses is set against income. The matter should, however, be given careful thought and not merely determined by reference to the usual rough and ready estimate. Certain expenses may, upon a careful analysis, be properly attributable to capital rather than income.

16.10.4   Tax credits and charities

From 6 April 1999 dividends paid by UK companies only carry tax credits of 10 per cent and can only be set off against a shareholder's liability for tax on the dividend.

Tax credits are no longer payable to shareholders with no tax liability. The tax credit continues to satisfy the tax liability of taxpayers in the lower and basic rate tax bands.

The result is that as charities are exempt from tax on dividends, they can no longer claim repayment of the tax credit, as they could prior to 6 April 1999. In order to compensate charities for the loss of repayable tax credits Finance (No.2) Act 1997, s.35 provided for transitional payment out of public funds of amounts calculated as a percentage of the dividend received by the charity. The rate was 21 per cent in 1999/2000 falling to 4 per cent by 2003/04. The transitional scheme ended in 2003/04.

16.10.5   Complaints about charities

The Charity Commissioners have a useful website (**www.charitycommission. gov.uk**). There are various helpful publications available there. See, in particular, CC47 *Complaints about Charities.*

CHAPTER 17

Probate practice checklists

Solicitors in private practice may adapt or adopt these checklists for the purpose set out on **page iv** of this Handbook, but not for any other purpose.

17.1 PERSONAL REPRESENTATIVES AND PLANNING CHECKLIST

Before you begin to deal with the assets and liabilities have you:

1. Obtained clear instructions from the personal representatives (PRs)?
2. Explained to the PRs:

   - their duties;
   - the nature and extent of the work to be done;
   - what is included in your retainer;
   - costs, charging, expenses;
   - Inheritance (Provision for Family and Dependants) Act 1975, statutory advertisements, deeds of variation, plus time limits – and noted relevant dates in your diary;
   - potential hold-ups: elapse of survival period, HMRC Capital Taxes, etc.;
   - any welfare benefits relevant and how to apply? (See **Chapter 9**.)

   Sent to PRs:

   - information letter (see **Chapter 3**);
   - client care letter/leaflet (see **Chapter 3**);
   - copy will?

3. Obtained your clients' addresses and phone and fax numbers and their availability? Agreed reporting frequency and logged dates in your diary? Agreed billing frequency and logged dates in your diary?
4. Established an anticipated, realistic, timetable for completion of the administration? Confirmed this to PRs?
   Established target dates for completion of each stage?
   Logged these into your diary? Plus six-month and 12-month anniversaries of death and other significant dates such as two-month anniversary of statutory advertisements? Established whether there is any need to obtain the grant urgently? If so, and if inheritance tax (IHT) is payable, checked with HMRC on possibility of submitting account with estimated valuations?

5. Checked will for validity? Contacted witnesses if affidavits are necessary?
6. Checked gifts for ademption, lapse, contingencies, etc.?
7. Checked form of ownership of assets (sole name, joint tenancy, co-ownership)? In case of assets which appear to have passed to the deceased by survivorship, checked whether there might have been severance by mutual agreement at an earlier stage?
8. Checked whether third parties allege rights in assets of the estate as a result of resulting or constructive trusts or proprietary estoppel?
9. Checked whether any lifetime gifts made by the deceased might be voidable on the basis of undue influence?
10. Obtained PRs' consent to contact residuary beneficiaries with copy will and estimated timescale? Obtained PRs' consent to contact legatees with estimated timescale?
11. Confirmed beneficiaries' and next of kin's addresses with PRs? Taken steps to trace any missing beneficiaries? Considered whether statutory advertisements are appropriate? The cost may not be justified where the executor is taking the entire estate. If appropriate, inserted statutory advertisements?
12. Informed:

- deceased's bank or building society;
- other professional advisers;
- insurers;
- others?

Obtained figures for balances of funds held, accrued interest, etc.?
13. Arranged valuations?
Instructed valuer to make valuation on basis of open market value and to state this on the valuation?
Included balances and valuations on draft accounts?
Obtained details of deceased's tax office and current position?
14. Established whether deceased was a member of Lloyd's?
If so, decided whether:

- it is safe to rely on indemnities or insurance,
- or whether it is necessary to apply to court under *Practice Statement: Chancery Division: Estates of Deceased Lloyd's Names* [2001] 3 All ER 765 for leave to distribute without making provision for contingent liability in the event of Equitas being inadequate?

Made application, if necessary?
15. Begun to prepare the accounts by:

- listing all assets and estimated values;
- deciding whether specialist advice is needed;
- listing all liabilities?

16. Prepared list of asset holders needing to see the grant of representation?
17. Considered with PRs the method of payment of IHT? Made the necessary arrangements?
18. Established the nature of money coming into the office in terms of the Solicitors' Accounts Rules 1998 requirements? (See **Chapter 5**.)
19. Considered whether variation desirable?

17.2 IMMEDIATE PRACTICAL ACTION CHECKLIST

Items   *For action by family/us*

1. Register death.
2. Check for directions re disposal of body in wills, personal assets log, and amongst papers.
3. Arrange funeral/cremation (as directed if appropriate).
4. Notify time, date and place to family.*
5. Deceased's house:

   - remove valuables (if to office, does our insurance cover value? Do any special conditions, e.g. regarding guns, apply?);**
   - arrange maintenance (e.g. drain water system) if appropriate;
   - cancel deliveries, e.g. milk, papers;
   - redirect mail;
   - lodge keys securely, not marked with address;
   - deal with insurers, landlord and council tax as appropriate.

6. Deceased's car:

   - inform insurers;
   - transfer insurance, etc., if to be used by family;
   - arrange for security if not to be used.

7. Livestock and pets:

   - arrange for their immediate welfare;
   - check if prior long-term arrangements have already been made with friends or family (the Law Society personal assets log includes a point on pets);
   - if not, pedigree pets may sometimes be returned to the breeder; otherwise the Kennel Club, Cat Fancy and welfare organisations could help (see **Useful addresses**).

---

* Some firms counsel clients not to announce the death in the local or national paper, nor the funeral, because many families have – almost unbelievably – come back from a funeral to find that the house has been burgled.
** See the helpful article on firearms in this context by Peter Sarony in [1995] *New Law Journal*, Probate Supplement, 29 September.

17.3 TESTATE ESTATE CHECKLIST

1. Is the will valid and properly signed and dated, with an appropriate attestation clause, and correctly witnessed? If not, list remedial action needed and advise the client.
2. Is this definitely the last will? Are there any codicils?
3. Is there likely to be any dispute about the validity of dispositions included in the will? Did the testator or testatrix marry or divorce after the date of the will? Are any of the presumptions, e.g. capacity, validity, etc., likely to be rebutted? If so, is there any evidence of the circumstances surrounding the execution? Can the witnesses be traced

if affidavits have to be obtained? List remedial action, and advise the client.

4. Does the will refer to unexecuted writings, chattels by memo, etc.? Is there a letter explaining why a person has not been provided for in the context of an IPFDA 1975 claim? Is a claim likely? (See **Chapter 10**.) Advise the client.
5. Is there any evidence of secret or half-secret trusts? If so, have the requirements for validity been met? If the will contains precatory words, can they be complied with?
6. Is there any evidence of an agreement that the will should be mutual? If so, where the death is of the first testator or testatrix make sure that the existence of the trust now binding on the property of the surviving testator is clearly recorded; if the death is of the surviving testator remember that the terms of any will left by the surviving testator cannot overrule the terms of the trust imposed on the death of the first testator.
7. If the will refers to contingencies, have they been satisfied?
8. Is all the property referred to in the will available for beneficiaries, or have any gifts adeemed?
9. Have all beneficiaries been traced? Do any gifts lapse?
10. Have any legacies been adeemed by subsequent lifetime gifts as a result of the doctrine of satisfaction?
11. Is the estate solvent?
12. Is there any evidence of PETs and other transfers?
13. Is a variation appropriate?

17.4 INTESTATE AND PARTIALLY INTESTATE ESTATE CHECKLIST

1. The death: if the deceased and spouse or partner died together in an accident, remember 14-day survivorship period applies to spouses but not to others. Does this affect this estate? Advise client.
2. Has a search for a will been made? (If it is thought a will was made, the 'Wills and Whereabouts' page in the *Gazette*, local solicitors, the deposit facility at the Principal Registry (see **Useful addresses**) and enquiry of the deceased's bank, friends and relatives may all be of assistance.)
3. Will the estate be solvent? Does it exceed statutory legacy limits of £125,000/£200,000? How will the existence of any undisposed-of property affect the payment of debts?
4. List the surviving relatives; in more complex cases drawing up a family tree is usually easier than describing relationship. Can they all be contacted? Will there be any problems establishing identity and relationship? Might there be an IPFDA 1975 claim? (See **Chapter 10**.)
5. Establish who will be entitled to the estate; note minor children's ages and the years in which they will attain majority.
6. Establish who will take the grant. Will two administrators be needed?
7. How will the statutory trusts apply, if at all?
8. Does the spouse wish to redeem the life interest and/or appropriate the matrimonial home? Log the 12 months' deadline from the issue of the grant into the diary. Does the value of the matrimonial home exceed

the value of the statutory legacy? If so, what arrangements need to be made to cover the difference?
9. Is there any evidence of PETs and other transfers?
10. Is a variation appropriate?

17.5 THE OATH AND AFTER CHECKLIST

1. List assets and liabilities.
2. Is IHT account required? (See **14.3–14.4.**) Which pages?
3. Prepare oath and HMRC account.
4. Send tax cheque to HMRC. Lodge papers and receipted D18 at probate registry. Order plenty of office copies – it is false economy to order too few. Does timetable need adjusting? If so, inform PRs.
5. Prepare for payment of debts. Will assets need to be sold? If so, contact PRs and residuary beneficiaries:
Which ones? Arrange valuations if necessary.
Consider tax implications – deed of variation?
6. Update draft accounts. Update other lists. Review file generally, especially initial letters, and check expiry dates and deadlines – review schedule if necessary and advise client. Are charities interested in estate? If so, check whether they wish assets to be appropriated to them to avoid unnecessary CGT. Check proceeds of sale of shares and land against probate valuations to see if assets qualify for IHT loss on sale relief (IHTA 1984, ss.178–189). If so, claim relief and file corrective account. Check proceeds of sale of assets generally against probate valuations to see if there are gains or losses for CGT purposes.
7. Log in diary due dates for IHT interest payments in relation to instalment option property, if appropriate.
8. Interim bill? (Did you agree this with the PRs in advance?)
9. Interim distribution? May be advisable to avoid a beneficiary receiving a large income receipt in one tax year pushing beneficiary into higher rate tax unnecessarily (see **Chapter 16**).

17.6 OBTAINING THE GRANT CHECKLIST

This checklist, with reminders, has been specially revised and reformulated by Kevin Donnelly, Chief Clerk at the Probate Registry, Somerset House, and we are most grateful to him for doing so, and for permission to use it.

Oath form YES/NO

1. *Extracting solicitors*

   • Has your name, address (including post code), DX number and reference (if required) been included at the heading of the oath?

2. *Name of deceased*

   • Does the name correspond with the will (if any)?

- If not, or if an alias is necessary for any other reason, has the true name been identified and the reason for the alias been set out in the oath by way of a footnote?
- Was the deceased known by any other name or was the death registered in any other name? If so, these should be included on the oath (although these names may not appear on the grant).

3. *Address of deceased*

- Has the last residential address been included? (A short stay in hospital can be ignored for these purposes.) Include post code.

4. *Names of applicants*

- Are these the true names?
- Do they correspond with the will (if any)?
- Is an affidavit of identity required?
- Has the applicant included any extra initials in his or her signature to the oath? (Any extra initials should be investigated and the oath resworn to show the true name if necessary.)
- Include address and post code.
- Does the will contain a clause providing that the executor or executrix must survive by a specified period before the appointment becomes effective?
- If yes, has the period expired?

5. *Survival clause in will*

- Does the will contain a clause providing that the executor or executrix must survive by a specified period before the appointment becomes effective?
- If yes, has the period expired?

6. *Date of death*

- Does the date of death given in the oath agree with that on the death certificate? (If the death certificate does not give a specific date of death, the oath should state when the deceased was last seen or known to be alive and when his or her body was found.)

7. *Codicil*

- Did the deceased leave any codicils to the will?
- If yes, has reference been made to them in the oath?
- If yes, have they been marked in accordance with Rule 10 of the Non-Contentious Probate Rules (NCPR) 1987 by the applicant and swearing Commissioner?

8. *Age of the deceased*

- Has the age and date of birth of the deceased been included in the oath?

9. *Domicile of the deceased*

- Has the domicile of the deceased been included in the oath? (If the deceased died domiciled out of England and Wales and different systems of law operate within the country, the state of domicile must be shown, e.g. the State of Victoria, the State of New Jersey.)

10. *Settled land*

- Has the clause concerning settled land been included/completed? (This clause must be included in every oath.)

11. *Life/minority interest*

- Did the deceased leave a will?
- If yes, is the executor or executrix appointed in it applying for the grant?
- If no, or if the deceased left no will, does a life or minority interest arise out of the estate?
- Has the appropriate section in the oath been included/completed? (The oath must state, in terms, whether a life or minority interest arises unless an executor or executrix is applying for the grant.)
- Have all the persons with a prior entitlement to the applicant been accounted for in the oath?
- Has the applicant's title been stated in full? (Unless all clearings have been included and the title stated in full the oath is certain to be queried and is likely to require reswearing.)

12. *Title*

- Have all the persons with a prior entitlement to the applicant been accounted for in the oath?
- Has the applicant's title been stated in full? (Unless all clearings have been included and the title stated in full the oath is certain to be queried and is likely to require reswearing.)

13. *Value of the estate: Is the estate an 'excepted estate'? (See **14.3**.)*

- If yes, have the band figures appropriate to the date of death been included in the oath?
- Has the net estate been stated to the nearest thousand?
- Have the words 'and this is not a case in which a HMRC account is required to be lodged' (or similar) been included in the correct clause? (Failure to include this clause will result in the oath having to be resworn.)
- If not, and the deceased died domiciled in England and Wales, has the total of all the estate passing under the grant been included?
- Does this total agree with that shown in the HMRC account?
- If not, has an explanation for the difference been included in the oath?
- If the deceased died domiciled out of England and Wales, has the relevant clause been amended to refer to estate only in England and Wales? (It is possible to have an 'excepted estate' for a deceased who died domiciled in Scotland.)

14. *Jurat*

- Has the oath and will/codicil(s) (if any) been signed by (all) the applicant(s) and swearing Commissioner(s)?
- Has the oath been dated and the place of swearing stated? (Please bear in mind that the oath and any supporting affidavits cannot be sworn before the solicitor extracting the grant or a member of his or her firm.)

Special types of application

1. *Attorney grants*

   - Has the limitation to be recited in the grant been included in the oath? (The usual limitation is 'for the use and benefit of – [*the donor*] and until further representation be granted'.)

2. *Grants for minors*

   - Are there two applicants?
   - Is it necessary to lodge a nomination of the second applicant?
   - If the application relies upon court orders, are court-certified copies available?
   - Does the oath state that a minority interest arises?
   - Does the oath have the correct limitation? (The usual limitation in such application is 'for the use and benefit of – [the minor(s)] until he/she/one of them shall attain the age of 18 years'.)

3. *Domicile out of England and Wales*

   - Has the domicile of the deceased been described correctly?
   - Have those facts upon which the deponent to the affidavit of law (if any) has relied when reaching his or her conclusions been included in the oath or another sworn document? (These facts are usually recited in the affidavit of law following the words 'I am informed and verily believe' or similar. If they are not sworn, the application will be delayed whilst the oath or affidavit is resworn.)
   - Have the words 'in England and Wales' been added to the clause dealing with the estate?
   - Are any foreign court documents to be used in support of the application copies certified by the court?
   - Has the correct form of HMRC account (IHT201) been completed and controlled by the Capital Taxes Office?
   - Has any necessary order under NCPR 1987 been obtained or approved? (It may not be necessary to have the order drawn before swearing the oath but prior approval of the district judge or district probate registrar must be obtained.)

4. *Lost wills*

   - Has the original will been seen since the deceased's date of death?
   - Was the will known to have been in the possession of the deceased up to the date of his or her death?
   - If the answer to the first question is no and the second yes, does the evidence in support of the application rebut the presumption of revocation of the will by the deceased in his or her lifetime?
   - Can the authenticity of the copy will be confirmed?
   - Does the affidavit in support of the application exhibit the copy will to be proved?
   - Does the oath in support of the application for the grant describe accurately the copy will being proved? (It is suggested that the affidavit(s) in support of the application be prepared in draft form in the first instance to enable any further evidence required by the district judge or registrar to be incorporated.)

Wills and codicils

1. Has the testator or testatrix signed the will?

    - Has the will been witnessed by two witnesses?
    - Does the will contain a properly worded attestation clause?
    - Has the will been dated?

    (Although these are obvious points, a large number of wills are rejected by the probate registries each year for these simple defects. The factors also apply to codicils. It may still be possible to prove a will/codicil with any of these defects if validity can be established under the Wills Act 1963.)

2. Does the will/codicil have any unattested alterations or additions?
3. Is there a valid appointment of executrix/executor(s)? (Care should be taken to ensure that the appointment is correctly worded; if there is any doubt, evidence of the testator's or testatrix's intention will be necessary.)
4. Did the deceased leave any codicils to his or her will?

    - If yes, are they all available?
    - Is the appointment of executors affected by the codicil?
    - Does the codicil confirm the will by the correct date? (If the date is not correct, evidence that the right will is being proved may be necessary.)

5. Have the will and codicils (if any) been marked by the applicant(s) and swearing Commissioner(s) in accordance with Rule 10 of NCPR 1987?

IHT accounts

1. Has the correct account, appropriate to the date of death and type of application, been used?
2. Has the account been signed and dated by the applicant(s)?

    - Does the account need to be controlled by HMRC? (Although any account may be controlled, generally speaking this need be done only in the estates of persons who die domiciled out of England and Wales.)
    - Is the date of death of the deceased before 13 March 1975?
    - If the answer is yes, has the IHT account been sworn? (NB This is a requirement.)
    - Has the certificate regarding payment of IHT been signed?

Fees

1. Has the correct fee been paid?
2. Does the payment include the fee for any copies ordered?

17.7 COLLECTING THE ASSETS, PAYING THE DEBTS CHECKLIST

1. Cancel/obtain refund/collect/return/pay/check:

    - council tax;
    - Department for Work and Pensions payments;
    - trade union or professional association subscription – and some death benefit may be payable;

- club and other memberships such as charities, libraries, pressure groups, voluntary organisations, political parties and consumer and motoring organisations;
- subscriptions: journals, magazines, book clubs;
- borrowed items: library books, records, videos, hospital equipment such as a wheelchair;
- payments made in advance by deceased, e.g. gas or electricity account may be in credit;
- payments due to deceased which may be in arrears, e.g. pension;
- laundry or dry cleaning, or items sent for valuation or repair;
- items on hire: TV or washing machine, computer, possibly evening or formal dress;
- relevant direct debits/standing orders, etc., at bank or building society;
- milk, papers and other deliveries;
- passport;
- credit cards.

2. List all the assets and refunds and include a column for noting what happened to the asset, its value and relevant dates.
3. Is there any property abroad? How will this be dealt with? Do foreign law rules conflict with the will or the intestacy rules? Specialist advice may be needed.
4. Valuation: some items may be more valuable than one might expect. Certain charities, such as the PDSA, offer house clearance services (others may advertise in local papers and free sheets) but ensure that nothing possibly of value is overlooked. See specialist valuers address list (see **Useful addresses**) for items needing an expert's opinion.
5. Send office copies of the grant to asset holders – use standard letters on a word processor to save time and get plenty of office copies, too few is a false economy. Include a request in letters to bank, building societies, etc., for all the necessary paperwork for closure of accounts to be sent.
6. Keep standard letters to creditors on a word processor to save time. Send these early so that relatives are not troubled by reminders about bills.
7. Make a list of all the deceased's liabilities, with columns for the dates and amounts of payments. Tick each off as it is dealt with.
8. Ensure that assets in your office are insured and listed, and any special regulations (e.g. re guns, antique or modern) are observed.
9. Pay bills promptly when funds becomes available – if this takes time, does the timetable need adjusting? If so, advise the client.
10. It may be helpful to keep all the paperwork related to paid debts (e.g. bills, receipts and correspondence, etc.) in a separate file once they are no longer current matters.

17.8 ACCOUNTING AND DISTRIBUTION CHECKLIST

1. Prepare any corrective account for IHT which has become necessary. For small amounts, correspondence may suffice.
2. Make interim distributions, but reserve enough money for outstanding tax, costs and other contingencies. Consider ensuring that PRs and

residuary beneficiaries are satisfied with the draft accounts before making large distributions.

3. Ensure arrangements for payment of tax by beneficiaries have been made, where necessary.

4. Offer beneficiaries receiving substantial legacies your firm's investment advice if you are authorised. See also **Chapter 4** on undertaking investment business.

5. Do any beneficiaries need:

- wills?
- codicils?
- tax advice?
- enduring powers of attorney?

6. Have all beneficiaries received forms R185E where appropriate? This is particularly important for charities who will need to obtain refunds of income tax.

7. If problems in obtaining a discharge arise consider insurance, payment into court under Trustee Act 1925, s.63, etc.

8. Have the important dates for protecting PRs passed – two months for statutory advertisements, six months from date of grant for IPFDA 1975 claims? (See **Chapter 8** on probate time limits.)

9. Prepare accounts (or have them prepared for you).

10. Obtain receipts and discharges from beneficiaries.

17.9 CLOSING YOUR FILE CHECKLIST

1. Is your file closure letter satisfactory? It is an important document as it should stand proof that you have completed your work satisfactorily. To perform this function it should incorporate the following points:

- It should explain why the file has been closed. This is usually because the matter has been completed. However, the client may have changed solicitors or decided to deal with the matter in person. This needs to be fully explained so that the client cannot allege later that you were still instructed. It is particularly important where you were retained to deal with only certain aspects of the administration.
- It should explain exactly what work your firm has done and what the outcome was. There may be a misunderstanding between what you have done and what the client thinks you have done. It is better for the client to realise this at a time when further instructions can be given easily.
- It should set out clearly any tasks which the client has to perform (for example, the payment of instalments of IHT) with, if necessary, exact timings and the consequences of failing to adhere to those timings.
- Consider sending two copies of the letter to your client asking for one to be signed and returned.

2. Which documents belong to the client? See *The Guide to the Professional Conduct of Solicitors 1999* (the Guide), Principle 12.11 and 12.12, and Annex 12A, 'Guidance: ownership, storage and destruction of documents'.

3. How long must the file be kept? See the Guide, Annex 12A para.4 'How long should I retain old files?'.
4. Which documents should be preserved? This list is not exhaustive:
   - documents belonging to the client;
   - documents of title;
   - significant correspondence with HMRC, returns, accounts, etc.;
   - court orders;
   - valuations (it may be advisable to supply probate valuations to non-residuary legatees – otherwise they will contact you in the future if CGT becomes an issue for them).
5. Consider asking the client if any old, but non-essential, documents could be of interest to a local history society or museum.
6. Could any of the letters or documents you prepared form the basis of stock letters for future use by you or within the office? If so, consider keeping these in a separate, indexed, precedent file.

17.10 EVALUATING CHECKLIST

Ten things I know now I wish I'd known then:

1.

2.

3.

4.

5.

6.

7.

8.

9.

10.

PART IV

Profitable Probate

Much of this Handbook is intended to help with cost-effective case and file management. This Part of the book looks more widely at practice management and the organisation of work in the office both generally and individually, so it is hoped it will be of interest to all solicitors, whether or not they have management responsibilities.

CHAPTER 18

Computing and technology issues

Charles Christian

18.1 INTRODUCTION

Thanks to the high profile coverage computer systems and information technology (IT) related matters now enjoy in the legal press, there is a growing belief among solicitors' practices that computerisation is the universal panacea for all problems. However, while it might be nice to think that if the firm is not making enough money out of probate practice, the easiest solution is to install a new 'probate case management software' application, not only is this a far too simplistic approach, but it could also prove to be commercially disastrous.

Leaving aside the cost and inevitable disruption (including the time taken up with administration matters that would otherwise be devoted to fee earning) associated with all computerisation projects, there is a risk of running foul of the old computer industry adage: GIGO – garbage in, garbage out. In other words, if the practice has problems, installing a computer will not fix those problems, it will merely computerise them.

That's the bad news. The good news is that a properly implemented law office computerisation project will yield positive benefits. And in the case of probate practitioners, at the very least this should include reducing the time and overheads associated with individual probate matters, so allowing them both to increase the volume of work they can handle and also to increase the profitability of that work. Or, to put it another way, technology is a tool that properly used will help you earn more money, get out of the office and away home earlier – and still keep the client satisfied.

18.2 TECHNOLOGY IN CONTEXT

The starting point for any discussion about legal technology must be with the premise that technology is not an end in itself but merely a tool to help implement a law firm's overall business and practice development plans. In other words the emphasis is upon the creation of a joined-up, rather than a semi-detached, strategy.

Unfortunately too many firms still approach computerisation projects from the wrong direction, putting the proverbial cart before the horse, and make the decision to invest in technology without fully thinking through its longer term implications. Just because the firm down the road has bought a new probate system is not a good enough reason for your firm to buy one as well, it is important to look at the bigger picture. For example, where is your firm planning to go over the next five years? Will it still be doing private client work? Are there plans to expand or contract its probate practice? Are there any obvious problems with the way that probate work is currently processed that could benefit from technology? And what benefits is it envisaged that technology will deliver?

The answers to all these questions will help determine the firm's priorities; however, particular emphasis should be paid to the issue of the anticipated benefits of technology – or the 'return on investment' (ROI). Solicitors' practices are notorious for fudging the answer to this question and despite the fact a firm can currently expect to spend about 5 per cent of its annual turnover each year on IT, the method of measuring the ROI is, to put it charitably, naive and unscientific. I've lost count of the number of times I've heard a firm justify some huge expenditure solely on the grounds that 'it will help us to provide a better service to our clients'.

Talk about stating the obvious – well, of course the firm hopes it is going to help provide a better service otherwise it would not be buying these systems. But warm, cosy, touchy-feely sentiments like that will not pay the bills – nor generate the fee income to keep the partnership happy. When assessing ROI the questions a firm should be asking are: 'How much money is this new system going to save us?' For example, will it be possible to cut down on the number of staff in the probate department? And: 'How much in extra fees is this system going to help us earn?' For instance, will the system enable the firm to handle more matters with the same staff resources?

Firms should also ensure that any ROI calculations focus upon profitability, as distinct from mere increases in turnover because more billable hours can be generated. If this increase in turnover has only been achieved by also increasing overheads, the slightest downturn in the economy will put pressure on profit margins, which once again will not please the rest of the partnership. Lecture over, now let's start looking at the technology options available.

18.3 PROBATE SYSTEMS

Probate systems are a confusing area of law office automation in that the same term is often loosely applied by suppliers to a broad range of applications covering everything from will writing software through to investment trust accounting and portfolio management systems. A listing and contact details of all the relevant systems suppliers are provided in **Appendix C.**

18.3.1   Will writing software and electronic forms and precedents

Providing the products that have clearly been designed for the DIY market or will writing businesses are ignored, there are nevertheless some good systems available which are suitable for probate solicitors in private practice. And, to repeat the old Law Society adage – that if you want to stay in practice, you need to get a niche – it may well be that the demographics of your local area means there is a commercially viable revenue stream to be had from offering will preparation services.

For example, in a rural area with limited public transport, sole practitioners may consider providing house calls, taking their laptop computers with them to provide will writing and other services to clients who would otherwise be unable to get to their offices. This also neatly highlights the true value of technology as a tool. It is not a universal panacea nor a one-size-fits-all solution but in the right hands can enhance the delivery of legal services to clients – in this instance, if the client cannot get into the office, the solicitor can take a 'virtual office' on a laptop to the client. Think outside the box.

Mention should also be made of the wide range of legal forms and precedents that now exist in an electronic format (typically on CD-Rom or via a download from the internet) so clauses can be selected and automatically incorporated within a document or deed without the need to retype any wording. For example, the Law Society's Probate Section is committed to building up the number of documents and deeds members can buy or download from its website (**www.probatesection.org.uk**). These include things such as a Client Retainer Guide.

18.3.2   Wills and deeds registers

This is really just another name for a computerised index of all the wills that the firm holds copies of and where they are physically located. Back in the days of stand-alone technology, specific software packages were sold to handle this type of application. Today, with the emphasis in law firm IT on central databases, this type of information will usually be stored within an overall client/matter section of a practice management system or else it will be one of the elements of a probate case management system.

18.3.3   Trusts and portfolio management systems

This area of legal work sees the practitioner moving beyond the conventional bounds of probate practice and into the broader private client/investment/financial services arena. Technically this is outside the scope of this book; however, with the rise in property prices and spread of financial investing (thanks to ISAs, etc.) bringing many more estates up into values where IHT becomes an issue, we are seeing many more 'ordinary members of the public' (as distinct from high net worth private clients) seeking advice on estate and tax planning matters where trusts may be relevant. A number of suppliers of probate systems also supply trust accounting and management systems.

18.3.4 Internet systems

This area has seen a lot of movement since the previous edition of this book was published, when we were just starting to move into the dotcom boom era and there was a lot of excitement about the possibility of law firms selling wills and related services online via the web. Now, the hype has subsided and the internet is now seen as primarily a communications medium, a resource and, in some types of work, a way to enhance or complement the delivery of legal services.

Although there are still some firms offering online wills-related services, two factors have effectively killed this market. The first was the realisation of the complexity of the compliance issue – how do you ensure you don't breach five professional conduct rules before breakfast (never mind avoiding falling foul of the anti-money laundering regulations) when you are dealing with a virtual client? However, the real killer was that firms found there was simply not a commercially viable volume of demand for online wills services. Indeed, firms that did go this route discovered that the fees generated failed to even recoup the cost of the systems needed to deliver such services.

That however still leaves three valuable roles for the internet. The first, as already mentioned, is as a communications medium. This is going to become more important over the next few years as more 'e-government' initiatives are rolled out and it becomes quicker, more convenient and cheaper (particularly if government agencies extend the practice of offering financial incentives to complete forms online) to turn to the web rather than use traditional paper-based form filling methods. The Court Service now has a section of its website devoted to the Probate Service, which includes links through to the HMRC capital taxes section (**www.hmcourts-service.gov.uk/cms/wills.htm**).

The second role of the internet is as a resource – a searchable repository of information. Here the Law Society's own website (**www.lawsociety.org.uk**) deserves praise as its usability has been greatly improved, as has the scope of its contents and the search engine to help locate those contents. One particularly useful feature, located at the time of writing at the bottom of the home page, is a link through to the Society's e-business newsletter, which chronicles all the latest e-government initiatives. Another link to bookmark is the legal resources website maintained by Delia Venables (**www.venables.co.uk**) which contains a link to every website in the UK that should be of interest to lawyers in their professional capacity.

The third and final role of the internet is in the delivery of legal services to clients and related third parties. This is particularly relevant in some areas of legal practice, such as residential conveyancing where typically the client, the estate agent and the mortgage lender (to whose panel the solicitor belongs) will be able to access matter progress reports online via a secure website known as an extranet. Increasingly 'client access extranets' are becoming a standard option within case management software although to date there has been very little demand for this facility by probate practitioners. To go back to my technology as a tool analogy – just because technology can do something, does not necessarily mean that your clients will actually want it or that you need to buy it.

18.3.5 Probate case (or workflow) management systems

These systems introduce an element of automation to probate work by building a workflow routine that effectively controls the way the work is processed. These can be very useful where work is being handled by a department and the partner in charge needs not only to be able to review and manage the progress of matters but also to ensure that tasks delegated to non-legally qualified staff take place within a sufficiently rigid framework, so there is no room for mistakes to be made.

For prospective purchasers there are a number of issues to consider here. The first is whether they have the volume of work or organisational structure to justify the workflow management approach? If lawyers are not prepared to delegate probate work to more junior staff the introduction of computerisation will merely turn fee earners in very expensive keyboard operators.

Another issue is whether the software is being sold on a stand-alone or integrated basis. For example, some suppliers sell software on a stand-alone basis, so you can buy a probate workflow application and run it out of the box, with or without link's to your firm's accounts or practice management software. (This is also sometimes called the 'best of breed' approach.) However, much of the software sold into the UK legal systems market consists of integrated products, so a firm cannot use one supplier's probate system unless that supplier's accounts system is also installed. If a firm is happy with its existing accounts/practice management system (the Law Society's own Software Solutions Guide has some relevance here and this will be discussed in more detail at **18.5.6**), the cheapest and most hassle free option will usually be to install that supplier's probate system.

18.3.6 Probate accounts software

This is used to help practitioners compile estate accounts, print interim statements for beneficiaries and prepare completed IHT returns. Most of these systems also contain some form of workflow management-style diary reminders and checklists. Bearing in mind that the preparation of estate accounts can be one of the most time-consuming features of probate work, this is a system many practitioners would benefit from using. But when talking to software sales staff, be certain that they do not fudge this issue. Can it really handle all aspects probate accounts – for example can it produce IHT forms? And do not be fobbed off with promises that although the system currently only offers workflow facilities 'an accounts module is under development'. That is no good, you need to know what it can do for you now, not what it might be able to do at some dim and possibly very distant date in the future.

18.4 HOW PROBATE SYSTEMS CAN HELP PRACTITIONERS

This is a potentially contentious topic, for it does not matter how good a computer system may be in theory because unless a practice is prepared to invest adequately in training – so that its members really know how to operate the computers on their desks – the full benefits of the system will never be realised. Whatever else you do, do not skimp on training. Leaving aside this important qualification, there are five potential areas of benefit.

18.4.1 Achieving immediate objectives

There are a number of situations that can arise where computerisation is successfully undertaken to achieve immediate, relatively limited, short-term objectives. For example, suppose an experienced probate practitioner is heading for retirement and planning to work on a part-time consultancy basis. If the firm still has a healthy probate practice then investing in a probate accounts system that can act as an *aide-mémoire* for another less experienced lawyer and take over some of the donkey work on the estate accounts preparation work may be a cost-effective alternative to replacement of the consultant.

Similarly, if the firm were to win a major commercial client, such as a financial institution, and with it the prospect of a major increase in the volume of its probate work, then installing IT would be a cost-effective alternative to recruiting additional probate department staff. This also meets one of the measurements for ROI, namely how much will this system help us save?

18.4.2   Better information

In discussing computerisation most people tend to focus on the 'technology' aspect of 'information technology'. However, the 'information' angle should also be remembered. Although computers have earned a poor reputation in the past for generating impenetrable reports of monumental length, modern systems are excellent tools for extracting valuable business information from large volumes of data – information that would be almost impossible to obtain (or at least take a long time and prevent staff from getting on with their normal work) using manual methods.

For example, access to detailed information about clients and work types allows firms to be more precise in their marketing and cross-selling efforts – which in the past probably involved little more than sending Christmas cards to every client name on the books, regardless of whether anyone in the firm had spoken to them in the last decade. (This aspect of legal software is increasingly referred to as 'client relationship management' or CRM.)

For firms who anticipate that most of their probate work will be generated from the results of earlier wills campaigns (such as the annual Law Society 'Wills Week'), a good information system also allows the firm to become proactive rather than reactive, so clients can be periodically contacted to see if they need to review and update their wills. After all, this year's happily married shopkeeper could be next year's lottery winner with a younger spouse, new family and an increasingly complex network of commercial interests.

18.4.3   Greater efficiency and productivity

One of the more obvious benefits of computerisation is that IT is very good at doing relatively dull repetitive tasks very quickly and accurately, such as adding up long columns of figures. In the probate department this means error-free estate accounts can be prepared within hours whereas previously staff could have been tied up for days. This in turn means that the firm will now have the capacity to handle more work with the same or fewer resources, thus avoiding the need to recruit extra staff and/or allowing existing staff to be allocated to other tasks. Once again this meets the ROI criteria for saving money and/or helping the firm to make more money.

It is also worth noting that workflow and case management systems primarily come into their own in the context of helping manage the delegation of routine aspects of work to more junior staff – a particular boon for firms handling high volumes of work. However, even in those firms where probate work is handled by just one highly skilled solicitor, there can still be productivity gains. For example, there is always a degree of routine work associated with any matter, such as sending out client care letters, replying to correspondence and to enquiries about the progress of a matter, cheque requisitions for official fees, plus associated diary entries and updates to files and archives. The important point here is that the computer is not in anyway diminishing the role of the lawyer by automating some of these tasks, it is merely taking over some of the boring but necessary non-legal aspects of the business process. In other words, it frees lawyers from pushing around bits of paper and allows them to concentrate on the more interesting – and financially rewarding – legal work.

This has led to the suggestion that if a workflow system can automate just some of these tasks, perhaps only saving a fee earner five or 10 minutes a day, in the long term this can add up to a substantial saving in time. Ten minutes a day is the equivalent of 50 hours a year – which is quite a chunk considering the average English solicitor only bills a total of 1250 hours a year. And, of course, if every fee earner in the firm enjoys the same benefits . . . In effect this is the 'little bang' approach to technology. The introduction of IT cannot be expected to dramatically change the firm's fortune in some kind of 'big bang' experience but the incremental benefits can be become substantial over time. This also brings us back to my original comment that the role of technology in a solicitors' practice is to help you earn more money, get home earlier and still keep the client satisfied.

18.4.4 Better service

Having an IT system also opens up the possibility of offering services to clients which previously firms would have been reluctant to offer because of the additional workload involved. For example, producing interim accounts for the beneficiaries of an estate becomes an automated click-of-a-button operation. Leaving aside the potential for generating extra fees (or taking less time to earn the same amount of fees) the ability to offer additional services is a plus point in terms of establishing a longer-term professional relationship with a client and helping to differentiate a firm from its competition. In broader practice development and marketing terms this is vital, because law firms cannot reduce their quality of service, competing on price is potentially ruinous, so the viable route is to offer a service that helps the firm to stand out from the rest of the crowd.

18.4.5 Increased profitability

If an IT system can help increase productivity among secretarial, clerical and fee earning staff, so that the same people can get through more work in the same or less time, then this will clearly have an impact upon the firm's profitability in that it frees them to get on with additional fee earning activities. However, computerisation can also bring about an increase in profitability by its potential for reducing overheads.

For example, it is not uncommon to find that smaller firms have an administrative 'tail' with a ratio of 1 to 2. In other words, for every fee earner in the firm, there are two back office staff (including secretaries). But, if IT is introduced, so fee earners can carry out jobs that would have previously involved dictating instructions to secretaries and waiting for these to be effected, it becomes possible to reduce the size of this tail.

A 1 to 1 ratio is the minimum to aim for, which typically will be achieved by sharing secretaries between fee earners, assigning some secretaries to quasi fee earning activities and reducing the reliance on 'temps'; however many firms have already achieved 2 to 1 or greater. Less reliance on support staff has, in turn, a number of other benefits. For example, it means it is possible to recruit more fee earners without also having to recruit a corresponding number of secretaries, which means that an expanding firm is likely to outgrow its existing office space less quickly than it would otherwise do.

Clearly employing proportionally fewer staff means that less is being spent on overheads, which in turn means increased profits. Equally, bearing in mind the competitive market in which solicitors operate, reducing overheads means that firms can also afford to compete on price (for example against banks and other financial institutions) by cutting their margins yet still manage to make some profit on a matter.

18.5   THE PRINCIPLES OF IT PROCUREMENT

Along with salaries, accommodation and professional indemnity (PI) insurance, for many solicitors' practices their investment in a new computer system, or some related form of IT, will be one of the single largest financial commitments they ever take on. Current research suggests firms spend between 2 per cent and 7 per cent of their total fee income each year on IT, with small firms averaging 3.5 per cent and larger firms just over 5.5 per cent.

Furthermore, unlike buying conventional office equipment, such as a new photocopier, an investment in IT will potentially alter the way in which the whole firm operates. Bookkeepers, secretaries, receptionists, fee earners, partners and clients will all find that the new technology has some impact upon them and the legal services they either supply or receive. It is, therefore, essential that the IT procurement process is as efficient and problem free as possible, because if a firm gets it wrong, not only will a lot of time, money and effort have been wasted but the firm's commercial viability and professional reputation may have been irreparably compromised.

18.5.1   Strategy

Most solicitors probably know of 'computing disasters' that have occurred within other firms. However what is not always appreciated is that the bulk of these disasters stem not from choosing inappropriate hardware or software but from attempts to implement fundamentally flawed IT strategies. The key element to bear in mind here (and I make no apology for repeating part of the message that appeared at the outset of this chapter because it is important) is that IT – even a stand-alone probate system – is not some self-contained entity but is instead merely an enabling technology or tool that should be regarded as an integral part of the practice's overall business development plan. If it wants to get its IT strategy right, a firm must first have (or devise) an appropriate general business strategy.

To give a simple example, there is no point spending time choosing a supplier of probate software, if the firm's only probate practitioner is considering retirement. In addition, any strategy should also take into account the firm's medium-term requirements and longer-term aspirations, for example opening new branch offices or diversifying into new areas of practice, such as trust and portfolio management. In other words, don't buy a system that meets only the immediate current needs, buy one that will also meet any future anticipated needs.

The first stage in devising an IT strategy therefore has nothing to do with computers but instead involves drawing up a business or practice development plan. Only once this is in place should partners begin considering how IT can be used to help implement that plan over the next few years.

Next comes the process of drawing up more detailed specifications and requirements – in effect a computerisation shopping list – that will help to realise the IT strategy. For example, is the proposed system intended to be used by one fee earner only as a productivity tool? In this case, a stand-alone software application that will run on a personal computer may be suitable. In contrast, is probate work to be handled by a department, with different tasks delegated between fee earning and secretarial staff? In this case, a networked case management product is going to be more appropriate. Whether or not a formal 'Invitation to Tender' (or ITT) document should be drawn up is a matter of policy, but the firm certainly must have a clear understanding of its requirements if prospective suppliers are to be properly briefed and their responses evaluated on a like-for-like basis.

18.5.2 Budgets

It is essential at this stage to consider budgets and the availability of finance to support the proposed investment in IT (whether from cash reserves, leasing, bank loans, etc.). An important factor to bear in mind is that calculating the overall IT spend is a lot more complicated than adding the cost of PC hardware and a single user software licence together and multiplying it by the total number of users.

Along with hardware and software, there is the cost of installing the supporting network cabling, which in older premises may mean major rewiring and redecorating exercises. There is also the cost of training, and it cannot be stressed strongly enough that it is essential to properly train everyone who is intended to use the computers. Then there are the ongoing running costs, including insurance, annual maintenance contracts, renewable software licences (where applicable), hardware and software upgrades, additional training for additional or replacement staff and computer 'consumables' such as replacement laser printer toner cartridges and pre-printed 'continuous' stationery.

As a rule of thumb today, in terms of capital costs, for a probate accounts software package, plus a PC to run it on and training, firms should budget on between £3,000 and £5,000 per user plus a further one-third of this capital cost for each subsequent year by way of ongoing running costs.

18.5.3 Finding a supplier

Having decided what it wants to buy and how much it is prepared to pay for it, the firm is now in a position to look for a suitable supplier. This may seem a daunting task, particularly when the total number of suppliers is considered. However, when broken down into logical stages, it becomes more manageable:

- First of all thin down the number of contenders – if trust accounts, the case management approach or will writing software are not required, drop them from the list.
- Contact the remaining suppliers for further information, such as brochures and promotional literature containing details of their track records and installations; visit their stands at exhibitions; attend any of the sales presentations you will inevitably be invited to, once they realise you are a prospect; talk to contacts within the profession; reference websites given by the supplier and anyone else who has experience of dealing with them.
- Given the size of the probate systems market, this process will help whittle down the total number of prospects to a shortlist of three or four suppliers. In fact, your choice may be even more restricted if you are looking for software that is compatible with your firm's existing practice management system. Send these shortlisted companies copies of the tender document (if this has been drawn up) so that responses can be evaluated on a like-for-like basis.
- Visit their premises or user reference sites for detailed system demonstrations and discussions about how they would propose to handle the implementation of the project, including training. Incidentally, ensure that the key staff who will actually be using the proposed new system attend these demonstrations.
- Follow up any user references that are given and start exploring the contractual terms that are being offered, as this is frequently a protracted

stage of the negotiations, not least because as lawyers you will inevitably find aspects of their contractual wording to disagree with!

- Take notice of your own business instincts. The relationship with the supplier does not end the day the new computer goes 'live' – the firm will be dealing with them for at least the next five to seven or even 10 years, so be certain these are people you feel you can trust and work with on a longer-term basis.
- Don't be blinded by science. A lot of suppliers are now claiming their respective products are better than those of their competition because they have been developed using 'better' software development tools. This is all 'under the bonnet' stuff. What really matters is the functionality of the software – does it do the job you want it to do, in the way you want it done?
- Be clear what the firm is getting for its money. For example, how does the supplier of a probate accounts package deal with the fact that IHT rules change at least once a year, which may require amendments both to the way the software calculates returns and the incorporation of new forms to be submitted to HMRC? Is an automatic update included as part of the ongoing software maintenance contract or is this a chargeable extra?
- Finally, do take into account that price should not be the key factor (sadly, in many firms it still appears to be the only issue) in the selection process. Along with the ROI issues mentioned earlier, for those firms that lack their own in-house IT resources (and most firms with 30 or fewer members of staff fall into this category) the availability of what is some-times called a 'trusted supplier' (someone who can be relied on to help out in a crisis) is essential. This kind of service is rarely provided by suppliers who have been selected purely on the basis of price. It is also arguable that 'implementation' (see **18.5.4**), including installation, training (especially of lawyers) and ongoing support, is even more important than selection.

18.5.4   Implementation

Now the firm is in a position to place an order. And is that it? Well actually no, for the firm is entering one of the most sensitive stages – implementation – where problems can frequently arise because insufficient management resources are devoted to this aspect of the project. By implementation we mean everything from the delivery of the system to the firm's premises, to the rolling out of the system and the completion of staff training. This is a management issue and at the very least a partner (i.e. someone who has sufficient 'clout' to make things happen if problems arise) should have responsibility for over-seeing its progress.

There is a co-ordination job to ensure that the installation of the network cabling, the delivery of the hardware, the loading of the software and the training of staff to use the new system is properly scheduled and takes place satisfactorily according to a mutually convenient and pre-agreed timetable. For example, it is probably wise to avoid the holiday season and the end of the firm's financial year – not least because the firm will normally be expected to pay for substantial chunks of the system on the completion of each of these stages.

Larger firms with experience of IT projects can probably manage implementation projects themselves but for smaller firms it makes more sense to leave the project management to its main systems supplier. This can be particularly important in multi-vendor situations, with hardware coming from one source, software from another, and yet another organisation installing the network cabling at your offices.

18.5.5   Training, training and more training

Although training should be part of the broader implementation process, I'm giving it an extra focus here because it is one area where law firms always try to make economies. At its most blatant this takes the form of 'sitting next to Nelly'. In other words the minimum possible number of people are sent on a formal training course and when they return to the office, they are expected to train up the other members of the staff, as well as trying to remember themselves how the new system works and continuing to do their day job. It may have worked in the past with some of the earlier (and simpler) legal systems but today it is a recipe for a dilution of knowledge in terms of the firm's overall understanding of how a system operates.

In effect, it is the training equivalent of Chinese whispers and can lead to serious problems when the original 'Nelly' has left the practice and those who sat next to her are now trying to train their own successors. There have been a number of occasions where firms have set out to purchase a replacement software system that can perform a specific function only to discover that their original system had that capability all along, but thanks to inadequate training no one in the firm realised it.

As mentioned before, computer systems are just tools whose value derives from how they are used. It therefore follows that if people are not trained in how to use them properly, the firm will not see a satisfactory return on its IT investments. Best advice is therefore that everyone who is going to use a particular system should receive full training in how to use that system. It should also be uninterrupted training, so the participants can concentrate on the course rather than being distracted by interruptions from clients and colleagues.

And, it also means that the fee earners, who will be working with the software, must attend these sessions. This is one reason why it helps to have a senior member of the firm in overall charge of implementation, so they can compel the fee earners to attend. If not, left to their own devices, fee earners will often claim that they are 'far too busy' to attend training and then complain that the software is 'hopeless' when they later discover that they do not know how to use it.

Firms should also consider periodic 'top up' (or remedial) training, to ensure that everyone remains up to speed on how to use systems – not least because not everything taught during the initial intensive training sessions will be remembered. And, the firm needs to be able to cope with any upgrades that come along. A larger firm with its own HR department will be able to monitor the requirements for staff training. For smaller firms, the impetus may come from the systems suppliers, if the support calls coming through to their help desks have been monitored and analysed. And don't forget to invest in proper training for any newcomers who join your firm – modern systems are too complex to leave to 'Nelly'.

18.5.6   The Law Society *Software Solutions Guide*

The Law Society's annual Software Solutions Guide has become a victim of its own success in that many, less IT-literate solicitors now believe it is the definitive guide to legal software and that if a supplier's name is not included, it should automatically be excluded from any IT procurement shortlist. There are two problems with this viewpoint: the first is that the guide only covers law office accounts and practice management systems, so if you are dealing with a specialist supplier of probate software that does not offer an accounts system, then not only will they be absent from the guide, but they could not be included even if they wanted to be. The second problem is that it is only a voluntary guide – as distinct from some kind of mandatory suppliers list. For example there are 15 suppliers listed in the latest (2006) edition guide (available from the Law Society's website, **www.lawsociety.org.uk**), whereas there are a further 33 suppliers of law office accounts and practice management systems who have chosen not to go into the guide, either because they think it reaches the wrong target market for their software or because they feel that the approx £10,000 that it costs to be included in the guide could be better spent elsewhere.

So, if looking for probate-related software, do not automatically discount a supplier who is not included in the Software Solutions Guide – not least because for some applications this may exclude all the potential suppliers. However, if a firm is in the process of an overall review of all its IT facilities (at the time of writing a number of firms are at this stage) and is considering buying new or replacing its practice management systems and its probate software, then may make sense to pick a supplier that is both *Software Solutions Guide* listed and can offer a probate package.

18.6 PROBATE SYSTEMS BUYERS GUIDE

The list in **Appendix C** gives the details of suppliers (in alphabetical order, with contact details) of probate systems and related software applications. Please note that software products are regularly upgraded in terms of their functionality. Suppliers who also appear in the latest *Software Solutions Guide* have 'SSG 2006' after their names. Finally, my own website (**www.legaltechnology.com**) contains a regularly updated probate systems buyers guide, which is intended to reflect any changes taking place between the publication of this book and any subsequent edition.

CHAPTER 19

Managing private client business for profit

Gill Steel

19.1 OVERVIEW

- Why plan at all?
- Obtaining commitment – stemming the decrease in profits
- Reviewing existing services and the competition
- Tactics, action plan and review
- Structure of department and staffing issues
- Knowledge management and IT
- Risk assessment and quality management systems
- Marketing

19.2 WHY PLAN AT ALL?

Pressure on the management of law firms is increasing day by day. The legal profession is in the midst of many major reforms and faces continued criticism from government and consumer groups. This is coupled, in the wider business world, with the development and introduction of sophisticated IT packages which streamline and improve performance, and the introduction of quality management procedures.

In broad terms, the immediate impact of these (and other) radical developments, such as the growth in anti-money laundering regulation, have to a large extent affected firms as a whole rather than probate practitioners in particular. There is, however, a noticeable trend towards withdrawal from private client work by some more commercially minded firms and a dearth in quality practitioners available to lead and develop private client teams, as senior people retire and firms find it hard to recruit to replace them. There still is too little investment within probate departments in integrated case management systems and general improvements in the use of technology, even when within the same firms other parts of the practice have successfully introduced equivalent products. Overt promotional activity for private client work is often more directed at will making than at probate work.

312

As a result, most probate departments, in management terms, have not had to cope with significant change in the way services are offered and delivered, even though there is pressure to do so from increasing actual and potential competition. Probate practitioners have been a steady, reliable but unchanging group producing constant, profitable fees in reasonable volume. In some firms this steady growth is criticised when other areas have significantly increased both turnover and profits. Whilst it is not possible to increase the number of probate cases available in the geographic area served by a practice, it is possible to generate an increase in the number of people who choose to use the firm and the range of services offered to clients and potential clients at appropriate rates.

So the perceptions of the probate department and the firm within which it operates may be divergent. The danger is that those owners and managers of the firm who have little or no knowledge of private client work will demand a more transactional approach and as a result may insist on unrealistic financial targets which eventually leads to withdrawal from this area of work. There is another way. Probate practitioners could become more entrepreneurial and put across to their colleagues that the long-term relationship approach is what has kept for the firm a steady and to date profitable private client department. It should operate differently from the other departments undertaking transactional work, but nevertheless adopt appropriate improved management techniques.

The profession is at a crossroads and is faced with an unpalatable economic scenario in which traditional sources of core income are under threat (e.g. e-conveyancing); more investment is needed in the use of technology and research; and there is increased bureaucracy, change of familiar procedures and regulatory pressures. Margins throughout the firm are becoming tighter. As a result, partnerships must develop remunerative areas of practice and this means the attention of the managing partner inevitably turns towards the ever-reliable probate department as a source of significant levels of fee income and profit. Probate practitioners need to respond to this challenge by providing not only an efficient and friendly service for clients, but also an increasingly profitable income stream for the practice.

Such a situation demands a reconsideration of the way in which probate is delivered. Without in any sense compromising on the quality of work delivered or the relationship with the client, efficiency must be sought, revenue must be maximised and systems must be streamlined.

Probate practitioners need to look to their management systems to improve efficiency and enhance performance.

19.3 OBTAINING COMMITMENT: STEMMING DECREASING PROFITABILITY

Some firms do not have an overall business plan, but hopefully, these may be few in number. Even with an overarching firm plan some probate lawyers may not be familiar with the idea of a departmental plan. However, without a business plan it is impossible to stretch or challenge existing perceptions of what is reasonable, and it will be difficult to evaluate progress and performance. A departmental plan will identify the strategy, set the objectives to be achieved and provide that yardstick against which to measure successful performance.

Having a business plan for a department is not a foolish notion. It does not matter how small or large the department is, the need to know what it is aiming to achieve and whether it has done so is just plain common sense. How else will it be evaluated whether investments made were cost effective? How else will appropriate staff be chosen in the future?

Sometimes it helps to get started if practitioners pose for themselves and their colleagues a really wild question just to get the creative juices flowing. For example, if £500,000 could be invested in the next year (over and above the firm's current available funds) with the goal of achieving a thriving, more competitive and secure practice:

- What would you spend it on?
- Why would you choose those particular things/actions?
- How would you set about it?
- Who would be responsible for actioning it?
- When would you expect to achieve it?
- How would you know you had achieved it?

Once the group has done some freewheeling with those questions for a large sum, ask why were those priorities chosen and can any of those ideas actually become reality? If this is to happen, the partners must recognise that there is a balance to be had between the short-term issues of maintaining cash flow and profitability whilst at the same time investing resources in the future success of the practice by developing new ways of meeting the clients' needs in the future. This includes finding enough time for managing the practice and the department. Time will be needed to reflect, plan and implement any changes effectively.

Concentrate on setting up a strategy for the firm's core business: if private client work is at the centre of the firm then it is important that you have a strategy for it to improve the overall profitability of the firm. Be creative about considering new ways of doing things! Is the firm's culture of 'but this is the way we do things around here'? Why? Trying to improve competitiveness requires changing habits – your habits and those of your partners. Change can be a painful process, and managing change needs new skills, management skills, not just professional skills.

Sveiby and Lloyd in their book *Managing Know-How: Add Value . . . by Valuing Creativity* (Bloomsbury, 1987) identified 10 success factors for a professional organisation. How does your firm match up?

- *Day-to-day leadership.* This is not just the technical ability to conduct the work but rather possessing the basic skills and attributes of the successful leader, which include: the ability to help others succeed, not just strive for personal success; the need to have a set of principles and to enthuse and motivate colleagues to achieve their roles; the ability to bring constructive new ideas on how to improve the practice and productivity of the team; and the ability to act as the team's coach, both collectively and individually nurturing and challenging everyone to achieve the identified goals.

- *Quality control.* There has never been a greater need to identify the client's real requirements and at the same time acknowledge the standards of professionalism required to meet those requirements and those of the regulators. The more people in the team or conducting work of this type, the more important it is to have control over the outputs to minimise disappointment for clients, reduce negligent errors and to enhance the reputation of the firm. It is widely accepted that clients do not take into account technical competence when evaluating the 'quality' of the service they experienced – unless they are lawyers themselves how can they know whether they have been given the 'right' advice? Instead they rely on how the service was delivered. Was it:

  - reliable?
  - responsive to their needs?
  - accessible?
  - courteous?
  - a process of communication: information provision and active listening?
  - credible?
  - secure?
  - tailored to the specific client?
  - performed in satisfactory offices, by appropriately dressed staff using effective equipment?

- *Respect for know-how.* Know-how is value-added information, the sort of information that arises out of complex problem solving. Law firms must therefore be know-how businesses since they are selling the ability to produce solutions to often complex problems. The probate team will often be dealing with technical details over taxation and sometimes difficult family problems, and the advice given will be based on solid experience gained from having tackled similar problems in the past. A firm needs to respect the building and sharing of know-how, as this is the main asset it is selling.

315

- *Combination of professional and managerial know-how.* It is important to identify, develop and share know-how not only about technical matters but also about the management of the department and firm. The successful head of department will not just have basic knowledge and information about the probate system and law but needs the skills and attributes of the manager such as analytical, problem-solving, decision-making skills; social skills and abilities; emotional resilience to cope with difficult situations; the ability to respond proactively to events; creativity; mental agility; balanced learning habits and skills (an independent learner with a 'helicopter mind' which can move between the theoretical and the practical) and plenty of self-knowledge so that he or she can identify when personal factors are influencing the decision-making process.
- *A strong, well-defined culture.* So often it is the culture of a firm that is either enabling or inhibiting successful change. Every firm has a culture whether it has been explicitly identified or not. Effective managers need awareness of and understanding of the power dynamics within their firm. To get things changed will require the ability to identify where a particular source of power is in play and whether there is a particularly under-used source of power that can be brought into play.
- *Focus on core know-how.* Firms that know what their clients actually want, as opposed to what the firm thinks they want, are on the right track to identifying what know-how is required to produce what the client wants. Firms that have focused on the main know-how to achieve what their client base wants have proved to be the most successful in terms of repeat business and recommendation.
- *Know-how preservation.* Since know-how is hard to come by, as it is as much about experience and practice as it is about technical knowledge, capturing and preserving it when key staff leave is difficult to do but some firms are led by people who have identified that it is a key success factor for the future of their firm.
- *Developing the people.* As we cannot do everything ourselves and remain sane it is vital that any professional service firm employs people who it recognises need to be continually developed to attain the changing skills relevant to the job in hand. More needs to be done by firms to help people find out what it is to serve a client, and about how to work with people, whether they are your juniors, your seniors or your colleagues.
- *Changing key people.* The marketing adage that 'people buy people' is certainly true of private client practice in law firms. A successful firm will properly ensure succession planning so that when people change a client is kept informed and retained rather than left floundering.
- *Stable structures.* If a successful firm is to be achieved or maintained, it will be necessary to create or preserve stability. Looking only at the short term does not help practitioners to develop policies for long-term stability.

The above ideas should have got your creative juices flowing. It will be apparent that if there is no commitment from all the equity partners (the owners of the business) to allow you, as head of department, to devote some time to planning, managing and implementing the plan (non-chargeable work), then if the firm focuses only on personal billing levels you will find yourself being criticised. Far better to explain what you propose to do, in order to ensure that your sanity and your partners' equilibrium are maintained. Also, if all the partners decided independently to reorganise their area of work or department at the same time, then the firm's cash flow would take a nose-dive!

If the head of department is to spend time thinking, planning and coming up with ideas to develop his or her area of practice then some fee earning work must be *delegated* to other people: junior people. Why is this not being done already?

- Great emphasis is placed on personal billing; in a recession there is a danger that senior people hoard what work there is to maintain their personal level of billing.
- The practice does not hold the individual partners responsible for finding ways of reducing the costs of the way the firm delivers the particular legal service; partners are usually only responsible for finding and doing the work.
- There is a reluctance to 'invest' time in coaching and supervising staff, and yet people are the key resource in know-how businesses.
- Fear: if you delegate you will have to find other work of a more complex nature to do and may feel out of your depth.

If planning for change is to be successful, the head of department will need the support not only of the owners of the firm but also of the staff in the department, office or firm – the team. It is vital to ensure that a well-integrated, effective and supportive team is in place. This requires talking to all in the team, both individually and as a group, about their concerns, views and ideas. Use this not as an opportunity to criticise but rather to listen and learn. Research and practice shows that a well-balanced team will outperform any other team.

A group of people become a team if they have:

- a strong leader;
- respect for one another;
- a clear idea of what is expected of them and why;
- an incentive to share resources for the benefit of each other;
- an ability to resolve conflict between themselves; and
- an interest in their own future.

19.4 IDENTIFYING THE BEST OPPORTUNITIES: REVIEW EXISTING SERVICES AND THE COMPETITION

As a team, you should review everything:

- Consider what is going on in the world at large: the demographic changes resulting in an ageing population; government policy making the provision of care for the elderly a major area of concern; the social structure making it less likely for families to care for elderly relatives; the technological revolution making it easier to work from home and find suppliers via the internet, so making it more important for firms to harness its power to remain competitive; the state of the economy which affects the 'feel good factor' of not just potential clients but also the partners and staff; the availability of appropriately trained staff.
- Examine what services are currently offered by the firm in this area, e.g. wills, probate, enduring powers of attorney, living wills, tax advice, help with care in the community decisions.
- Identify current and future potential competition in the area from all sources for these services, e.g. other law firms now (name rivals and identify their strengths and weaknesses), but also will-writing companies and individuals making their own wills (as they represent substitutes for your service) and accountants or large investors such as companies with a consumer focus e.g. supermarkets, looking to expand into probate services in the future (as these represent threats from new entrants into the field).
- Review which of the services currently offered are profitable and why, and which are not and why. What determines profitability?

  - How much does it cost to deliver the service, e.g. overheads, staff salaries?
  - How much are buyers prepared to pay for the service? If they can do it themselves and see no perceived value in what you can do, then will they really pay?
  - Can you minimise the costs and maximise the price?

- Consider any agencies and bodies locally which might provide services and information to the elderly. To what extent are they also substitutes for the service offered by your department? To what extent could some clients, who could not afford to pay your fees but need appropriate help, be referred to them? What can be learnt from the way these bodies approach this potential client group?
- Decide what resources the firm already has available or is prepared to commit to this project, e.g. money, time, people (with their particular strengths and weaknesses) and technology.
- Examine what services are often needed but which are not currently provided, e.g. independent financial advice, something solicitors are well placed to offer.

318

19.5   TACTICS, ACTION PLAN AND REVIEW

19.5.1   Defining aspirations

At the outset of the planning process, management needs to set acceptable standards of financial performance. Questions which need to be resolved include:

- What are acceptable billing figures?
- What are acceptable profit levels?
- What are the required levels of growth?

These targets will be affected by the factors which motivate the practice as a whole. Different firms are driven by different motivations and the business plan must reflect these differences. Motivation will generally be composed of a balance between:

- money;
- power;
- material gain;
- promotion;
- status;
- improving the environment;
- job satisfaction; and
- helping others.

19.5.2   Content of the business plan

Having defined departmental aspirations, an analysis of how to meet those aspirations must be undertaken. There are two simple but effective tools which assist with this task.

PESTE analysis

A PESTE analysis is a review of the external influences and factors operating on the department. It covers the following issues:

P: Political
E: Economic
S: Sociological
T: Technological
E: Environmental

A PESTE analysis within a probate department might consider the following:

1. *Political*

   (a) Structural reforms, recent political decisions that have made an impact:

      (i)   abolishing the professional prohibition on 'touting' for work;
      (ii) abolishing monopolies in probate;
      (iii) authorised probate practitioners;
      (iv) taxation issues.

   (b) Financial changes with political origins, e.g. reductions in fee rates.
   (c) Legislative changes, changes in the law you advise on, and changes in how you practise.

2. *Economic*: general economic forces impacting on:

   (a) ownership of more than one property;
   (b) increasing wealth based largely on property values;
   (c) declining estate values due to lifetime giving, care fees and equity release.

3. *Sociological*

   (a) Social attitude influencing demand, e.g.

      (i)   towards home ownership;
      (ii) towards cohabitation, divorce and the second family;
      (iii) towards civil partnership.

   (b) Consumer awareness affecting client expectations, e.g.

      (i)   price awareness;
      (ii) heightened consumer awareness of legal rights;
      (iii) greater service standard expectations.

   (c) Demographic trends, e.g.

      (i) population trends;
      (ii) age structures, nationally and regionally.

4. *Technological*: office equipment:

   (a) computers have revolutionised business;
   (b) methods of doing business, e.g. online banking facilities, telegraphic transfers, e-mail, video-links and others.

5. *Environmental*

   (a) office location;
   (b) use of 'green' products such as recycled paper.

SWOT analysis

A SWOT analysis is a review of the internal influences and factors operating on the department. It covers the following issues:

S: Strengths
W: Weaknesses
O: Opportunities
T: Threats

Consider the internal strengths and weaknesses of the department or team, and then seek to address planning in order to:

• maximise opportunities (capitalising upon strengths); and
• minimise threats (in order to eliminate weaknesses).

A SWOT analysis is often carried out by examining the department's strengths, weaknesses, opportunities and threats in the context of:

• structure;
• administration;
• finance;
• services;
• partners;
• staff;
• clients;
• know-how and IT; and
• marketing.

A SWOT analysis carried out against these management disciplines within a probate department might consider the following:

1. *Structure*

   (a) Does the department have a suitable shape? What are the partner/ fee earner/support staff ratios?
   (b) Is the department's management structure appropriate?

2. *Administration*

   (a) Who is responsible for administration?
   (b) Does the quality of that administration meet client and staff needs?

(c) Do the department's systems have their intended effects? What are their intended effects? Could the systems be streamlined to make them more efficient?

Be ruthless with office procedures. Question everything. Are there any gaps in what you perceive your clients want and what the individual client expects of your service because of that client's:

  (i) past experience of your firm?
  (ii) own needs?
  (iii) view of your competitors' services?
  (iv) knowledge through word of mouth recommendation?
  (v) knowledge of any promotional information you have supplied?

Probate is a process that lends itself to standardisation. Wills are tailor made for the client but are built up from a set of tried and tested precedents. There are well-known steps for the mitigation of IHT. Where possible, aim to develop uniform procedures within the team. Retain only those steps in the process that are essential, and deliver a quality service in the way the type of clients that the firm serves will recognise as 'quality'.

3. *Finance*

  (a) Are you charging enough?
  (b) What are your profit/billing expectations?
  (c) Is your credit control effective?
  (d) Are you effective at recovering all your chargeable time?

4. *Partners*

  (a) Do the partners have the necessary management skills to develop the department?
  (b) What is the partnership's attitude towards delegation, teamwork and communication?

5. *Staff*

  (a) Do you have the right calibre of staff? Do they understand their jobs?
  (b) Are your staff properly trained? Do they have skills which are different and more valuable than the competition, e.g. bereavement counselling skills, the ability to communicate well with the deaf and blind?
  (c) Are they motivated?
  (d) Are you over/under staffed?
  (e) How do you monitor staff performance?

6. *Clients*

    (a) Who are your clients?
    (b) Where are your clients?
    (c) What do they want of you?
    (d) Are your clients satisfied with your performance?
    (e) Do you converse and write in plain English and in such a way as to get the best out of every interaction with your clients?
    (f) Ask yourself why do clients ask a law firm to undertake probate work?

        (i)   they do not know how to do it themselves;
        (ii)   they do not have the time to do it;
        (iii) it would not be an effective use of their time;
        (iv) the particular case is too complicated;
        (v)   there is a dispute and someone independent is required to deal with it;
        (vi) they have no choice, the testator or testatrix appointed partners in the firm as executors.

There are many more reasons but whichever reason applies in a particular case will have an effect on how that client perceives the quality of the service you are providing. If the case is complicated the client may be looking to you because your firm is regarded as having an acknowledged expert and the client may only want to deal with that expert. The 'client' may have no choice about dealing with your firm, as members of the firm are the executors. This may be resented, e.g. where the 'client' has acted in an estate personally before and the process holds no mystique. He or she may well focus on how quickly you finish the job and how cheaply you do so.

7. *Know-how and IT*

    (a) What will the future impact of technology be?
    (b) Can you use IT more effectively?
    (c) Can you make better use of existing equipment?
    (d) Consider how technology can serve you and provide meaningful systems that manual methods could not. Do not just seek to computerise what you already do. Try to see if there is a better way of delivering the service that can be computerised. Often manual systems have grown up over the years in a piecemeal fashion and have become 'the way it has to be done'. Yet the only reason the existing way was developed was because with a manual system it was not possible to organise it in any other way; whereas now you are not limited to manual solutions – computers are there to help!

(e) The client expects you to do things in the most cost-effective way. Why should the client pay for your time to do something manually when the job could be done at a fraction of the price and more efficiently if a computer system was used?

(f) Can you make it easy to share skills and experience gained by one person with others in the team, and thus keep those skills and knowledge even if that person chooses to leave? It is no good investing in an IT system, and finding out that only one person knows how to use the system/package just as that person goes on maternity leave!

8. *Marketing*

(a) Have you thought through an effective marketing strategy?

(b) Are you providing the right services? Can you keep in touch with the developments in this area to such an extent that you know before your competitors about any changes to rules, services (such as social service delivery in your area), law?

(c) Is your marketing spend sufficient to meet your strategic goals?

19.5.3 Strategic plan

Having carried out the PESTE and SWOT analyses in the light of the department's aspirations, the strategic goals of the department will become clear. Strategic goals will often be very simply expressed and, depending on the aspirations of the firm, will probably be about achieving improved profitability or sustaining profits. It is a good idea not to have too many strategic goals but rather to focus on the key goals which must be achieved under the main headings of:

- Information Technology
- Human Resources
- Finance
- Quality and Risk
- Marketing
- Management

Examples might include:

- to increase the profitability of the private client department by 5 per cent by 31 December 200–; or
- to implement the use of an estate accounts software package before 1 August 200–.

In today's volatile trading conditions, an appropriate 'strategic window' for planning purposes is perhaps two to three years. Anything longer is unrealistic, as the PESTE and SWOT factors affecting the department are likely to change radically over such a length of time.

Developing a strategy and implementing it is about wanting to succeed. It is hard work! Features of a strategy that contributes to success are:

- it comprises goals that are simple, consistent and long term;
- it displays a profound understanding of the competitive environment;
- it contains an objective review of resources available; and
- it is effectively implemented.

19.5.4 Operational plan

Once the strategic goals have been established, the next step is to consider the implementation issues and develop an operational plan. The operational plan defines the activities the department must undertake in order to achieve its strategic goals. For example, if the strategic goal was to increase the private client department's profitability by 5 per cent by 31 December 2007 this might translate into a number of operational goals including for example 'to increase the number of wills written per month by 20 from 120 to 140 by 31 December 2006'. This is often the main part of any business plan. It is generally short or medium term in character, covering only a one- to two-year period.

The team's commitment to any plans is essential. Without it the plans will never get off the drawing board. Developing a workable strategy needs the people at the 'bottom' to contribute – after all, it is the team who will have to carry it out.

Consult people; encourage ideas; develop suggestions; assess skills

This is where involving the team is essential. Play to their strengths and minimise their weaknesses. As head of department, do you know what are their personal career goals? Could the attainment of those goals be involved in the delivery of the firm's goals? Is an environment where people will freely express their areas of weakness without fear of criticism encouraged? Why not agree with your partners that the team has a combined fee target, whilst agreeing with the team a division that allows you development time, as team leader?

Is sufficient management information available to review fee income at least monthly against the team target? To check how and where the fees were generated? (Always thank introducers of business.) Can you review overheads and identify the cost of supplying the services offered in the way you do?

Structure actions; allocate jobs; delegate; set targets

A useful exercise is to take separate sheets of paper for each of the team's goals and draw up a table to be completed of:

- what needs to be done to achieve it;
- who is to take responsibility for each of these actions;

- how much time will be needed or is available to spend on each action;
- what is the deadline for completion of the action;
- how the team will know that the action has been achieved; and
- what budgets have been set for the activity.

Give people a few weeks to consider what actions they are prepared to commit to and then arrange a follow-up meeting. For example, the strategic goal of increasing the volume of wills written demands consideration of a wide range of issues – research into the marketplace, promotional activity, allocation of additional work, and so on. As the team leader, ensure that the end result is a workable and practical set of actions, which different members of the team have taken responsibility for implementing. Ensure that the team agree a fixed date in the future to conduct an evaluation.

Budgeting is vital but often poorly thought through. Unless there is a strategic reason which justifies it, there is little point in undertaking a promotional campaign if the expenditure involved will be greater than the level of profit that the promotion is anticipated to yield. The budget should therefore include profit and loss and cash flow projections for the period under consideration.

19.5.5   Goals

At all stages of the planning process goals need to be SMART:

- *Specific*: stated in such a way as to aid verification. What evidence would be required to establish success?
- *Measurable*: so that specific data can be collated to identify achievement (or otherwise).
- *Achievable*: to stretch but not over-challenge the individual and the team.
- *Realistic*: avoid arbitrary quantifications such as stipulating a 20 per cent reduction when there are no grounds for thinking this is any more or less attainable than a 50 per cent or 100 per cent reduction.
- *Timed*: how far ahead is it necessary or sensible to set certain objectives – one month/one year? Without imposed deadlines the plan will lose impetus as short-term priorities intervene.

19.5.6   Evaluation and review

If you have not documented what you are trying to achieve, by whom and by when, then the chances are you will not achieve your goals. If you have not considered what 'success' will look like, how will you know whether or not you have achieved it?

Periodically examine how you are doing, what worked and what did not. Were the actions identified successfully completed within budget and on time? If not, why not? What lessons were learnt as a result of trying to achieve the goals set? How can this experience inform the next stage of planning? Then continue with the next stage of action planning.

Ensure that your strategies keep up with the market place in which you operate by ongoing review and action. If you do, then you are certain to succeed.

Continually ask yourself the question: how can we get better at what we do?

19.6   STRUCTURE OF DEPARTMENT AND STAFFING ISSUES

The single largest overhead incurred in any probate department is likely to be the payroll and its associated costs. Given the very high ratio of payroll costs to income generated, it is vital to ensure that the best possible value is obtained from the firm's investment in staff.

As a simple example, a significant impact of poor personnel management is often high staff turnover. This not only subjects the department to the disruption encountered when a key member of staff moves on, there are also the significant costs incurred in replacing that member of staff and a learning curve to be overcome when a new member of staff begins work.

Good personnel management practices will ensure that staff are properly motivated, committed to the practice, properly trained and resourced and dedicated to meeting the needs of clients.

Within the department, however small, various roles will be performed:

- *Head of department* holds principal responsibility for the effective and profitable operation of the department. The role encompasses responsibility for:

    - development and implementation of departmental operating plans geared to meeting targets established by the firm;
    - establishment and achievement of departmental budgets and targets;
    - provision of coherent leadership and management support;
    - supervision, training and development of departmental staff; and
    - marketing of the department and development of the department's client base.

- *Fee earners* hold principal responsibility for the delivery of prompt, effective and accurate advice and services. The role encompasses:

    - provision of legal advice and assistance to the firm's clients;
    - development of excellent working relationships with clients and referring agencies alike;
    - familiarisation with and use of the department's IT systems;
    - familiarisation with and adherence to the department's prescribed operating systems and procedures;
    - maintenance and development of relevant technical legal knowledge and skills;

327

- direction of support staff to maximise the performance of the department; and
- resolution of client/referrer enquiries which cannot be dealt with by the support staff.

- *Support staff* hold principal responsibility for providing secretarial and administrative support to the collective fee earning staff. The role encompasses:

  - provision of word processing services and the completion of forms as directed by the fee earners;
  - attending to clients on the telephone and taking messages accurately;
  - establishment and maintenance of accurate filing facilities on behalf of the fee earners and head of department;
  - data input of time records;
  - maintenance of fee earners' diaries and appointments;
  - provision of photocopying services to the department;
  - preparation and sorting of incoming and outgoing mail;
  - familiarisation with and adherence to the firm's prescribed operating systems and procedures; and
  - answering routine enquiries relating to progress.

It may be that one person fulfils all the roles or that there are several people fulfilling the same roles. When reviewing the structure of the department and its ability to deliver the operational and strategic plans which have been devised, a review of the functions which have to be performed, the roles of the team members in conducting each of the functions and the relevant competencies of personnel to conduct them, is essential.

Some practitioners battle on with unrealistic caseloads believing the firm will not agree to any further staff assistance because overall fee income is low, without looking at why the income is low. If the same person is responsible for organising the way work is done, attracting the work, as well as doing it, it is inevitable that too much emphasis will be placed by that person on doing the work rather than on the significant question of how the work could be achieved in a more cost-effective way.

A cheaper member of staff can justify his or her salary and contribute to the profits much more quickly than a senior member of the firm. The workload of the senior manager could be made more realistic and real improvements to the bottom line achieved just by changing the staffing mix.

The larger the team the more essential it is that the department head is relieved of day-to-day fee earning and allowed to concentrate on the management of the team and its development in line with the strategic goals it has to achieve. This is always hard for professional people, who have undoubtedly been chosen to head up the department or team because of their seniority or technical legal know-how. Whilst their experience will still be called into use and their knowledge of particular clients will inevitably involve them in client contact the effective manager will try to delegate most of the routine matters to free up valuable planning and implementing time.

Gaining commitment from others in the team to take on some of these more routine matters and caseload will only be achieved if promises to deliver on matters only a partner or manager can implement are kept. This means setting an exemplary example of being a person who can manage their time and their work to beneficial effect. There are only 24 hours in the day and seven days in the week for each and every one of us. The Prime Minister has no more time each day than the head of a department in a law firm. So it is not about having more time, it is about how we use the time available. Achievement is about being focused, organised and effective.

There are plenty of courses, books and programmes to help people to rethink how they manage themselves, but the biggest hurdle is to recognise that this may be a weakness; arrange to do something about it and keep an open mind as to what you may need to alter in your life to change what are essentially bad habits. Remember, it is easy to make New Year's resolutions but so much harder to achieve them.

When the services that the department is to offer clients and the ways in which those services will be delivered have been explored, it will be apparent what legal skills are needed in the team. However, it is also important to work through the processes that are necessary to have in place to deliver these services, and the non-legal skills required in order to operate the processes that are just as essential to the fulfilment of the plan. It then becomes easier to identify what competencies are needed to perform these functions and therefore what mix of staff skills, behaviours and attitudes will be required.

The more you can involve the team in identifying these competencies the easier it will be to develop a guide to job roles, comprising the critical success factors needed for each person to perform his or her role, and to identify any gaps in knowledge and skills which need to be filled by the recruitment of suitable additional staff, the utilisation of appropriate IT, or by the development of existing staff.

The more everyone in the team is involved in this exercise, the more likely it is that you will build a successful team where each member knows what is expected of them and the others in the team, how the individual skills fit together and who is responsible for what activities. It also helps when it comes to setting a pay structure where salaries can be set for the combination of factors within a person's job role for which that person is accountable. The critical success factors for which that person is accountable also provide the yardstick against which his or her own personal performance can be measured both on the job and when implementing regular appraisals to update training and development plans.

19.7 KNOWLEDGE MANAGEMENT AND IT

There are three kinds of knowledge:

- improvement of a process or service;
- exploitation of existing knowledge to develop new processes and services; and
- innovation by applying existing knowledge to produce new knowledge.

19.7.1 Developing knowledge

Managing information successfully means getting the right information, in the right form, to the right person at the right time to add value.

Hugh Garai in *Managing Information* (Gower Publishing, 1997) identified four principles of information management which he argued can turn worthless data into powerful intelligence, which, when applied, will generate effective change:

1. Data + Relevance + Purpose = Information
2. Information + Insight = Understanding
3. Understanding + Communication = Intelligence
4. Intelligence + Action = Effectiveness

So to work smarter you need to be able to:

- distinguish between useful information and data;
- sort, order and display information in the most communicative way; and
- identify innovative ways of using the information to add value.

The huge increase in the use of specialist software applications in law firms and departments is changing staffing levels, so that departments are being asked to do more with fewer people. Clients want the ability to have 24-hour a day, seven days a week access to the progress of their matters. Without harnessing the use of IT how can this realistically be done? Case management systems accessed via a web-based product and secured by codes and encryption are already used by some firms, and those who have yet to address these issues and make the investment required are already behind the game.

Management must be allowed to invest development time in order to address these issues, and training time to ensure that equipment and software is being used properly. Otherwise, you will still have to perform to your clients' chosen standards – which may mean working until you drop – or you will eventually lose those clients to other organisations who are prepared to invest and learn.

The result of focusing on developing the knowledge that the client actually wants to access and making it available to them is an improvement in your service which adds value for which a client will pay.

19.7.2   Knowledge from resources such as books, lectures, cases, conferences, precedents

In the search for profit, one of the most popular ways of boosting the bottom line is to reduce the overhead costs, so advocating expenditure on sources of knowledge may not be well received. Actually, what would make both common sense and economic sense would be if the business made a better return on its expenditure on gaining knowledge. Instead of individuals being trained or seeing training as merely gathering continuing professional development points, the firm should want to see more focus in the choice of training and more use by all relevant practitioners in the firm of the information gained by the individual.

Basically, lawyers are selling knowledge based on their experience and skill. It therefore makes sense for a firm to take the explicit knowledge gained from these sources and to enable all who need to access this knowledge to do so freely at any time, e.g. by having access to the firm's precedents via laptop and portable printer when visiting a terminally ill client to prepare an emergency will.

For more information about knowledge management see Chapter 8 'Knowledge management' of Peter Scott (ed.), *Practice Management Handbook* (Law Society, 2004).

19.7.3   Personal knowledge gained from experience and practical observation

A powerful selling point for any organisation is the experience and skill of its people. This is often the most difficult source of knowledge to capture but as any firm will know if a senior lawyer has died suddenly, or retired without some succession planning having been done, once a source of tacit knowledge about individual clients or tried and tested schemes or just plain human psychology which comes from a lifetime of dealing with people disappears, it can take years to recover, if it ever is.

Trying to identify this kind of experience as knowledge is the first step to being able to design systems to capture it.

If the firm adopts the 'eat what you kill' approach to profit sharing rather than the traditional 'lockstep approach', where rewards reflect a person's long-term contribution to the firm not just current personal profitability, then it is hard to change the culture to one where individual knowledge and experience needs to be captured for the long-term good of the firm, whether or not that individual is there. There is no incentive on the individual partner to encourage 'his' clients to be 'firm' clients.

19.7.4   Sharing knowledge

Of systems

It is not just legal knowledge that needs to be shared but experience of the use of any systems in place in the firm, such as file management systems, accounting procedures, how the firm prefers to set out its estate accounts, etc.

Understanding why a particular procedure is undertaken helps newcomers contribute to how systems might be improved or streamlined. Systems that ossify are an impediment to progress but equally checks and safeguards, recognised as such, will more likely be honoured if the people obliged to follow them understand the reason for them.

Of access to information

We need to recognise the old adage 'knowledge is power'. If people are rewarded for keeping information to themselves, then the power is held by individuals and this stops people from being open and willing to share. Shared knowledge is greater power in the marketplace for your firm and that means encouraging understanding of the means of access to as much information as possible within your firm, e.g. enabling fee earners and administrative staff to obtain billing guides and client account balances, rather than this being done only in the accounts department.

Availability

Sharing personal knowledge and experience requires senior people to be available to the more junior. This can be expensive in the short term but over time the investment in developing the younger individuals will be securing the succession to your firm for the future. People may want increasing salaries but they also want opportunities to develop and the chance to see a career path. If senior partners take time to talk to younger lawyers and help them to understand why a problem is usually approached a particular way, this can smooth the transition for clients when the time comes and the senior partner is no longer available. However, if the culture of your firm generally is not positively disposed to this kind of approach, who will carry it forward and so keep these people in whom you have invested within the firm when you retire?

Rewarding the creation of 'firm's knowledge' not just personal knowledge

People often need incentives to change their behaviour. If people are to share what they know, it must become positively pointless to hoard knowledge and it must be made much more financially rewarding to share it. For example, promotion may depend on how well someone acts for the benefit of the team by entering course summaries into the department's knowledge bank for sharing internally.

19.7.5 Training

In developing systems

To what extent does the firm encourage people to learn how to solve a problem? Do solicitors ever attend courses on large changes, such as pre-owned assets income tax charge, and then never develop the systems needed in the firm to address the changes?

Training in technical matters tends to dominate the training budgets of many firms; however training on how to go about designing and implementing a system for use in the firm, or how to manage a project like the selection and installation of a new IT system, will often be much more useful to senior people. A large organisation may have specialist people to organise this sort of thing, but unless they also have input from you as the probate practitioner, the resulting system may have severe shortcomings that you and your team have to deal with on a daily basis.

In use of systems

It is a common complaint of staff that partners produce a new system, particularly IT systems, and simply say 'there you are, now get on with it'. This type of 'sink or swim' approach is far from cost effective. Work output plummets, stress levels soar and everyone is unhappy. If only the installation and training budget for new IT were at the top of the list of items when purchasing a new system, then some of the 'hidden' costs of change would be properly identified and dealt with in a positive way.

How can a member of staff show a new employee how to use something when they have only learnt by trial and error, which often means half of what the system has to offer is never used? It is human nature to learn enough to get your daily work done and not spend time on learning what else the system can do, even if this might mean missing out on useful shortcuts or safety procedures.

In technical aspects

Achieving strength and depth in the wider areas of law within the probate department helps once more to sell the services of the firm. There is the need to have the ability to undertake estate planning, living wills, financial services, community care planning, as well as the core services of will drafting, enduring power of attorney preparation and administration, probate and intestate succession and trust drafting and administration.

19.7.6 Using software and the internet

Estate accounts packages

There are a number of companies offering estate accounts packages for probate and trusts. The Legal Technology Insider website (**www.legaltechnology.com**) contains a regularly updated copy of what is available.

Some companies offer integrated systems which include probate as part of a suite of software but this is often not as good as the stand-alone systems, several of which have originally been the brainchild of probate practitioners who have developed the program to help themselves with their day-to-day work.

Case management software

This is where the system acts as a comprehensive supporter of the work-flow in the probate field, supplying as it does templates, databases of contacts, probate registries, local authorities, standard letters and the forms used in the process. The idea is that you enter the details once about the deceased and the deceased's estate and those databases are interrogated by the system as required to complete the IHT200, the oath, letters to institutions, beneficiaries, executors, etc.

The main advantage is that this enables paralegals to help with the work and reminds the practitioner what to do next, often through the use of task lists or diary reminders.

Forms: data entry only, self-calculating, integrated

Whether or not case management systems are necessary (most firms will have a series of good manual systems which can deal with most of the probate process adequately), the use of technology to complete forms, particularly tax forms, is a must.

Simple forms are available on screen where the details are entered every time. Apart from saving the storage of hard copy stationery and ensuring, through a maintenance package with the supplier, that the most up-to-date form is always used, this data entry type of form does not provide the practitioner with very much more.

Some tax forms are integrated with the production of estate accounts. There are estate accounts packages which include e.g. IHT200, as the information needed for the one activity is clearly needed for the other, and this might be set up to extract the data when input once and then utilise it for the other use. It is important to ensure that the government department concerned has formally approved any official form that might be included.

Some types of tax form are self-calculating. HMRC itself has now put the IHT200 on its website, allowing the practitioner to download it from the website, enter the client's data offline, save it, and have the program calculate the tax due. Once all the information has been entered, it can be printed off and submitted in the usual way. This software is free, and all that is needed for saving and printing is an additional piece of low-priced software from Adobe (**www.adobe.com**).

As with all software, it takes time to become familiar with it, but once it has been mastered it can save so much time and therefore money. It can also mean that the quality of service to the client improves, as practitioners can produce a set of accounts at the push of a button rather than struggling with the file for half a day!

Library information

The excellent *Internet Newsletter for Lawyers* produced by Delia Venables (see **www.venables.co.uk**) has debated the pros and cons of developing an electronic library in comparison with a print library. Electronic libraries are useful research tools, and avoid the danger of 'losing' books and periodicals within an office just when they are needed. It is easier to keep the electronic files up to date (simply by loading the update CD), rather than having to file paper updates, an important but time-consuming job.

However, lawyers are often working not on current law but on the law that applied some time earlier when the cause of action arose, for example, and therefore still need access to paper versions that may contain the relevant information rather than the 'current' information provided electronically.

Another difficulty is that there is no industry standard as to how systems are updated. Whilst it is easy to update stand-alone PCs with update CDs, it can be impossible to do so over a network. This may require individual machines to be loaded with relevant CDs, a logistical nightmare and hard to police in order to ensure that your firm complies with user licence conditions.

Websites and e-mail alerts

We live in an age of information overload and certainly within the law there is a plethora of ways that we can access information over the Internet. A series of web portals has grown up to help find a simple way through to the most useful sites, for example **www.venables.co.uk** and **www.infolaw.co.uk**, the latter of which is run by Nick Holmes.

As many commentators have noted, the law on the internet is not comprehensive nor is it easily accessible for research purposes. This is because the approach taken by each website is independent of the others. Government-supplied statutes are available going back to around 1988 but not statutes still current which date from before then. Some case reports are available free of charge on the internet, but only since around 1996 and for some areas such as Employment Appeal Tribunals only from 2000. Alongside the freely available information are the subscription-only sites and these are often set up so that users can indicate their chosen area of interest and have delivered to their computer each day an e-mail of developments and articles upon any of those selected subjects.

The daily or periodic update via e-mail is, in theory, a wonderful tool – but how many people actually read them and then save what they need and delete the rest? Are you one of those people who print them all out and add the paper to the growing heaps of reading which are the lawyer's lot? New means of acquiring knowledge need new skills in harnessing it and making it work for you.

19.8   RISK ASSESSMENT AND QUALITY MANAGEMENT SYSTEMS

19.8.1   Risk assessment

To ensure that professional indemnity insurance premiums are kept at manageable levels, risk assessments need to be undertaken. If the firm is committed to the provision of quality services then file management will be at the heart of the office's systems and procedures. The two are linked, as those firms that have gained the Lexcel Quality Mark promoted by the Law Society have found that the premiums quoted for indemnity insurance are reduced by between 10 and 25 per cent. More detailed guidance on Risk Management can be found in Chapter 9 'Risk management' of Peter Scott (ed.) *Practice Management Handbook* (Law Society, 2004).

It is acknowledged that implementing a file management system will inevitably incur administrative time, but at some stage it is likely that this will become a professional standard, so as always it is better to experiment with it whilst it is not compulsory rather than be faced with having to instigate systems under pressure. There are many firms and individuals who will testify to the advantage of having to implement similar approaches in the litigation areas of practice to continue to offer publicly funded work.

One way of checking whether systems and procedures are safe and reliable is to identify the possible risks that can arise in the probate process and check if robust safety systems are in place.

A few common risks are identified below with their obvious risk management actions alongside.

Risks	Actions
Delay – giving rise to complaints	File management system for keeping files under review and moving
Failure to attend to tax matters – giving rise to penalties	Software to help complete forms; training to understand compliance during the administration; checklist/diary to recognise due dates
Missed deadlines – leaving you exposed to negligence	Central diary system
Over-distribution to beneficiaries – giving rise to personal (if PRs) or firm liability to meet shortfall	Estate accounts package should minimise risk of paying out before IHT paid but still need file management system review before distribution
Sending money to wrong person/address – breach of confidence and potential loss	Accurate database, properly trained staff, file management system to review
Overlooking usefulness of deeds of variation – leaving you exposed to negligence claims	Knowledge and skill as to whether relevant and how to conduct it; diary system to record by when it should be done
Failure actively to manage investments – giving rise to personal liability for any loss	Training to obtain knowledge and skill over asset management and realisation to deal promptly to best effect

19.8.2 Quality management systems

There are a number of quality management standards which are appropriate for incorporation within law offices and probate departments. They are:

- ISO 9001;
- Investors in People;
- Lexcel, the Law Society's Practice Management Standards.

ISO 9001

ISO 9001 is an externally audited management standard with its roots in the American defence industry. It is a self-defined standard: users establish their own management and file systems against the framework requirements of the standard itself, and are then audited against their own written systems. The standard is not specific to the legal profession but can be interpreted within a legal context. ISO 9001 tends to enjoy higher popularity within larger firms with commercial practices since it may be required by potential clients in tender situations.

Investors in People

Investors in People (IIP) is a management standard developed within the United Kingdom and applied and audited in England and Wales through the national network of Learning and Skills Councils. IIP is based upon the premise that a business will be successful if:

- it has a clear set of objectives which are communicated to all staff;
- all staff understand their contribution to those objectives;
- all staff are properly trained and equipped to fulfil their responsibilities; and
- performance is continually evaluated and reviewed.

As with ISO 9001, IIP is not specific to the legal profession, but fits very well within it.

Lexcel

The Law Society's Practice Management Standards (PMS) represent Law Society guidance on good management practice. Specific to the legal profession, the Lexcel system covers:

- management structure;
- services and forward planning;
- financial management;
- managing people;
- office administration;
- case management;
- file management.

The Law Society arranges external accreditation and audit of the standard under the brand name of 'Lexcel'. Accredited practices are able to make use of the Lexcel logo and take part in Lexcel promotional initiatives. The audit process is simplified for those firms which are already accredited under other quality management standards. For an up-to-date statement of the Practice Management Standards and Lexcel, see Matthew Moore, *Lexcel Assessment Guide and Lexcel Office Procedures Manual*, 3rd edn (Law Society, 2004).

There are several shared characteristics between these standards:

- all require external assessment and audit of the firm seeking accreditation;
- all measure the quality of the management systems in place within the practice, and not the quality of the legal advice and experience on offer;
- all require a measure of strategic planning to have been carried out;
- all require defined systems to be in place for the delivery of the product or service on offer; and

- all require effective mechanisms for personnel management, training and development to be in place.

The quality management standards provide a framework within which efficient management practices can be developed and implemented. In particular, systems for the efficient running of client files, incorporating safeguards to minimise the possibility of error or client dissatisfaction, are a key feature of quality management systems within the legal environment.

The need for such systems is clear. When the Solicitors' Indemnity Fund (SIF) was the profession's main insurer 5 per cent of claims by number and 4 per cent by settlement amount were attributable to wills and probate matters. Penalty deductibles (effectively, an additional deductible of 50 per cent) arose from failure to:

- execute a deed of variation within two years (IHTA 1984, s.142(1));
- give written notice to HMRC within the six months permitted under IHTA 1984, s.142(2).

The main problems encountered by SIF within the probate arena include:

- wills:

  - delay in preparing wills – disappointed beneficiaries;
  - failure to comply with formalities for attestation;
  - failure to consider tax implications;
  - ineffective gifts (e.g. no severance of joint tenancy);

- administration:

  - delay – loss of value in assets;
  - failure to submit tax returns as trustees;
  - failure to review fund investments;
  - failure to act promptly in sale of shares/stocks/currency;
  - shares sold at loss within 12 months of death – failure to substitute lower value for value of shares at time of death;

- deeds of arrangement:

  - failure to consider tax consequences;
  - failure to meet time limits – deeds of variation;
  - failure to give notice of election within six months;

- beneficiaries:

  - failure to verify IHT liability prior to payment of beneficiaries;
  - failure to verify correct beneficiaries/address;
  - duty to disappointed beneficiaries;

- trusts:
  - failure to ensure trust drafted to make favourable tax treatment available.

19.8.3 File management systems

The checks and balances inherent in an efficient file management system can be broken down into a series of key areas:

- response to enquiry and collection of marketing information;
- providing costs information and follow-up;
- allocation of work;
- opening a file;
- use of checklists;
- undertakings;
- arrangement of file contents;
- file supervision to include fee earner review, file review and the legal process;
- updating the client;
- file closure; and
- complaint handling systems.

19.8.4 Response to enquiries

The provision of telephone quotations is often seen as a mere irritant. Many probate practitioners, when asked to give a quotation over the phone, will do so briefly and without any attempt at 'selling' the service or the department. It is important to:

- give responsibility for responding to enquiries to the person who is best equipped to do it – not necessarily a partner but ideally someone with:
  - a good telephone manner;
  - sales experience; and
  - an outgoing personality;

- prepare a checklist of all the information that must be provided to the client;
- take a positive approach: not a defensive attitude to competitive pricing;
- cross-sell: ensure that the client is well aware of all the issues and services attached to his initial enquiry. You may, for example, encourage clients to consider an enduring power of attorney whilst discussing wills (see **Chapter 20** on marketing);
- capture information: it is vital to keep a record of the enquiry and to find out from the client what prompted the enquiry in the first place. Knowing the source of the enquiry will enable firms to monitor and plan their marketing strategy for the future.

19.8.5   Information on costs and follow-up

This is a major source of client dissatisfaction and complaint. It is compulsory under Practice Rule 15 to address how costs will be calculated at the outset and in particular to provide terms of business setting out whether the 'value' element will be used in calculating the bill in a probate matter.

Even if it was not compulsory it is certainly true that the full and adequate provision of information about the likely costs of the matter, at the start and during its progress, will assist the client by providing a clear expectation. Failure to provide this information inevitably leads to shock at the size of the final bill. One of the most frequent complaints in probate matters is the unexpected nature of the bill.

It is important to agree the funding arrangements and payment terms. To help convert an enquiry into firm instructions, it is essential to follow up initial enquiries with a personalised letter. Ensure that the response is made on the day of receipt of the initial enquiry, unless this is patently unreasonable, and that it is accompanied by appropriate sales or promotional literature, particularly information concerning related services.

The details of the quotation, the client and the source of the enquiry should be recorded for future follow-up and in order to monitor sources of work and conversion rates.

19.8.6   Allocation of work

The successful probate department will be efficient in confirming instructions in writing to the client and obtaining the necessary data from the client to progress the matter.

Upon receipt of the confirmed instructions, allocate the work to the most appropriate fee earner. This means achieving a balance between:

* experience;
* workloads;
* nature of the instructions; and
* value of the work.

Failure to control the workload being handled by an individual fee earner spells potential disaster, particularly if file management/supervision procedures are absent.

At the same time, undertake a case planning exercise to try to identify problem areas as the matter progresses. In a probate matter, such a planning exercise might cover:

* difficult interpretations of law;
* beneficiaries lacking capacity;
* insolvent estate;

- all assets in possession of deceased; outstanding tax or other liabilities;
- whether deed of variation necessary/appropriate;
- IHT implications;
- whether statutory advertisement for creditors required; and
- whether charities have been properly identified.

The case planning exercise might also seek to establish targets and key dates relating to:

- assets collected;
- liabilities settled;
- time limits (variation, etc.);
- interim billing;
- grant of probate; and
- distribution, interim and final.

19.8.7 Opening a file

By now, the vast majority of the information required in order to carry out this function should be available. Client details are available and must be transferred on to the file and on to any electronic database or case management software, if in place.

19.8.8 Use of checklists

Fee earners should complete professional checklists at key stages in the conduct of the matter. The purpose of a checklist is to act as an *aide-mémoire* to ensure that all relevant professional issues have been properly addressed prior to moving forward to the next stage in the matter.

If all is as it should be, the checklist will act as evidence on the file to confirm this: if the checklist throws up an omission, no matter how major or minor, the fee earner will be prompted to go back into the file to rectify the identified problem.

19.8.9 Undertakings

Strict control is required over the granting of undertakings, which bind the firm and its partners. Any undertakings, other than standard wording undertakings (e.g. those recommended by the Law Society in a conveyancing transaction), should receive a partner's prior authority.

A central register of undertakings granted should be established in addition to a clear record being placed on the file. Many firms now use a system of synopsis sheets on the front covers of files, which summarise key data relating to the file: it is sensible to include space on the synopsis sheet to show when an undertaking has been granted. Verbal undertakings should always be confirmed in writing.

19.8.10   Arrangement of file contents

Case files should be laid out neatly to ensure easy accessibility to all information by all fee earners and support staff and to enable supervisors regularly to review work. Working papers should be arranged so that:

- all correspondence is in sequence on a filing clip;
- all file notes/attendance notes are stored in sequence on the correspondence clip;
- a synopsis sheet is prominently attached to all files;
- deeds and other documents of title are stored in secure filing facilities, properly cross-referred to the file; and
- any other papers are neatly arranged on the file, if necessary in a plastic wallet.

19.8.11   File supervision

Supervision of the management of the matter breaks down into two areas:

- fee earner supervision; and
- file review.

Fee earner supervision

Supervision equates to effective support of the fee earner. The objective of supervision is to ensure that:

- all fee earners know who is supervising them;
- arrangements to ensure supervision of the conduct of case work are in place and understood within the department;
- arrangements are in place for a regular independent review of case files in terms of procedural and legal content; and
- arrangements are in place to supervise the conduct of work carried out by non fee-earning staff.

The supervision process tends to be divided into three areas:

- checking of incoming post;
- checking (but not necessarily signing) of all outgoing post; and
- regular supervision meetings.

The level of supervision required will depend upon the experience of the fee earner concerned. Fee earners who are considered to be of sufficient experience should be granted the ability to supervise their own post, but they should still be subject to regular supervision meetings by their supervisor.

Base the frequency of supervision meetings on the fee earner's experience. Meetings should include coverage of issues such as:

- new cases taken on;
- existing workloads;
- progress on current cases;
- problem clients;
- the outcome of cases;
- training needs;
- undertakings granted or given;
- any other problems encountered.

The purpose of the meeting is for the supervisor to guide and assist the fee earner in the delivery of legal services.

File review

All files should be subject to independent periodic review. The review should cover both procedural matters and substantive legal issues. A supervisor who is independent from the day-to-day conduct of the matter should carry out the review.

The frequency of reviews is dependent upon the experience of the fee earner involved: five files per quarter will give an accurate, cross-sectional overview of the workload of most fee earners. The file review should be evidenced by means of a file review sheet which should be signed off and agreed by both parties to the review process. The review should check at least the following issues:

- substantive legal issues properly addressed;
- papers referenced;
- file notes used consistently;
- undertakings recorded;
- conflict of interest check conducted;
- requirements or instructions of the client recorded;
- advice given recorded;
- action to be taken recorded;
- costs arrangements recorded;
- terms of business despatched;
- key dates recorded and backed up;
- client properly updated;
- changes in costs notified.

Any poor levels of compliance should be drawn to the fee earner's attention and rectified within an agreed period of time.

19.8.12 Updating the client

Fee earners should ensure that clients are appropriately updated throughout the matter and this includes ensuring that:

- information about action taken in a case, or its handling, is given to the client promptly;
- information relating to delays is passed on to the client immediately.

Both of the above points should be evidenced on file, either by attendance notes or by means of a copy letter to the client.

19.8.13 At the end of the matter

Proper procedures need to be put in place to ensure that any outstanding points are properly dealt with before the file is closed formally within the firm. This is best achieved by means of a file closure checklist. Issues addressed on the checklist should include:

- that the client has been informed of the outcome of the matter;
- that the client (or beneficiary in a probate) has been accounted to for any outstanding money;
- that interest on the client account has been calculated (where applicable);
- that original documents have been returned to the client unless storage arrangements have been agreed;
- that, where appropriate, the client has been informed about arrangements for storage and retrieval of papers;
- that the client has been advised whether the matter should be reviewed in the future, and if so, when;
- that final bills have been received and settled and that account balances are zero;
- that a future review date (if applicable) has been diaried forward and that a file destruction date has been allocated.

19.8.14 Complaint systems

Complaint systems are not put in place simply to provide clients with the ability to whinge. Complaint systems are a part of the process of assessing client satisfaction. They are a means of identifying problems, resolving those problems and ensuring that the resulting benefit is passed on to the client base. Complaint systems should include a means not only of resolving the initial client complaint, but also of planning to ensure that the problem which gave rise to it never recurs.

In probate matters it is possible that complaints are received from residuary beneficiaries, particularly in cases where members of the firm are the only executors, and our rules dictate that the residuary beneficiaries would have to approve the costs in any event.

19.9 MARKETING

19.9.1 New customers versus existing clients

Profitable organisations recognise that the best source of profit and sustainable revenue is gained by focusing on existing clients. It costs far more to convert a prospective client into an actual client than to sell more services to an existing client.

This assumes, however, that the client is a potential repeat buyer of the services offered and that the segment of the market being targeted will generate good and profitable business. If the type of client and the type of service are not in a profitable segment of the market, no amount of selling to them will generate good business.

The current emphasis stresses customer relationship management (CRM), i.e. that a firm should develop close alignment with its clients, being able to customise its messages and activities to the different needs and values of its clients.

19.9.2 Customer relationship management

The smaller firm has probably been practising CRM for years: it offers a service that is personal to each client. This works for as long as only one person deals with that client, but as the firm grows and as the personnel change it is inevitable that the 'closeness' of the service offered originally is weakened, and faced with this clients often choose to take the opportunity to move to another practice.

To learn enough to differentiate between clients the firm will need to have a system for capturing each individual's contact with the client (particularly if it wishes to cross-sell probate services to clients who have only used the litigation or conveyancing services) so that it can keep track of the dialogues and interactions which will help with your side of the work that the firm proposes to do for the client.

Clients find it much more difficult to start over with another firm, so you need to help them to create their own barrier to leaving your firm behind. You are trying to build and keep their trust. To keep them biased towards your firm, you need to find out what the client values from the way your firm delivers its services and then make sure that this is what you deliver to the client.

Clients are always going to value things that make their life easier – the challenge is to find out what this might be for the probate service. Can frequent visits to the office be avoided, thus saving them time, by giving clients regular reports, or allowing them access to basic information over the internet? The more your marketing can identify what the individual client is doing (behaviour) and thinking (feelings) the more emotional attachment there will be to your firm if you address these behaviours and feelings, and the more likely it is they will stick with you.

Everyone in the team needs to be able to adapt his or her delivery to suit the level of sophistication of the particular client. Do be clear about:

- what the service offered actually entails;
- how much this service is actually going to cost;
- how the level of cost is justified for the type of service provided; and
- how any problems will be dealt with.

Make contact with the bodies who are providing services to the elderly locally: provide free advice, join the local committee, discover what they are looking for from the lawyer. In this way, the profile of the firm to undertake work in this field in your area will be raised, encouraging referral of work.

Market the team's services by undertaking seminars to local groups, to clients, with the local care agencies, and write editorials for publications. However, you cannot market successfully until you are clear about what it is you are marketing.

When the firm has developed its own specific value chain to its satisfaction it can promote this value to its clients, e.g. by having better IT and systems than rival firms to collect all information necessary both accurately and efficiently (lower cost advantage), or by performing activities in a unique way, such as producing the will at the person's place of work or home to increase greater perceived value to the client (differentiation advantage).

In the will drafting sector, solicitors are not the only people offering the service, so it is important to benchmark not just other solicitors' value chains (which is difficult outside groups such as LawNet or outside local areas) but other organisations or firms that might see this as a service to offer.

Several years ago the Law Society commissioned a benchmarking study of other professions and commercial companies in relation to client care. The result of this was that solicitors were advised to manage expectations and communications. The report recommended that:

- You are specific and clear in all communications:

    - use of plain English – have you ever appraised the competence of the practitioners in your firm in this respect?
    - use of guidance notes and leaflets – does your firm have clear terms and conditions of business or client care guide? Do you use explanatory leaflets that you have tried and tested for understanding by lay people?

- You know the concerns of your audience, i.e. the different needs of different types of client:

  - scenario 1: you are invited to speak at an Age Concern lunch club about what is involved in making a will; you are permitted to promote your own firm's will-making service. What would you say?
  - scenario 2: the Excess Bank plc invites you to a seminar it is holding for some of its high net worth clients. The Bank does not have its own will-drafting service. It is recognised as being expert at putting its customers first. Do you offer to make a presentation? What would you say?
  - scenario 3: the local branch of the Institute of Directors is holding a trade fair. Do you take part? How would you present the firm's will-writing service?

- You match content and style to your market, i.e. if you only act for scenario 1 clients, it is no good offering a scenario 3 service.
- You never commit without being able to deliver: it is a marketing adage that you should always under-promise and over-deliver, i.e. promise to produce a new will in two weeks time and produce it in one week.
- You make rules and guidelines accessible to all:

  - internally, involve staff in designing and monitoring;
  - externally, ensure lay people can understand what is intended.

Interestingly, the Fact Sheet produced by the Law Society's Research and Policy Planning Unit identified that firms can strengthen and expand their client bases through good client care. The Fact Sheet pointed out:

- Private clients and smaller businesses usually choose solicitors on the basis of past experience or recommendation. Existing clients are more likely to be retained and new clients attracted if clients are satisfied with the service purchased.
- The public is demanding higher levels of service from all professionals. Firms which demonstrate first class client care will gain a competitive edge in the market place.
- There is a strong correlation between good colleague care and good client care. Developing good client care is likely to lead to improved relationships between members of the firm whereas poor client care can seriously damage internal relationships.
- The Legal Services Ombudsman has called for solicitors to adopt a more 'consumerist' mentality to complaints from clients about processes and service, rather than negligent professional service.
- Effective client-centred complaint handling may increase client loyalty. Research has shown that where a complaint is satisfactorily resolved, 75 per cent of consumers were likely to go back.

- There is also evidence that excellent complaint handling can lead to even higher customer loyalty than amongst those clients who experience no problems at all.
- If clients are not adequately cared for the reputation of the profession as a whole suffers.

The Fact Sheet went on to identify the areas that comprise good client care as:

- developing appropriate interpersonal and organisational skills such as effective interviewing, communication and managerial skills;
- the setting up of efficient management systems;
- the gathering of clients' opinions about completed work;
- the provision of 'client friendly' office accommodation and information;
- a regime of regulation which reinforces good client care practice, through training, appraisal, monitoring and compliance mechanisms;
- appropriate mechanisms for the swift handling and resolution of clients' complaints at the right level; and
- the development in law firms of a culture of client care which values complaints and reports of clients' dissatisfaction as crucial feedback which can be used to improve the legal services offered.

19.10 SUMMARY

1. Take your firm's business objectives.
2. Apply them to your department's strategic aspirations.
3. Review your firm's competition for similar services.
4. Conduct a PESTE and SWOT analysis of your department and its service provision.
5. Compare these with the competition and set your department some benchmarks.
6. Set down the department's agreed operational plan and allocate responsibilities for achievement between people in the team.
7. Be clear and precise about how you will know whether you have achieved your operational goals.
8. Implement your plan.
9. Review your performance against the plan.
10. Take forward what you have learnt to the next planning cycle.

CHAPTER 20

Marketing wills and probate

Kim Tasso

20.1　INTRODUCTION

This chapter aims to achieve the following:

- to dispel the myths about marketing and business development and to explain the core concepts of marketing that are relevant to wills and probate practitioners;
- to provide an analysis and planning framework to help probate practitioners understand their present position, articulate what they want to achieve and to develop effective marketing action plans;
- to provide practical guidance on selecting which of the many marketing approaches are appropriate for probate practitioners in their different markets; and
- to provide insight through comments and marketing case studies from a variety of probate practitioners around the UK.

Marketing is not a concept that is comfortable for many wills, trust and probate practitioners. There is still a feeling that those in 'the death department', as it was put to me the other day, should resist the modern management approaches that their colleagues in the commercial departments have embraced and that by simply doing great work and keeping clients satisfied they will continue to prosper. Whilst I wholeheartedly agree that you must have strong technical expertise and provide excellent service at the foundation of a successful probate practice, I – and many probate practitioners – know that much more must be done to secure the future of a probate practice. I hope this chapter helps persuade you of the merits of this view and provides the tools you need to embrace marketing.

It should be noted that the markets for and marketing of wills can be significantly different from the markets for tax planning, trusts and probate. Also, the marketing approaches accessible and suitable for sole practitioners and High Street firms are very different from those used by their colleagues in the larger firms. This chapter will try to address these different perspectives and needs.

20.2 UNDERSTANDING THE BASIC PRINCIPLES OF MARKETING

20.2.1 What is marketing?

Some people think that marketing is the preserve of those in the marketing department – managing the production of brochures, seminars and websites. But this is only a small part of the picture, because real marketing involves all those who provide wills or probate advice, and extends to issues such as market research, analysis of present clients, strategic decisions of what services will be provided to whom and how and at what price.

'Marketing is the management process responsible for anticipating and meeting client needs profitably' is the Chartered Institute of Marketing's official definition and one that few professionals would argue with – after all, isn't every lawyer there to meet the needs of their clients whilst making a modest profit?

Marketing is a philosophy that focuses – at every point in the firm – on the needs of the client. From a service delivery perspective, every member of the firm who has contact with clients and referrers (whether as a receptionist, switchboard operator, secretary, trainee, legal executive, etc.) creates an impression of the firm and the probate team and either supports or undermines the marketing effort. From a cross-selling perspective, everyone in the firm must be aware of what the probate team has to offer, including its particular strengths and how to introduce clients to the services available.

Marketing comprises a number of elements that are blended together into what is called 'the marketing mix':

- *Product* – the legal expertise and the way in which advice is delivered. Very often clients of the wills and probate team will be unable to determine whether the legal advice they receive is good or bad. However, they will make a judgment about the service depending on how that advice is delivered to them. Was the receptionist friendly? Were the meeting rooms pleasant? Did the solicitor make an effort to understand their particular concerns? Were things explained in a way that was easy to understand? Were letters and documents in a consistent style? Was it easy to contact the solicitor concerned? Were messages answered promptly? Were the benefits and value received good enough? To what extent is the service from your firm different from or better than the service available from other providers – whether these are will writers, other solicitors or internet-based services?
- *People* – It follows then that the lawyers and their support staff who are the marketers, sellers, producers and deliverers of the wills or probate services are a critical part of the marketing process and must therefore be included in the marketing, planning and service delivery process. This is likely to involve training and communications programmes for them.

- *Place* – The various markets where the services are promoted and delivered or the channels involved, e.g. web-based services. There are many different markets for wills and probate practitioners, such as the general public, financial advisers, and directors within commercial organisations. These markets will also have different needs; for example young married couples will have concerns relating to their own families and their relatives, different from the concerns of older people living on their own or in care homes. Similarly, those with little wealth and few assets will have needs that are different from the needs of those with significant assets that may be within trusts or overseas.
- *Price* – Some markets may choose their advisers on the basis of price alone whereas others will be more concerned with the reputation of the adviser, their past relationship, the other services provided, or the particular service or value provided.
- *Promotion* – This concerns all those activities designed to alert clients, referrers and potential clients to your wills and probate services and to generate new clients and new work.

These different elements are explored further in the remainder of this chapter but it is important that all elements are considered together. A promotional campaign alone is unlikely to succeed.

There is often some confusion within the legal profession about the terms 'marketing', 'selling' and 'business development'. They are distinct activities aimed at different parts of an ongoing and integrated cycle (see **Figure 20.1**).

Marketing
(ëAnticipating and meeting client needs profitably')

- Analysis
- Strategic planning
- General needs
- Service development
- Market development
- Profile/brand building
- One to many

Client development

- CRM
- Retaining/developing
- Cross-selling
- Specific client/referrer
- (Key) Account management
- Many to one

Selling

- Opportunity to talk/meet
- Tactical
- Converting enquiries/RFPs/ITTs
- Pitches and presentations
- Specific client/needs
- One to one

Figure 20.1   The business development cycle in law firms

20.2.2　What is selling?

Marketing is concerned with identifying needs in the market (therefore research and analysis are important), identifying or developing the services that meet those needs and communicating the appropriate messages to the market. Marketing is also concerned with developing the reputation or brand of the firm, service or individual. If marketing is successful then enquiries and opportunities to meet with potential referrers and clients will be generated.

When you move from communicating with a market to communicating with a particular individual or organisation, you have moved into the selling phase. Here the focus is on the specific needs of that one individual rather than the generalised needs of the whole market. Some argue that selling is more orientated to 'pushing' the product or service being sold, although in the legal market the most successful selling is driven by the needs of the buyer. Typically in a law firm, selling is the preserve of the lawyers who talk to and meet with clients and who have the experience and knowledge to promote their own and the firm's services. Sometimes, there is a formal tendering process (or 'beauty parade') involved if there is a large volume of work or a legal panel at the client organisation.

Converting a prospect through successful selling results in the firm gaining a client. However, one set of instructions does not a client make. Continued marketing and selling to that client (within the framework of a CRM programme) will be needed to ensure that further instructions are received for additional or new services. This is a vital activity in every law firm, as usually around 80 per cent of a firm's income is from existing clients. Typically, this area of client or relationship development is where the majority of lawyers focus their efforts. Whilst some will argue that you only undertake one probate per client, the essence of this is true – but a wills client who is looked after through many years will continue to instruct the firm. An accountant or independent financial adviser (IFA) who refers a number of clients and matters across will continue to do so as long as the relationship is good and contact is regular.

This view of marketing should dispel the myth that it is only about new business: a major component of law firm marketing is about developing the existing client and referrer base through relationship marketing.

20.2.3　Consumer (private client) versus business-to-business (commercial) marketing

Before we embark on a practical framework to get you marketing your probate and wills practice, you need to appreciate that marketing techniques vary depending on the nature of your target clients. The importance of segmenting the market into smaller, more manageable segments with common characteristics or needs must also be considered. Clever segmentation can result in a highly profitable niche practice, which makes achieving a premium fee for specialist work easier.

When promoting wills, you are typically targeting private individuals or families. There are over 58 million people in the UK and they can be grouped by socio-economic group, by age, by location, by household, by lifestyle and in various other ways. Even though the firm may have focused on a particular group, it would be difficult and not very cost effective to try to mail all members of that group or to spend hours in one-to-one meetings. So, more indirect methods of marketing might be adopted, such as advertising or media relations. The members of each group or segment will have common interests or needs that can be addressed within a marketing campaign. The smaller and more focused the segment, the easier it will be to reach the members with a suitable marketing tool and the easier it will be to tailor your message to address their specific needs.

Some elements of the private client market are keen to use the internet, and there are a number of examples of successful websites that provide an efficient online solution to simple wills and probate matters. Similarly, other elements of the private client market might appreciate a much greater level of face-to-face interaction when dealing with legal matters, perhaps even in their own home environment. By segmenting the market, the service, the price and the promotional activity can be tailored more precisely to their needs.

For example, you might adopt a radically different approach and decide to target businesses in your area, offering a will-writing service to their employees. There are significantly fewer businesses than individuals and there is a greater wealth of information about them in various public directories and publications. Business people are less likely to be reached effectively through advertising so it might be appropriate to adopt a more direct approach to marketing to this group: by direct mail, through seminars or perhaps by arranging for a lawyer make visits to employers' premises. Their needs will be different too: whereas individuals might need a will for peace of mind, to provide for their children, to minimise their tax liabilities on death, etc., a business will have different priorities. If a company offers a will-writing service to its employees it might be because it is genuinely concerned with staff welfare, it might be more concerned with minimising time away from the place of employment, or it might wish to minimise difficulties for the company's pension scheme in the event of death in service. Therefore, the way of reaching the business audience will be different and the message communicated needs to be different.

A further alternative might be to decide to reach referrer organisations to generate will or probate business, such as retirement homes, hospices, doctors, accountants, advice centres, charities or even banks. Here you are targeting organisations so the business-to-business techniques are more likely to be effective.

In marketing terms, this is the difference between consumer (private client) and business-to-business (commercial client or referrer) marketing. Often, lawyers do not make this distinction and use the wrong technique as a result. As a rule of thumb (there are always exceptions), if you are marketing to consumers you use indirect methods, while for businesses you use more direct approaches. The following are the various techniques that could perform these tasks:

Indirect methods	Direct methods
advertising	networking
signs/posters	selling (presentations and visits)
media relations	tenders
sponsorship	direct marketing
literature (left on display)	literature (mailed)
websites	seminars/briefings
word of mouth	hospitality
	telemarketing

20.2.4 A marketing framework for probate practitioners

What follows is a framework to guide practitioners through the various steps to prepare them for effective marketing and to prepare a marketing plan to focus their marketing, selling and client development activities. It may seem that a lot of analysis, thinking and planning has to take place before taking any real 'action'. However, most solicitors' marketing fails because insufficient attention is paid to precisely these issues.

20.3 ANALYSING THE PRESENT SITUATION

20.3.1 Analysing current work, clients and sources

Let us start by looking at the sorts of sources of work and clients that a probate practioner might have:

Those inside the firm	Those outside the firm
private clients	private individuals
matrimonial	low income
personal	people with ageing parents
residential conveyancing	high net worth/rich clients
financial services	company directors
Commercial clients	**Referring individuals**
corporate/commercial: directors, senior employees, shareholders employment: senior employees	existing/past clients those who know the solicitor personally

Other	Referring organisations
staff, friends and family	accountants
	surveyors/agents
	advice centres/bureaux
	banks
	carers
	hospitals/homes
	funeral directors
	other law firms

Or it may be possible to produce a diagram of the particular dynamics in this market, like the example in **Figure 20.2**.

This illustrates the great variety of clients and prospective clients (both private and commercial), sources of referral, or work and needs with which wills and probate practitioners must get to grips. Prepare a similar diagram for your own firm. If the firm does not have the necessary information then an early priority is to ensure that systems (usually a client and contact database and a work referral or lead tracking system) are established to collect this information in the future. Marketing without sound information is rather like building on sand – it is without foundation and liable to crumble away.

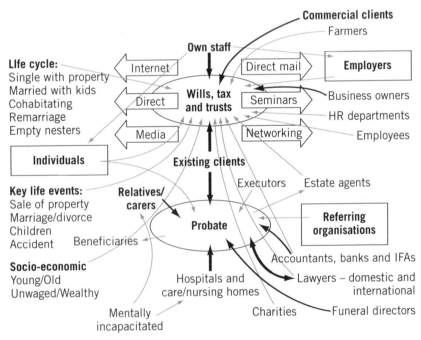

Figure 20.2 Market mapping example

Case study: Analysis at Thomson Snell & Passmore

Jeremy Passmore, Partner and head of Private Client at Thomson Snell & Passmore in Kent. The private client team comprises 19 people, five of whom focus exclusively on probate, and generates around 20 per cent of the firm's income.

Before you develop a marketing strategy, you must have a clear view of where your work comes from at present. To capture the information we needed we diverted all new client forms through our marketing team and it took around two years before we had an accurate picture of what was happening. Our analysis – which confirmed our suspicions – showed that 74% of our work came from existing clients. Of the 26% of work from new clients 36% was from professional referrals (quite a significant amount from firms in London), 25% existing client referrals and 21% from partners and staff. The balance was from the website, our seminars and our newsletter 'Your wealth law' – where we always place wills and probate related material – that is sent three times a year to clients, contacts and referrers. This information enables us to focus our marketing and to measure our results accurately.

This analysis should provide three or four areas on which you need to concentrate. Or it may show that the marketing challenge is to alter radically the nature of clients and work being generated.

If the time is available, talking to existing clients and referrers will be an invaluable aid to future marketing. It will help you to identify why people come to your firm, what they like (and do not like) about the service, what additional help or advice they would like and what it is about your firm that is different from others. It will also provide insight into the clients' point of view and their existing and emerging needs. Time and effort spent investigating the perceptions and satisfaction of existing clients is always paid back.

20.3.2 Reviewing your skills, staff and services

The next thing is to review the skills and abilities of the staff who are promoting and servicing the wills and probate work. Do they have any specialist expertise, for example, in complicated tax issues, in contested wills, in situations with cohabiting couples, with overseas assets? If your firm has some expertise that is unlikely to be found in comparable firms then this may provide a key point of difference which will make targeting and marketing much easier.

Case study: Specialist expertise at Rix & Kay

Lisa Jones, a partner at Rix & Kay. The firm has 14 partners and in excess of 100 staff in offices based in Uckfield, Heathfield and Seaford in Sussex. There are four partners and 18 staff in the Wills Trusts and Probate team.

We are fortunate in that we have a specialist – Martin Terrell – for Court of Protection work. He has extremely good links with the Court of Protection and

357

much work is referred to him. His reputation and networking also means that he gets referrals from barristers.

Are there any gaps in your expertise? You might identify areas where new or different skills need to be developed within the wills and probate team. Alternatively, your research may reveal that the service provided by some parts of your team is not generating sufficient client satisfaction or is the source of complaints. Training may be needed, or changes in systems and procedures. If there are weaknesses, it may be sensible to concentrate marketing efforts on only those areas where you know you are strong.

Are staff able and motivated to provide great service and to sell? Perhaps interpersonal skills training to develop their enthusiasm, confidence or 'bedside manner' should be considered. It may be useful to review the rewards system so that they are encouraged to invest time and energy in winning new business. Even if you decide to take on the major share of marketing yourself, it is still vital to ensure that all those who have contact with clients understand what you are trying to achieve, and that they deliver the services in the way you have promised and achieve a high level of client satisfaction.

20.3.3   Analysing the market

Now that you understand where your work comes from, and the resources available to develop and deliver work in the future, it is time to look outside your firm to consider issues that may affect your future marketing success. A starting point may be some online research to get a feel for the overall size of the market; for example, there are around 600,000 deaths per annum in the UK, around 300,000 marriages and 160,000 divorces. That will provide a starting point – but how do these figures apply to your particular geographic area? Standard Life research indicates that 57 per cent of UK adults have no will and a further 19 per cent have experienced significant changes that are not reflected in their wills. When the increasing wealth and rising property prices in the UK are considered, it becomes apparent that the importance of making a will and planning for IHT will become an issue for many more thousands of people than in the past.

The long-term changes in the market that might affect future needs for wills and probate should also be taken into account. A review of political, sociological, technological and economic factors may alert you to imminent changes that will drive different client needs and different services. There are many changes that might impact on the future flow of your work: for example deregulation, the impact of the introduction of civil partnership, or the increasing number of second and third marriages leading to increasingly complex potential claims on estates.

Case study: Comments from Boodle Hatfield

Boodle Hatfield is based in Mayfair in London and Oxford. It has a total of 27 partners, with eight in the private client department.

There is a general feeling that Clementi won't have too much impact on the higher end of the market, because the service that firms like us provide is part of an integrated package that high net worth individuals will probably continue to use for their overall planning much as they have done in the past. However, it will have an impact on the lower end of the market. All the research indicates that the general public, and particularly younger people, are likely to start going to large organisations such as Tesco or their banks. The attraction of a known and trusted brand is very strong and the image of solicitors is often of being expensive and unapproachable. We are concerned at the impact of change to section 55 of the Courts and Legal Services Act in terms of the quality of advice and protection of the public. Clearly there is a danger that if people with no formal qualifications, no insurance and no regulation are allowed to write wills then mistakes will happen and the public will not be as protected.

On the more positive side, as house prices continue to rise, more people will need tax planning advice and this may encourage them to continue to seek advice from solicitors. HMRC is becoming more demanding in terms of having correct values before the grant of probate is granted so we may see more people seeking legal advice as a result. There is also a growing need to interact with lawyers in other jurisdictions as people become more mobile and own more assets overseas. There is therefore a greater need for assistance on issues such as residence, domicile and international taxation and succession from solicitors. Furthermore, the world is becoming more litigious and therefore the demand for contentious probate support will increase – there are more fragmented and complicated family structures now and increases in individual wealth will probably lead to further increases in disputes over wills/will trusts.

Case study: Comments from Nelsons

Richard Grosberg, Partner and head of Private Client of Nelsons in the Midlands and former National Chair of the Law Society's Probate Section.

There are a number of different regulatory issues that should be considered by those thinking about how their probate sections will develop in the future. The first is the growth of will writers – from a handful a few years ago to many thousands today. Clementi raises the issues of whether will writers should be regulated – it is unlikely that they would be so on the same basis as us yet it would give them an air of respectability and perhaps widen their appeal thus further eroding our market. Secondly, there has been a prohibition on anyone applying for grants of probate for a fee except solicitors yet the 1990 Courts and Legal Protection Act indicates – in sections 54 and 55 – that this could be extended to banks, building societies and insurance companies. Thirdly, the outside ownership of law firms in the White Paper may herald the arrival of 'Tesco Law' and the large financial institutions entering the wills and probate market. It is unlikely that they would set up operations like law firms from scratch – they may acquire parts of or whole law firms, they may establish entirely computer based operations backed up with call centres and sophisticated customer services operations. This would lead to the further deskilling and commoditisation of our services and remove yet another element of the mass/low end of the market. These threats mean that solicitors must remain alert to the nature of the service they provide – and the value they bring and the way that those services are delivered. It also means that the importance of niche marketing approaches – where specialist knowledge or experience is valued – may increase for probate practitioners.

Case study: Comments from Forshaws

Forshaws is a 12-partner firm in the North West with offices in Warrington, Stockton Heath and Frodsham. Emma Stride is an associate solicitor who qualified in 1990.

Over the past 15 years, there has been a significant change in the awareness and expectations of clients. Their demands have increased. They are entitled to more information in writing than ever used to be the case and thus, quite rightly, have greater knowledge about the standard of service they should receive. Beneficiaries expect to receive their entitlements without delay. Many clients from the older generation have embraced the IT revolution and now quite happily use e-mail. Being retired and having time on their hands often means that they are waiting at their computer for a swift response. To alleviate the pressure, practices and procedures need to be streamlined to become as efficient as possible. Where specialist advice is being offered, it is important to be able to demonstrate that this is the case and membership of professional bodies, such as STEP and ACTAPS, is always beneficial. We are living in an ageing population. Life expectancy is increasing. According to the Office for National Statistics, the number of people over pensionable age (taking account of the change in the woman's retirement age) is projected to increase from nearly 11.4 million in 2006 to 12.2 million in 2011 and will rise to nearly 13.0 million by 2026, reaching over 15.2 million in 2031. It is still a fact that 60% of people die without having made a will which, when set against the above figures, leaves an enormous proportion of the population who will potentially die intestate.

Case study: Comment from Kaye Tesler

Michael Kaye, of two-partner High Street practice Kaye Tesler & Co., uses an innovative website to target a very different segment.

People my age ask each other for recommendations. Those at university and the younger generation think nothing of getting online and seeking the information they need that way. It is a fundamental attitude and buying shift.

The next step is to think about local demands and needs. The demand in your area may be different from that in other parts of the country depending on, for example, the demographic socio-economic spread of the local population, the prevailing attitudes towards planning, the extent of nursing and private care homes and facilities and the nature of the competition in the area. This information can be found by researching at local reference libraries or contacting local government agencies who often have concise overviews of areas and the main economic and social trends. Networking at local events will also enable you to learn about the dynamics within your local marketplace and will provide vital marketing intelligence. It will have the added benefit of raising your firm's profile for all its services.

Case study: Local market analysis at Rix & Kay

Our three offices operate in very different markets. Uckfield has relatively young and affluent residents who are in well paid jobs or running businesses. We have done talks for groups of professionals – GPs on the subject of IHT and we plan to extend this to groups of dentists, vets and even school teachers in due course. However, at the other two offices the majority of the population is older and retired. This means that we have to adapt the services we offer and the marketing approach for the different markets.

A key issue to consider will obviously be the strengths and weaknesses, strategies and activities of your competitors. These may not all be solicitors, and you will also need to consider banks, accountants (especially those with tax and trust departments), financial advisers and independent will writers. In any market you will face a variety of competitors – but just collecting information about your competitors is not sufficient. The information must then be used to modify your approach and activities in order to find a different market position offering different benefits.

Case study: Comment from Thomson Snell & Passmore

Yes, there is greater competition in the wills market but we are holding our ground. That's partly a factor that we are long established and very well known in our local market. We have segmented the market carefully and target the more sophisticated clients who are likely to have a range of demanding tax planning needs.

20.3.4 Pulling your research together

An analysis of your internal strengths and weaknesses and how these translate into external opportunities and threats may help to identify the key issues on which you need to act. As you consider each opportunity and threat, think what needs to be done – as a specific action – to resolve or grasp the situation. The more time spent synthesising the key findings of your internal and external research, the easier it will be to develop a marketing strategy and action plan that works for you. Encourage all members of your probate team to participate in a discussion about the market and how it is changing – they are a good source of additional information and ideas, and if they are to participate in any changes in the way that the service is delivered or in any specific marketing activities, they will need to know what you are doing and why.

20.4 DECIDING WHAT WORKS FOR YOU

20.4.1 Setting objectives

By looking at the business plan for the firm, you will see the firm's overall objectives, both the financial targets and in terms of the perception and impression that the firm wishes to create in the market and the nature of the key clients it wishes to target. It is at this stage that many wills and probate practitioners find a difficulty, especially if the firm is focusing on developing commercial work rather than private client work. It may also be difficult if there are other practice groups targeting similar client and referrer groups to those targeted by the probate and wills team. All of these groups will need to work together carefully in this case to produce an integrated plan for marketing to private clients.

Case study: An integrated approach at Boodle Hatfield

At Boodle Hatfield we take an integrated approach to marketing our private client services. Our clients are generally high net worth individuals to whom we provide long-term, complex tax, trusts and succession planning advice, often acting for one family over a number of generations. Probate services and will writing are therefore part of that integrated package of advice we provide, usually over a number of years (and often to generations of the same family).

Once the firm-wide and short-term (usually one year) objectives have been identified, it will be possible to go on to develop short-term and longer-term objectives for the wills and probate team. Setting objectives that are measurable and realistic (see the discussion of SMART goals at **19.5.5** above) is hard, but without these it will be difficult to focus your marketing efforts appropriately and it will be impossible to measure the success of your marketing.

20.5 AGREEING A STRATEGY

The external and internal analyses are complete and your objectives are set. The next challenge is to agree an overall strategy for the future – this involves making a number of hard decisions, which will enable efforts to be focused on those areas most likely to yield the results you seek. These decisions might include:

- the markets which will be targeted;
- the particular services and benefits to be offered;
- how the teams for service delivery and marketing are to be organised;
- the balance of effort between marketing to existing as opposed to new clients;
- whether a largely indirect (to individuals) or direct (to referrers) approach will be adopted; and
- the particular marketing techniques that will be deployed.

Case study: Marketing strategy at Forshaws

Forshaws is a long established practice and we have a large bank of wills. In the past, we have always been able to rely on the work generated by those wills and the associated existing clients. Clearly, the climate is changing and it is no longer enough to sit back and wait for the work to come to us. We therefore feel that it is important for us to be preparing and completing enough wills now so as to be retaining a sufficient percentage to generate future probate work for the Wills and Probate Department, particularly given the threat of authorised probate practitioners. We also feel that greater emphasis needs to be given to pre-death work in our marketing strategy – wills, powers of attorney, planning for future care and the like – again especially in light of the recent consultation papers on reviewing probate work.

Case study: Marketing strategy at Thomson Snell & Passmore

A safe full of wills is no guarantee of future business (although if we are named as executors there is a high likelihood of this happening) so an active marketing programme is needed. We do little direct marketing. We post a wide range of fact sheets on different topics onto our website. We integrate the marketing of the wills, trusts and probate team into all those marketing efforts within the firm aimed at private individuals. We have a list of target referrers – accountants, banks and IFAs – where we try to maintain regular contact and pass on leads where appropriate.

Case study: Marketing strategy at Nelsons

Our marketing strategy was established some years ago and has served us well. It is built on three planks:

(a) **Keep in contact with existing clients** – We stopped producing our newsletter five years ago and this we learned was a short-sighted decision and a grave mistake. Whilst it is hard to measure the immediate impact it seems that sending regular information to existing clients has a cumulative effect. We have extended this with e-mails to selected clients of important changes that occur between editions of the newsletter. We also issue a letter to our wills clients every five years prompting them to consider whether they have experienced any significant changes that should be reflected in revised wills. We get a 10% response rate on these letters – although some of it is to alert us to changes in address which are valuable to have. The 'pain barrier' of getting your client database and information correct must be broken. It is time intensive and ongoing effort is vitally important.

(b) **Organise seminars** – We also offer seminars to existing clients although we extend the invitation to potential clients as well. We are also always prepared to provide talks to non-professionals – for example at retirement seminars, rotary clubs, Third Age. Our Derby office does a quarterly talk at a local Council for all those employees who are thinking about retirement planning.

(c) **Raise our profile** – When changes occur we respond with comments and articles in the media. A recent example was the day after a Panorama documentary about NHS fees and care homes we sent information to the local press. We devote a lot of time to developing relationships with those at the local Law Society – having a high profile in this area supports recommendations for the specialist services we provide.

20.5.1   Agreeing your target market and position

The market and client analyses should be used to identify which particular segments of the market you will focus on. Typical choices include high net worth individuals, as opposed to the lower value mass market. Other segments might include those, for example, with agricultural estates or international assets. Other approaches may segment on particular demographics such as age, gender or occupation. Lifestyle segmentation is another approach. There are many ways to segment the market and the choice will dictate the best methods of marketing – through intermediaries or directly, through advertising or seminars, and so on.

The next stage is to decide what position you want to achieve in the market. If all the other wills and probate service providers are pushing the low cost, prepackaged wills 'product', then look at whether there are opportunities for firms offering a higher priced, more tailored 'service'. If others are targeting the low income families, consider targeting the wealthy. If others are focusing on reaching the 'man in the street', why not consider reaching the executive in the boardroom or local employers?

A key element of your positioning will be trying to identify what it is that your firm offers that others do not. This may be expertise in a particular area, it may be your accessibility, it may be your client care philosophy, it may be innovative use of IT (for example providing internet delivery) or the degree of integration with other legal and financial services. Unless a 'cost leadership' strategy is being pursued, a suitable differentiation strategy must be identified.

If it is not possible to differentiate your firm across the whole market, then a particular niche in the market must be identified and selected. For example, a suitable 'segment' might be accounting firms over a certain size with no tax planning capabilities, or agricultural estates.

It is important that your strategy takes a slightly longer-term view as well. Use the positioning stage to identify where you want your wills and probate practice to be in, say, three or four years' time.

20.5.2   Balance of effort between targeting existing or new clients

Once your desired position in the market is agreed, you then need to decide to what extent you are focusing on developing existing clients and referrers compared to the development of new business. Long-established firms will probably devote more effort to developing and extending existing relationships, whereas newer or smaller firms are more likely to focus on winning new clients.

Case study: Boodle Hatfield client relationships development

We work very hard at nurturing the relationship with the clients themselves to ensure that they stay loyal and hopefully recommend others. Enthusiastic clients are a great way of obtaining opportunities with others in their social group. Of course, the most important thing is to provide proactive and high-quality legal advice, but it is also important to deliver this through a lawyer with whom the client builds empathy over a period of time. We try to match the personality of our lawyers to a family as well as their legal skills, we also introduce lawyers to the younger generations so that they start to build their own relationships. We encourage the lawyers to visit the families in their own homes if appropriate. We also maintain regular contact with our clients through newsletters, newsflashes and client entertainment. We have just held a large party at the Wallace Collection for clients and intermediaries, and we also invite small groups of people to cultural events such as Garsington, the London Handel Singing Competition or the theatre.

20.5.3   Direct or indirect approach

As discussed above, another key decision is the extent to which the firm will seek to market to individuals with wills, trusts and probate needs, compared to an approach through intermediaries. Most probate practices will concentrate on targeting accountants, charities, care organisations and such like for referral work. When marketing wills, however, it is more likely that the individuals themselves will be approached. It is likely, therefore, that different strategies and marketing campaigns will be appropriate, depending on the specific needs and services being promoted.

Case study: Boodle Hatfield and referral management

The most valuable source of referrals tends to be from intermediaries and we have developed a shortlist of key intermediaries with whom we work regularly. This has been carefully researched to identify firms who have the same

365

approach to clients as we do and with whom we can build a good working relationship on mutual client activity. We try to refer work to them whenever we can and hope to receive referrals from them as well! We have get-togethers to share technical knowledge – from the occasional meeting to a regular legal clinic that we hold for some private client bankers. This helps the bankers to get to know our lawyers – their personal style and technical skills, so they can choose an appropriate lawyer for the client if asked for a recommendation. We also regularly socialise with them, both at events organised by ourselves and at industry events. An increasingly significant part of our business is the contentious trust/probate market. These large cases are often international, always extremely complex and usually involve several firms of lawyers from different jurisdictions. The referral network is strong, and lawyers tend to recommend lawyers with whom they have worked well in the past. Marketing in this area is therefore primarily relationship building. During a case it is important to build a rapport and to introduce younger members of the team as much as possible to deepen the relationship. Once the matter is over, it is important to keep in touch through visits, e-mails and newsletters – and sometimes a gentle reminder that another firm 'owes' you a referral doesn't do any harm! The relationship activity should be backed up by PR activity so that the firm's brand in the international arena is strong, the right directory listings are obtained, and the lawyers attend the type of conferences where international intermediaries gather.

20.5.4 Packaging the product and the people

An integral part of deciding strategy and positioning will be agreeing what it is the firm is selling in the market. Some firms have differentiated the services of their wills and probate team by packaging together a range of services such as wills, living wills, enduring powers of attorney and advice on financing long-term care either in an 'elderly citizens' package or as a 'families with ageing relatives' package. Some firms 'package in' tax, financial, trust and conveyancing services in different combinations to suit the particular needs of slightly different audiences.

The actual legal 'product' is similar in all such packages: what differs is the particular needs of the particular target audience being addressed and the emphasis. The packaging can shift the emphasis away from things people are reluctant to consider (the lack of a will when they die) to more positive issues, such as financing the education of any grandchildren. Another approach might be to package the way the advice is offered or delivered. For example, there are some highly innovative websites which offer a fixed price procedure for straightforward grants of probate in low value estates or will drafting.

Case study: Web-based services at Kaye Tesler

We are targeting those in the 35–50 year age group whose parents or elderly relatives have smaller estates – there is rarely any inheritance tax. They don't want advice – they know how to gather and distribute the estate – they want a finished product in applying for the relevant grant. The interactive website makes them read through some explanatory material and prompts them for the information we require. This information then goes direct into our computer system so the relevant forms and documentation are produced. We state the relevant warnings and disclaimers for those with more complicated needs. Our site has generated enquiries and probate work. More surprisingly, it has generated a lot of enquiries from the United States (which of course we cannot service). However, the USA is a little ahead of the UK in terms of internet use so we will be ready when the UK catches up. Technology means we can provide an efficient, interactive service that meets the specific needs of our target clients. The internet environment means that the small firms like mine are on an even playing field with the largest firms in the country.

In addition to packaging what the firm is actually offering, you need to consider the way in which the advice is delivered and this involves taking a long and hard look at everyone (lawyers, paralegals, secretaries and switchboard staff) involved in client communications for wills and probate services. Ensuring that everyone becomes a valued and integral part of the service promise will require training, communication and involvement in the marketing, planning and implementation process, so if you have not involved them in the process so far, do so now. This can be achieved through team meetings, where you explain what you are trying to achieve and ask those present to discuss the barriers they perceive to those goals and the help they will require in delivering the promise. An alternative approach would be to appoint people to specialist roles, such as handling telephone enquiries, explaining the service, or first meeting management.

20.5.5 Pricing

If they perceive no other differences in what is being offered by different suppliers, clients will choose on price alone. Therefore, if there is no perceived difference in the will writing or probate service offered by your firm or any other provider, price will dominate the decision. A key element of marketing is to move clients away from thinking about the price to thinking about the benefits of the service and other factors, such as speed, accessibility, ease of use, friendliness, personal service, etc. This is called differentiation.

The price must equate to the value of the service as perceived by clients. They are not interested in the cost of providing that service (i.e. the time taken to produce a perfect document). Therefore, price must be considered in both strategic terms (what are my broad hourly or fixed fee rates and what level of profitability does the firm wish to achieve?) and in tactical terms (how much for this particular piece of work?). Some firms are becoming more creative in pricing, moving away from hourly rates to fixed price deals, value billing, retainer arrangements or shared risk arrangements and bonus arrangements. This gives clients the benefit of certainty.

Case study: Pricing at Thomson Snell & Passmore

We are moving towards a fixed price approach for probate work – we usually indicate a fixed fee and indicate those elements that may require an additional time-based fee. This is around 1% plus a time element which is still less than the banks who might charge at 3–4% overall.

For those operating at the lower end of the market, attention must be paid to the pricing strategies of the online providers as these will shape client expectations. At the time of writing, a quick search reveals the following: **www.tenminutewill.co.uk** offers a will for £29.95 and an enduring power of attorney for £27.95 (£39.95 for a pair); **www.lawpack.co.uk** appeals to business owners with a will for £14.99; **www.doityourselfwills.co.uk** offers a will at £9.95. Increasingly, banks and charities are offering wills free of charge, as a loss leader, in order to gain loyalty and custom in other areas.

20.5.6 Promotion and internal marketing

The objectives, analyses and strategies should reveal where the firm's marketing efforts are to be focused and should have indicated the types of marketing tool that will be most effective in achieving them. The following section identifies some of the key issues to consider when planning to use some of the most common marketing tools.

20.5.7 Advertising

Advertising is where a media owner (e.g. a directory, a newspaper, a magazine, a radio station, a poster site operator, a TV channel) is paid to reproduce your message exactly as you require. There are two elements to the cost: the cost of designing and producing the advert, and the cost of the media space.

Advertising is a tool to get a simple message to a large audience that is perhaps difficult to reach by other means. It is generally more suited to winning legal aid or private client work. Common places where probate practitioners advertise for private client work include telephone directories, local newspapers and poster sites near advice centres. There are a growing number of magazines targeted at the older generation and some firms place adverts in magazines produced by charities or other advisers. There are over 1,400 trade and technical journals which are targeted at specific business, professional or trade audiences. For example, there are magazines aimed at accountants, independent financial advisers, funeral directors, nursing home staff and those who care for the elderly.

One-off adverts are rarely effective, so if advertising is the chosen tool, it will be important to make sure that adverts will appear on more than one occasion over a suitable period of time as part of a campaign. You must be clear on the following points before any advertising is attempted:

- Who is my target audience and what media will reach them efficiently?
- What key message am I trying to convey?
  - Is it simple and clear?
  - Does it focus on a specific need and mention benefits?
  - Is it sufficiently different from other solicitors' advertisements?
- What action does it prompt the reader/viewer to take?

With all marketing activities, be sure that the firm can respond to any enquiries that are generated (have switchboard and reception staff been briefed?) and that the response to the advert can be measured to assess its effectiveness.

Most solicitors focus on display adverts. Other types to explore include: inserts in printed media; messages on appointment cards; posters; give-aways; leaflets in counter top dispensers; door-to-door leaflets; cable television (considerably cheaper than national or terrestrial television and much more focused on particular areas or audiences); local radio and the promotional materials of non-competing organisations targeting the same audience. The internet is another important advertising medium – specialists can advise you on how to get your website to the top of search engine enquiries or how to use online advertisements to drive traffic to your website.

Case study: Advertising at Forshaws

We have also embarked on advertising through a TV concept at a local gym. Advertisements are played at regular intervals throughout the day on television screens in front of cardio exercising equipment. On the basis that there is not much else you can do when exercising apart from listen to music or watch the screens provided, we are hoping that the 'captive audience' will produce positive results.

20.5.8 Direct mail

Direct mail is a cost-effective method of reaching commercial clients and referring organisations. The starting point is some form of database which contains, as well as the name of the individual, their position, the name of the organisation, its address, telephone number and e-mail address. Other useful information would be specific areas of interest (e.g. tax advice), other relationships or services used within the firm, a list of past contacts and any other information that helps with analysis and segmentation. There are many mailing lists that can be purchased or hired from organisations which specialise in list development or from those, such as magazine owners, who make their lists of subscribers commercially available.

Short, simple letters or e-mails following the AIDA rule (Attention, Interest, Desire and Action) are effective, especially when the follow-up action is low commitment (e.g. sending in for an information pack, requesting a copy of a helpful checklist or visiting a website) rather than high commitment (e.g. attending a meeting). A covering letter will increase the chances of any brochure or newsletters being read. It may be helpful to facilitate an easy response by providing reply-paid envelopes, freephone telephone numbers or pro forma fax sheets. Most firms have websites with further information – and sections that are tailored to particular issues or campaigns – and some have invested in setting up modest call centres to manage enquiries.

Be creative in thinking what might be sent to people that will be of value – items should be focused on specific messages or issues. Copies of articles or of speeches delivered by partners in the firm, feedback or testimonials from clients facing similar situations, invitations to informal briefings or receptions, notification of books or speeches in preparation, could all be used. Although there has been a tendency for law firms to produce high quality, glossy promotional materials, direct mail will work just as well (sometimes even better) if the materials are produced smartly and inexpensively in-house. Such items can often feel more immediate and personal than their glossy counterparts. They can also be tailored to specific needs, topical issues or special audiences with ease.

Direct mail can be used to communicate on a regular basis with existing clients and referrers as well, helping to build relationships, provide added-value service and keep your firm's name 'front of mind'. This is particularly cost-effective and easy to do if an e-mail alert system is employed.

Case study: Educational video at Sugdens

Kevin Ludgate, a partner at Sugdens solicitors in Huddersfield, produced a short video called 'Making a Will – Explained' which comes complete with a glossary which explains terms such as executor, intestate, residue, trust and witness in the video case cover. He also produced a short colour flier that he mailed out to promote the video. The video is rated 18 with an explanatory statement saying 'Essential viewing for all adults in England and Wales!'. The video explains very simply why you need a will and the likely contents through some realistic examples – a young couple, a middle-aged couple and an older single woman. The feedback he received was excellent and he provides the leaflets and video to intermediaries, building societies, accountants and the like. Kevin's rationale for this exercise was that he had found from research that although people were interested in learning more about wills, they were rather put off by the prospect of meeting a solicitor and the possible cost that might be incurred. A video that they could watch in their own homes at their leisure would overcome both potential problems. He also considers that if a potential client spends 30 minutes watching a video – rather than asking him questions for an hour on general background and common issues – it will make his life easier too: a win-win situation.

20.5.9 Public relations (including media relations)

'Public relations' is a broad term which covers a whole range of activities involving the firm in two-way communications with the various publics it serves. Relevant publics for probate practitioners might include existing wills/probate clients, other clients of the firm, potential clients, local referrers, the local media, existing staff, potential staff, the legal profession and government officials.

Media relations

This is one of the most useful tools for probate practitioners, i.e. communications with the printed and broadcast media. Timely press releases about topical issues, offering the expert views of the firm's tax, probate or private client experts, short articles providing practical advice, articles containing checklists to help readers assess their situation and 'legal problem pages' are all inexpensive (but time intensive) ways of getting your message across. If you regularly scan the main newspapers you can be ready to provide comments and advice when a high profile will or probate case hits the headlines. However, unlike in advertising, the editor will always have the final say on what items are used and the manner in which the material is used, so you have much less control. Unless you have some experience of dealing with the media it is often useful to employ the services of someone who does – freelance press officers can be used on an occasional basis and their rates are often very reasonable. It should be possible to find a public relations officer with good knowledge of and contacts within the media you have targeted. Sue Stapely's book *Media Relations for Lawyers*, 2nd edn (Law Society, 2003) is an excellent introduction.

Case study: Boodle Hatfield and media relations

Public relations is an important part of our marketing. Our partners speak regularly on key conference platforms, we write articles in technical journals in the UK and those aimed at offshore intermediaries, and also write less technical articles in the type of 'lifestyle' magazines which are read by our clients.

Publications

Typical publications might include a firm brochure, a private client brochure or leaflets describing the services offered by the wills/probate team. Again, the key words here are 'focus' and 'benefits'. Too many solicitors' publications focus on 'we' the firm rather than 'you' the client and contain features rather than benefits. Truly client-facing publications will be written from the clients' point of view (e.g. problems, needs, questions, concerns, issues, etc.) rather than the firm's point of view (location, departments, services, etc.). Newsletters will serve a number of purposes. Whether they are general and aimed at of the firm's clients, or focused on the needs of particular groups (such as private clients, elderly clients, professional carers, etc.), they will:

- alert readers to changes in the law;
- educate them on possible needs they might have;
- provide simple advice so that they can help themselves;
- explain difficult legal issues in simple terms;
- remind them that the firm is proactive and able to assist;
- cross-sell services of the firm; and
- secure the loyalty and memory of existing or dormant clients.

Events

Events which target existing or potential clients or referrers would also fall under the public relations umbrella. Some firms take exhibition or stand space at local county or town shows – an opportunity to meet, face-to-face, local people who might be clients or potential clients. Stands at trade exhibitions (e.g. for professional careers or home operators) can also be useful if targeted properly.

Speakers

The firm might be able to provide 'expert' speakers to address the audiences of local business, trade or social groups. Organisations such as the Institute of Directors, the Chambers of Commerce and Business Links are often heavily targeted by other solicitors, so seek out more unusual organisations. Similarly, representatives of the firm could be sent to network at these events, the aim being both to develop contacts that might generate or refer business in the future and also to gather vital information or market intelligence about local needs and competitors and to ensure that the firm's name appears regularly at local events.

Seminars

Seminars are covered separately below.

20.5.10 Internal marketing

This area of public relations – communicating with those within the firm – is vitally important to will and probate practitioners because other members of the firm will be an important source of referrals for your department and because sometimes you may be targeting similar audiences to others in the firm. In smaller firms it is easier to talk informally to the partners, assistants, trainees and secretaries within other departments without having to arrange special meetings or prepare lists of the services provided, the clients served and ways in which you can help each other develop business.

Internal marketing is important because limited resources will be available within the wills and probate team. However, the marketing and communication load can be significantly spread if all members of the firm understand what the team is offering, to whom, the relative benefits and how to 'pass across' clients or referrers who have the sorts of questions or problems with which the probate and wills team can help.

Case study: Internal marketing at Rix & Kay

Internal marketing is important too. All departments are aware of the need to cross-sell the firm's services and do, especially the family and commercial teams. The directors of our commercial clients are keen to make wills and look at ways to save tax. We are proactive too – with these clients we talk about succession planning and confirm that they have arrangements in place in case circumstances relating to their family or children change.

Case study: Internal marketing and cross-selling at Forshaws

Although we have dipped our toes into the marketing foray in the past by advertising and the publication of articles, we have found that the response rate has been low. For the first time, we are now putting in place an active marketing strategy and exploring marketing ideas. Initially, we have decided that we will focus on cross-selling within the practice on the basis that we already have a strong client base from which to take advantage. We feel that this is particularly so in the case of the Conveyancing and Matrimonial Departments. In these increasingly litigious days, our Wills and Probate Department now also regularly works in conjunction with the Litigation Department. Work relating to contentious probate matters and family provision claims, grants of representation required in connection with compensation claims arising out of fatal accidents and trusts in relation to personal injury awards is referred between the two Departments.

Case study: Internal marketing at Thomson Snell & Passmore

Internal marketing and communications are important to us to support recommendations from staff. We hold monthly 'Getting to know you' sessions where teams from different departments present an overview of their services, work and clients to others in the firm. We have found that the stronger the personal relationships between people in our department and others in the firm, the more referrals we get. It is also true that probate work tends to follow through from wills and tax planning work – so we support each other and make our efforts as integrated as we can. We have also worked closely with our commercial teams to identify the directors at large organisations who might be interested in our private client services. Our buddy system encourages lawyers to get together to talk about each others' clients and identify the possible need for their respective expertise.

20.5.11   Organising events and networking

Organising events can take a huge amount of time and preparation. Support staff will need to assist with preparing invitation lists, monitoring the response and the myriad of logistical arrangements (e.g. room preparations, catering, cloakrooms, handouts, audio-visual materials, etc.). At the most informal level, a selection of clients, potential clients or referrers could be invited to your office for lunch or a glass of wine. This provides them with an opportunity to network with other people. However, people may be often invited to 'plain' cocktail parties and receptions, so it will help considerably if there is something that will make your event different, for example, an external guest of honour or by giving the event a theme. Better still, provide a business rationale for the event: so, for example, invite a group of staff involved in residential and nursing homes to an informal round table discussion where issues of common concern (with a legal flavour but not entirely legally focused) can be discussed.

The events taking most effort are those where your legal expertise is being presented or showcased – for example, a briefing for small firms of accountants on IHT planning, or a seminar for high net worth people on the impact of the Chancellor's annual budget. It is often better with high net worth clients to package any wills, tax and probate topics with other private client topics such as property transactions, overseas investment funds, and so on. Inviting external speakers to these events will both increase the attractiveness to your invitees and reduce the burden on your staff of preparing materials.

Case study: Seminars at Rix & Kay

Seminars, or rather open evenings, have worked very well for us. We had an article in the *Sussex Express* newspaper and got all 25 of our seminar attendees that way. We held it at the end of the day and ran it in conjunction with an IFA. We always generate work from seminars as people are always keen to save tax. We have also operated seminars with IFAs where we bring 12 or so of our clients and contacts and they bring the same.

Networking can be used to achieve a number of purposes and can be done at your own and other people's events. For example, you can raise the profile of your firm in the local business community or amongst a particular audience (e.g. local social services people or local GPs). You can effect introductions and start to establish personal relationships with referrers or potential clients. Networking may also be used to help develop your understanding of the needs, interests and motivations of your target audience.

Talking to people (and listening carefully to what they say) is one of the best ways to gather market intelligence. Regular attendance at a particular organisation's meetings or events will increase your chances of being recognised and establishing ongoing contacts. Offering to present topical subjects or to explain complicated legal issues with a wide appeal in a simple way and being seen on speaker's platforms will help to raise your profile. People at the events will then feel a little easier about approaching you.

Case study: Theatre sponsorship

A small practice in the West Country places a range of inexpensively produced but attractive leaflets on all its services in dispensers at a local theatre. A wills leaflet states that it has members of the Society of Trust and Estate Practitioners and that it also offers an investment management service. This is an example of integrated marketing, where the firm's sponsorship of a popular local arts venue provides: (a) an excellent opportunity to entertain clients and intermediaries in a location where there is a clear link to the firm; (b) publicity and awareness raising from the strong branding in the signage supporting the sponsorship; (c) advertisements in event programmes; and (d) marketing materials on display in a location where they know members of their target audience – better off people of a slightly older generation – will see and read them.

20.5.12   Presentations

After establishing contact (or, indeed, having created an opportunity to establish contact), a short presentation about a topical issue alongside some information about the credentials and experience of your firm, your team and your services will ensure that the relevant information is conveyed efficiently and accurately. Yet not everyone is comfortable making presentations and some lawyers have little experience in public speaking. It is helpful to prepare audio-visual materials (whether these be pre-written sheets to talk against, overhead projector slides or CD or web-based presentations) to guide the speaker and provide additional interest for the audience. Advance planning and rehearsals are vitally important if a poor quality presentation is not to undermine your professional skills. Summaries of talks should always be distributed, with your name, the firm's name and contact details marked discreetly but clearly on each separate sheet.

20.6   DEVELOPING AND IMPLEMENTING YOUR PLAN

20.6.1   Developing a marketing and action plan

A marketing plan will be needed in order to draw together the results of your analysis, objective setting, strategy development and consideration of the various marketing tools available. A typical marketing plan would address the following issues:

1. Introduction
2. Where are we now? An analysis of the current situation

    •   External analysis – general trends, competition, local market
    •   Internal analysis – fees, clients, sources of work, services, skills, people
    •   Summary of critical issues to address

3. Where do we want to be? Our goals

    •   The firm's goals – financial, clients, work, reputation
    •   The probate, trusts and wills teams goals – short, medium and long term
    •   How we will monitor and measure effectiveness

4. How will we get there? Our overall strategy

    •   How we will organise and resource our marketing and business development effort
    •   Additional research and preparation required (e.g. development of database)
    •   Product – legal expertise, service delivery, relationships and brand
    •   People – recruitment, training, communications, work process, service standards
    •   Place – market segmentation, target markets, referrers/clients
    •   Price – charging methods and payment plans
    •   Promotion – choice of public relations, direct marketing and other tools in appropriate campaigns

5. Budgets and action plan (see below)

Case study: Marketing planning at Rix & Kay

The major challenge for us is prioritisation. We have lots of ideas about what we could do to generate interest in different areas from the various markets. We are also very conscious of the need to match the different lawyers to the various markets and to their preferred style of marketing. There is a firm-wide marketing plan and it is adaptable to the different areas of work – some elements are highly relevant to the wills, trust and probate team and others less so. We recognise that we have only limited time for marketing so we need to spend time considering the different opportunities so that we focus our efforts accordingly. Developing a marketing plan for the WTP team is the process that will enable us to do this.

The next stage is to prepare a short, clear, task-orientated action plan, assigning the names of the responsible individuals and the target dates by which the tasks will be completed. The action plan will achieve a number of things:

- ensure that those activities which will help to achieve the objectives are selected;
- ensure priorities are assigned to those actions;
- ensure that you are realistic about what can be achieved with the human and financial resources available;
- communicate to everyone in the probate team (and in the wider firm) exactly what is planned and their role and responsibilities; and
- help you to monitor progress.

An example of a suitable action plan for a solicitor in a probate department is shown below:

Week	Month	Activity
1	January	Analyse past information about sources of work
1	January	Analyse past information about nature/types of client
2	January	Talk to 10 intermediaries to ask them for their views on the services provided by the team
3	January	Attend two meetings with other private client practice groups in the firm to identify ways in which joint marketing can be conducted
1	February	Research a list of 30 local financial advisers
2	February	Research a list of the 20 nearest small accounting firms
3	February	Attend a meeting of the corporate and commercial group to identify 10 high net worth directors who may be interested in estate planning
4	February	Identify the main local business and consumer media and read some back copies to identify opportunities for placing articles
1	March	Prepare a checklist of the sorts of legal questions most likely to be asked by elderly clients/nursing home residents and their families
2	March	Prepare a short article for the local hospital about the issues surrounding relatives and enduring powers of attorney
3	March	Visit the three main referrers of past work
3	March	Identify two local organisations which should be targeted for networking

377

20.6.2 Agreeing a budget

The main cost in marketing probate services will be the time of the solicitors involved in the marketing. Firms often budget out-of-pocket marketing expenditure very carefully but fail to think about how much time will be used and whether sufficient return on that time investment will be achieved. Many great marketing plans never deliver the desired results because the lawyers are simply too busy to devote sufficient time to implementing them.

Therefore, the budget should be prepared in two parts. The first is the out-of-pocket expenditure and should cover items such as advertising (especially directory entries), postage for mailings, catering for events, website design, membership and attendance of local events, entertaining people at lunches and dinners, the production of marketing materials such as leaflets and presentation aids (although many of these can be produced in-house at no cost by using advanced word processing or desktop publishing facilities) and sponsorship. As a rule of thumb, professional firms should spend around 2 per cent of their gross annual fee income on marketing and business development. Consider the overall fee income of the probate team and think about what proportion of that should be spent on marketing. Remember that if little or no marketing has been done in the past, slightly more cash might be needed in the first year than in subsequent years.

The second and more important part of your budget is agreeing how much time each solicitor and support person will spend on marketing each week or each month. The action list, having broken down the various marketing activities into their component tasks, might help with estimating. Alternatively, a specific amount of time each week or month can be allocated for each fee earner to spend on marketing and selling. It may be necessary to adjust the time recording system to capture and report on non-chargeable time spent on marketing. One of the main reasons why solicitors (particularly non-partners) do not invest time in marketing is because they feel that they only receive recognition and reward for chargeable time.

Case study: Boodle Hatfield organising for marketing

Marketing private client services is hard work. The most effective activity is relationship building with carefully targeted people, and that has to be done by the lawyers themselves. Their marketing teams have an important role to play in identifying the right targets, organising the right events and ensuring everything is carefully recorded in a good CRM system.

20.6.3 Monitoring results

After an initial burst of enthusiasm, the marketing initiatives of many law firms flounder and fade away. This is often because there are no mechanisms for:

- monitoring what is happening (and taking action to ensure that it does happen); and
- feeding back results and success stories to keep motivation high.

Two parts of your marketing need to be monitored: the process and the results. In the early days there may be few results, and it is likely to take a few months before any results materialise. The action plan can be used to tick off what actions have been completed. The amount of non-chargeable time being spent by various solicitors on marketing activities can be reviewed. A record should be kept of how many events are attended, how many mailings are issued, how many press releases or articles are produced, and so on.

Monitoring the results may require some changes to the firm's internal systems. It will be useful to be able to monitor additional work from existing clients or referrers and to pinpoint enquiries and work as a direct result of each marketing activity. Logging calls, enquiries, meetings, instructions, income or the amount of press coverage are all valid ways to measure the success of marketing. Most websites now have the ability to monitor how many visitors there have been to the site, the number of enquiries generated and the number of subscribers to e-mail alert or newsletter lists.

However, at the end of the day the only true measure will be whether the marketing activity delivers the objectives which were set at the beginning of the planning process. That is why it is so important that time is spent ensuring that the objectives are clear and measurable at the outset.

Anti-Money Laundering Guidance for Solicitors Conducting Private Client Work[1]

INTRODUCTION

1. This work draws heavily on work already published by the Law Society to help solicitors comply with the UK's anti money laundering regime, which is available from **www.lawsociety.org.uk**, or from Professional Ethics: 0870 606 2577. Family lawyers will have a particular interest in the guidance on *Bowman* v. *Fels* [2005] EWCA Civ 225, which is referred to below.

2. Private client work which involves learning about, or dealing with, a client's assets can lead a solicitor to form knowledge or suspicion, or gives rise to reasonable grounds for suspicion, of money laundering. However, whether a money laundering report is required in any individual situation will require a detailed examination of the relevant criminal offences within Part 7 of POCA as most recently interpreted by the case of *Bowman* v. *Fels*. Full guidance on *Bowman* v. *Fels* [2005] EWCA Civ 226 is available, and solicitors conducting private client work should carefully consider their approach in the light of this judgment.

3. Solicitors could be at risk of money laundering if their work involves assisting with the management or distribution of assets which include suspected 'criminal property', whether they take a principal role themselves or act for others, e.g. trust work, administration of estates, Powers of Attorney, Court of Protection work, or wealth management. Such work can risk commission of a principal money laundering offence under sections 327–329 of POCA, see paragraphs 2.13–2.18 of the Law Society's Money Laundering Guidance – pilot January 2004 – ('the Guidance') available from **www.lawsociety.org.uk**. However, a defence may be available if a report is made to the National Criminal Intelligence Service ('NCIS'), or after 1 April to the Serious and Organised Crime Agency ('SOCA'), and if relevant, 'appropriate consent' is obtained or can be deemed through lapse of time, see paragraph 2.23–2.27 of the Guidance. However, because of the judgment in *Bowman* v. *Fels*, before a solicitor reports to NCIS/SOCA a key consideration will be whether their knowledge or suspicion of money laundering is based on information received in legally professionally privileged circumstances.

4. If a solicitor takes a principal role in a matter, for example by acting as an executor or trustee, it may mean that there are fewer alternative ways to deal with a money laundering situation than when acting for others, e.g. termination of the retainer may not be possible.

5. Solicitors undertaking private client work should remain alert to the warning signs outlined in chapter 6 of the Guidance. For example, private client instructions which fall outside a solicitor's expertise need careful consideration, see paragraph 6.16–6.19 of the Guidance. Solicitors may benefit from discussing the

---

[1] © Law Society, 23 February 2006.

issues with Professional Ethics before accepting instructions, or at a later stage if reasons for suspicion emerge: Tel 0870 606 2577.

MONEY LAUNDERING REGULATIONS 2003

6. Whenever a solicitor is conducting any 'relevant business' for a client, they will need to comply with the Money Laundering Regulations 2003, see paragraph 3.6–3.15 of the Guidance. Suggested identification methods for individuals, estates, and trusts are also covered in chapter 3 of the Guidance.
7. Although will writing is not 'relevant business' for the purposes of the Money Laundering Regulations 2003 as no trust exists until death, ancillary services provided by solicitors when drafting wills may be 'relevant business'. For example, tax advice is covered by the definition of relevant business in Regulation 2(2)(i). Similarly trust services are covered in Regulation 2(2)(m), see paragraph 3.12 of the Guidance, and administration of estates is likely to fall within the meaning of 'financial transaction' within Regulation 2(2)(l), see paragraph 3.9 of the Guidance. However, obtaining a Grant of Probate may fall outside the definitions.

NOTE:

Whether or not work being undertaken is covered by the Money Laundering Regulations 2003 solicitors should take a risk based approach when considering what anti money laundering procedures they wish to implement, bearing in mind the level of money laundering risk posed by the nature of the work they are being asked to undertake. When taking clients' instructions it may already be necessary, or at least helpful, to obtain information about the purpose of those instructions, e.g. the reason for forming or winding up a trust, or for the execution of a Power of Attorney. Aside from providing clients with the best possible service, assessing the information provided, and if appropriate asking more questions, may help resolve any money laundering concerns. Making careful notes of questions posed and answers received may assist if a solicitor's conduct is questioned later.

RISK AREAS

Administration of estates

8. Administration of estates is likely to fall within the definition of 'financial transaction' within Regulation 2(2)(l), (see paragraph 3.9–3.12 of the Guidance). Therefore, as well as being aware of the principal offences, see paragraphs 2.13–2.31 of the Guidance, solicitors need to be aware of the section 330 failure to report (regulated sector) offence; see paragraphs 2.40–2.43 of the Guidance.
9. When a solicitor is either acting as executor, or for executors, there is no blanket requirement that a solicitor should be satisfied as to the provenance of all of the funds which form a part of the estate they are administering. However, solicitors should be alive to factors which can increase the money laundering risk of the work they are undertaking and act accordingly, see chapter 6 of the Guidance. For example, where estate assets have been earned in a foreign jurisdiction, solicitors should be aware of the wide definition of 'criminal conduct' in section 340(2)(b), namely the provision in POCA relating to overseas criminal conduct, see paragraph 2.7 (Also, see footnote). Suspect territories in particular should prompt solicitors to make more checks, see paragraphs 6.31–6.34 of the Guidance.

NOTE:

It does not matter when the underlying criminal offence occurred as the definition of 'criminal conduct' in s.340(2) has unlimited retrospective effect.

10. The wide nature of the offence of 'acquisition, use and possession' in section 329 offence of POCA may lead to a money laundering offence being committed at an early point in the administration. The section 328 arrangements offence may also be relevant. This is one reason why solicitors need to be alert from the outset, and throughout, so that any reporting can be considered as soon as knowledge or suspicion is formed to avoid problems with delayed appropriate consent, see paragraph 2.26 of the Guidance. However, a key advantage achieved by the *Bowman* v. *Fels* judgment is that a solicitor who makes a report is able to continue work on the matter short of transferring funds or taking some other irrevocable step.

11. An extreme example of when administration of an estate may constitute a money laundering offence would be where a solicitor dealing with administration knows or suspects that the deceased was accused or convicted of acquisitive criminal conduct during their lifetime, perhaps because their firm acted in the relevant criminal litigation.

12. Where a solicitor forms knowledge or suspicion that the deceased improperly claimed welfare benefits during their lifetime, for example because the capital of the deceased took them over the financial threshold for the relevant benefit they claimed, there will be 'criminal property' included in the estate, and so usually a money laundering report may be required. More information on the financial thresholds for benefits can be obtained from **www.dwp.gov.uk**, However, a practical solution to consider in these circumstances is whether any outstanding liability to the Department of Work and Pensions can be repaid prior to collation of the assets or administration, as this may rid the estate of any 'criminal property' and so avoid the risk of committing a money laundering offence by administering the estate. The extent of the liability should be established from the Department of Work and Pensions.

NOTE:

The definition of 'criminal property' in section 340(3)(a) does not have a financial minimum which applies to solicitors. Any proceeds of criminal conduct, including deemed proceeds from obtaining a pecuniary advantage, may be defined as criminal property, however small the amount.

14. It may be helpful to consider the general warning signs for money laundering in chapter 6 of the Guidance if there is concern about beneficiaries. In high risk circumstances, such as terrorism, solicitors may wish to refer to the Bank of England consolidated sanctions list, see paragraph 2.36 of the Guidance and **www.bankofengland.co.uk**.

15. Whilst administering an estate a solicitor may form knowledge or suspicion that beneficiaries are not intending to pay the correct amount of tax, or are avoiding some other financial penalty, e.g. creditors, or the Assets Recovery Agency. For example, beneficiaries may be reluctant to disclose gifts they have received from the deceased less than seven years before death. Dependent on the circumstances these types of matters may not in fact constitute money laundering because no criminal conduct has yet occurred, and therefore there is no 'criminal property', but a solicitor should carefully consider their position in conduct terms under Principle 12.02 because they may be in breach of the law or Professional Conduct rules. Further help can be obtained from Professional Ethics: 0870 606 2577.

GRANT OF PROBATE

16. Simply obtaining a grant of probate may not fall within the definition of 'financial transaction' in Regulation 2(2)(l), see paragraph 3.9–3.12.

Deceased non-UK domiciled persons

17. A UK grant of probate may be required before UK assets can be released, whilst for overseas assets the relevant local laws will apply. Solicitors should remain alert to money laundering warning signs, e.g. where the deceased or their business interests are based in a suspect territory. Information about non cooperative territories is available from **www.fatf-gafi.org**, and information about countries where corruption/bribery is a problem is available from **www.transparency.org**. In appropriate circumstances it may be helpful to ask the lawyer dealing with the matter in the home country for information about the deceased to gain some reasonable assurances that there are no suspicious circumstances surrounding the provenance of their estate. The issue of the tax payable on the estate may depend upon the relevant jurisdiction, see paragraph 14 above regarding the future potential tax evasion.

Trusts

18. Trust work is covered by Regulation 2(2)(m). Guidance on possible methods of identification is given at paragraphs 3.104–3.107 of the Guidance.
19. Although trusts are most commonly used for legitimate reasons, they can also be used as money laundering vehicles. Discretionary trusts and complex offshore trusts are most vulnerable to money laundering. When setting up trusts, solicitors should remain alive to the warning signs of money laundering, and consider whether the purpose of the trust could be money laundering. Information about the purpose of the trust, including why any unusual structure or jurisdiction has been used, can help allay concerns. Similarly information about the provider of the funds, and those who have control over the funds, may also assist, see *Re: the Esteem settlement, Grupo Torras SA* v. *Al-Sabah* [2004] WTLR 1.
20. Whether solicitors act as trustees themselves, or for trustees, the nature of work may already require information which will assist in assessing money laundering risk, e.g. location of assets, identity of trustees, see paragraph 3.105 of the Guidance. Again, any involvement of suspect jurisdictions, especially those with strict bank secrecy and confidentiality rules, or in jurisdictions without equivalent money laundering procedures, may mean that further enquiries are helpful, see paragraphs 6.31–6.34 of the Guidance.
21. Solicitors may form knowledge or suspicion of money laundering in relation to money or property which either already forms a part of trust property, or is intended to do so. Such knowledge or suspicion may arise from information about the circumstances of historic events, e.g. where there has been a sale of a property overseas and tax was not paid on that sale. In these circumstances solicitors should consider whether their instructions may involve them in a section 328 arrangement offence, and if so what options are open to them in accordance with the *Bowman* v. *Fels* guidance.

Charities

22. Whether the Money Laundering Regulations 2003 apply to work undertaken for charities depends upon whether 'relevant business' is being undertaken, see

chapter 3. Where the work will constitute 'relevant business' the charity will need to be identified, see paragraphs 3.9–3.15. Identification will need to be to an objective and subjective standard, see paragraph 3.28 of the Guidance. In cases where a charity is not the solicitor's client, but is involved in some way in the solicitor's instructions, the solicitor may still wish to make some checks.

NOTE:

The Charity Commission provides some information about registered charities in England and Wales, **www.charity-commission.gov.uk** or tel: 0870 333 0123, The information available includes the charities' objects, contact details, the names of its trustees, its broad areas of activity as well as overall financial information including when annual returns have been filed and accounts. Charities which are household names may pose a lower risk. However, not all charities in England and Wales are required to register, or the charity may be based in a country which does not have a registration system. Solicitors may make enquiries about the level of regulation in the host country, or seek advice from Professional Ethics.

23. In common with trusts, whilst the majority of charities are used for legitimate reasons, they can also be used as money laundering/terrorist financing vehicles. Solicitors who act for charities may need to consider the purpose of the charity itself. Remaining alert to the warning signs of money laundering may assist with this, see Chapter 6. An extreme example of the misuse of charities may be terrorist purposes, and where there is concern, reference should be made to the Bank of England terrorist lists see paragraph 14 above.

24. Where a solicitor is acting for a charity and is due to receive money on their behalf from an individual or company donor, the solicitor needs to be alert to unusual circumstances including significant sums. Where the charity is due to receive a bequest from an estate similar considerations apply.

Powers of Attorney/Receivership

25. Execution of a Power of Attorney for clients does not itself constitute a 'financial transaction' for the purposes of Regulations 2(2)(l), see paragraph 3.9 of the Guidance. However, a solicitor acting for an attorney, or as an attorney themselves, is likely to be undertaking 'relevant business'. Similarly solicitors acting for receivers appointed by the Court of Protection, or who are appointed as receivers themselves, are likely to be undertaking 'relevant business'.

26. All these areas of work can give rise to money laundering issues. For example, where a solicitor acts as an attorney they may learn financial information about the donor, such as their non payment of tax, or wrongful receipt of welfare benefits. Whether this is a matter which is reportable to NCIS/SOCA as money laundering will depend upon a detailed analysis of the *Bowman* v. *Fels* guidance, especially whether knowledge or suspicion has been formed from information received in legally professionally privileged circumstances. Where the Court of Protection has an interest because of a receivership or registered enduring power of attorney, consideration will need to be given as to whether the Master needs to be informed. Informing the Master is unlikely to be tipping off because it is unlikely to prejudice an investigation, which is a necessary criterion for either of the tipping off offences, see paragraph 2.57–2.61 of the Guidance.

27. Principle 24.03 of the Guide to the Professional Conduct of Solicitors contains information for solicitors regarding Powers of Attorney, e.g. if a solicitor forms knowledge or suspicion that a donee is acting improperly, for example not dealing

with the donor's assets in the donor's best interests, the solicitor should seek confirmation of instructions from the donor.

28. If a solicitor forms knowledge or suspicion that a donee has already completed an improper financial transaction, that may amount to a money laundering suspicion, and a money laundering report to NCIS/SOCA may be required, dependent on whether legal professional privilege applies. However, solicitors may find it hard to decide whether they have a suspicion if the background is a family dispute, and it can help to discuss matters with Professional Ethics: 0870 606 2577.

Reporting Issues

29. The case of *Bowman* v. *Fels* has drastically altered how private client solicitors undertaking private client work should approach their reporting obligations because of the increased importance of legal professional privilege. Administration of estates or other types of private client work should lead solicitors to consider in detail the *Bowman* v. *Fels* guidance referred to above.

30. Legal professional privilege is a key consideration and recent case law has defined privilege in transactional work widely, see paragraph 5.6 onwards in the *Bowman* v. *Fels* guidance. For example instructions to prepare wills are likely to be covered by legal professional privilege (unless there is a criminal intention behind the instructions), and after death but before publication of wills, rights to legal professional privilege vest in the Personal Representatives.

Solicitors in need of guidance should contact: Professional Ethics tel: 0870 606 2577

Footnote to Paragraph 9: Once section 102 of the Serious Organised Crime and Police Act 2005 comes into force, usually a money laundering offence will not be committed if a solicitor knows or believes on reasonable grounds that the relevant criminal conduct occurred outside the UK and was not, at the time it was committed, a crime in that country or territory. Up to date information about this future change to POCA can be obtained on this subject from Professional Ethics: 0870 606 2577.

Complaints and Complainants in Probate Matters[1]

WHO IS THE CLIENT?

A question that seems to vex Probate practitioners more than any other relates to a solicitors *responsibilities under Rule 15* and to whom those responsibilities are owed. The question is: who should the practitioner regard as his client in Probate matters and what, if any, duties does he owe to those who are not his clients? To answer this it is necessary to begin with some basic points.

Firstly, in dealing with an estate, the only person who can be the solicitor's *client is the executor*, or, obviously, the executors if there are more than one.

It follows that the executor is the only person to whom a solicitor owes a duty under Rule 15 and so is the only person to whom a solicitor is obliged to give costs information and, subject to the exception mentioned below, is the only person who can raise a service complaint which the solicitor is obliged to deal with.

Secondly, only a client can benefit from a compensatory award in the event of a finding of inadequate professional service (IPS) by the OSS, so that a compensatory award can only be made in favour of an executor.

Thirdly, the OSS does not need a complaint from a client to enable it to investigate complaints of IPS. Any doubts about this were removed by *Schedule 7 para 11(2)(c) of the Access to Justice Act 1999.*

Having said that, the OSS will not normally accept complaints of inadequate service from someone who is not a client of the solicitor complained of. The reason is that solicitors only owe a duty of service to their own clients. Usually, when complaints come from another source, they either come from the other party in a matter ie the opponent whose interests are diametrically opposed to those of the solicitor's own client, or from interfering relatives who don't like the result achieved, even though the client may be quite content.

However, that situation does not hold good in Probate matters and it does not take much thought to realise why.

As will be readily appreciated, it would be nonsensical to have a situation where beneficiaries, who are not clients of the solicitor because he himself is the executor and is therefore his own client, had to refer complaints to the solicitor because he was the executor, and, as executor, he could then just tell the beneficiaries that they had no grounds for complaint and he was satisfied that he, with his solicitor's hat on, was dealing with things perfectly properly.

If *residuary beneficiaries*, who are more interested than anyone else in the adequate handling of the estate, were not able raise genuine complaints with the OSS, they would, in fact, have no redress and no-one they could turn to for help if, for instance,

---

[1] © Law Society, 2004.

there was unreasonable delay in the winding up of the estate without having to embark on potentially expensive litigation.

If such complaints are found to be substantiated, the only sanction available is a reduction in the solicitor's fees, with, obviously, a consequent increase in the size of the residuary estate which would benefit the residuary beneficiaries.

Applying the above principles, it would now be appropriate to examine the three scenarios that can arise.

1. **Where the *executors* of a Will *are laymen* and have no connection with the solicitor's firm and the solicitor is instructed by the executors to obtain Probate and to act in the administration of the estate.**

In that case, the situation is clear. It is the executor (or both of them if there is more than one) who is the client and it is the executor to whom all the information required by Practice Rule 15 should be given and he is the only person entitled to make a complaint with which the solicitor is obliged to deal in accordance with his firm's Complaints Procedure.

In practice it is found that many complaints arise out of disagreements between beneficiaries and executors. If a complaint is received from a beneficiary, whether specific or residuary, there is no compulsion on a solicitor to deal with it and the beneficiary can be politely referred to the executor with an accompanying explanation that it is the executor who is the client and that it would, therefore not be correct for you, the solicitor, to correspond with the beneficiary, eg for reasons of confidentiality. However, where there is no over-riding reason why the solicitor should not answer the matters raised by the Residuary Beneficiary, it would be preferable for him to tell the Residuary Beneficiary that, subject to him obtaining his client's (the executor's) consent, he will deal with the matters raised. It might also be good public relations to give residuary beneficiaries costs information and to let them know how matters are progressing. After all, it is the Residuary Beneficiary who is, in effect, paying the bill!

2. **Where the *solicitor*, or a member of his firm, is appointed to be the *executor* of the Will and he so acts in obtaining Probate and administering the estate. (The following observations will, of course, apply equally to cases where there is more than one executor and all the executors are members of the same firm.) In those circumstances the solicitor/executor is his own client and there is no obligation upon the solicitor to give costs, or any other Rule 15, information to anyone else and the solicitor will not suffer a costs reduction or be required by the OSS to pay compensation for failing, for example, to give costs information to a residuary beneficiary.**

With regard to the question of general service complaints eg delay, failing to account etc. the position, as indicated above, is somewhat different.

It is to guard against that kind of situation, where, in effect, a solicitor can act as judge in his own cause, that the OSS *will* contemplate complaints by a residuary beneficiary where there is no lay executor who can take up the complaints on behalf of the residuary beneficiaries. Likewise, the solicitor should deal with such complaints.

3. **Where the solicitor is a *joint executor with a layman*. Here the situation is more complicated and less definite.**

All really depends on the nature, or standing, of the lay executor. This is where it all becomes something less than an exact science, as one has to make a judgement about the standing of the lay executor.

In these circumstances, as, hopefully, will now be readily appreciated, it is the solicitor and the lay executor together who are the clients. The lay executor is the person who is entitled to the Rule 15 information and from whom the solicitor has to accept complaints.

If the lay co-executor is not even a beneficiary of any kind and has been appointed simply because he was an old friend of the deceased and someone the deceased felt could be relied upon to see that his wishes were carried out, his function with regard to the realisation of the estate being restricted to signing forms, he may well not have sufficient personal interest to pursue any complaint raised by a beneficiary. Under those circumstances, particularly if the lay executor is elderly, the situation would not be regarded in the same way.

It is still the lay executor who is the solicitor's client and who is the person solely entitled to the relevant information under Rule 15 and there would, therefore, still be no redress for a residuary beneficiary who received no costs information, but he could get redress, albeit indirectly by way of a costs reduction, for other complaints related to the service afforded.

The position is different with regard to *dealing with complaints*, because it is more akin to that under 2. above, and, consequently, the OSS would expect a solicitor to deal with complaints that come from any one, or more, of the residuary beneficiaries. The difficulty, of course, is that the position may not be quite so clear cut as it is in the examples given above so that one would be forced into making a subjective decision as to whether or not complaints ought to be dealt with under the firm's Complaints Procedure.

Perhaps the better view would be, as suggested above, and it is an attitude that the OSS would encourage, and indeed one which, on reflection, you as the solicitor may think makes commercial sense, that, no matter what the strict interpretation may be, it would be in the interests of good client relations to *treat all residuary beneficiaries as if they were clients*, even if, strictly speaking, they are not. Certainly, as indicated above, the OSS would prefer solicitors to deal with service complaints from residuary beneficiaries as if they were clients. That would also seem to be the view taken by the Ombudsman and Consumer organisations who, it would appear, would like to see a harder line taken whereby solicitors were obliged to accept, and deal with, complaints from residuary beneficiaries.

However, it is possible to conceive of circumstances where that may not be desirable, for example if the complaint arises from a family squabble, or if just one of many residuary beneficiaries seeks to raise a matter when all the others are perfectly happy. There was, for instance, one complaint referred to the OSS by a residuary beneficiary who refused to sign the accounts until his complaints had been dealt with to his satisfaction, thus holding up the distribution of the estate to each of the other 22 beneficiaries, all of whom had no complaint whatsoever.

It is also fair to say that, subject to how many of them there are, the OSS would like solicitor/executors to *give Rule 15 information to residuary beneficiaries* and keep them informed of progress, although there is no obligation to do so. Indeed, you may think it sensible from both a public relations and a 'potential client' point of view, to do this, thus treating such people at all times as if they are clients.

Perhaps the best way of addressing that type of situation, assuming you are prepared to do so, would be for you to write to the residuary beneficiaries at the outset of the matter giving them the normal costs information and explaining that, although it is the executor who, strictly speaking, is the client, you are prepared, if the *residuary beneficiaries all agree*, to keep them informed as to progress at set intervals and also setting out the anticipated cost of giving them that information, or explaining how the cost will be calculated. You can explain that it is necessary for them all to agree in order to avoid a complaint from any beneficiary who later maintains they did not want such information and that costs have been wasted.

One final point.

It should also be born in mind that, in cases where there is no lay executor, residuary beneficiaries have the specific right to apply for a Remuneration Certificate.

APPENDIX A3

'Who is the probate client? And when should non-clients be given rule 15 information?'[1]

The case studies section of the Office for the Supervision of Solicitors' newsletter, the Bulletin, has recently carried a series of pointers on the vexed subject of solicitor/executors and Law Society practice rule 15.

But, from the responses received, it would appear that the situation vis-a-vis solicitors' responsibilities is still far from clear.

(These observations will, of course, apply equally to cases where there is more than one executor and all the executors are members of the same firm). The questions are: who should the practitioner regard as his client in probate matters? And are there circumstances in which he or she should be giving rule 15 information to, or dealing with complaints by, those who are not his or her clients? There are three possible scenarios.

WHERE THE EXECUTORS OF A WILL ARE LAYMEN

In this scenario, the executors will have no connection with the solicitor's firm and the solicitor is instructed by the executors to obtain probate and to act in the administration of the estate. In that case, the situation is clear.

It is the executor – or both of them if there is more than one – who is the client and it is the executor to whom all the information required by practice rule 15 should be given.

The executor is the only person entitled to make a complaint with which the solicitor is expected to deal in accordance with his firm's complaints procedure. In practice it is found that many complaints arise out of disagreements between beneficiaries and executors.

If a complaint is received from a beneficiary, whether specific or residuary, that beneficiary can be politely referred to the executor with an explanation that it is the executor who is the client and that it would, therefore, not be correct for the solicitor to correspond with the beneficiary.

WHERE THE SOLICITOR, OR A MEMBER OF THE FIRM, IS APPOINTED TO BE THE EXECUTOR

In this instance the solicitor, or a member of the firm, will be appointed as executor of the will and he so acts in obtaining probate and administering the estate. In those circumstances solicitor/executors are their own client, and there is no compulsion on them to give costs information to anyone else.

---

[1] © The Law Society 2000. This article was written by Mike Frith, see [2000] *Gazette*, 10 February, 38.

They will not be penalised in any way by the Office for the Supervision of Solicitors (OSS) for failing to give costs information, for example, to a residuary beneficiary. With regard to the question of general service complaints, for example, those involving delay or failing to account, the position is somewhat different.

It would be nonsensical to have a situation where beneficiaries, who were not clients of the solicitor/executor, had to refer complaints to the solicitor as executor and, as executor, that solicitor could tell the beneficiaries that they had no grounds for complaint and he was satisfied that he, with his solicitor's hat on, was dealing with things perfectly properly. It is to guard against that kind of situation that the OSS will contemplate complaints by a residuary beneficiary where there is no lay executor or in circumstances such as those described below.

It is also in these circumstances where, subject to how many of them there are, the OSS would like solicitor/executors to give rule 15 information to residuary beneficiaries and keep them informed of progress, although there is no compulsion on them to do so.

Indeed, solicitors themselves may think it sensible from both a public relations and a 'potential client' point of view, to treat such people as if they are clients, even if, strictly speaking, they are not. Perhaps the best way of addressing that type of situation, assuming the solicitor is prepared to do so, would be to write to the residuary beneficiaries at the outset of the matter giving them the normal costs information and explaining that – although they are not clients in the strict sense of the word – the solicitor is prepared, if they all agree, to keep them informed as to progress.

The solicitor should also set out the anticipated cost of giving them that information, or explain how the cost will be calculated.

The reason why they all need to agree is to avoid the later possibility of any who did not in fact agree accusing the solicitor of wasting costs. The reason why the OSS will accept complaints from persons who are not clients of the solicitor, is that, if it were otherwise, residuary beneficiaries would have nowhere, and no one, to whom they could have recourse, should a complaint arise, without embarking on expensive litigation.

This would result in manifest unfairness if, for example, it was taking an unreasonable time for the estate to be realised and distributed.

WHERE THE SOLICITOR IS A JOINT EXECUTOR WITH A LAYMAN

Here the situation is more complicated and less definite.

All really depends on the nature, or standing, of the co-executor.

This is where it all becomes something less than an exact science, as one has to make a judgment about the standing of the co-executor. In these circumstances it is the lay executor, together with the professional executor, who are the clients.

The lay executor is the person who is entitled to the Rule 15 information and from whom the solicitor has to accept complaints. If the co-executor is not a beneficiary of any kind – and has been appointed simply because he was an old friend of the deceased, and someone the deceased believed could be relied on to see that his wishes were carried out – he may not have sufficient personal interest to pursue any complaints.

Under those circumstances, particularly if the co-executor is elderly, the situation would not be regarded in the same way. It is still the lay executor who is the solicitor's client and who is the person solely entitled to the relevant information under rule 15. However, the position is different with regard to dealing with complaints, because it is more akin to that under the second point above, and the OSS would, in those circumstances, expect the solicitor to deal with complaints which come from any one, or more, of the residuary beneficiaries. The difficulty is that the position may not be quite so clear-cut as it is in the examples given earlier.

Perhaps the better view would be that, no matter what the strict interpretation might be, it would be in the interests of good client relations to treat all residuary beneficiaries as though they were clients, even if, strictly speaking, they are not. Certainly, as indicated above, the OSS would prefer solicitors to deal with complaints from residuary beneficiaries as though they were clients and that is certainly the line taken by the Legal Services Ombudsman and consumer organisations. However, it is possible to conceive of circumstances where that may not be desirable, for example if the complaint arises from a family squabble, or if just one of many residuary beneficiaries seeks to raise a matter when all the others are perfectly happy.

There was, for instance, one complaint referred to the OSS by a residuary beneficiary who refused to sign the accounts until his complaints had been dealt with to his satisfaction, thus holding up the distribution of the estate to each of the other 22 beneficiaries, all of whom had no complaint whatsoever. But perhaps, from the practitioner's point of view, the more important aspect of all this is: what penalty might the OSS impose if a complaint is made to it by someone who is not, in reality, a client? The powers of the OSS, from a purely financial point of view, are, in cases where there is a finding of inadequacy of service, to reduce a solicitor's profit costs and/or to make a compensatory award.

However, compensation can only be awarded to a client.

It follows that such an award can only be made to a residuary beneficiary when that person is also a client in the strict sense of the word.

Therefore, where a complaint is made by someone who is not a client of the solicitor complained of, the only power available to the OSS is to reduce the solicitor's costs, which would, of course, have a knock-on effect of increasing the residuary estate which would benefit all of the residuary beneficiaries. It should be noted that the OSS does not need a complaint to be made to it in order to empower it to investigate the quality of service afforded by a solicitor.

Any previous uncertainty about this was finally removed by the provisions of schedule 7, para 11 (2) (c) of the Access to Justice Act 1999. One final observation.

Many firms, as a matter of good practice – and, no doubt with an eye to trying to recruit clients – treat residuary beneficiaries as clients.

They then provide those residuary beneficiaries with rule 15 information, particularly in instances where there are not so many of them that to give such information might lead to another complaint of wasting money. It should also be borne in mind that, in cases where there is no lay executor, residuary beneficiaries have the specific right to apply for a remuneration certificate.

Solicitors' Costs Information and Client Care Code 1999[1]

Code dated 3rd September 1999 made by the Council of the Law Society with the concurrence of the Master of the Rolls under Rule 15 of the Solicitors' Practice Rules 1990, regulating the English and Welsh practices of solicitors, registered European lawyers, registered foreign lawyers and recognised bodies in giving information to clients and operating complaints procedures.

1. Introduction

(a) This code replaces the written professional standards on costs information for clients (see paragraphs 3–6) and the detail previously contained in Practice Rule 15 (client care) (see paragraph 7).

(b) The main object of the code is to make sure that clients are given the information they need to understand what is happening generally and in particular on:

    (i) the cost of legal services both at the outset and as a matter progresses; and

    (ii) responsibility for clients' matters.

(c) The code also requires firms to operate a complaints handling procedure.

(d) It is good practice to record in writing:

    (i) all information required to be given by the code including all decisions relating to costs and the arrangements for updating costs information; and

    (ii) the reasons why the information required by the code has not been given in a particular case.

(e) References to costs, where appropriate, include fees, VAT and disbursements.

2. Application

(a) The code is of general application, and it applies to registered foreign lawyers as well as to solicitors of the Supreme Court and registered European lawyers (subject to note (v) to Practice Rule 15). However, as set out in paragraph 2(b), parts of the code may not be appropriate in every case, and solicitors should consider the interests of each client in deciding which parts not to apply in the particular circumstances.

(b) The full information required by the code may be inappropriate, for example:

    (i) in every case, for a regular client for whom repetitive work is done, where the client has already been provided with the relevant information, although such a client should be informed of changes; and

[1] © The Law Society. Last amended 8 June 2006.

(ii) if compliance with the code may at the time be insensitive or impractical. In such a case relevant information should be given as soon as reasonably practicable.

(c) Employed solicitors should have regard to paragraphs 3–6A of the code where appropriate, e.g. when acting for clients other than their employer. Paragraph 7 does not apply to employed solicitors.

(d) Solicitors should comply with paragraphs 3–6 of the code even where a client is legally aided if the client may have a financial interest in the costs because contributions are payable or the statutory charge may apply or they may become liable for the costs of another party.

(da) If appropriate solicitors should also comply with paragraph 6A of the code where a client is legally aided.

(e) The code also applies to contingency fee and conditional fee arrangements and to arrangements with a client for the solicitor to retain commissions received from third parties.

3. Informing the client about costs

(a) Costs information must not be inaccurate or misleading.

(b) Any costs information required to be given by the code must be given clearly, in a way and at a level which is appropriate to the particular client. Any terms with which the client may be unfamiliar, for example 'disbursement', should be explained.

(c) The information required by paragraphs 4 and 5 of the code should be given to a client at the outset of, and at appropriate stages throughout, the matter. All information given orally should be confirmed in writing to the client as soon as possible.

4. Advance costs information – general

The overall costs

(a) The solicitor should give the client the best information possible about the likely overall costs, including a breakdown between fees, VAT and disbursements.

(b) The solicitor should explain clearly to the client the time likely to be spent in dealing with a matter, if time spent is a factor in the calculation of the fees.

(c) Giving 'the best information possible' includes:

    (i) agreeing a fixed fee; or

    (ii) giving a realistic estimate; or

    (iii) giving a forecast within a possible range of costs; or

    (iv) explaining to the client the reasons why it is not possible to fix, or give a realistic estimate or forecast of, the overall costs, and giving instead the best information possible about the cost of the next stage of the matter.

(d) The solicitor should, in an appropriate case, explain to a privately paying client that the client may set an upper limit on the firm's costs for which the client may be liable without further authority. Solicitors should not exceed an agreed limit without first obtaining the client's consent.

(e) The solicitor should make it clear at the outset if an estimate, quotation or other indication of cost is not intended to be fixed.

Basis of firm's charges

(f) The solicitor should also explain to the client how the firm's fees are calculated except where the overall costs are fixed or clear. If the basis of charging is an hourly charging rate, that must be made clear.

(g) The client should be told if charging rates may be increased.

Further information

(h) The solicitor should explain what reasonably foreseeable payments a client may have to make either to the solicitor or to a third party and when those payments are likely to be needed.

(i) The solicitor should explain to the client the arrangements for updating the costs information as set out in paragraph 6.

Client's ability to pay

(j) The solicitor should discuss with the client how and when any costs are to be met, and consider:

    (i) whether the client may be eligible and should apply for legal aid (including advice and assistance);

    (ii) whether the client's liability for their own costs may be covered by insurance;

    (iii) whether the client's liability for another party's costs may be covered by pre-purchased insurance and, if not, whether it would be advisable for the client's liability for another party's costs to be covered by after the event insurance (including in every case where a conditional fee or contingency fee arrangement is proposed); and

    (iv) whether the client's liability for costs (including the costs of another party) may be paid by another person e.g. an employer or trade union.

Cost-benefit and risk

(k) The solicitor should discuss with the client whether the likely outcome in a matter will justify the expense or risk involved including, if relevant, the risk of having to bear an opponent's costs.

5. Additional information for particular clients

Legally aided clients

(a) The solicitor should explain to a legally aided client the client's potential liability for the client's own costs and those of any other party, including:

    (i) the effect of the statutory charge and its likely amount;

    (ii) the client's obligation to pay any contribution assessed and the consequences of failing to do so;

    (iii) the fact that the client may still be ordered by the court to contribute to the opponent's costs if the case is lost even though the client's own costs are covered by legal aid; and

    (iv) the fact that even if the client wins, the opponent may not be ordered to pay or be capable of paying the full amount of the client's costs.

Privately paying clients in contentious matters (and potentially contentious matters)

(b) The solicitor should explain to the client the client's potential liability for the client's own costs and for those of any other party, including:

    (i) the fact that the client will be responsible for paying the firm's bill in full regardless of any order for costs made against an opponent;

    (ii) the probability that the client will have to pay the opponent's costs as well as the client's own costs if the case is lost;

    (iii) the fact that even if the client wins, the opponent may not be ordered to pay or be capable of paying the full amount of the client's costs; and

    (iv) the fact that if the opponent is legally aided the client may not recover costs, even if successful.

Liability for third party costs in non-contentious matters

(c) The solicitor should explain to the client any liability the client may have for the payment of the costs of a third party. When appropriate, solicitors are advised to obtain a firm figure for or agree a cap to a third party's costs.

Clients represented under a conditional fee agreement (including a collective conditional fee agreement)

(d) Where a client is represented under a conditional fee agreement, the solicitor should explain:

    (i) the circumstances in which the client may be liable for their own costs and for the other party's costs;

    (ii) the client's right to assessment of costs, wherever the solicitor intends to seek payment of any or all of their costs from the client; and

    (iii) any interest the solicitor may have in recommending a particular policy or other funding.

6. Updating costs information

The solicitor should keep the client properly informed about costs as a matter progresses. In particular, the solicitor should:

(a) tell the client, unless otherwise agreed, how much the costs are at regular intervals (at least every six months) and in appropriate cases deliver interim bills at agreed intervals;

(b) explain to the client (and confirm in writing) any changed circumstances which will, or which are likely to affect the amount of costs, the degree of risk involved, or the cost-benefit to the client of continuing with the matter;

(c) inform the client in writing as soon as it appears that a costs estimate or agreed upper limit may or will be exceeded; and

(d) consider the client's eligibility for legal aid if a material change in the client's means comes to the solicitor's attention.

6A. Disclosure of solicitor's arrangements with third parties

(a) The solicitor should disclose to the client any relationship with a third party (for example a funder, fee sharer or introducer) which affects the steps which the solicitor can take on the client's behalf.

(b) The solicitor should explain any constraints or conditions which affect the client.

(c) All information given orally concerning (a) and (b) above should be confirmed in writing to the client as soon as possible.

7. Client care and complaints handling

Information for clients

(a) Every solicitor in private practice must ensure that the client:

    (i) is given a clear explanation of the issues raised in a matter and is kept properly informed about its progress (including the likely timescale);

    (ii) is given the name and status of the person dealing with the matter and the name of the principal, or director (in the case of a recognised body which is a company), or member (in the case of a recognised body which is a limited liability partnership) responsible for its overall supervision;

    (iii) is told whom to contact about any problem with the service provided; and

    (iv) is given details of any changes in the information required to be given by this paragraph.

Complaints handling

(b) Every principal in private practice (or, in the case of a recognised body, the body itself) must:

    (i) ensure the client is told the name of the person in the firm to contact about any problem with the service provided;

    (ii) have a written complaints procedure and ensure that complaints are handled in accordance with it; and

    (iii) ensure that the client is given a copy of the complaints procedure on request.

APPENDIX A5

Death certificate verification form and protocol letter

For use by Solicitors

DEATH CERTIFICATE VERIFICATION FORM[1]

Registration District: ....

Place of death ....

Parish (if specified) ....
& County

Entry number ....

Date of death ....

Cause of death[2] ....

....

....

....

Name of doctor[3] ....
certifying death

Name of informant[4] ....

Name of registrar[5] ....

Date of birth[6] ....

Sex[7] ....

Maiden name[8] ....
(if applicable)

Previous married name ....
(if applicable/known)

Occupation ....

I/We certify that I/we have examined the death certificate of

(client's name) ....

(client's address) ....

.... and that the said certificate contains the information as recorded above. **A copy is kept on the client file for my/our information to which you may request access.**

Signed: (Partner) .... Date: ....

Full name ....

Firm Name: ....

Firm Law Society number ....

Firm's stamp

GUIDANCE NOTES

1 Only information contained in the certificate may be recorded on this form. Where information for a particular field is not recorded in the certificate, or not known, please state 'not recorded on certificate' or 'not known'.

  This form is not appropriate for use in lieu of an interim death certificate or a foreign death certificate.

2 This information is important in the event of an early claim on an underwritten policy. Each and every cause of death must be recorded as they appear in the certificate.

3 On occasion, usually in connection with an attempted fraud, the name of the doctor certifying the death may be important.

4 This information may be important in the context of an attempted fraud and in helping to identify if there is a spouse which may be relevant in the case of protected rights or guaranteed minimum pensions under pension plans where the provider has discretion over the beneficiary.

5 In some cases the signature may be illegible (and the name is not printed). If this is the case, please state 'signature illegible'. This does, at least, confirm that the Registrar has signed the certificate.

6 Identifies any possible mis-statements of age.

7 Allows comparisons with information provided at date of inception. (gender is not always obvious from the forenames).

8 Confirms identity of a woman who has married since policy inception but omitted to provide this information.

Dear

Re: [. . .] deceased Ref: [. . .] [*account/policy/pension number*]

We regret to inform you that [. . .] [*full name*] died on [. . .] at [. . .]. We act for [. . .], who are personal representatives of [. . .].

We are in possession of a certified copy of the entry of the death, the full details of which can be found in the attached schedule.* We confirm that we will forward the copy of the death certificate if the [. . .] [*bank/insurer/pension provider*] requires it.

We would be grateful if you would please note the fact of this death and take such action as is required.

We would be grateful if you could also provide precise details of all [. . .] [*accounts/insurance policy/assets*] held by you and their value as at [. . .] [*date of death*] for the purpose of administering the estate.

Yours faithfully

*Insurers/Pension providers will also require birth and
marriage forms to be completed for certain purposes.

Non-Contentious Probate Rules 1987 (SI 1987/2024)

The President of the Family Division, in exercise of the powers conferred upon him by section 127 of the Supreme Court Act 1981, and section 2(5) of the Colonial Probates Act 1892, and with the concurrence of the Lord Chancellor, hereby makes the following Rules:

1. Citation and commencement

These Rules may be cited as the Non-Contentious Probate Rules 1987 and shall come into force on 1st January 1988.

2. Interpretation

(1) In these Rules, unless the context otherwise requires –

'the Act' means the Supreme Court Act 1981;
'authorised officer' means any officer of a registry who is for the time being authorised by the President to administer any oath or to take any affidavit required for any purpose connected with his duties;
'the Crown' includes the Crown in right of the Duchy of Lancaster and the Duke of Cornwall for the time being;
'district judge' means a district judge of the Principle Registry;
'grant' means a grant of probate or administration and includes, where the context so admits, the resealing of such a grant under the Colonial Probates Acts 1892 and 1927;
'gross value' in relation to any estate means the value of the estate without deduction for debts, incumbrances, funeral expenses or inheritance tax (or other capital tax payable out of the estate);
'judge' means a judge in the High Court;
'oath' means the oath required by rule 8 to be sworn by every applicant for a grant;
'personal applicant' means a person other than a trust corporation who seeks to obtain a grant without employing a solicitor or probate practitioner, and 'personal application' has a corresponding meaning;
'registrar' a district probate registrar of the district probate registry –

  (i) in which an application for a grant made or is proposed to be made,
  (ii) in rules 26, 40, 41 and 61(2) from which the grant is issued, and
  (iii) in rules 46, 47 and 48, from which the citation has issued or is proposed to be issued.

'registry' means the Principal Registry or a district probate registry;

'the senior district judge' means the Senior District Judge of the Family Division or, in his absence, the senior of the district judges in attendance at the Principal Registry;

'the Treasury Solicitor' means the solicitor for the affairs of Her Majesty's Treasury and includes the solicitor for the affairs of the Duchy of Lancaster and the solicitor of the Duchy of Cornwall;

'trust corporation' means a corporation within the meaning of section 128 of the Act as extended by section 3 of the Law of Property (Amendment) Act 1926.

(2) A form referred to by number means the form so numbered in the First Schedule; and such forms shall be used wherever applicable, with such variation as a registrar may in any particular case direct or approve.

3. Application of other rules

(1) Subject to the provisions of these rules and to any enactment, the Rules of the Supreme Court 1965 as they were in force immediately before 26th April 1999 shall apply, with any necessary modifications to non-contentious probate matters, and any reference in these rules to those rules shall be construed accordingly.

(2) Nothing in Order 3 of the Rules of the Supreme Court shall prevent time from running in the Long Vacation.

4. Application for grants through solicitors or probate practitioners

(1) A person applying for a grant through a solicitor or probate practitioner may apply at any registry or sub-registry.

(2) Every solicitor or probate practitioner through whom an application for a grant is made shall give the address of his place of business within England and Wales.

5. Personal applications

(1) A personal applicant may apply for a grant at any registry or sub-registry.

(2) Save as provided for by rule 39 a personal applicant may not apply through an agent, whether paid or unpaid, and may not be attended by any person acting or appearing to act as his adviser.

(3) No personal application shall be proceeded with if –

(a) it becomes necessary to bring the matter before the court by action or summons, unless a judge, district judge or registrar so permits;

(b) an application has already been made by a solicitor or probate practitioner on behalf of the applicant and has not been withdrawn; or

(c) the district judge or registrar so directs.

(4) After a will has been deposited in a registry by a personal applicant, it may not be delivered to the applicant or to any other person unless in special circumstances the district judge or registrar so directs.

(5) A personal applicant shall produce a certificate of the death of the deceased or such other evidence of the death as the district judge or registrar may approve.

(6) A personal applicant shall supply all information necessary to enable the papers leading to the grant to be prepared in the registry.

(7) Unless the district judge or registrar otherwise directs, every oath or affidavit required on a personal application shall be sworn or executed by all the deponents before an authorised officer.

(8) No legal advice shall be given to a personal applicant by an officer of a registry and every such officer shall be responsible only for embodying in proper form the applicant's instructions for the grant.

6. Duty of district judge or registrar on receiving application for grant

(1) A district judge or registrar shall not allow any grant to issue until all inquiries which he may see fit to make have been answered to his satisfaction.

(2) Except with the leave of a district judge or registrar, no grant of probate or of administration with the will annexed shall issue within seven days of the death of the deceased and no grant of administration shall issue within fourteen days thereof.

7. Grants by district probate registrars

(1) No grant shall be made by a probate registrar –

    (a) in any case in which there is contention, until the contention is disposed of; or

    (b) in any case in which it appears to him that a grant ought not to be made without the directions of a judge or a registrar of the Principal Registry.

(2) In any case in which paragraph (1)(b) applies, the registrar shall send a statement of the matter in question to the Principal Registry for directions.

(3) A district judge may either confirm that the matter be referred to a judge and give directions accordingly or may direct the registrar to proceed with the matter in accordance with such instructions as are deemed necessary, which may include a direction to take no further action in relation to the matter.

8. Oath in support of grant

(1) Every application for a grant other than one to which rule 39 applies shall be supported by an oath by the applicant in the form applicable to the circumstances of the case, and by such other papers as the district judge or registrar may require.

(2) Unless otherwise directed by a district judge or registrar, the oath shall state where the deceased died domiciled.

(3) Where the deceased died on or after 1st January 1926, the oath shall state whether or not, to the best of the applicant's knowledge, information and belief, there was land vested in the deceased which was settled previously to his death and not by his will and which remained settled land notwithstanding his death.

(4) On an application for a grant of administration the oath shall state in what manner all persons having a prior right to a grant have been cleared off and whether any minority or life interest arises under the will or intestacy.

9. Grant in additional name

Where it is sought to describe the deceased in a grant by some name in addition to his true name, the applicant shall depose to the true name of the deceased and shall specify some part of the estate which was held in the other name, or give any other reason for the inclusion of the other name in the grant.

10. Marking of wills

(1) Subject to paragraph (2) below, every will in respect of which an application for a grant is made –

(a) shall be marked by the signatures of the applicant and the person before whom the oath is sworn; and

(b) shall be exhibited to any affidavit which may be required under these Rules as to the validity, terms, condition or date of execution of the will.

(2) The district judge or registrar may allow a facsimile copy of a will to be marked or exhibited in lieu of the original document.

11. Engrossments for purposes of record

(1) Where the district judge or registrar considers that in any particular case a facsimile copy of the original will would not be satisfactory for purposes of record, he may require an engrossment suitable for facsimile reproduction to be lodged.

(2) Where a will –

(a) contains alterations which are not to be admitted to proof; or

(b) has been ordered to be rectified by virtue of section 20(1) of the Administration of Justice Act 1982,

there shall be lodged an engrossment of the will in the form in which it is to be proved.

(3) Any engrossment lodged under this rule shall reproduce the punctuation, spacing and division into paragraphs of the will and shall follow continuously from page to page on both sides of the paper.

12. Evidence as to due execution of will

(1) Subject to paragraphs (2) and (3) below, where a will contains no attestation clause or the attestation clause is insufficient, or where it appears to the registrar that there is doubt about the due execution of the will, he shall before admitting it to proof require an affidavit as to due execution from one or more of the attesting witnesses or, if no attesting witness is conveniently available, from any other person who was present when the will was executed; and if the registrar, after considering the evidence, is satisfied that the will was not duly executed, he shall refuse probate and mark the will accordingly.

(2) If no affidavit can be obtained in accordance with paragraph (1) above, the registrar may accept evidence on affidavit from any person he may think fit to show that the signature on the will is in the handwriting of the deceased, or of any other matter which may raise a presumption in favour of due execution of the will, and may if he thinks fit require that notice of the application be given to any person who may be prejudiced by the will.

(3) A district judge or registrar may accept a will for proof without evidence as aforesaid if he is satisfied that the distribution of the estate is not thereby affected.

13. Execution of will of blind or illiterate testator

Before admitting to proof a will which appears to have been signed by a blind or illiterate testator or by another person by direction of the testator, or which for any other reason raises doubt as to the testator having had knowledge of the contents of the will at the time of its execution, the district judge or registrar shall satisfy himself that the testator had such knowledge.

14. Evidence as to terms, condition and date of execution of will

(1) Subject to paragraph (2) below, where there appears in a will any obliteration, interlineation, or other alteration which is not authenticated in the manner prescribed by section 21 of the Wills Act 1837, or by the re-execution of the will or by the execution of a codicil, the district judge or registrar shall require evidence to show whether the alteration was present at the time the will was executed and shall give directions as to the form in which the will is to be proved.

(2) The provisions of paragraph (1) above shall not apply to any alteration which appears to the district judge or registrar to be of no practical importance.

(3) If a will contains any reference to another document in such terms as to suggest that it ought to be incorporated in the will, the district judge or registrar shall require the document to be produced and may call for such evidence in regard to the incorporation of the document as he may think fit.

(4) Where there is a doubt as to the date on which a will was executed, the district judge or registrar may require such evidence as he thinks necessary to establish the date.

15. Attempted revocation of will

Any appearance of attempted revocation of a will by burning, tearing, or otherwise destroying and every other circumstance leading to a presumption of revocation by the testator, shall be accounted for to the district judge's or registrar's satisfaction.

16. Affidavit as to due execution, terms, etc., of will

A district judge or registrar may require an affidavit from any person he may think fit for the purpose of satisfying himself as to any of the matters referred to in rules 13, 14 and 15, and in any such affidavit sworn by an attesting witness or other person present at the time of the execution of a will the deponent shall depose to the manner in which the will was executed.

17. Wills proved otherwise than under section 9 of the Wills Act 1837

(1) Rules 12 to 15 shall apply only to a will that is to be established by reference to section 9 of the Wills Act 1837 (signing and attestation of wills).

(2) A will that is to be established otherwise than as described in paragraph (1) of this rule may be so established upon the district judge or registrar being satisfied as to its terms and validity, and includes (without prejudice to the generality of the foregoing) –

(a) any will to which rule 18 applies; and

(b) any will which, by virtue of the Wills Act 1963, is to be treated as properly executed if executed according to the internal law of the territory or state referred to in section 1 of that Act.

18. Wills of persons on military service and seamen

Where the deceased died domiciled in England and Wales and it appears to the district judge or registrar that there is prima facie evidence that a will is one to which section 11 of the Wills Act 1837 applies, the will may be admitted to proof if the registrar is satisfied that it was signed by the testator or, if unsigned, that it is in the testator's handwriting.

19. Evidence of foreign law

Where evidence as to the law of any country or territory outside England and Wales is required on any application for a grant, the district judge or registrar may accept –

(a) an affidavit from any person whom, having regard to the particulars of his knowledge or experience given in the affidavit, he regards as suitably qualified to give expert evidence of the law in question; or
(b) a certificate by, or an act before, a notary practising in the country or territory concerned.

20. Order of priority for grant where deceased left a will

Where the deceased died on or after 1 January 1926 the person or persons entitled to a grant in respect of a will shall be determined in accordance with the following order of priority, namely –

(a) the executor (but subject to rule 36(4)(d) below);
(b) any residuary legatee or devisee holding in trust for any other person;
(c) any other residuary legatee or devisee (including one for life) or where the residue is not wholly disposed of by the will, any person entitled to share in the undisposed of residue (including the Treasury Solicitor when claiming bona vacantia on behalf of the Crown), provided that –

    (i) unless a district judge or registrar otherwise directs, a residuary legatee or devisee whose legacy or devise is vested in interest shall be preferred to one entitled on the happening of a contingency, and
    (ii) where the residue is not in terms wholly disposed of, the district judge or registrar may, if he is satisfied that the testator has nevertheless disposed of the whole or substantially the whole of the known estate, allow a grant to be made to any legatee or devisee entitled to, or to share in, the estate so disposed of, without regard to the persons entitled to share in any residue not disposed of by the will;

(d) the personal representative of any residuary legatee or devisee (but not one for life, or one holding in trust for any other person), or of any person entitled to share in any residue not disposed of by the will;
(e) any other legatee or devisee (including one for life or one holding in trust for any other person) or any creditor of the deceased, provided that, unless a district judge or registrar otherwise directs, a legatee or devisee whose legacy or devise is vested in interest shall be preferred to one entitled on the happening of a contingency;
(f) the personal representative of any other legatee or devisee (but not one for life or one holding in trust for any other person) or of any creditor of the deceased.

21. Grants to attesting witnesses, etc

Where a gift to any person fails by reason of section 15 of the Wills Act 1837, such person shall not have any right to a grant as a beneficiary named in the will, without prejudice to his right to a grant in any other capacity.

22. Order of priority for grant in case of intestacy

(1) Where the deceased died on or after 1 January 1926, wholly intestate, the person or persons having a beneficial interest in the estate shall be entitled to a grant of administration in the following classes in order of priority, namely –

(a) the surviving spouse or civil partner;
(b) the children of the deceased and the issue of any deceased child who died before the deceased;
(c) the father and mother of the deceased;
(d) brothers and sisters of the whole blood and the issue of any deceased brother or sister of the whole blood who died before the deceased;
(e) brothers and sisters of the half blood and the issue of any deceased brother or sister of the half blood who died before the deceased;
(f) grandparents;
(g) uncles and aunts of the whole blood and the issue of any deceased uncle or aunt of the whole blood who died before the deceased;
(h) uncles and aunts of the half blood and the issue of any deceased uncle or aunt of the half blood who died before the deceased.

(2) In default of any person having a beneficial interest in the estate, the Treasury Solicitor shall be entitled to a grant if he claims bona vacantia on behalf of the Crown.

(3) If all persons entitled to a grant under the foregoing provisions of this rule have been cleared off, a grant may be made to a creditor of the deceased or to any person who, notwithstanding that he has no immediate beneficial interest in the estate, may have a beneficial interest in the event of an accretion thereto.

(4) Subject to paragraph (5) of rule 27, the personal representative of a person in any of the classes mentioned in paragraph (1) of this rule or the personal representative of a creditor of the deceased shall have the same right to a grant as the person whom he represents provided that the persons mentioned in sub-paragraphs (b) to (h) of paragraph (1) above shall be preferred to the personal representative of a spouse or civil partner who has died without taking a beneficial interest in the whole estate of the deceased as ascertained at the time of the application for the grant.

23. Order of priority for grant in pre-1926 cases

Where the deceased died before 1st January 1926, the person or persons entitled to a grant shall, subject to the provisions of any enactment, be determined in accordance with the principles and rules under which the court would have acted at the date of death.

24. Right of assignee to a grant

(1) Where all the persons entitled to the estate of the deceased (whether under a will or on intestacy) have assigned their whole interest in the estate to one or more persons, the assignee or assignees shall replace, in the order of priority for a grant of administration, the assignor or, if there are two or more assignors, the assignor with the highest priority.

(2) Where there are two or more assignees, administration may be granted with the consent of the others to any one or more (not exceeding four) of them.

(3) In any case where administration is applied for by an assignee the original instrument of assignment shall be produced and a copy of the same lodged in the registry.

25. Joinder of administrator

(1) A person entitled in priority to a grant of administration may, without leave, apply for a grant with a person entitled in a lower degree, provided that there is

no other person entitled in a higher degree to the person to be joined, unless every other such person has renounced.

(2) Subject to paragraph (3) below, an application for leave to join with a person entitled in priority to a grant of administration a person having no right or no immediate right thereto shall be made to a district judge or registrar, and shall be supported by an affidavit by the person entitled in priority, the consent of the person proposed to be joined as administrator and such other evidence as the district judge or registrar may direct.

(3) Unless a district judge or registrar otherwise directs, there may without any such application be joined with a person entitled in priority to administration –

(a) any person who is nominated under paragraph (3) of rule 32 or paragraph (3) of rule 35;

(b) a trust corporation.

26. Additional personal representatives

(1) An application under section 114(4) of the Act to add a personal representative shall be made to a district judge or registrar and shall be supported by an affidavit by the applicant, the consent of the person proposed to be added as personal representative and such other evidence as the district judge or registrar may require.

(2) On any such application the district judge or registrar may direct that a note shall be made on the original grant of the addition of a further personal representative, or he may impound or revoke the grant or make such other order as the circumstances of the case may require.

27. Grants where two or more persons entitled in same degree

(1) Subject to paragraphs (1A), (2) and (3) below, where, on an application for probate, power to apply for a like grant is to be reserved to such other of the executors as have not renounced probate, notice of the application shall be given to the executor or executors to whom power is to be reserved; and, unless the district judge or registrar otherwise directs, the oath shall state that such notice has been given.

(1A) Where power is to be reserved to executors who are partners in a firm, notice need not be given to them under paragraph (1) above if probate is applied for by another partner in that firm.

(2) Where power is to be reserved to partners of a firm, notice for the purposes of paragraph (1) above may be given to the partners by sending it to the firm at its principal or last known place of business.

(3) A district judge or registrar may dispense with the giving of notice under paragraph (1) above if he is satisfied that the giving of such a notice is impracticable or would result in unreasonable delay or expense.

(4) A grant of administration may be made to any person entitled thereto without notice to other persons entitled in the same degree.

(5) Unless a district judge or registrar otherwise directs, administration shall be granted to a person of full age entitled thereto in preference to a guardian of a minor, and to a living person entitled thereto in preference to the personal representative of a deceased person.

(6) A dispute between persons entitled to a grant in the same degree shall be brought by summons before a district judge or registrar.

(7) The issue of a summons under this rule in a registry shall be noted forthwith in the index of pending grant applications.

(8) If the issue of a summons under this rule is known to the district judge or registrar, he shall not allow any grant to be sealed until such summons is finally disposed of.

28. Exceptions to rules as to priority

(1) Any person to whom a grant may or is required to be made under any enactment shall not be prevented from obtaining such a grant notwithstanding the operation of rules 20, 22, 25 or 27.

(2) Where the deceased died domiciled outside England and Wales rules 20, 22, 25 or 27 shall not apply except in a case to which paragraph (3) of rule 30 applies.

29. Grants in respect of settled land

(1) In this rule 'settled land' means land vested in the deceased which was settled prior to his death and not by his will, and which remained settled land notwithstanding his death.

(2) The person or persons entitled to a grant of administration limited to settled land shall be determined in accordance with the following order of priority:

   (i) the special executors in regard to settled land constituted by section 22 of the Administration of Estates Act 1925;

   (ii) the trustees of the settlement at the time of the application for the grant; and

   (iii) the personal representatives of the deceased.

(3) Where there is settled land and a grant is made in respect of the free estate only, the grant shall expressly exclude the settled land.

30. Grants where deceased died domiciled outside England and Wales

(1) Subject to paragraph (3) below, where the deceased died domiciled outside England and Wales, a district judge or registrar may order that a grant, limited in such way as the district judge or registrar may direct, do issue to any of the following persons –

   (a) to the person entrusted with the administration of the estate by the court having jurisdiction at the place where the deceased died domiciled; or

   (b) where there is no person so entrusted, to the person beneficially entitled to the estate by the law of the place where the deceased died domiciled or, if there is more than one person so entitled, to such of them as the district judge or registrar may direct; or

   (c) if in the opinion of the district judge or registrar the circumstances so require, to such person as the district judge or registrar may direct.

(2) A grant made under paragraph (1)(a) or (b) above may be issued jointly with such person as the district judge or registrar may direct if the grant is required to be made to not less than two administrators.

(3) Without any order made under paragraph (1) above –

   (a) probate of any will which is admissible to proof may be granted –

      (i) if the will is in the English or Welsh language, to the executor named therein; or

      (ii) if the will describes the duties of a named person in terms sufficient to constitute him executor according to the tenor of the will, to that person; and

(b) where the whole or substantially the whole of the estate in England and Wales consists of immovable property, a grant in respect of the whole estate may be made in accordance with the law which would have been applicable if the deceased had died domiciled in England and Wales.

31. Grants to attorneys

(1) Subject to paragraphs (2) and (3) below, the lawfully constituted attorney of a person entitled to a grant may apply for administration for the use and benefit of the donor, and such grant shall be limited until further representation be granted, or in such other way as the district judge or registrar may direct.

(2) Where the donor referred to in paragraph (1) above is an executor, notice of the application shall be given to any other executor unless such notice is dispensed with by the district judge or registrar.

(3) Where the donor referred to in paragraph (1) above is mentally incapable and the attorney is acting under an enduring power of attorney, the application shall be made in accordance with rule 35.

32. Grants on behalf of minors

(1) Where a person to whom a grant would otherwise be made is a minor, administration for his use and benefit, limited until he attains the age of eighteen years, shall, unless otherwise directed, and subject to paragraph (2) of this rule, be granted to

(a) a parent of the minor who has, or is deemed to have, parental responsibility for him in accordance with –

(i) section 2(1), 2(2) or 4 of the Children Act 1989,

(ii) paragraph 4 or 6 of Schedule 14 to that Act, or

(iii) an adoption order within the meaning of section 12(1) of the Adoption Act 1976 or section 46(1) of the Adoption and Children Act 2002; or

(aa) a person who has, or is deemed to have, parental responsibility for the minor by virtue of section 12(2) of the Children Act 1989 where the court has made a residence order under section 8 of that Act in respect of the minor in favour of that person; or

(ab) a step-parent of the minor who has parental responsibility for him in accordance with section 4A of the Children Act 1989; or

(b) a guardian of the minor who is appointed, or deemed to have been appointed, in accordance with section 5 of the Children Act 1989 or in accordance with paragraph 12, 13 or 14 of Schedule 14 to that Act; or

(ba) a special guardian of the minor who is appointed in accordance with section 14A of the Children Act 1989; or

(bb) an adoption agency which has parental responsibility for the minor by virtue of section 25(2) of the Adoption and Children Act 2002; or

(c) a local authority which has, or is deemed to have, parental responsibility for the minor by virtue of section 33(3) of the Children Act 1989 where the court has made a care order under section 31(1)(a) of that Act in respect of the minor and that local authority is designated in that order

provided that where the minor is sole executor and has no interest in the residuary estate of the deceased, administration for the use and benefit of the minor limited as aforesaid, shall, unless a district judge or registrar otherwise directs, be granted to the person entitled to the residuary estate.

(2) A district judge or registrar may by order appoint a person to obtain administration for the use and benefit of the minor, limited as aforesaid, in default of, or jointly with, or to the exclusion of, any person mentioned in paragraph (1) of this rule; and the person intended shall file an affidavit in support of his application to be appointed.

(3) Where there is only one person competent and willing to take a grant under the foregoing provisions of this rule, such person may, unless a district judge or registrar otherwise directs, nominate any fit and proper person to act jointly with him in taking the grant.

33. Grants where a minor is a co-executor

(1) Where a minor is appointed executor jointly with one or more other executors, probate may be granted to the executor or executors not under disability with power reserved to the minor executor, and the minor executor shall be entitled to apply for probate on attaining the age of eighteen years.

(2) Administration for the use and benefit of a minor executor until he attains the age of eighteen years may be granted under rule 32 if, and only if, the executors who are not under disability renounce or, on being cited to accept or refuse a grant, fail to make an effective application therefor.

34. Renunciation of the right of a minor to a grant

(1) The right of a minor executor to probate on attaining the age of eighteen years may not be renounced by any person on his behalf.

(2) The right of a minor to administration may be renounced only by a person appointed as guardian under paragraph (2) of rule 32, and authorised by the district judge or registrar to renounce on behalf of the minor.

35. Grants in case of mental incapacity

(1) Unless a district judge or registrar otherwise directs, no grant shall be made under this rule unless all persons entitled in the same degree as the incapable person referred to in paragraph (2) below have been cleared off.

(2) Where a district judge or registrar is satisfied that a person entitled to a grant is by reason of mental incapacity incapable of managing his affairs, administration for his use and benefit, limited until further representation be granted or in such other way as the district judge or registrar may direct, may be granted in the following order of priority –

  (a) to the person authorised by the Court of Protection to apply for a grant;
  (b) where there is no person so authorised, to the lawful attorney of the incapable person acting under a registered enduring power of attorney;
  (c) where there is no such attorney entitled to act, or if the attorney shall renounce administration for the use and benefit of the incapable person, to the person entitled to the residuary estate of the deceased.

(3) Where a grant is required to be made to not less than two administrators, and there is only one person competent and willing to take a grant under the foregoing provisions of this rule, administration may, unless a registrar otherwise directs, be granted to such person jointly with any other person nominated by him.

(4) Notwithstanding the foregoing provisions of this rule, administration for the use and benefit of the incapable person may be granted to such other person as the district judge or registrar may by order direct.

(5) Unless the applicant is the person authorised in paragraph (2)(a) above, notice of an intended application under this rule shall be given to the Court of Protection.

36. Grants to trust corporations and other corporate bodies

(1) An application for a grant to a trust corporation shall be made through one of its officers, and such officer shall depose in the oath that the corporation is a trust corporation as defined by these Rules and that it has power to accept a grant.

(2) (a) Where the trust corporation is the holder of an official position, any officer whose name is included on a list filed with the senior district judge of persons authorised to make affidavits and sign documents on behalf of the office holder may act as the officer through whom the holder of that official position applies for the grant.

(b) In all other cases a certified copy of the resolution of the trust corporation authorising the officer to make the application shall be lodged, or it shall be deposed in the oath that such certified copy has been filed with the senior district judge, that the officer is therein identified by the position he holds, and that such resolution is still in force.

(3) A trust corporation may apply for administration otherwise than as a beneficiary or the attorney of some person, and on any such application there shall be lodged the consents of all persons entitled to a grant and of all persons interested in the residuary estate of the deceased save that the district judge or registrar may dispense with any such consents as aforesaid on such terms, if any, as he may think fit.

(4) (a) Subject to sub-paragraph (d) below, where a corporate body would, if an individual, be entitled to a grant but is not a trust corporation as defined by these Rules, administration for its use and benefit, limited until further representation be granted, may be made to its nominee or to its lawfully constituted attorney.

(b) A copy of the resolution appointing the nominee or the power of attorney (whichever is appropriate) shall be lodged, and such resolution or power of attorney shall be sealed by the corporate body, or be otherwise authenticated to the district judge's or registrar's satisfaction.

(c) The nominee or attorney shall depose in the oath that the corporate body is not a trust corporation as defined by these Rules.

(d) The provisions of paragraph (4)(a) above shall not apply where a corporate body is appointed executor jointly with an individual unless the right of the individual has been cleared off.

37. Renunciation of probate and administration

(1) Renunciation of probate by an executor shall not operate as renunciation of any right which he may have to a grant of administration in some other capacity unless he expressly renounces such right.

(2) Unless a district judge or registrar otherwise directs, no person who has renounced administration in one capacity may obtain a grant thereof in some other capacity.

(2A) Renunciation of probate or administration by members of a partnership –

(a) may be effected, or

(b) subject to paragraph (3) below, may be retracted by any two of them with the authority of the others and any such renunciation or retraction shall recite such authority.

(3) A renunciation of probate or administration may be retracted at any time with the leave of a district judge or registrar; provided that only in exceptional circumstances may leave be given to an executor to retract a renunciation of probate after a grant has been made to some other person entitled in a lower degree.

(4) A direction or order giving leave under this rule may be made either by the registrar of a district probate registry where the renunciation is filed or by a district judge.

38. Notice to Crown of intended application for grant

In any case in which it appears that the Crown is or may be beneficially interested in the estate of a deceased person, notice of intended application for a grant shall be given by the applicant to the Treasury Solicitor, and the district judge or registrar may direct that no grant shall issue within 28 days after the notice has been given.

39. Resealing under Colonial Probates Acts 1892 and 1927

(1) An application under the Colonial Probates Acts 1892 and 1927 for the resealing of probate or administration granted by the court of a country to which those Acts apply may be made by the person to whom the grant was made or by any person authorised in writing to apply on his behalf.

(2) On any such application an Inland Revenue affidavit or account shall be lodged.

(3) Except by leave of a district judge or registrar, no grant shall be resealed unless it was made to such a person as is mentioned in sub-paragraph (a) or (b) of paragraph (1) of rule 30 or to a person to whom a grant could be made under sub-paragraph (a) of paragraph (3) of that rule.

(4) No limited or temporary grant shall be resealed except by leave of a district judge or registrar.

(5) Every grant lodged for resealing shall include a copy of any will to which the grant relates or shall be accompanied by a copy thereof certified as correct by or under the authority of the court by which the grant was made, and where the copy of the grant required to be deposited under subsection (1) of section 2 of the Colonial Probates Act 1892 does not include a copy of the will, a copy thereof shall be deposited in the registry before the grant is resealed.

(6) The district judge or registrar shall send notice of the resealing to the court which made the grant.

(7) Where notice is received in the Principal Registry of the resealing of a grant issued in England and Wales, notice of any amendment or revocation of the grant shall be sent to the court by which it was resealed.

40. Application for leave to sue on guarantee

An application for leave under section 120(3) of the Act or under section 11(5) of the Administration of Estates Act 1971 to sue a surety on a guarantee given for the purposes of either of those sections shall, unless the district judge or registrar otherwise directs under rule 61, be made by summons to a district judge or registrar and notice of the application shall be served on the administrator, the surety and any co-surety.

41. Amendment and revocation of grant

(1) Subject to paragraph (2) below, if a district judge or registrar is satisfied that a grant should be amended or revoked he may make an order accordingly.

(2) Except on the application or with the consent of the person to whom the grant was made, the power conferred in paragraph (1) above shall be exercised only in exceptional circumstances.

42. Certificate of delivery of Inland Revenue affidavit

Where the deceased died before 13th March 1975 the certificate of delivery of an Inland Revenue affidavit required by section 30 of the Customs and Inland Revenue Act 1881 to be borne by every grant shall be in Form 1.

43. Standing searches

(1) Any person who wishes to be notified of the issue of a grant may enter a standing search for the grant by lodging at, or sending by post to any registry or sub-registry, a notice in Form 2.

(2) A person who has entered a standing search will be sent an office copy of any grant which corresponds with the particulars given on the completed Form 2 and which –

    (a) issued not more than twelve months before the entry of the standing search; or

    (b) issues within a period of six months after the entry of the standing search.

(3) (a) Where an applicant wishes to extend the said period of six months, he or his solicitor or probate practitioner may lodge at, or send by post to, the registry or sub-registry at which the standing search was entered written application for extension.

    (b) An application for extension as aforesaid must be lodged, or received by post, within the last month of the said period of six months, and the standing search shall thereupon be effective for an additional period of six months from the date on which it was due to expire.

    (c) A standing search which has been extended as above may be further extended by the filing of a further application for extension subject to the same conditions as set out in sub-paragraph (b) above.

44. Caveats

(1) Any person who wishes to show cause against the sealing of a grant may enter a caveat in any registry or sub-registry, and the district judge or registrar shall not allow any grant to be sealed (other than a grant ad colligenda bona or a grant under section 117 of the Act) if he has knowledge of an effective caveat; provided that no caveat shall prevent the sealing of a grant on the day on which the caveat is entered.

(2) Any person wishing to enter a caveat (in these Rules called 'the caveator'), or a solicitor or probate practitioner on his behalf, may effect entry of a caveat –

    (a) by completing Form 3 in the appropriate book at any registry or sub-registry; or

    (b) by sending by post at his own risk a notice in Form 3 to any registry or sub-registry and the proper officer shall provide an acknowledgement of the entry of the caveat.

(3) (a) Except as otherwise provided by this rule or by rules 45 or 46, a caveat shall be effective for a period of six months from the date of entry thereof, and

where a caveator wishes to extend the said period of six months, he or his solicitor or probate practitioner may lodge at, or send by post to, the registry or sub-registry at which the caveat was entered a written application for extension.

(b) An application for extension as aforesaid must be lodged, or received by post, within the last month of the said period of six months, and the caveat shall thereupon (save as otherwise provided by this rule) be effective for an additional period of six months from the date on which it was due to expire.

(c) A caveat which has been extended as above may be further extended by the filing of a further application for extension subject to the same conditions as set out in sub-paragraph (b) above.

(4) An index of caveats entered in any registry or sub-registry shall be maintained and upon receipt of an application for a grant, the registry or sub-registry at which the application is made shall cause a search of the index to be made and the appropriate district judge or registrar shall be notified of the entry of a caveat against the sealing of a grant for which the application has been made.

(5) Any person claiming to have an interest in the estate may cause to be issued from the nominated registry in which the caveat index is maintained a warning in Form 4 against the caveat, and the person warning shall state his interest in the estate of the deceased and shall require the caveator to give particulars of any contrary interest in the estate; and the warning or a copy thereof shall be served on the caveator forthwith.

(6) A caveator who has no interest contrary to that of the person warning, but who wishes to show cause against the sealing of a grant to that person, may within eight days of service of the warning upon him (inclusive of the day of such service), or at any time thereafter if no affidavit has been filed under paragraph (12) below, issue and serve a summons for directions.

(7) On the hearing of any summons for directions under paragraph (6) above the district judge or registrar may give a direction for the caveat to cease to have effect.

(8) Any caveat in force when a summons for directions is issued shall remain in force until the summons has been disposed of unless a direction has been given under paragraph (7) above or until it is withdrawn under paragraph (11) below.

(9) The issue of a summons under this rule shall be notified forthwith to the nominated registry in which the caveat index is maintained.

(10) A caveator having an interest contrary to that of the person warning may within eight days of service of the warning upon him (inclusive of the day of such service) or at any time thereafter if no affidavit has been filed under paragraph (12) below, enter an appearance in the nominated registry in which the caveat index is maintained by filing Form 5; and he shall serve forthwith on the person warning a copy of Form 5 sealed with the seal of the court.

(11) A caveator who has not entered an appearance to a warning may at any time withdraw his caveat by giving notice at the registry or sub-registry at which it was entered, and the caveat shall thereupon cease to have effect; and, where the caveat has been so withdrawn, the caveator shall forthwith give notice of withdrawal to the person warning.

(12) If no appearance has been entered by the caveator or no summons has been issued by him under paragraph (6) of this rule, the person warning may at any time after eight days of service of the warning upon the caveator (inclusive of the day of such service) file an affidavit in the nominated registry in which the caveat index is maintained as to such service and the caveat shall thereupon

cease to have effect provided that there is no pending summons under paragraph (6) of this rule.

(13) Unless a district judge or, where application to discontinue a caveat is made by consent, a registrar by order made on summons otherwise directs, any caveat in respect of which an appearance to a warning has been entered shall remain in force until the commencement of a probate action.

(14) Except with the leave of a district judge, no further caveat may be entered by or on behalf of any caveator whose caveat is either in force or has ceased to have effect under paragraphs (7) or (12) of this rule or under rule 45(4) or rule 46(3).

(15) In this rule, 'nominated registry' means the registry nominated for the purpose of this rule by the senior district judge or in the absence of any such nomination the Leeds District Probate Registry.

45. Probate actions

(1) Upon being advised by the court concerned of the commencement of a probate action the senior district judge shall give notice of the action to every caveator other than the plaintiff in the action in respect of each caveat that is in force.

(2) In respect of any caveat entered subsequent to the commencement of a probate action the senior district judge shall give notice to that caveator of the existence of the action.

(3) Unless a district judge by order made on summons otherwise directs, the commencement of a probate action shall operate to prevent the sealing of a grant (other than a grant under section 117 of the Act) until application for a grant is made by the person shown to be entitled thereto by the decision of the court in such action.

(4) Upon such application for a grant, any caveat entered by the plaintiff in the action, and any caveat in respect of which notice of the action has been given, shall cease to have effect.

46. Citations

(1) Any citation may issue from the Principal Registry or a district probate registry and shall be settled by a district judge or registrar before being issued.

(2) Every averment in a citation, and such other information as the registrar may require, shall be verified by an affidavit sworn by the person issuing the citation (in these Rules called the 'citor'), provided that the district judge or registrar may in special circumstances accept an affidavit sworn by the citor's solicitor or probate practitioner.

(3) The citor shall enter a caveat before issuing a citation and, unless a district judge by order made on summons otherwise directs, any caveat in force at the commencement of the citation proceedings shall, unless withdrawn pursuant to paragraph (11) of rule 44, remain in force until application for a grant is made by the person shown to be entitled thereto by the decision of the court in such proceedings, and upon such application any caveat entered by a party who had notice of the proceedings shall cease to have effect.

(4) Every citation shall be served personally on the person cited unless the district judge or registrar, on cause shown by affidavit, directs some other mode of service, which may include notice by advertisement.

(5) Every will referred to in a citation shall be lodged in a registry before the citation is issued, except where the will is not in the citor's possession and the district judge or registrar is satisfied that it is impracticable to require it to be lodged.

(6) A person who has been cited to appear may, within eight days of service of the citation upon him (inclusive of the day of such service), or at any time thereafter if no application has been made by the citor under paragraph (5) of rule 47 or paragraph (2) of rule 48, enter an appearance in the registry from which the citation issued by filing Form 5 and shall forthwith thereafter serve on the citor a copy of Form 5 sealed with the seal of the registry.

47. Citation to accept or refuse or to take a grant

(1) A citation to accept or refuse a grant may be issued at the instance of any person who would himself be entitled to a grant in the event of the person cited renouncing his right thereto.

(2) Where power to make a grant to an executor has been reserved, a citation calling on him to accept or refuse a grant may be issued at the instance of the executors who have proved the will or the survivor of them or of the executors of the last survivor of deceased executors who have proved.

(3) A citation calling on an executor who has intermeddled in the estate of the deceased to show cause why he should not be ordered to take a grant may be issued at the instance of any person interested in the estate at any time after the expiration of six months from the death of the deceased, provided that no citation to take a grant shall issue while proceedings as to the validity of the will are pending.

(4) A person cited who is willing to accept or take a grant may, after entering an appearance, apply ex parte by affidavit to a district judge or registrar for an order for a grant to himself.

(5) If the time limited for appearance has expired and the person cited has not entered an appearance, the citor may –

    (a) in the case of a citation under paragraph (1) of this rule, apply to a district judge or registrar for an order for a grant to himself;

    (b) in the case of a citation under paragraph (2) of this rule, apply to a district judge or registrar for an order that a note be made on the grant that the executor in respect of whom power was reserved has been duly cited and has not appeared and that all his rights in respect of the executorship have wholly ceased; or

    (c) in the case of a citation under paragraph (3) of this rule, apply to a district judge or registrar by summons (which shall be served on the person cited) for an order requiring such person to take a grant within a specified time or for a grant to himself or to some other person specified in the summons.

(6) An application under the last foregoing paragraph shall be supported by an affidavit showing that the citation was duly served.

(7) If the person cited has entered an appearance but has not applied for a grant under paragraph (4) of this rule, or has failed to prosecute his application with reasonable diligence, the citor may –

    (a) in the case of a citation under paragraph (1) of this rule, apply by summons to a district judge or registrar for an order for a grant to himself;

    (b) in the case of a citation under paragraph (2) of this rule, apply by summons to a district judge or registrar for an order striking out the appearance and for the endorsement on the grant of such a note as is mentioned in sub-paragraph (b) of paragraph (5) of this rule; or

    (c) in the case of a citation under paragraph (3) of this rule, apply by summons to a district judge or registrar for an order requiring the person cited to take a grant within a specified time or for a grant to himself or to some other person specified in the summons;

and the summons shall be served on the person cited.

48.   Citation to propound a will

(1)   A citation to propound a will shall be directed to the executors named in the will and to all persons interested thereunder, and may be issued at the instance of any citor having an interest contrary to that of the executors or such other persons.

(2)   If the time limited for appearance has expired, the citor may –

(a)   in the case where no person has entered an appearance, apply to a district judge or registrar for an order for a grant as if the will were invalid and such application shall be supported by an affidavit showing that the citation was duly served; or

(b)   in the case where no person who has entered an appearance proceeds with reasonable diligence to propound the will, apply to a district judge or registrar by summons, which shall be served on every person cited who has entered an appearance, for such an order as is mentioned in paragraph (a) above.

49.   Address for service

All caveats, citations, warnings and appearances shall contain an address for service in England and Wales.

50.   Application for order to attend for examination or for subpoena to bring in a will

(1)   An application under section 122 of the Act for an order requiring a person to attend for examination may, unless a probate action has been commenced, be made to a district judge or registrar by summons which shall be served on every such person as aforesaid.

(2)   An application under section 123 of the Act for the issue by a district judge or registrar of a subpoena to bring in a will shall be supported by an affidavit setting out the grounds of the application, and if any person served with the subpoena denies that the will is in his possession or control he may file an affidavit to that effect in the registry from which the subpoena issued.

51.   Grants to part of an estate under section 113 of the Act

An application for an order for a grant under section 113 of the Act to part of an estate may be made to a district judge or registrar, and shall be supported by an affidavit setting out the grounds of the application, and

(a)   stating whether the estate of the deceased is known to be insolvent; and

(b)   showing how any person entitled to a grant in respect of the whole estate in priority to the applicant has been cleared off.

52.   Grants of administration under discretionary powers of court, and grants ad colligenda bona

An application for an order for –

(a)   a grant of administration under section 116 of the Act; or

(b) a grant of administration ad colligenda bona,

may be made to a district judge or registrar and shall be supported by an affidavit setting out the grounds of the application.

53. Applications for leave to swear to death

An application for leave to swear to the death of a person in whose estate a grant is sought may be made to a district judge or registrar, and shall be supported by an affidavit setting out the grounds of the application and containing particulars of any policies of insurance effected on the life of the presumed deceased together with such further evidence as the district judge or registrar may require.

54. Grants in respect of nuncupative wills and copies of wills

(1) Subject to paragraph (2) below, an application for an order admitting to proof a nuncupative will, or a will contained in a copy or reconstruction thereof where the original is not available, shall be made to a district judge or registrar.

(2) In any case where a will is not available owing to its being retained in the custody of a foreign court or official, a duly authenticated copy of the will may be admitted to proof without the order referred to in paragraph (1) above.

(3) An application under paragraph (1) above shall be supported by an affidavit setting out the grounds of the application, and by such evidence on affidavit as the applicant can adduce as to –

(a) the will's existence after the death of the testator or, where there is no such evidence, the facts on which the applicant relies to rebut the presumption that the will has been revoked by destruction;

(b) in respect of a nuncupative will, the contents of that will; and

(c) in respect of a reconstruction of a will, the accuracy of that reconstruction.

(4) The district judge or registrar may require additional evidence in the circumstances of a particular case as to due execution of the will or as to the accuracy of the copy will, and may direct that notice be given to persons who would be prejudiced by the application.

55. Application for rectification of a will

(1) An application for an order that a will be rectified by virtue of section 20(1) of the Administration of Justice Act 1982 may be made to a district judge or registrar, unless a probate action has been commenced.

(2) The application shall be supported by an affidavit, setting out the grounds of the application, together with such evidence as can be adduced as to the testator's intentions and as to whichever of the following matters as are in issue: –

(a) in what respects the testator's intentions were not understood; or

(b) the nature of any alleged clerical error.

(3) Unless otherwise directed, notice of the application shall be given to every person having an interest under the will whose interest might be prejudiced, or such other person who might be prejudiced, by the rectification applied for and any comments in writing by any such person shall be exhibited to the affidavit in support of the application.

(4) If the district judge or registrar is satisfied that, subject to any direction to the contrary, notice has been given to every person mentioned in paragraph (3) above,

and that the application is unopposed, he may order that the will be rectified accordingly.

56. Notice of election by surviving spouse or civil partner to redeem life interest

(1) Where a surviving spouse or civil partner who is the sole or sole surviving personal representative of the deceased is entitled to a life interest in part of the residuary estate and elects under section 47A of the Administration of Estates Act 1925 to have the life interest redeemed, he may give written notice of the election to the senior district judge in pursuance of subsection (7) of that section by filing a notice in Form 6 in the Principal Registry or in the district probate registry from which the grant issued.

(2) Where the grant issued from a district probate registry, the notice shall be filed in duplicate.

(3) A notice filed under this rule shall be noted on the grant and the record and shall be open to inspection.

57. Index of grant applications

(1) The senior district judge shall maintain an index of every pending application for a grant made in any registry or sub-registry.

(2) Every registry or sub-registry in which an application is made shall cause the index to be searched and shall record the result of the search.

58. Inspection of copies of original wills and other documents

An original will or other document referred to in section 124 of the Act shall not be open to inspection if, in the opinion of a district judge or registrar, such inspection would be undesirable or otherwise inappropriate.

59. Issue of copies of original wills and other documents

Where copies are required of original wills or other documents deposited under section 124 of the Act, such copies may be facsimile copies sealed with the seal of the court and issued either as office copies or certified under the hand of a district judge or registrar to be true copies.

60. Costs

(1) Order 62 of the Rules of the Supreme Court 1965 shall not apply to costs in non-contentious probate matters, and Parts 43, 44 (except rules 44.9 to 44.12), 47 and 48 of the Civil Procedure Rules 1998 ('the 1998 Rules') shall apply to costs in those matters, with the modifications contained in paragraphs (3) to (7) of this rule.

(2) Where detailed assessment of a bill of costs is ordered, it shall be referred -

   (a) where the order was made by a district judge, to a district judge, a costs judge or an authorised court officer within rule 43.2(1)(d)(iii) or (iv) of the 1998 Rules;

   (b) where the order was made by a registrar, to that registrar or, where this is not possible, in accordance with sub-paragraph (a) above.

(3) Every reference in Parts 43, 44, 47 and 48 of the 1998 Rules to a district judge shall be construed as referring only to a district judge of the Principal Registry.

(4) The definition of 'costs officer' in rule 43.2(1)(c) of the 1998 Rules shall have effect as if it included a paragraph reading –

'(iv) a district probate registrar.'

(5) The definition of 'authorised court officer' in rule 43.2(1)(d) of the 1998 Rules shall have effect as if paragraphs (i) and (ii) were omitted.

(6) Rule 44.3(2) of the 1998 Rules (costs follow the event) shall not apply.

(7) Rule 47.4(2) of the 1998 Rules shall apply as if after the words 'Supreme Court Costs Office' there were inserted ', the Principal Registry of the Family Division or such district probate registry as the court may specify'.

(8) Except in the case of an appeal against a decision of an authorised court officer (to which rules 47.20 to 47.23 of the 1998 Rules apply), an appeal against a decision in assessment proceedings relating to costs in non-contentious probate matters shall be dealt with in accordance with the following paragraphs of this rule.

(9) An appeal within paragraph (8) above against a decision made by a district judge, a costs judge (as defined by rule 43.2(1)(b) of the 1998 Rules) or a registrar, shall lie to a judge of the High Court.

(10) Part 52 of the 1998 Rules applies to every appeal within paragraph (8) above, and any reference in Part 52 to a judge or a district judge shall be taken to include a district judge of the Principal Registry of the Family Division.

(11) The 1998 Rules shall apply to an appeal to which Part 52 or rules 47.20 to 47.23 of those Rules apply in accordance with paragraph (8) above in the same way as they apply to any other appeal within Part 52 or rules 47.20 to 47.23 of those Rules as the case may be; accordingly the Rules of the Supreme Court 1965 and the County Court Rules 1981 shall not apply to any such appeal.

61. Power to require applications to be made by summons

(1) Subject to rule 7(2) a district judge or registrar may require any application to be made by summons to a district judge or registrar in chambers or a judge in chambers or open court.

(2) An application for an inventory and account shall be made by summons to a district judge or registrar.

(3) A summons for hearing by a district judge or registrar shall be issued out of the registry in which it is to be heard.

(4) A summons to be heard by a judge shall be issued out of the Principal Registry.

62. Transfer of applications

A registrar to whom any application is made under these Rules may order the transfer of the application to another district judge or registrar having jurisdiction.

62A. Exercise of a registrar's jurisdiction by another registrar

A registrar may hear and dispose of an application under these Rules on behalf of any other registrar by whom the application would otherwise have been heard, if that other registrar so requests or an application in that behalf is made by a party making an application under these Rules; and where the circumstances require it, the registrar shall, without the need for any such request or application, hear and dispose of the application.

63. Power to make orders for costs

On any application dealt with by him on summons, the registrar shall have full power to determine by whom and to what extent the costs are to be paid.

64. Exercise of powers of judge during Long Vacation

All powers exercisable under these Rules by a judge in chambers may be exercised during the Long Vacation by a district judge.

65. Appeals from district judges or registrars

(1) An appeal against a decision or requirement of a district judge or registrar shall be made by summons to a judge.
(2) If, in the case of an appeal under the last foregoing paragraph, any person besides the appellant appeared or was represented before the registrar from whose decision or requirement the appeal is brought, the summons shall be issued within seven days thereof for hearing on the first available day and shall be served on every such person as aforesaid.
(3) This rule does not apply to an appeal against a decision in proceedings for the assessment of costs.

66. Service of summons

(1) A judge or district judge or, where the application is to be made to a district probate registrar, that registrar, may direct that a summons for the service of which no other provision is made by these Rules shall be served on such person or persons as the judge, district judge or registrar may direct.
(2) Where by these Rules or by any direction given under the last foregoing paragraph a summons is required to be served on any person, it shall be served not less than two clear days before the day appointed for the hearing, unless a judge or district judge or registrar at or before the hearing dispenses with service on such terms, if any, as he may think fit.

67. Notices, etc.

Unless a district judge or registrar otherwise directs or these Rules otherwise provide, any notice or other document required to be given to or served on any person may be given or served in the manner prescribed by Order 65 Rule 5 of the Rules of the Supreme Court 1965.

68. Application to pending proceedings

Subject in any particular case to any direction given by a judge or district judge or registrar, these Rules shall apply to any proceedings which are pending on the date on which they come into force as well as to any proceedings commenced on or after that date.

69. Revocation of previous rules

(1) Subject to paragraph (2) below, the rules set out in the Second Schedule are hereby revoked.
(2) The rules set out in the Second Schedule shall continue to apply to such extent as may be necessary for giving effect to a direction under rule 68.

FIRST SCHEDULE – FORMS

FORM 1

Rule 42

Certificate of delivery of inland revenue affidavit

And it is hereby certified that an Inland Revenue affidavit has been delivered wherein it is shown that the gross value of the said estate in the United Kingdom (exclusive of what the said deceased may have been possessed of or entitled to as a trustee and not beneficially) amounts to £.................... and that the net value of the estate amounts to £....................

And it is further certified that it appears by a receipt signed by an Inland Revenue officer on the said affidavit that £.................... on account of estate duty and interest on such duty has been paid.

FORM 2

Rule 43(1)

Standing search

In the High Court of Justice

Family Division

The Principal or District Probate Registry

I/We apply for the entry of a standing search so that there shall be sent to me/us an office copy of every grant of representation in England and Wales in the estate of –

Full name of deceased ....

Full address: ....

Alternative or alias names: ....

Exact date of death: ....

which either has issued not more than 12 months before the entry of this application or issues within 6 months thereafter.

Signed: ....

Name in block letters ....

Full address: ....

....

....

....

....

Reference No. (if any) ....

FORM 3

Rule 44(2)

Caveat

In the High Court of Justice

Family Division

The Principal *or* District Probate Registry.

Let no grant be sealed in the estate of (*full name and address*) deceased, who died on the .... day of .... 19 .... without notice to (*name of party by whom or on whose behalf the caveat is entered*).

Dated this .... day of .... 19 ....

(*Signed*) (*to be signed by the caveator's solicitor or probate practitioner or by the caveator if acting in person*)

whose address for service is: ....

Solicitor/probate practitioner for the said .... (*If the caveator is acting in person, substitute 'In person'.*)

FORM 4

Rule 44(5)

Warning to caveator

In the High Court of Justice

Family Division

The *nominated registry as defined by rule 44(15)*

To .... of .... a party who has

entered a caveat in the estate of .... deceased.

You have eight days (starting with the day on which this warning was served on you):

(i) to enter an appearance either in person or by your solicitor or probate practitioner, at the [*name and address of the nominated registry*] setting out what
   interest you have in the estate of the above-named ....
   of .... deceased contrary to that of the party at whose
   instance this warning is issued; or

(ii) if you have no contrary interest but wish to show cause against the sealing of a
   grant to such party, to issue and serve a summons for directions by a district judge
   of the Principal Registry or a registrar of a district probate registry.

If you fail to do either of these, the court may proceed to issue a grant of probate or
administration in the said estate notwithstanding your caveat.

Dated the .... day of .... 19 ....

Issued at the instance of ....

[*Here set out the name and interest (including the date of the will, if any, under which
the interest arises) of the party warning, the name of his solicitor and the address for
service. If the party warning is acting in person, this must be stated.*]

Registrar

FORM 5

Rules 44(10), 46(6)

Appearance to warning or citation

In the High Court of Justice

Family Division

The Principal [*or* .... District Probate] Registry

Caveat No. ....

dated the .... day of .... 19 ....

[Citation dated the .... day of .... 19 ....]

Full name and address of deceased: ....

....

....

....

....

Full name and address of person warning [*or* citor]:

....

....

....

....

(*Here set out the interest of the person warning, or citor, as shown in warning or citation.*)

Full name and address of caveator [or person cited].

....

....

....

(*Here set out the interest of the caveator or person cited, stating the date of the will (if any) under which such interest arises.*)

Enter an appearance for the above-named caveator [*or* person cited] in this matter.

Dated the .... day of .... 19 ....

(*Signed*)

whose address for service is:

Solicitor/probate practitioner (*or* 'In person').

FORM 6

Notice of election to redeem life interest

In the High Court of Justice

Family Division

The Principal [*or* .... District Probate] Registry

In the estate of .... deceased. Whereas ....

of .... died on the .... day of

.... 19 .... wholly/partially intestate leaving his/her/lawful

wife/husband/civil partner and .... lawful issue of the said

deceased;

And whereas Probate/Letters of Administration of the estate of the said

.... were granted to me, the said .... [and to

.... of ....] at the Probate Registry on the

.... day of .... 19 .... ;

And whereas [the said .... has ceased to be a personal representative

because ....] and I am [now] the sole personal representative;

Now I, the said .... hereby give notice in accordance with section

47A of the Administration of Estates Act 1925 that I elect to redeem the life interest

to which I am entitled in the estate of the late .... by retaining

£ .... its capital value, and £ .... the costs of

the transaction.

Dated the .... day of .... 19 ....

(Signed)

To the district judge of the Family Division.

Non-Contentious Probate Fees Order 2004 (SI 2004/3120)

The Lord Chancellor, in exercise of the powers conferred upon him by sections 92 and 108(6) of the Courts Act 2003, and section 128 of the Finance Act 1990 with the consent of the Treasury under section 92(1) of the Courts Act 2003 and after consultation with the Lord Chief Justice, the Master of the Rolls, the President of the Family Division, the Vice-Chancellor, the Head of Civil Justice and the Deputy Head of Civil Justice and the Civil Justice Council under section 92(5) and (6) of the Courts Act 2003, hereby makes the following Order:

Citation, commencement and interpretation

1. (1) This Order may be cited as the Non-Contentious Probate Fees Order 2004 and shall come into force on the 4th January 2005.

    (2) In this Order –

        (a) a fee referred to by number means the fee so numbered in Schedule 1 to this Order;

        (b) 'assessed value' means the value of the net real and personal estate (excluding settled land if any) passing under the grant as shown –

            (i) in the Inland Revenue affidavit (for a death occurring before 13th March 1975), or

            (ii) in the Inland Revenue account (for a death occurring on or after 13th March 1975), or

            (iii) in the case in which, in accordance with arrangements made between the President of the Family Division and the Commissioners of the Inland Revenue, or regulations made under section 256(1)(a) of the Inheritance Tax Act 1984 and from time to time in force, no such affidavit or account is required to be delivered, in the oath which is sworn to lead to the grant,

    and in the case of an application to reseal means the value, as shown, passing under the grant upon its being resealed;

        (c) 'authorised place of deposit' means any place in which, by virtue of a direction given under section 124 of the Supreme Court Act 1981 original wills and other documents under the control of the High Court (either in the principal registry or in any district registry) are deposited and preserved;

        (d) 'grant' means a grant of probate or letters of administration;

        (e) 'district registry' includes the probate registry of Wales, any district probate registry and any sub-registry attached to it;

(f) 'the principal registry' means the Principal Registry of the Family Division and any sub-registry attached to it.

Fees to be taken

2. The fees set out in column 2 of Schedule 1 to this Order shall be taken in the principal registry and in each district registry in respect of the items described in column 1 in accordance with and subject to any directions specified in column 1.

Exclusion of certain death gratuities

3. In determining the value of any personal estate for the purposes of this Order there shall be excluded the value of a death gratuity payable under section 17(2) of the Judicial Pensions Act 1981 or section 4(3) of the Judicial Pensions and Retirement Act 1993, or payable to the personal representatives of a deceased civil servant by virtue of a scheme made under section 1 of the Superannuation Act 1972.

Exemptions, reductions, remissions and refunds

4. Where it appears to the Lord Chancellor that the payment of any fee prescribed by this Order would, owing to the exceptional circumstances of the particular case, involve undue financial hardship, he may reduce or remit the fee in that case.

5. (1) Subject to paragraph (2) where a fee has been paid at a time –

    (a) where the Lord Chancellor, if he had been aware of all the circumstances, would have reduced the fee under article 4, the amount by which the fee would have been reduced shall be refunded; and

    (b) where the Lord Chancellor, if he had been aware of all the circumstances, would have remitted the fee under article 4, the fee shall be refunded.

    (2) No refund shall be made under paragraph (1) unless the party who paid the fee applies within 6 months of paying the fee.

    (3) The Lord Chancellor may extend the period of 6 months referred to in paragraph (2) if he considers that there is good reason for an application being made after the end of the period of 6 months.

6. (1) Where by any convention entered into by Her Majesty with any foreign power it is provided that no fee shall be required to be paid in respect of any proceedings, the fees specified in this Order shall not be taken in respect of those proceedings.

    (2) Where any application for a grant is withdrawn before the issue of a grant, a registrar may reduce or remit a fee.

    (3) Fee 7 shall not be taken where a search is made for research or similar purposes by permission of the President of the Family Division for a document over 100 years old filed in the principal registry or a district registry or another authorised place of deposit.

Special exemption – Armed Forces

7. Where a fee has been paid or fees have been paid for the application of a grant (other than fee 3.2) and at the time of payment of that fee or those fees –

(a) the application for the grant was in respect of an estate exempt from Inheritance Tax by virtue of section 154 of the Inheritance Tax Act 1984 (exemption for members of the armed forces etc); and

(b) was in respect of a death occurring before 20th March 2003;

the Lord Chancellor shall upon receiving a written application refund the difference between any fee or fees paid and fee 3.2.

Revocation

8. The Order specified in Schedule 2 in so far as it was made under section 128 of the Finance Act 1990 shall be revoked.

SCHEDULE 1	**FEES TO BE TAKEN**	**Article 2**

Column 1 Number and description of fee   *Column 2 Amount of fee*

1. Application for a grant

On an application for a grant (or for resealing a grant) other than on an application to which fee 3 applies, where the assessed value of the estate exceeds £5,000   £40

2. Personal application fee

Where the application under fee 1 is made by a personal applicant (not being an application to which fee 3 applies) fee 2 is payable in addition to fee 1, where the assessed value of the estate exceeds £5,000   £50

3. Special applications

3.1 For a duplicate or second or subsequent grant (including one following a revoked grant) in respect of the same deceased person, other than a grant preceded only by a grant limited to settled land, to trust property, or to part of the estate   £15

3.2 On an application for a grant relating to a death occurring on or after 20th March 2003 and in respect of an estate exempt from inheritance tax by virtue of section 154 of the Inheritance Tax Act 1984 (exemption for members of the armed forces etc)   £8

4. Caveats

For the entry or the extension of a caveat   £15

5. Search

On an application for a standing search to be carried out in an estate, for each period of six months including the issue of a copy grant and will, if any (irrespective of the number of pages)   £5

6. Deposit of wills

On depositing a will for safe custody in the principal registry or a
district registry £15

7. Inspection

On inspection of any will or other document retained by the registry
(in the presence of an officer of the registry) £15

8. Copy documents

On a request for a copy of any document whether or not provided as
a certified copy:

(a) for the first copy £5
(b) for every subsequent copy of the same document if supplied at the
same time £1
(c) where copies of any document are made available on a computer
disk or in other electronic form, for each such copy £3
(d) where a search of the index is required, in addition to fee 8(a), (b)
or (c) as appropriate, for each period of 4 years searched after the
first 4 years £3

9. Oaths

Except on a personal application for a grant, for administering an oath,

9.1 for each deponent to each affidavit £5
9.2 for marking each exhibit £2

10. Determination of costs

For determining costs   The same fees as are payable from time to time for
determining costs under the Civil Proceedings Fees
Order 2004, (the relevant fees are set out in fee 5 in
Schedule 1 to that Order)

11. Settling documents

For perusing and settling citations, advertisements, oaths, affidavits,
or other documents, for each document settled £10

SCHEDULE 2   **ORDER REVOKED**   **Article 8**

Title   *Reference*

The Non-Contentious Probate Fees (Amendment) Order 2000 S.I. 2000/642

APPENDIX B3

Court of Protection and enduring power of attorney fees

The following is the appendix to the Court of Protection Rules 2001 as amended. The fees stated are effective from 1 April 2006.

COURT OF PROTECTION FEES

The following is Schedule 2 of the Court of Protection (Enduring Powers of Attorney) Rules 2001, as amended. The fees stated are effective from 1 April 2005.

ENDURING POWER OF ATTORNEY FEES

Item	Fee
Registration Fee 1. On lodging an application for registration of an enduring power of attorney.	£120.00
Search Fee 2. On application for a search of the register.	£20.00
Fee for passing of accounts 3. On the passing of an attorney's accounts by the court.	£100.00
Fee for certain directions 4. On making an application for, or, as the case may be, on the making of, a direction under section 8(2)(d) or (e) of the Act, or for a direction under section 5 of the Act which, if the power were registered, would be a direction under section 8(2)(d) or (e).	£100.00, or, in a special case – (a) a standard fee of – (i) £100.00 or (ii) in a case to which rule 26(4) applies, £360.00; and (b) an additional fee of £500.00. provided that no fee under this item shall be taken if the property is worth less than £100.00.

Solicitors (Non-Contentious Business) Remuneration Order 1994 (SI 1994/2616)

The Lord Chancellor, the Lord Chief Justice, the Master of the Rolls, the President of the Law Society, the president of Holborn law society and the Chief Land Registrar (in respect of business done under the Land Registration Act 1925, together constituting the committee authorised to make orders under section 56 of the Solicitors Act 1974, in exercise of the powers conferred on them by that section and having complied with the requirements of section 56(3), hereby make the following Order:

Citation, commencement and revocation

1. (1) This Order may be cited as the Solicitors' (Non-Contentious Business) Remuneration Order 1994.
   (2) This Order shall come into force on 1st November 1994 and shall apply to all non-contentious business for which bills are delivered on or after that date.
   (3) The Solicitors' Remuneration Order 1972 is hereby revoked except in its application to business for which bills are delivered before this Order comes into force.

Interpretation

2. In this Order:

   'client' means the client of a solicitor;
   'costs' means the amount charged in a solicitor's bill, exclusive of disbursements and value added tax, in respect of non-contentious business or common form probate business;
   'entitled person' means a client or an entitled third party;
   'entitled third party' means a residuary beneficiary absolutely and immediately (and not contingently) entitled to an inheritance, where a solicitor has charged the estate for his professional costs for acting in the administration of the estate, and either

   (a) the only personal representatives are solicitors (whether or not acting in a professional capacity); or
   (b) the only personal representatives are solicitors acting jointly with partners or employees in a professional capacity;

   'paid disbursements' means disbursements already paid by the solicitor;
   'recognised body' means a body corporate recognised by the Council under section 9 of the Administration of Justice Act 1985;

'remuneration certificate' means a certificate issued by the Council pursuant to this Order;

'residuary beneficiary' includes a person entitled to all or part of the residue of an intestate estate; 'solicitor' includes a recognised body; 'the Council' means the Council of the Law Society.

Solicitors' costs

3.   A solicitor's costs shall be such sum as may be fair and reasonable to both solicitor and entitled person, having regard to all the circumstances of the case and in particular to:

(a)   the complexity of the matter or the difficulty or novelty of the questions raised;

(b)   the skill, labour, specialised knowledge and responsibility involved;

(c)   the time spent on the business;

(d)   the number and importance of the documents prepared or perused, without regard to length;

(e)   the place where and the circumstances in which the business or any part thereof is transacted;

(f)   the amount or value of any money or property involved;

(g)   whether any land involved is registered land;

(h)   the importance of the matter to the client; and

(i)   the approval (express or implied) of the entitled person or the express approval of the testator to:

(i)   the solicitor undertaking all or any part of the work giving rise to the costs or

(ii)   the amount of the costs.

Right to certification

4.   (1)   Without prejudice to the provisions of sections 70, 71 and 72 of the Solicitors Act 1974 (which relate to taxation of costs), an entitled person may, subject to the provisions of this Order, require a solicitor to obtain a remuneration certificate from the Council in respect of a bill which has been delivered where the costs are not more than £50,000.

(2)   The remuneration certificate must state what sum, in the opinion of the Council, would be a fair and reasonable charge for the business covered by the bill (whether it be the sum charged or a lesser sum). In the absence of taxation the sum payable in respect of such costs is the sum stated in the remuneration certificate.

Disciplinary and other measures

5.   (1)   If on a taxation the taxing officer allows less than one half of the costs, he must bring the facts of the case to the attention of the Council.

(2)   The provisions of this Order are without prejudice to the general powers of the Council under the Solicitors Act 1974.

Commencement of proceedings against a client

6. Before a solicitor brings proceedings to recover costs against a client on a bill for non-contentious business he must inform the client in writing of the matters specified in article 8, except where the bill has been taxed.

Costs paid by deduction

7. (1) If a solicitor deducts his costs from monies held for or on behalf of a client or of an estate in satisfaction of a bill and an entitled person objects in writing to the amount of the bill within the prescribed time, the solicitor must immediately inform the entitled person in writing of the matters specified in article 8, unless he has already done so.

(2) In this article and in article 10, 'the prescribed time' means:

    (a) in respect of a client, three months after delivery of the relevant bill, or a lesser time (which may not be less than one month) specified in writing to the client at the time of delivery of the bill, or

    (b) in respect of an entitled third party, three months after delivery of notification to the entitled party of the amount of the costs, or a lesser time (which may not be less than one month) specified in writing to the entitled third party at the time of such notification.

Information to be given in writing to entitled person

8. When required by articles 6 or 7, a solicitor shall inform an entitled person in writing of the following matters:

    (a) where article 4(1) applies:

        (i) that the entitled person may, within one month of receiving from the solicitor the information specified in this article or (if later) of delivery of the bill or notification of the amount of the costs, require the solicitor to obtain a remuneration certificate; and

        (ii) that (unless the solicitor has agreed to do so) the Council may waive the requirements of article 11(1), if satisfied from the client's written application that exceptional circumstances exist to justify granting a waiver;

    (b) that sections 70, 71 and 72 of the Solicitors Act 1974 set out the entitled person's rights in relation to taxation;

    (c) that (where the whole of the bill has not been paid, by deduction or otherwise) the solicitor may charge interest on the outstanding amount of the bill in accordance with article 14.

Loss by client of right to certification

9. A client may not require a solicitor to obtain a remuneration certificate:

    (a) after a bill has been delivered and paid by the client, other than by deduction;

    (b) where a bill has been delivered, after the expiry of one month from the date on which the client was informed in writing of the matters specified in article 8 or from delivery of the bill if later;

    (c) after the solicitor and client have entered into a non-contentious business agreement in accordance with the provisions of section 57 of the Solicitors Act 1974;

    (d)   after a court has ordered the bill to be taxed;

    (e)   if article 11(2) applies.

Loss by entitled third party of right to certification

10. An entitled third party may not require a solicitor to obtain a remuneration certificate:

    (a)   after the prescribed time (within the meaning of article 7(2)(b)) has elapsed without any objection being received to the amount of the costs;

    (b)   after the expiry of one month from the date on which the entitled third party was (in compliance with article 7) informed in writing of the matters specified in article 8 or from notification of the costs if later;

    (c)   after a court has ordered the bill to be taxed.

Requirement to pay a sum towards the costs

11. (1)   On requiring a solicitor to obtain a remuneration certificate a client must pay to the solicitor the paid disbursements and value added tax comprised in the bill together with 50% of the costs unless:

    (a)   the client has already paid the amount required under this article, by deduction from monies held or otherwise; or

    (b)   the solicitor or (if the solicitor refuses) the Council has agreed in writing to waive all or part of this requirement.

   (2)   The Council shall be under no obligation to provide a remuneration certificate, and the solicitor may take steps to obtain payment of his bill if the client, having been informed of his right to seek a waiver of the requirements of paragraph (1), has not:

    (a)   within one month of receipt of the information specified in article 8, either paid in accordance with paragraph (1) or applied to the Council in writing for a waiver of the requirements of paragraph (1); or

    (b)   made payment in accordance with the requirements of paragraph (1) within one month of written notification that he has been refused a waiver of those requirements by the Council.

Miscellaneous provisions

12. (1)   After an application has been made by a solicitor for a remuneration certificate the client may pay the bill in full without invalidating the application.

   (2)   A solicitor and entitled person may agree in writing to waive the provisions of sub-paragraphs (a) or (b) of articles 9 or 10.

   (3)   A solicitor may take from his client security for the payment of any costs, including the amount of any interest to which the solicitor may become entitled under article 14.

Refunds by solicitor

13. (1)   If a solicitor has received payment of all or part of his costs and a remuneration certificate is issued for less than the sum already paid, the solicitor must immediately pay to the entitled person any refund which may be due (after taking into account any other sums which may properly be payable to the solicitor whether for costs, paid disbursements, value added tax or otherwise) unless the solicitor has applied for an order for taxation within one month of receipt by him of the remuneration certificate.

(2) Where a solicitor applies for taxation, his liability to pay any refund under paragraph (1) shall be suspended for so long as the taxation is still pending.

(3) The obligation of the solicitor to repay costs under paragraph (1) is without prejudice to any liability of the solicitor to pay interest on the repayment by virtue of any enactment, rule of law or professional rule.

Interest

14. (1) After the information specified in article 8 has been given to an entitled person in compliance with articles 6 or 7, a solicitor may charge interest on the unpaid amount of his costs plus any paid disbursements and value added tax, subject to paragraphs (2) and (3) below.

(2) Where an entitlement to interest arises under paragraph (1), and subject to any agreement made between a solicitor and client, the period for which interest may be charged may run from one month after the date of delivery of a bill, unless the solicitor fails to lodge an application within one month of receipt of a request for a remuneration certificate under article 4, in which case no interest is payable in respect of the period between one month after receiving the request and the actual date on which the application is lodged.

(3) Subject to any agreement made between a solicitor and client, the rate of interest must not exceed the rate for the time being payable on judgment debts.

(4) Interest charged under this article must be calculated, where applicable, by reference to the following:

(a) if a solicitor is required to obtain a remuneration certificate, the total amount of the costs certified by the Council to be fair and reasonable plus paid disbursements and value added tax;

(b) if an application is made for the bill to be taxed, the amount ascertained on taxation;

(c) if an application is made for the bill to be taxed or a solicitor is required to obtain a remuneration certificate and for any reason the taxation or application for a remuneration certificate does not proceed, the unpaid amount of the costs shown in the bill or such lesser sum as may be agreed between the solicitor and the client, plus paid disbursements and value added tax.

Application by solicitor

15. A solicitor, when making an application for a remuneration certificate in accordance with the provisions of this Order, must deliver to the Council the complete relevant file and working papers, and any other information or documentation which the Council may require for the purpose of providing a remuneration certificate.

Probate systems buyers guide

As with all software systems, it is essential to clarify just how much or how little accounts functionality is available. For example, can they handle estate accounts?

How flexible are their workflows? Can they automatically perform IHT200 calculations? And, if so, can they also populate and produce facsimiles of the official forms?

Supplier	Product	Telephone and web address	Type of system	SSG 2006
AIM Professional Systems	Evolution Probate	01482 326971 www.aimlegal.com	Probate case management	SSG 2006
Axxia Systems	Case Manager	0118 960 2602 www.axxia.com	Probate case management	SSG 2006
Civica Systems	Galaxy Probate	0121 359 4861 www.civica.co.uk	Probate case management	SSG 2006
Cognito Software	Custodiens	01279 821400 www.cognitosoftware.co.uk	Full function probate, accounts and trusts system	
Documents Plus (DPL)	Chameleon Wills	01732 867792 www.chamnet.com	CD-based will writing system	SSG 2006
DPS Software	DPS Probate	020 8804 1022 www.dpssoftware.co.uk	Probate case management	SSG 2006
Eclipse Legal Systems	Proclaim Probate	01274 704100 www.eclipselegal.co.uk	Probate case management	SSG 2006
Excelsior LawDesk	ProbateDesk + FormDesk	01273 494978	Handles IHT 200 and R185 calculations	
FinApps	Troika	01403 322900 www.finapps.co.uk	Specialist trusts system	
Isokon Systems	Isokon 2	020 7482 6555 www.isokon.com	Full function probate, accounts and trusts system	Sold by TFB (SSG 2006)
Laserform	Probate CaseControl	01925 750020 www.laserform.co.uk	Full function probate case and accounts management	

Supplier	Product	Contact	Description	Notes
Lawbase	Probate Accounts & Case Management	0161 480 4420 www.lawbase.co.uk	Full function probate case and accounts management	
LexisNexis Butterworths	Wills Creator	0845 608 1188 www.lexisnexis.co.uk	CD-based will writing system incorporates Williams precedents	
Linetime	Liberate Probate	0113 250 0020 www.linetime.co.uk	Probate case management	SSG 2006
Mountain Software	Probate Accounts & Support	01476 573718 www.mountainsoftware.co.uk	Probate case management	SSG 2006
MYOB	Trust Accounts	020 8997 5500 www.myob.com	Specialist trusts system	
Paula Accounts	Paula for Probate	020 8940 3798 www.paula-accounts.co.uk	Probate case and accounts management	
Sweet & Maxwell	Express Wills	020 7449 1111 www.sweetandmaxwell.co.uk	CD-based will writing system incorporates Kessler precedents	
Sweet & Maxwell	Probate Plus	020 7449 1111 www.sweetandmaxwell.co.uk	CD-based, handles IHT 200 calculations and forms	
Timeslice	Probate & Trust Manager	020 7231 0073 www.timeslice.co.uk	Probate and trust management	
Videss	Legal Office Probate	01274 851577 www.videss.co.uk	Probate case management	
Visualfiles	SolCase Probate	0113 226 2000 www.visualfiles.com	Probate case and accounts management	Sold by SOS (SSG 2006)

Further reading

1. PROBATE AND ESTATE ADMINISTRATION

Bedworth, G. and Waterworth, M. (2006) *Rossdale: Probate and the Administration of Estates: A Practical Guide*, 3rd edn, Legalease.

Biggs, A.K. and Gaudern, E. (2003) *Probate and the Administration of Estates: The Law and Practice*, Callow Publishing.

Butcher, C. and King-Jones, A. (1996) *Probate Practice Manual*, 19th edn, Sweet & Maxwell (looseleaf).

Caddick, N. and Martyn, J. (2007) *Williams, Mortimer & Sunnocks – Executors, Administrators and Probate*, Sweet & Maxwell.

D'Costa, R., Synak, T., Winegarton, J. (2001/2005 supplement) *Tristram and Coote's Probate Practice*, LexisNexis.

Dew, R. and Russell, C. (2005) *Ranking Spicer and Pegler: Executorship Law, Trusts and Accounts,* 25th edn, LexisNexis.

King, L. and Whitehouse, C. (2000) *Administration of Estates*, LexisNexis (looseleaf).

Saker, A. and Wright, C. (1996) *Butterworths Wills, Probate and Administration Service*, LexisNexis (looseleaf).

2. INHERITANCE TAX

Arnfield, R. and Waterworth, M. (2006) *Tolley's Inheritance Tax Planning*, LexisNexis.

Arthur, S., Wilson, R., Rowell, D. (2006) *The Practical Lawyer Guide to Inheritance Tax Planning*, Legalease.

Golding, J. (2006) *Tolley's Inheritance Tax 2006/07*, LexisNexis.

McCutcheon, M. (2004/2006 supplement) *McCutcheon on Inheritance Tax*, Sweet & Maxwell.

Wallington, R.A. (Gen. Ed.) *et al.* (1991) *Foster's Inheritance Tax*, LexisNexis (looseleaf).

3. WILLS AND WILL PRECEDENTS

Barlow, R., Sherrin, C., Wallington, R., Meadway, S., Waterworth, M. (2002) *Williams on Wills*, 8th edn, LexisNexis.

Bridge, S., Martyn, J., Oldham, M. (2001) *Theobald on Wills*, Sweet & Maxwell.

Endicott, D. and Jones, A. (2002) *Brighouse's Precedents of Wills*, 13th edn, Sweet & Maxwell.

Riddett, R. (2004) *Will Draftsman's Handbook*, 8th edn, Law Society.

Withers (1987) *Practical Will Precedents*, Sweet & Maxwell (looseleaf and CD-ROM).

4. TRUSTS AND TRUST PRECEDENTS

Clutton, O. and Jennings, S. (1999) *Administration of Trusts*, LexisNexis (looseleaf).

Hayton, D.J. (2002) *Underhill and Hayton: Law Relating to Trustees*, 16th edn, LexisNexis.

Kessler, J. (2006) *Drafting Trusts and Will Trusts: A Modern Approach*, 8th edn, Sweet & Maxwell (hardback and CD-ROM).

Mowbray, J., Tucker, L., Le Poidevin, N., Simpson, E. (2006) *Lewin on Trusts*, 18th edn, Sweet & Maxwell.

Oakley, A.J. (2006) *Parker and Mellows: The Modern Law of Trusts*, 9th edn, Sweet & Maxwell.

Steel, G. (2005) *Trust Practitioner's Handbook*, Law Society.

Withers (1986) *Practical Trust Precedents*, Sweet & Maxwell (looseleaf).

5. JOURNALS AND NEWSLETTERS

PS (Magazine of the Probate Section), Law Society.

Elderly Client Adviser, Ark Publishing.

Private Client Business, Sweet & Maxwell.

STEP Journal, Society of Trust and Estate Practitioners.

6. LAW SOCIETY BOOKS AND MATERIALS

Trusts, Wills and Probate

Angus, T., Clarke, A., Hewitt, P., Reed, P. (2007) *Inheritance Act Claims: A Practical Guide*, Law Society.

Bielanska, C., Terrell, M., Ashton, G. (due 2007) *Elderly Client Handbook*, 4th edn, Law Society.

BMA and the Law Society (2004) *Assessment of Mental Capacity*, 2nd edn, BMJ Books/Blackwells.

Greaney, N., Morris, F., Taylor, B. (2005) *Mental Capacity Act 2005: A Guide to the New Law*, Law Society.

King, P. and Ward, C. (2007) *Lasting Powers of Attorney: A Practical Guide*, Law Society.

Riddett, R. (2004) *Will Draftsman's Handbook*, 8th edn, Law Society.

Steel, G. (2005) *Trust Practitioner's Handbook*, Law Society.

Leaflets

Making a Will Won't Kill You (pack of 25).

Personal Assets Log

Questionnaire for Personal Representative Clients

Your Will: Client Questionnaire

Management

Adam, L. (2001) *Marketing Your Law Firm: A Solicitors' Manual*, Law Society.

Adler, M. (2006) *Clarity for Lawyers: Effective Legal Writing*, 2nd edn, Law Society.

Archbold, C. (2003) *E-Business Basics for Law Firms*, Law Society.

Boutall, T. and Blackburn, B. (2001) *Solicitors' Guide to Good Management*, 2nd edn, Law Society.

Bown-Wilson, D. and Courtney, G. (2002) *Marketing, Management and Motivation: Successful Business Development for Professional Service Firms*, Law Society.

Camp, P. (2006) *Solicitors and the Accounts Rules: A Compliance Handbook*, Law Society.

Camp, P. (2007) *Solicitors and Money Laundering: A Compliance Handbook*, 2nd edn, Law Society.

Kendrick, R. (2002) *Managing Cyber Risks: Strategic Approaches for Law Firms*, Law Society.

Law Society and Moore, M. (2004) *Lexcel Practice Excellence Kit*, 3rd edn, Law Society.

Scott, P. (2004) *Practice Management Handbook*, Law Society.

Smith, M. (2002) *Setting Up and Managing a Small Practice,* 2nd edn, Law Society.

Stapely, S. (2003) *Media Relations for Lawyers*, 2nd edn, Law Society.

Stewart, H. (2003) *Excellent Client Service: Strategies for Success*, Law Society.

Webb, N. (2003) *Internet Marketing: Strategies for Law Firms*, Law Society.

Young, S. (2003) *New Partner's Guide to Management*, Law Society.

Young Solicitors Group (2003) *Becoming a Partner*, 5th edn, Law Society.

Useful addresses

PROBATE REGISTRIES

London Probate Department

Principal Registry
First Avenue House
42–49 High Holborn
London WC1V 6NP
Tel: 020 7947 6939
Fax: 020 7947 6946
DX: 941 Lond/Chancery Ln

District registries

Birmingham

The Priory Courts
33 Bull Street
Birmingham B4 6DU
Tel: 0121 681 3414
Fax: 0121 236 2465
DX: 701990 Birmingham-7

Brighton

William Street
Brighton
East Sussex BN2 2LG
Tel: 01273 573 510
Fax: 01273 625 845
DX: 98073 Brighton-3

Bristol

Ground Floor
The Crescent Centre
Temple Back
Bristol BS1 6EP
Tel: 0117 927 3915/926 4619
Fax: 0117 925 3549
DX: 94400 Bristol-5

Ipswich

Ground Floor
8 Arcade Street
Ipswich IP1 1EJ
Tel: 01473 284 260
Fax: 01473 231 951

Leeds

3rd Floor, Coronet House
Queen Street
Leeds LS1 2BA
Tel: 0113 386 3540
Fax: 0113 247 1893
DX: 26451 Leeds Park Sq

Liverpool

The Queen Elizabeth II Law Courts
Derby Square
Liverpool L2 1XA
Tel: 0151 236 8264
Fax: 0151 227 4634
DX: 14246 Liverpool-1

Manchester

9th Floor, Astley House
23 Quay Street
Manchester M3 4AT
Tel: 0161 837 6070
Fax: 0161 832 2690
DX: 14387 Manchester-1

Newcastle

Number One
Waterloo Square
Newcastle upon Tyne NE1 4 AL
Tel: 0191 211 2170

Fax: 0191 211 2184
DX: 61081 Newcastle

Oxford

Combined Court Building
St Aldates
Oxford OX1 1LY
Tel: 01865 793 055
Fax: 01865 793 090
DX: 96454 Oxford

Winchester

4th Floor, Cromwell House
Andover Road
Winchester
Hants SO23 7EW
Tel: 01962 897 029
Fax: 01962 840 796
DX: 96900 Winchester-2

Cardiff Probate Registry of Wales

PO Box 474
2 Park Street
Cardiff CF10 1TB
Tel: 029 2037 6479
Fax: 029 2022 9855
DX: 122782 Cardiff-13

Sub-Registries

Bangor

City Council Offices
Ffordd Gwynedd
Bangor LL57 1DT
Tel: 01248 362 410
Fax: 01248 364 423
DX: 23186 Bangor–2

Bodmin

Market Street
Bodmin
Cornwall PL31 2JW
Tel: 01208 72279
Fax: 01208 2690047
DX: 81858 Bodmin

Carlisle

Courts of Justice
Earl Street
Carlisle CA1 1DJ
Tel: 01228 521 751
DX: 63034 Carlisle

Carmarthen

14 King Street
Carmarthen SA31 1BL
Tel: 01267 236 238
Fax: 01267 242 560
DX: 51420 Carmarthen

Chester

5th Floor, Hamilton House
Hamilton Place
Chester CH1 2DA
Tel: 01244 345 082
Fax: 01244 346 243
DX: 22162 Chester (Northgate)

Exeter

2nd Floor
Exeter Crown and County Courts
Exeter
Devon EX1 1UH
Tel: 01392 415 370
Fax: 01392 415 608
DX: 98442 Exeter-2

Gloucester

3rd Floor, Combined Courts Building
Kimbrose Way
Gloucester GL1 2DG
Tel: 01452 834 966
Fax: 01452 834 970
DX: 98663 Gloucester-5

Lancaster

Room 111, Mitre House
Church Street
Lancaster LA1 1HE
Tel: 01524 36625
Fax: 01524 35561
DX: 63509 Lancaster

Leicester

Crown Court Building
90 Wellington Street
Leicester LE1 6HG
Tel: 0116 285 3380
Fax: 0116 285 3382
DX: 17403 Leicester-3

Lincoln

360 High Street
Lincoln LN5 7PS
Tel: 01522 523 648
DX: 703233 Lincoln-6

Maidstone

Law Courts
Barker Road
Maidstone
Kent ME16 8EQ
Tel: 01622 202 002
Fax: 01622 202 047
DX: 130066 Maidstone-7

Middlesbrough

Combined Court Centre
Russell Street
Middlesbrough
Cleveland TS1 2AE
Tel: 01962 430 001
DX: 60536 Middlesbrough

Norwich

Combined Court Building
The Law Courts
Bishopsgate
Norwich NR3 1UR
Tel: 01603 728 267
Fax: 01603 627 469
DX: 5202 Norwich

Nottingham

Butt Dyke House
33 Park Row
Nottingham NG1 6GR
Tel: 0115 941 4288
Fax: 0115 950 3383
DX: 10055 Nottingham

Peterborough

1st Floor, Crown Building
Rivergate
Peterborough PE1 1EJ
Tel: 01733 562 802
DX: 12327 Peterborough-1

Sheffield

PO Box 832
The Law Courts
50 West Bar
Sheffield S3 8PH
Tel: 0114 281 2596
Fax: 0114 281 2598
DX: 26054 Sheffield-2

Stoke on Trent

Combined Court Centre
Bethesda Street
Hanley
Stoke on Trent ST1 3BP
Tel: 01782 854 065
Fax: 01782 274 916
DX: 703363 Hanley

York

Castle Chambers
5 Clifford Street
York YO1 9RG
Tel: 01904 666 777
Fax: 01904 666 776
DX: 720629 York-21

ANIMAL WELFARE CHARITIES

The Blue Cross

Shilton Road
Burford
Oxon OX18 4PF
Tel: 01993 822 651
Fax: 01993 823 083
www.bluecross.org.uk

Cats Protection

National Cat Centre
Chelwood Gate
Haywards Heath

Sussex RH17 7TT
Tel: 08707 708 649
www.cats.org.uk

Dogs Trust

17 Wakley Street
London EC1V 7RQ
Tel: 020 7837 0006
www.dogstrust.org.uk

Governing Council of the Cat Fancy

5 King's Castle Business Park
The Drove
Bridgwater
Somerset TA6 4AG
Tel: 01278 427 575
www.gccfcats.org

Kennel Club

1 Clarges Street
London W1J 8AB
Tel: 0870 606 6750
Fax: 020 7518 1058
E-mail: info@the-kennel-club.org.uk
www.the-kennel-club.org.uk

People's Dispensary for Sick Animals (PDSA)

Whitechapel Way
Priorslee
Telford
Shropshire TF2 9PQ
Tel: 01952 290 999
Fax: 01952 291 035
www.pdsa.org.uk

RSPCA

Wilberforce Way
Southwater
Horsham
West Sussex RH13 9RS
Tel: 0870 333 5999
Fax: 0870 753 0284
www.rspca.org.uk

COUNSELLING AND SUPPORT

Age Concern England

Astral House
1268 London Road
London SW16 4ER
Tel: 020 8765 7200
E-mail: ace@ace.org.uk
www.ace.org.uk

Age Concern Cymru

13–14 Neptune Court
Vanguard Way
Cardiff CF24 5PJ
Tel: 029 2043 1555
www.accymru.org.uk

British Association for Counselling and Psychotherapy

BACP House
35–37 Albert Street
Rugby
Warwickshire CV21 2SG
Tel: 0870 443 5253
www.bacp.co.uk

Child Poverty Action Group (CPAG)

94 White Lion Street
London N1 9PF
Tel: 020 7837 7979
Fax: 020 7837 6414
E-mail: staff@cpag.demon.co.uk
www.cpag.org.uk

Counsel and Care

Twyman House
16 Bonny Sreet
London
NW1 9PG
Tel: 020 7241 8555
Fax: 020 7267 6877
www.counselandcare.org.uk

CRUSE Bereavement Care

126 Sheen Road
Richmond
Surrey TW9 1UR

449

Tel: 020 8939 9530
Fax: 020 8940 7638
www.crusebereavementcare.org.uk

Dignity in Dying (formerly VES)

13 Prince of Wales Terrace
London W8 5PG
Tel: 0870 777 7868
E-mail: info@dignityindying.org.uk
www.dignityindying.org.uk

EXIT (formerly Scottish Voluntary Euthanasia Society (VESS)

17 Hart Street
Edinburgh EH1 3RN
www.euthanasia.cc

Gingerbread

307 Borough High Street
London SE1 1JH
Tel: 020 7403 9500
Fax: 020 7403 9533
E-mail: office@gingerbread.org.uk
www.gingerbread.org.uk

Mind

Granta House
15–19 Broadway
London E15 4BQ
Tel: 020 8519 2122
Legacy Officer (for publications): 020 8215 2241
E-mail: contact@mind.org.uk
www.mind.org.uk

National Association of Widows

3rd Floor
48 Queens Road
Coventry
CV1 3EH
Tel: 0845 838 2261
www.nawidows.org.uk

Terrence Higgins Trust

314–320 Gray's Inn Road
London WC1X 8DP

Tel: 020 7812 1600
Fax: 020 7812 1601
E-mail: info@tht.org.uk
www.tht.org.uk

COURTS

Court of Protection/Public Guardianship Office

Archway Tower
2 Junction Road
London N19 5SZ
Tel: 0845 330 2900
DX: 141150 Archway-2
www.guardianship.gov.uk

Principal Registry of the Family Division

First Avenue House
42–49 High Holborn
London WC1V 6NP
Tel: 020 7947 6000
Fax: 020 7947 6995
DX: 396 Lond/Chancery Ln

Royal Courts of Justice

The Strand
London WC2A 2LL
Tel: 020 7947 6000
DX: 44450 Strand WC2

GOVERNMENT

Department for Constitutional Affairs

Selborne House
54–60 Victoria Street
London SW1E 6QW
Tel: 020 7210 8500
Fax: 020 7210 8549
Email: general.queries@dca.gsi.gov.uk
www.dca.gov.uk

Department for Work and Pensions

www.dwp.gov.uk
www.jobcentreplus.gov.uk

HM Revenue and Customs (Capital Taxes)

Ferrers House
PO Box 38
Castle Meadow Road
Nottingham NG2 1BB
Tel: 0115 974 2400
Fax: 0115 974 2432
DX: 701201 Nottingham-4
www.hmrc.gov.uk/cto/
Tel: 0845 302 0900 (IHT and Probate forms)
Forms adviser: 0115 974 2706
Heritage team: 0115 974 2488

HM Revenue and Customs (Charities)

Unit 361
St John's House
Merton Road
Bootle
Merseyside L69 9BB
Tel: 0845 302 0203
E-mail: charities@inlandrevenue.gov.uk

Legal Services Commission

85 Gray's Inn Road
London WC1X 8TX
Tel: 020 7759 0000
Fax: 020 7759 1798
DX: 328 Lon/Ch'ry Ln WC2
www.legalservices.gov.uk

Official Solicitor and Public Trustee

81 Chancery Lane
London WC2A 1DD
Tel: 020 7911 7127
Fax: 020 7911 7105
DX: 0012 Lond/Chancery Ln
www.officialsolicitor.gov.uk

Treasury Solicitor's Department

1 Kemble Street
London WC2B 4TS
Tel: 020 7210 3000
www.tsol.gov.uk

REGULATORY ORGANISATIONS

Adjudicator's Office

6th Floor
Haymarket House
28 Haymarket
London SW1Y 4SP
Tel: 020 7930 2292
Fax: 020 7930 2298
E-mail: adjudicators@gtnet.gov.uk
www.adjudicatorsoffice.gov.uk

Advertising Standards Authority

Mid City Place
71 High Holborn
London WC1V 6QT
Tel: 020 7492 2222
Fax: 020 7242 3696
www.asa.org.uk

The Charity Commission

PO Box 1227
Liverpool L69 3UG
Tel: 0845 300 0218
Fax: 0151 7031 555
www.charity-commission.gov.uk

Financial Ombudsman Service

South Quay Plaza
183 Marsh Wall
London E14 9SR
Tel: 0845 080 1800
Switchboard: 020 7964 1000
Fax: 020 7964 1001
E-mail: complaint.info@
   financial-ombudsman.org.uk
www.financial-ombudsman.org.uk

Financial Services Authority

25 The North Colonnade
Canary Wharf
London E14 5HS
Tel: 020 7066 1000
Fax: 020 7066 1099
www.fsa.gov.uk

SOLICITOR'S ASSOCIATIONS

Association of Contentious Trust and Probate Specialists (ACTAPS)

c/o Henry Frydenson
Baker & Mackenzie LLP
100 New Bridge Street
London EC4V 6JA
Tel: 020 7919 1000
E-mail: henry.frydenson@bakernet.com

The Law Society

113 Chancery Lane
London WC2A 1PL
Tel: 020 7242 1222
Fax: 020 7831 0344
DX: 56 Lond/Chancery Lane
www.lawsociety.org.uk
www.probatesection.org.uk
Consumer Complaints Service:
  0845 608 6565
Law Management Section:
  020 7316 5707
Lawyer Line: 0870 606 2588
Library Enquiries: 0870 606 2511
Practice Advice: 0870 606 2522
Probate Section: 020 7316 5678
Professional Ethics: 0870 606 2577
Public Enquiries: 0870 606 6575
Sole Practitioners' Group 020 7320 5801

Society for Computers and Law

Administrative Secretary
10 Hurle Crescent
Clifton
Bristol BS8 2TA
Tel: 0117 923 7393
Fax: 0117 923 9305
E-mail: caroline.gould@scl.org
www.scl.org

Society of Trust and Estate Practitioners (STEP)

26 Grosvenor Gardens
London SW1W 0GT
Tel: 020 7838 4890
Fax: 020 7838 4886
www.step.org

Solicitor Sole Practitioners Group

www.spg.uk.com

Solicitors Benevolent Association

1 Jaggard Way
London SW12 8SG
Tel: 020 8675 6440
Fax: 020 8675 6441
DX: 41608 Balham
E-mail: sec@sba.org.uk
www.sba.org.uk

SPECIALIST VALUERS

Central Association of Agricultural Valuers

Market Chambers
35 Market Place
Coleford
Gloucestershire GL16 8AA
Tel: 01594 832 979
Fax: 01594 810 701
E-mail: enquiries@caav.org.uk
www.caav.org.uk

Fleurets

Chartered Surveyors – Hotel and
Licensed Property Valuers
4 Roger Street
London WC1N 2JX
Tel: 020 7280 4700
Fax: 020 7280 4750
E-mail: london@fleurets.com
www.fleurets.com

Institute of Revenues, Rating and Valuation

41 Doughty Street
London WC1N 2LF
Tel: 020 7831 3505
www.irrv.net

LAPADA, The Association of Art and Antique Dealers

535 Kings Road
Chelsea
London SW10 0SZ

Tel: 020 7823 3511
Fax: 020 7823 3522

National Association of Goldsmiths

78a Luke Street
London EC2A 4XG
Tel: 020 7613 4445
Fax: 020 7613 4450
www.jewellers-online.org

Society of Fine Art Auctioneers and Valuers (SOFAA)

London Road
Send
Woking
Surrey GU23 7LN
Tel: 01483 225 891
Fax: 01483 222 171

Stanley Gibbons Ltd

399 Strand
London WC2R 0LX
Tel: 020 7836 8444
Fax: 020 7836 7342
www.stanleygibbons.com
Valuation of postage stamps and postal history. Philatelic auctioneers.

Wildy & Sons Ltd

Lincoln's Inn Archway
Carey Street
London WC2A 2JD
Tel: 020 7242 5778
Fax: 020 7430 0897
E-mail: info@wildy.com
Valuation of legal books

MISCELLANEOUS

British Bankers' Association,

Joint Money Laundering Steering Group
Pinners Hall
105–108 Old Broad Street
London
EC2N 1EX
E-mail: david.swanney@jmlsg.org.uk
www.jmlsg.org.uk

British Medical Association

BMA House
Tavistock Square
London WC1H 9JP
Tel: 020 7387 4499
Fax: 020 7383 6400
www.bma.org.uk

British Red Cross

UK Office
44 Moorfields
London EC2Y 9AL
Tel: 0870 170 7000
Fax: 020 7562 2000
www.redcross.org.uk

Clarity

c/o Mark Adler
April Cottage
Logmore Green
Dorking
Surrey RH4 3JN
Tel: 01306 741 055
Fax: 01306 741 066
E-mail: adler@adler.demon.co.uk
www.clarity-international.net

Companies House

Crown Way
Cardiff CF14 3UZ
Tel: 0870 333 3636
DX: 33050 Cardiff-1
www.companieshouse.gov.uk

Ergonomics Society

Elms Court
Elms Grove
Loughborough
Leicestershire LE11 1RG
Tel: 01509 234 904
Fax: 01509 235 666
E-mail: ergsoc@ergonomics.org.uk
www.ergonomics.org.uk

Ergonomics and Safety Research Institute

Holywell Building
Holywell Way
Loughborough

Leicestershire LE11 3UZ
Tel: 01509 22 6900

General Council of the Bar

289–293 High Holborn
London WC1V 7HZ
Tel: 020 7242 0082
Fax: 020 7831 9217
www.barcouncil.org.uk

Insolvency Service

Bankruptcy Search Room
Ladywood House
45 Stephenson Street
Birmingham B2 4UP
Tel: 0121 698 4000
Fax: 0121 698 4406

Institute of Advanced Legal Studies

University of London
Charles Clore House
17 Russell Square
London WC1B 5DR
Tel: 020 7862 5800
E-mail: ials@sas.ac.uk
www.ials.sas.ac.uk

UK Transplant

NHS Organ Donor Line: 0845 606 0400
www.uktransplant.org.uk

The National Archives

Ruskin Avenue
Kew
Richmond
Surrey TW9 4DU
Tel: 020 8876 3444
Fax: 020 8392 5286
www.nationalarchives.gov.uk

Traceline (Office for National Statistics)

PO Box 106
Southport
PR8 2WA
Traceline team: 0151 471 4811
www.gro.gov.uk

Solicitors Assistance Scheme

Helpline: 020 7320 5795
www.solicitorsassistancescheme.org.uk

LawCare

LawCare Ltd
PO Box 2071
Shoreham by Sea
Sussex
BN43 5AH
Tel: 0870 774 3663
E-mail: admin@lawcare.org.uk
www.lawcare.org.uk
Helpline (England and Wales): 0800 279 6888
Helpline (Scotland): 0800 279 6869

Index

stemming decreasing profitability
314–17
Property
collecting assets checklist 291–2
failing to clarify property owned
132–3
foreign assets 156, 185–6
inheritance tax and 209
Internet wills and 156
joint property 132–3, 169–70
Proprietary constructive trusts 66
Public funding 125–6
Public Guardianship Office 239
Public relations 371–2
Publications 372

Quality management 315, 337–46
Questionnaires 152–3
Quick succession relief 92, 194
Quotations on costs 20–1
time limits 23

Receipts for legacies 262–3
Receivership
money laundering and 176–7
Reconciliation of bank statements 55, 59
Record-keeping requirements 53–5, 59
retention of will files 145
Rectification of the will 118
time limits 87–8
Refund monies 15–16
Registers
probate registries 240
wills and deeds 299
Relatives
deceased with no known relatives
212–14
intestacy and 168
Reminders
general 5–6
Removal of personal representatives 115,
182, 228–9
Remuneration certificate 14–15, 17
Renunciation 3–4, 235
Residence orders 81
Residuary legacies 166
Benham and *Ratcliffe* problem
269–79
Response to probate claim 119
Restraint orders 76
Resulting trusts 111
Retainers 139–40
termination 243

Retired solicitors
as executors 9
Retirement of trustees 181–2, 183
Review of files 344
Revocation of grant
action regarding 114–15
Risk assessment 336–7

S.57 agreements 18
Security
Internet wills and 147–8
Self-dealing
rule against 3
Seminars 372, 374
Service levels 27–30
Signature
electronic/digital 148–9
Social security system
attendance allowance 98
bereavement allowance 96
bereavement payment 96
child benefit 97
funeral costs and 96
incapacity benefit 97–8
widowed parent's allowance 97
Solicitors
appointment of solicitor/executor
121–2
charging for acting in relation to
insolvent estate 223–4
claims against 118
clients of *see* Clients
instructions
difficulty with 6
general reminders 5–6
involved in dishonest transactions
72–3
parting company with clients
243
retainers 139–40
termination 243
retired and non-practising 9
specialist 241–2
witnessing the will 237
Solicitors' Account Rules 45, 46
accountants' reports 57–8
classification of money 47–8
how Rules affect probate work
58–60
interest 55–7, 59–60
record-keeping requirements 53–5,
59